Effective
Leadership

First, I dedicate this book to all the scholars who have done research on leadership. It has been my great pleasure to read your articles. Without your contributions this book would not have been possible. I truly believe that your work is exciting—leadership is one of the most thrilling topics that we can possibly study. It has all the drama of life—the struggle for success, self-esteem, and recognition; the need for social relationships, friendships, and even love; and finally the need for meaning and purpose in life. Your research reveals the importance of all of these needs to leadership. When describing your research, I have tried to use a writing style that will capture the imaginations of our students and let them see how exciting your work on leadership really is. I hope that I have done your great work justice.

Second, I dedicate this book to all the inspiring leaders that I have profiled in this book. During the time that I was writing this book, I was going through an unusually difficult time in my own life. Many of the people that I love most, including my family and friends, began to suffer many of the tragedies that afflict humanity: accidents requiring hospitalization and long-term therapy; chronic, long-lasting illnesses; and even death. Naturally these tragedies weighed down my spirits and made it hard for me to write the optimistic and cheerful book that I envisioned. During this difficult time, something helped me recover my optimistic attitude: your biographies and life stories. I read about how you overcame your own problems, difficulties, and crisis situations and went on to achieve amazing personal and financial success. Moreover, you achieved this success while creating innovative products and services that benefited customers, while providing great jobs for employees, and while donating generously to charities. Your careers have inspired me, and I hope that I have managed to capture the inspiring nature of your life stories within the pages of this book.

Third, I dedicate this book to the students and other readers of this book. I hope that the leadership cases inspire you to success in your own life. We all go through difficulties in life, and I hope that whenever you go through your own troubles that you remember the inspiring examples in this book and persevere to your own success. And I hope you realize that leadership can be fun as well. The leaders in this book have lived life on their own terms, and they have been true to themselves while having a great time being leaders. The true life stories in this book are also backed up by solid academic research done by thousands of scholars. Millions of people have participated in the studies done by these researchers. So you can have confidence that you are getting not just an inspiring message but also a scientifically valid one. You are the future leaders of the world, and I hope this book helps you in your quest for personal happiness and financial well-being.

Effective Leadership
Theory, Cases, and Applications

Ronald H. Humphrey

Virginia Commonwealth University

Los Angeles | London | New Delhi
Singapore | Washington DC

Los Angeles | London | New Delhi
Singapore | Washington DC

FOR INFORMATION:

SAGE Publications, Inc.
2455 Teller Road
Thousand Oaks, California 91320
E-mail: order@sagepub.com

SAGE Publications Ltd.
1 Oliver's Yard
55 City Road
London EC1Y 1SP
United Kingdom

SAGE Publications India Pvt. Ltd.
B 1/I 1 Mohan Cooperative Industrial Area
Mathura Road, New Delhi 110 044
India

SAGE Publications Asia-Pacific Pte. Ltd.
3 Church Street
#10-04 Samsung Hub
Singapore 049483

Acquisitions Editor: Patricia Quinlin
Associate Editor: Maggie Stanley
Assistant Editor: Megan Koraly
Editorial Assistant: Katie Guarino
Production Editor: Stephanie Palermini
Copy Editor: Beth Hammond
Typesetter: C&M Digitals (P) Ltd.
Proofreader: Annie Lubinsky
Indexer: Kathy Paparchontis
Cover Designer: Janet Kiesel
Marketing Manager: Liz Thornton
Permissions Editor: Jennifer Barron

Copyright © 2014 by SAGE Publications, Inc.

Printed in the United States of America

Library of Congress Cataloging-in-Publication Data

Humphrey, Ronald H.

Effective leadership : theory, cases, and applications / Ronald H. Humphrey, Virginia Commonwealth University.

pages cm
Includes bibliographical references and index.

ISBN 978-1-4129-6355-8 (alk. paper)

1. Leadership. 2. Leadership—Case studies. I. Title.

HD57.7.H85 2014
658.4′092—dc23   2013000546

This book is printed on acid-free paper.

12 13 14 15 16 10 9 8 7 6 5 4 3 2 1

Brief Contents

Detailed Contents

Preface

W hy I Wrote This Book: Many inventors or entrepreneurs come up with their inventions or start their businesses because none of the existing products meet their needs. In the same way, my frustration with the existing textbooks inspired me to write this textbook. Many of the comprehensive leadership textbooks in the market are in their sixth or seventh editions, and some had their first editions published well over a quarter of a century ago. Although these books have been updated, their basic approach still reflects the leadership viewpoints that predominated at the time of their first edition. The world has changed a lot in the last quarter century, and businesses and nonprofit organizations alike have changed with it. Modern organizations have had to become more flexible and adaptable, and better educated employees now want more than a just a paycheck from their jobs.

I entered the field during the transition between the newer and the older approaches, so I was educated in the older leadership models and I've even done some research on these more traditional approaches. Many of the findings from these older studies still hold up. So I wanted a book that covered the traditional models, but that also included the newer approaches. A number of new leadership theories and philosophies have emerged in the last 25 years that reflect the changes in leadership that have taken place in the world. I have been actively involved in researching and developing these new approaches, so it is important to me to use a textbook that is up to date and that includes these newer leadership models. For example, I began researching the value of emotions to the workplace when few other management faculty were investigating emotions. I attended the first conference on Emotions in the Workplace in 1998. At that time, it was a small conference, but the network that was formed then has since gained official recognition by the Academy of Management (which hosts its website) and now has 1,300 faculty members around the world. I was also one of the founding members of the Network of Leadership Scholars, and this network has brought me into contact with researchers doing innovative research in a wide variety of areas. Many of these researchers have become my friends and colleagues, and I wanted to use a book that included the great work that they are doing. I was also one of the early management researchers in the area of identity theory, and I've been happy to see so many other faculty move into this area. In addition, I've been an active participant in the authentic leadership caucuses at the Academy of Management, and I am currently researching authentic leadership. Much of my early work focused on perceptual biases that caused managers to underestimate the abilities of lower-level employees, so my leadership philosophy also matches the *leadership at every level*, self-leadership, and shared leadership approaches.

I also wanted a book with cases that profiled great leaders who could serve as role models. Some of the textbooks were almost all theory and research and did not use in-depth cases. Others used short, fictionalized, unrealistic-sounding leadership cases that seemed tailored to exactly match some theory. Why use fictionalized cases when there are so many fascinating leaders around? It seems to me that if you can't find a real leader whose life experiences match the theory then it's probably a pretty poor theory! There were a few leadership books with exciting leadership cases, but these lacked the current theory and research to back up their leader profiles. So this is why I wrote a book that covers the traditional leadership theories and the exciting research that is being done right now, and one that has inspiring real-life leadership cases.

Appropriate Classes for This Book: Every year I teach a graduate leadership course targeted to students across the university from a wide variety of academic disciplines. These students come from a variety of applied disciplines, such as education, nursing and health care administration, social work, sports leadership, public administration, engineering, information systems, accounting, finance, and human resources. The students also come from academic areas such as psychology, sociology, and other liberal arts. In addition, I teach leadership courses for MBA students. My own research also has an interdisciplinary focus, and I have published with faculty from at least five different academic areas. Thus, I am aware of the leadership issues that are relevant to a wide range of disciplines, and I have made sure that the *Effective Leadership* textbook includes research that has been done in these different areas. I have also profiled leaders from a wide range of occupations and industries. As a result, *Effective Leadership* is appropriate for classes in various schools and disciplines.

Appropriate Level: Although I used the draft chapters of *Effective Leadership* in my graduate leadership classes, I have written the textbook in a clear and readable style that should be equally accessible to both undergraduates and graduate students. Many of the reviewers for the textbook teach under-graduate leadership classes, and they felt that the book's engaging writing style would work with undergraduates. The free online course pack that is on the textbook website also helps professors tailor the rigor of the course. Instructors can add to the class rigor by assigning articles from the course pack. Some of the articles are qualitative studies that include interesting quotes from leaders, and undergraduates might find these articles interest-ing. Other articles may have more of an appeal to graduate students. The low cost and concise nature of *Effective Leadership* also leaves room for instructors to assign their favorite readings without unduly burdening stu-dents with excessive reading or expenses. However, most professors will probably find that the material in each chapter is more than enough to keep the discussion going for the entire class time and that assigning extra read-ings is not necessary. In these cases, students may find the articles in the online course pack useful when doing research for term papers or class presentations.

Textbook Features

Companion Website: To access additional online learning tools go to **www .sagepub.com/humphreyel**

On the **Instructor Teaching Site** you will find the following resources:

- A **Microsoft® Word® test bank**, is available containing multiple choice, true/false, and essay questions for each chapter. The test bank provides you with a diverse range of pre-written options as well as the opportunity for editing any question and/or inserting your own personalized questions to effectively assess students' progress and understanding.
- A **Respondus electronic test bank**, is available and can be used on PCs. The test bank contains multiple choice, true/false, and essay questions for each chapter and provides you with a diverse range of pre-written options as well as the opportunity for editing any question and/or inserting your own personalized questions to effectively assess students' progress and understanding. Respondus is also compatible with many popular learning management systems so you can easily get your test questions into your online course.
- Editable, chapter-specific **Microsoft® PowerPoint® slides** offer you complete flexibility in easily creating a multimedia presentation for your course. Highlight essential content, features, and artwork from the book.
- **Learning Objectives** are provided to guide instructors and students in a chapter by chapter listing of takeaway learning goals.
- **The Leader's Bookcase:** *A Free Online Course Pack*. Every chapter includes a free article that can be downloaded from the textbook website. Students can

read these articles on their own to learn more about the topics covered in each chapter, or faculty can assign these articles to supplement the textbook.

- And more!

The **Student Study Site** is open access and provides students with the following study tools:

- **Self-Assessments:** Each chapter also includes online self-assessments so that students can learn more about their own leadership styles. After taking the online assessments, students can also read tips about how to improve their performance as a leader.
- **Web resources:** *Videos of leaders* describing their leadership techniques are included for every chapter.
- And more!

Chapter Features: Every chapter includes the following features:

Chapter Road Map: Each chapter begins with a listing of the major headings in the chapter. This gives students a quick overview of the chapter. The introduction to each chapter also lists several key questions that will be answered by reading the chapter.

Real Leadership Cases: Although some leadership books use fictional cases, *Effective Leadership* uses 100% real leadership cases about actual leaders and organizations. Each chapter features three or four cases that demonstrate leadership principles while also showing the excitement, passion, and power of leadership. Most of these cases feature inspiring leaders who have become successful while also contributing to society. A few cases, however, demonstrate what happens when leaders abuse their power or make strategic mistakes.

Personal Reflections: This conversationally written feature encourages students to reflect on their own experiences as they relate to the course material.

Applications: There are application questions scattered throughout each chapter. These questions are useful for stimulating classroom discussion and for getting students to apply the material to their own lives.

Put It in Practice: This feature summarizes the material learned in each chapter in a way that highlights the practical implications of the material.

Exercises: Each chapter ends with two or more exercises that can be done in class to engage students and to create an active learning environment.

Extended Coverage of Key Leadership Theories: In the last 20 years, perhaps more research has been done on transformational leadership theory than on any other leadership theory. Another leadership theory, leader-member exchange theory, has also been extensively researched. Before these theories became prominent, the older Ohio State model of leadership was also widely studied. Because of their prominence, these three theories are described in Chapter 1. The research on personality traits, teams, etc., often uses leadership scales from these three theories to measure leadership, so the research on these models is covered throughout the book. Many leadership textbooks use a single chapter to cover charismatic, transactional, and transformational leadership. Transformational leaders often use charismatic appeals, and there is a separate chapter on charisma. Moreover, the leadership techniques that transactional leaders use are substantially different from those used by transformational leaders. Transactional leaders use goal setting and contingent rewards to motivate followers, and these tactics are covered in Chapter 14. In contrast, transformational leaders rely more on inspiration to motivate followers, and these types of motivational techniques are covered in Chapter 15, the capstone chapter for the book. By having separate chapters on charisma, transactional leadership, and transformational leadership, this book can go into more depth on these leadership styles. Leader-member exchange theory also has its own chapter instead of sharing a chapter with several other theories. Likewise, the Ohio State model predominates in the chapter on the behavioral approach to leadership.

Coverage of New and Emerging Leadership Models: This book also covers the latest models of leadership. There are chapters on identity theory, authentic leadership and servant leadership, self-leadership, empowerment, shared/distributed leadership, and on the importance of affect to leadership. This book gives considerable attention to the importance of affect, so the research on affect and leadership is covered throughout the book. Many of the newer leadership models emphasize how leadership occurs at every level of the organization, and this perspective also runs throughout the *Effective Leadership* textbook.

Ethics and Social Responsibility: There are numerous examples throughout the book that show the importance of ethics and social responsibility to leadership. The book covers abusive leadership, fraud, and other unethical and illegal behaviors. On the positive side, this book also profiles leaders who develop environmentally friendly corporate policies, feed the hungry, risk their lives to help the sick or injured, improve worker safety, hire the disabled, mentor teenagers and support foster homes, help employees cope with personal problems, support education, and contribute generously to charity. The chapter on authentic leadership and servant leadership in particular shows the importance of ethics to leadership, but social responsibility is a theme that resonates throughout the book.

Global Research and Leadership: I have copublished with researchers located in universities in seven countries, so I am aware of the excellent research on leadership being done in countries besides the United States of America. Thus, this book has a very strong focus on leadership around the world. Every chapter features research that was done in a variety of countries. In addition, Chapters 1, 5, 11, 12, and 15 cover large scale cross-cultural research on leadership. Moreover, the leaders profiled in the book come from a wide range of countries and demographic backgrounds.

Women and Leadership: When I first started teaching management, few MBA students were women. However, times have changed, and leadership textbooks need to change with the times. In my interdisciplinary leadership classes, over half the students are female, and in my management classes, almost half are female as well. In order to provide role models for these students, I have included 15 outstanding female leader profiles in *Effective Leadership*. Chapter 5 covers women in leadership by reporting on a study of male and female leaders around the globe. In addition, the opening and closing cases for the chapter demonstrate that women can use a variety of leadership styles, including those stereotypically portrayed as more typical of men. Moreover, the coverage of women leaders is not restricted to a single chapter. Indeed, the textbook opens and closes with case studies of outstanding female leaders.

Featured Research Articles: Each chapter features several research articles that are covered in depth. This lets students appreciate how leadership research is conducted. This also helps students understand the value of an *evidence-based approach* to leadership. Although many popular leadership books are based on the author's own opinions, *Effective Leadership* draws upon the scientific method and literally thousands of studies to evaluate which leadership approaches really work. By reading about these featured research studies, students can judge for themselves how strong the evidence is for any particular theory or approach.

An Interdisciplinary Approach: This book reports on the leadership research that has been done in the applied professions such as management, health care, education, social work, public administration, sports leadership, and military leadership, as well as the research done in core academic areas such as psychology, social psychology, sociology, history, political science, and other disciplines. The case studies also profile leaders from a similar range of occupations and professions. The book not only features a large number of entrepreneurial leaders and corporate leaders but also leaders from nonprofits and governmental agencies.

Thanks to the Reviewers: *Effective Leadership* has gone through several rounds of reviews, and at each stage it has benefited from excellent feedback from the reviewers. There is definitely a learning curve when it comes to writing a text-book. At each round of reviews, the reviewers helped point me in the right direction with regard to writing style and textbook features. I wanted to make *Effective Leadership* a concise and affordable book, and that meant I had to make some tough choices about what to include and what to leave out. The reviewers provided invaluable advice in this regard, and I've done my best to include the theories and features that they wanted. My thanks go to these reviewers who have given generously of their time while providing me with feedback:

Dr. Mesut Akdere, University of Wisconsin-Milwaukee

Pauline J. Albert, St. Edward's University

Scott J. Allen, John Carroll University

Anthony C. Andenoro, Gonzaga University

Lucy A. Arendt, University of Wisconsin-Green Bay

Neal M. Ashkanasy, PhD, Professor of Management, The University of Queensland

Karla M. Back, State University of New York, Alfred State College

Kristin Backhaus, State University of New York at New Paltz

Myrna L. Bair, Ph.D., Director, Women's Leadership Development Program, Institute for Public Administration, University of Delaware

Emily Balcetis, New York University

Mark Beattie, Gonzaga University

Alice Black, PhD, nonprofit consultant, formerly affiliated with The Ohio State University

Eric B. Dent, PhD, Professor, University of North Carolina, Pembroke

Professor Peter Gronn, AcSS, Faculty of Education, University of Cambridge, England

Sheneice M. Hughes, M.A.P., Tarrant County Community College, Southeast

Deborah R. Litvin, Bridgewater State University

Luigi F. Lucaccini, School of Management, University of San Francisco

Christopher P. Neck, Associate Professor of Management, University Master Teacher, Arizona State University, W. P. Carey School of Business, Department of Management

Sherry H. Penney, PhD, Sherry H. Penney Professor of Leadership, College of Management, University of Massachusetts Boston

Dr. Sharon Perry-Nause, Tiffin University

Kira Kristal Reed, PhD, Syracuse University

Ronald E. Riggio, Claremont McKenna College

Machelle K. Schroeder, University of Wisconsin-Platteville

Dr. Denise Trudeau Poskas, MSED, PhD, Associate Professor of Leadership, Center for Community Vitality, University of Minnesota

Leigh E. Wallace, University of Wisconsin-Milwaukee

Jane V. Wheeler, PhD, Bowling Green State University

Jon R. Whitford, DBA, Rio Hondo College

Thanks to SAGE's Editorial Team: I also owe a great deal of thanks to the late Al Bruckner, the Senior Acquisitions Editor who invited me to submit a book proposal to SAGE. Lisa Shaw took over from Al when he retired, and Lisa helped me through the first few rounds of reviews. She gave me good advice about finding the golden mean between sounding too academic and sounding too low level. Because of her advice, I worked hard at creating a consistent tone for the book. Lisa's able assistant Julie also worked with me to find ways to meet the reviewer's concerns while staying true to my original intentions for the book. After Lisa took a promotion with another division in SAGE (congrats, Lisa!), Patricia (Pat) Quinlin took over as my editor. Pat's team includes Maggie Stanley, Associate Editor, and Katie Guarino, Editorial Assistant. Together, they worked hard to find the perfect set of reviewers who fit my target market and who could give me some useful feedback to help me polish the last and final draft of the book. Stephanie Palermini is the production editor for the book and she has done a wonderful job getting the book through the various stages of the production process. I also owe thanks to Beth Hammond, who carefully copyedited the manuscript and corrected all of my mistakes—thanks for making me look good. The art department also did a beautiful job with the cover and the layout of the book does a wonderful job of displaying the various features in each chapter.

PART I

INTRODUCTION

1

Introduction: Leaders Matter

Chapter Road Map

Case: *Ursula Burns—Xerox's Inspiring Leader*
What Is Leadership?
Leadership as Power and Influence
Leaders as Representatives and Problem Solvers
Leadership and Power Differences Around the Globe
Levels of Leadership
Check Your Egos at the Door: Leader Development Occurs at Every Level
Leader Development and Mentors
Some Specific Types of Leaders
What Do We Want From Leaders? Genuine Concern
Leaders Matter
Case: *Spotlight on Sustainable Practices*
Personal Reflections: *It's Easy to Become a Leader!*
Values, Ethics, and Corporate Social Responsibility
Evidence-Based Leadership
The Best of Every Theory
Case: *Jib Ellison (Environmentalist) and Lee Scott (Former CEO, Wal-Mart): Sustainability Saves Money and the Environment*
Put It in Practice
Exercises: (1) Perceptions of Leaders and (2) Leaders as Role Models

Case: *Ursula Burns—Xerox's Inspiring Leader*

Few CEO's have a more inspiring life story than Ursula Burns. In July of 2009, she was named CEO of Xerox—the first African American woman to be CEO of such a large Fortune 500 company. She rose to an even higher rank when she added the Xerox chairwoman duties to her CEO role on May 20, 2010. But she didn't start at the top, and she wasn't born with a silver spoon in her mouth. Her mother was of Irish and German American heritage, and her father was African American. Ursula was raised by her single mother in a New York City housing project. Although she grew up in a tough neighborhood, her mother inspired her to be a success. Ursula

Ursula Burns, Chairwoman and CEO of Xerox

Source: Wikipedia/U.S. Government Printing Office, 2004

recalls her mother frequently stating, "Where you are is not who you are" (Bryant, 2010). Her mother also taught her two important lessons: the first about being a good person and the second about being successful. Her mother taught her that she needed to give back to the world more than she received from it. In terms of success, her mother encouraged her to be curious, to get a good education, and to not see herself as a victim.

Ursula followed her mother's advice about education by earning degrees in engineering from Polytechnic Institute of New York University and from Columbia University. And it was Ursula's curiosity and forthright speaking manner that attracted the attention of her first mentor at Xerox, Wayland Hicks, a corporate vice president who made her his executive assistant and protégé. Later, her curiosity and willingness to ask tough questions favorably impressed the president of Xerox at that time, Mr. Allaire. President Allaire had declared during his monthly executive meetings that Xerox would stop hiring people, yet Burns noticed that Xerox kept hiring a thousand people a month. She boldly asked him why Xerox was still hiring more people. President Allaire rewarded her honesty by making her his own executive assistant. Ursula Burns credits both Hicks and Allaire with teaching her leadership skills. Together, they taught her about the need to communicate diplomatically with others and to give credit to others as a way of motivating them. As their executive assistant, she could learn by example from watching them lead Xerox.

During the 1990s, Ursula was assigned to lead important projects and she supervised teams in two of Xerox's high growth areas: faxes and office network printing. In

1999, she became vice president of Xerox's global manufacturing. Then, Xerox went through some turbulent times with accounting scandals, falling stock prices, and even rumors of impending bankruptcy. Burns thought about leaving, but she felt an obligation to help Xerox survive. Fortunately, Xerox soon thereafter made Anne Mulcahy CEO, and she and Ursula developed a true partnership in their efforts to transform Xerox. Ursula was given rapid promotions and was placed in charge of important initiatives, and for the next several years, Anne and Ursula worked together before Anne passed the CEO job (and then the chairwoman title) on to Ursula.

Ursula has continued to be recognized for her outstanding leadership, and in March 2011, she was recognized by *Working Mother Magazine* as one of the Most Powerful Moms in STEM (Science, Technology, Engineering, and Math). Truly, she's an inspiration for us all.

Applications: Ursula's mother taught her to be both a good person and to be successful. Can being a good person who wants to give back to others help one succeed? Ursula was good at establishing mentorship relations early in her career. How important is it to have mentors who can teach you leadership skills? What are the best ways to establish a mentorship relationship with senior leaders? Are there any leaders you can learn from?

Sources: NPR Staff. (2012, May 23). *Xerox CEO: 'If you don't transform, you're stuck'.* Retrieved from http://www.npr.org/2012/05/23/153302563/xerox-ceo-if-you-don-t-transform-you-re-stuck

Bourne, L. (2011, February). Most powerful moms in STEM. In H. Jonsen (Ed.), *Working Mother.* Retrieved from http://www.workingmother.com/BestCompanies/most-powerful-moms/2011/02/most-powerful-moms-in-stem

Bryant, A. (2010, February 21). Xerox's new chief tries to redefine its culture. *The New York Times.* Retrieved from http://www.nytimes.com/2010/02/21/business/21xerox.html?_r=1

Burns, Ursula. Retrieved April 3, 2011 from http://en.wikipedia.org/wiki/Ursula_Burns

As the preceding case illustrates, Ursula Burns developed her leadership skills throughout her life. She was particularly good at establishing protégé-mentorship relationships with her superiors. She also illustrates some of the best qualities of leaders. In particular, she is forthright in her communications, which allows her to establish good ties with others and to influence them as well. As the definition of leadership below illustrates, the ability to influence others is one of the key attributes of leadership. She also represents Xerox's corporate values by believing in the value of education and innovation, and her dedication to helping Xerox survive during tough times shows her commitment to the organization. As we'll see from the following definitions, leaders also help their group, organization, or society fulfill their mission. This chapter will also discuss some of the following key questions:

- What are the common ways to define leadership?
- How do cultures around the world rate on power distance and assertiveness, and how does this influence leadership?
- At what levels does leadership take place?
- Why do the top companies value leadership at every level? What is the difference between leader development and leadership development?
- Why do leaders matter to organizations even when taking into account environmental factors?

What Is Leadership?

There are many definitions of leadership. Some definitions emphasize the way leaders influence others. Northouse (2007, p. 3), for example, argues that "Influence is the sine qua non of leadership. Without influence, leadership does not exist." Other definitions, however, emphasize how leaders reflect the will of the majority—that people emerge as leaders because they are supported by the group, organization, or society they lead. In other words, leaders have to follow the people. Many scholars recognize that leadership involves a little bit of both, but let's consider these two ends of the continuum in the sections below.

Leadership as Power and Influence

According to a *power perspective definition of leadership*, leaders command, control, direct, and influence followers to achieve group, organizational, or societal goals. Notice that achieving goals is an important part of leadership. From this perspective, leaders set the goals or vision and then motivate others to achieve these goals by using either their powers of persuasion or their authority over their subordinates. Thus, the effectiveness of a leader depends upon (1) the degree to which the leader picked or devised the right strategy and vision and (2) the leader's ability to motivate and influence the group to carry out the strategy. An underlying premise of this perspective is that effective leaders may have to persuade others to change their views to match the leader's views or to directly command sometimes reluctant subordinates to carry out their assigned tasks. However, advocates of this perspective recognize that sometimes leaders have to consult their followers in order to gain information necessary to formulate the correct strategy or goals. Moreover, in order to motivate their followers, they have to consider their followers' needs and desires.

Leaders as Representatives and Problem Solvers

At the other end of the continuum from the power perspective is the viewpoint that people emerge as leaders when they best represent the values of the group, organization, or society they seek to lead. According to this perspective, people emerge as leaders because they are better at articulating the values and desires of the group or are in some way seen as best representing the group. In particular, they are seen as the ones best able to solve the group or organization's problems in a way that the members value. Leaders are those who are most engaged in the group's activities (Bass, 1990). In social groups, the leaders may be those who add fun and excitement to the activities that the group members prefer. In small work groups, the leaders may be the ones who work hardest at the group tasks, come up with solutions to the group problems, and in general, best help the group members achieve their goals. In many small work groups, the leaders often end up doing more than their fair share of the work. Even in an organization with a strict hierarchy of command, people are often selected for promotion based on the degree to which they represent the organization's core culture and are involved in carrying out the organization's core mission. At the national level, leaders are elected when the public perceives that the leaders share their values. This perspective assumes that leaders in essence conform to the group, organization, or society they lead. As the British Prime Minister Disraeli stated, "I must follow the people. Am I not their leader?" Thus, from the *leaders as representatives perspective, leaders are those who (1) best represent the values of their followers and (2) are better at solving their followers' problems and achieving their goals.*

> **Applications:** Should politicians vote their own conscience on key pieces of legislation, or should they follow the will of the people and vote the way the majority of their constituents think they should vote? How about in the work world? How much should leaders listen to their subordinates versus following their own instincts?

Some companies practice a high degree of empowerment and expect their employees to speak up about organizational issues; leaders in these organizations may follow the leaders as representatives' philosophy with regard to

many decisions (although probably not all) and let their followers participate in making decisions. In contrast, other organizations give most of the
power and decision-making authority to leaders who hold top management
positions. How often companies give a high degree of power to top leaders
varies by national culture. The next section covers two important cultural
differences related to power that leaders should take into account when leading people from diverse cultures.

Leadership and Power Differences Around the Globe

The extent to which leaders are best characterized by the power perspective
or the representative perspective varies by culture. Researchers use the term
power distance to refer to *the degree to which there are differences in status,
authority, privileges, respect, and right to participate in decision making
between managers and their subordinates* (Hofstede, 2001; House, Hanges,
Javidan, Dorfman, & Gupta, 2004). In high power distance countries, subordinates show great deference to their leaders, whereas in low power distance countries, subordinates may regard managers as their social equals and
may expect their managers to listen to their advice. In high power distance
countries, leaders may look out for the welfare of their subordinates but in
a more paternalistic way. Even in low power distance countries, leaders may
still have considerable influence over their subordinates.

An impressive amount of evidence about cross-cultural differences in
leadership and in power distance has been collected by House and his colleagues in the Global Leadership and Organizational Behavior Effectiveness
(GLOBE) project (House et al., 2004). This study examined leaders in 62
societies and had a sample size of 17,000. House and his colleagues also
studied a related cultural norm, that of assertiveness (the other cultural
characteristics in the GLOBE study will be described in later chapters).
According to House and his colleagues, *assertiveness* refers to *the willingness and desire to freely express both positive and negative messages to
others, as well as the willingness to express one's feelings and thoughts
to others*. In highly assertive Western cultures, employees are expected to
communicate their opinions directly and openly, whereas in other cultures,
communication may be more indirect. Den Hartog (2004) argued that
in some cultures it would be expected that employees would express disagreements with their leaders, whereas in other cultures, such signs of
disagreement would be unacceptable.

Atwater, Wang, Smither, and Fleenor (2009) used a subsample of the
GLOBE data set to test some intriguing hypotheses about the relationships

between leaders and followers. The subsample examined 21 countries and had 964 managers with 3,576 direct reports, as well as 3,616 peer ratings of the managers. The majority of the managers were upper midlevel (46.9%) or executive level (32.1%). Roughly three quarters (74.1%) were male. Atwater and her colleagues wanted to examine leaders' self-ratings of their leadership abilities and compare the leaders' ratings to the subordinates' ratings of their leaders. Across all cultures, the leaders' self-ratings and subordinates' ratings of the leaders were positively correlated, thus indicating a small to moderate level of agreement in how the leaders were rated.

Table 1.1 Assertiveness and Power Distance, by Country

	Assertiveness	Power Distance
Austria	4.62	4.95
Brazil	4.20	5.33
Canada	4.05	4.82
China	3.76	5.04
Denmark	3.80	3.89
Finland	3.81	4.89
France	4.13	5.28
Hong Kong	4.67	4.96
India	3.73	5.47
Ireland	3.92	5.15
Italy	4.07	5.43
Mexico	4.45	5.22
Netherlands	4.32	4.11
Poland	4.06	5.10
Russia	3.68	5.52
South Korea	4.40	5.61
Singapore	4.17	4.99
Spain	4.42	5.52
Sweden	3.38	4.85
United Kingdom	4.15	5.15
United States	4.55	4.88

Sources: Adapted from Atwater, L., Wang, M., Smither, J. W., & Fleenor, J. W. (2009). Are cultural characteristics associated with the relationship between self and others' ratings of leadership? *Journal of Applied Psychology, 94*(4), 876–886. doi: 10.1037/a0014561. Used with permission from the American Psychological Association.

Atwater and her colleagues (Atwater et al., 2009) also hypothesized that the cultural norms relating to power distance and assertiveness would influence the degree to which the managers' self-ratings agreed with the subordinates' ratings of their leadership abilities. *As Table 1.1 indicates, there are substantial differences among cultures in assertiveness and power distance.* The researchers reasoned that in more assertive cultures, subordinates should be freer to express their true feelings to their managers and that as a result, the managers would have more accurate self-images about their own leadership abilities. This is a powerful test of the willingness of subordinates to express their feelings—if they are willing to speak up to their managers about managerial weaknesses, then they certainly shouldn't be shy about expressing their views about various work options, strategies, or other issues that would normally be less threatening to the supervisors' self-esteem. As Atwater and her colleagues had hypothesized, *leaders' self-ratings were more consistent with their subordinates' ratings of their leadership in cultures high on assertiveness.* However, the study did not find that leaders' self-ratings were more consistent with subordinate ratings in low power distance countries. Overall, the study results demonstrate that cultures do differ in their expectations about how much power distance there should be between leaders and subordinates and about how free subordinates should be to express their attitudes about a wide variety of workplace issues—even about the performance of their boss.

Applications: How easy is it for you to express your opinions about work-related issues to your manager? Are you allowed to call your manager by his or her first name, or must you use a title instead? Do you think that the cultures that are high in assertiveness and low on power distance would have an advantage in terms of being productive? How could being willing to express your opinions about work to your leader increase productivity?

Self-Assessment: *Assertiveness.* Go to the textbook website to take a self-assessment of your assertiveness skills and to learn some tips about how to become appropriately assertive.

Levels of Leadership

Many leadership theories are about how managers can lead and influence the people directly under them—people that the leaders interact with on a face-to-face basis. Because this is the type of leadership situation that most people are likely to be in, it makes sense to focus on this type of leadership. This face-to-face type of leadership is also useful for working with teammates and peers in committees and small workgroups, sports teams, clubs, and so forth. However, organizational leaders who advance up the ranks of large organizations eventually have to lead people they rarely, if ever, interact with on a personal level. Leadership can take place at many different levels and with people who may not even be in your organization. Models of political leaders, for example, describe how these leaders influence millions of people they may never have met and who are not their employees or subordinates. Even business and nonprofit leaders often have to lead vast numbers of people they do not have the chance to interact with on a face-to-face level. In these cases, organizational leaders may have to use some of the same strategies political leaders use to communicate their vision and goals for the organization. For example, Steve Jobs, former CEO of Apple, held meetings for his employees in large auditoriums and spoke to them in carefully orchestrated speeches that were broadcast around the world to other employees and to potential customers. His charismatic appeal and communication techniques matched that of some of the world's best political leaders. Conversely, politicians can benefit from studying business leaders; mayors and other political administrators sometimes supervise thousands of employees, and they need to know modern managerial leadership skills.

Some leadership techniques may apply only to certain levels and certain types of industries or settings. Moreover, someone who is good at leading a small group or team may not necessarily be good at leading a large organization; likewise, there are some famous leaders of large organizations and nations who have had trouble establishing close ties with those around them.

Leadership takes place at multiple levels (Dansereau, Yammarino, & Markham, 1995; Yammarino, Dionne, Chun, & Dansereau, 2005). Leadership can occur at the following levels:

Within person: People lead themselves when they set personal goals, motivate themselves to stay on task, and develop their own leadership skills and competencies.

Individual personality differences: Leadership can be examined at the individual level—for example, what are the personality differences between leaders and followers or between different types of leaders?

Perceptual: People's perceptions of leaders are also important—in other words, leadership is in the eye of the beholder more than in the behavior of the leader.

Processes and behaviors: Instead of thinking about leadership in terms of person-ality traits, we can also think about leadership in terms of a set of processes and behaviors that leaders perform. For example, leaders engage in processes and behaviors such as planning, scheduling, and recognizing employees who have performed well.

Group level: Sometimes leaders focus on leading groups and they interact with followers primarily as members of a group. For example, leaders may establish departmental policies and procedures that regulate group activities and that treat all departmental members the same, and they may communicate with the follow-ers primarily in group meetings.

One-on-one relationships: At other times, leaders need to treat people as indi-viduals and establish one-on-one relationships with each follower. Thus, leaders may need to find time to meet individually with each follower. To establish good one-on-one interactions, leaders have to take into account the differing needs of followers.

Peer group leadership and empowered teams: Leadership does not always require formal managerial leaders. The leadership interactions among peer group mem-bers are also important. For example, in empowered work teams, the members lead themselves and each other.

Followers: Leaders also have to take into account the characteristics of followers—followers with different personalities, values, or skill levels may prefer different leadership styles. Thus, leaders may have to adjust their lead-ership behaviors to take into account the personalities and other characteristics of their followers.

Environmental factors: Leaders also have to take into account a wide variety of environmental factors, including job characteristics, the organizational structure, and the overall environment. In some situations, leaders may need to focus most of their attention on these environmental factors.

Macro level: At the macro level, leaders have to lead organizations or even societ-ies, and leading at these levels requires additional skills.

Yammarino and Dansereau (2008) argued *that problems occur when managers attempt to lead at the wrong level.* For example, a leader may interact with subordinates as individuals when the leader really needs to lead at the group level by addressing group work norms, group cohesiveness, or other group level problems.

Models of self-leadership, shared leadership, and distributed leader-ship, in particular, emphasize that leadership takes places at all levels of an organization. These models, which will be discussed in detail in later chapters, argue that employees and organizational members do not have to have formal managerial titles in order to initiate leadership and make things happen. The following section describes how the leading companies in the world recognize that leadership takes place at all levels of the organizations.

Check Your Egos at the Door: Leader Development Occurs at Every Level

Some corporate executives think it's beneath them to listen to those far below them in rank and status. As a VP, CEO, or even Chair, it's easy to believe you know more than a lower-level employee. Why should you listen to a custodian, factory worker, or truck driver? Or, for that matter, to a midlevel manager? But this snobbish attitude doesn't fly at the top companies for leadership development. As Rick Lash stated, "Leadership in the twenty-first century is about leading at all levels; not restricting it to title. As organizations become flatter, the best leaders are learning they must check their egos at the door." Rick is a director in the Hay Group's Leadership and Talent Practice unit and coleader of the sixth annual Best Companies for Leadership Study. In this study, the Hay Group surveyed 3,769 individuals from 1,827 organizations located in 96 countries. It found that *the top 20 companies nurtured leadership abilities among employees at every level of the organization.* All of the top companies give every employee the opportunity to develop leadership abilities. In contrast, only 70% of companies not in the top 20 give employees at all levels leadership development opportunities. Moreover, 90% of the top 20 companies expect that employees should demonstrate leadership regardless of whether they have managerial positions or not; only 59% of other companies expect their nonsupervisory employees to be leaders.

These top companies aren't empowering their employees just to be democratic. They believe that listening to lower-level employees and managers boosts their efficiency. *Although only 72% of companies not in the top 20 encourage local leaders to participate in decisions made at headquarters, all of the top 20 encourage this type of participation.* Indeed, 19 of the top 20 companies believe that ideas generated by subsidiary leaders are just as likely to be implemented as are those that originate at headquarters; subsidiary leaders are just as influential at only 76% of the other companies.

What are the best companies? The Hay Group identified the top five companies for leadership as General Electric, Procter & Gamble, Intel Corporation, Siemens, and Banco Santander.

Leader Development and Mentors

As David Day (2000) observed, there is a difference between leader development and leadership development. *Leader development refers to developing individuals' leadership skills, competencies, and overall leadership ability.* In contrast, **leadership development** *refers to the development of social structures and processes that facilitate leadership effectiveness throughout the organization.* In order to become an outstanding leader, potential leaders need to develop a wide range of skills. Day (2011, p. 38) lists these skills this way:

> Leader development includes individual *self-management capabilities* (e.g., self-awareness, balancing conflicting demands, ability to learn, and leadership values), *social capabilities* (e.g., ability to build and maintain relationships, building effective workgroups, communication skills, and ability to develop others), and *work facilitation capabilities* (e.g., management skills, ability to think/act strategically and creatively, and ability to initiate and implement change) (Van Velsor & McCauley, 2004).

People often learn leadership skills from their mentors. Employees who develop protégé-mentorship relationships and who receive career mentoring are more likely to be promoted, to have higher salaries, and to have higher job satisfaction and career satisfaction (Kammeyer-Mueller & Judge, 2008) Protégé-mentor relationships are important to the career success of both men and women (O'Brien, Biga, Kessler, & Allen, 2010). People with mentors tend to have better interpersonal relationships, are more motivated, and suffer slightly less work stress (Eby, Allen, Evans, Ng, & DuBois, 2008). Although learning from mentors is important, formal education has a larger effect on objective career outcomes, so taking advantage of both gives you the best results (Kammeyer-Mueller & Judge, 2008).

For an excellent overview of the research on leader and leadership development, download the following article from the textbook website:

> **The Leader's Bookcase:** Day, D. V. (2011). Leadership development. In A. Bryman, D. Collinson, K. Grint, B. Jackson, & M. Uhl-Bien (Eds.), *Sage handbook of leadership* (pp. 37–50). London, UK: Sage Publications

Some Specific Types of Leaders

Although Chapters 14 and 15 cover transactional and transformational leadership, many of the studies reported in the earlier chapters also used measures of transactional and transformational leadership in their studies on leadership traits, leadership effectiveness, communication styles, and so forth. For example, researchers may want to know what personality traits are related to leadership and thus might use transactional and transformational leadership scales to assess whether someone is a leader. Thus, it will be useful to briefly define transformational and transactional leadership in this chapter. According to researchers Bass and Avolio (1994), *transactional leaders rely on contingent rewards and routine managerial procedures to motivate and influence subordinates.* By **contingent rewards**, *they mean that leaders set up clear expectations for performance, specify what should be done, and reward employees based on their meeting goals and expectations.* There are also two types of transactional leaders: **management by exception—active**, and **management by exception— passive.** *As their names suggest, the former type is characterized by leaders who take a more active role in spotting and correcting problems before they become major issues, whereas the more passive leaders wait until problems become more noticeable.* Another type of leader, called *laissez- faire, is basically a manager who fails to exert leadership and avoids making decisions and carrying out other leadership responsibilities.* **Transformational leaders** *use idealized influence, inspirational motivation, intellectual stimulation, and individualized consideration to transform followers' beliefs and to create a new, more motivating vision* (Avolio, 2011; Bass & Riggio, 2006/2007). Thus, transformational leaders inspire people and develop innovative solutions, although they may also use transactional leadership as well. These two styles will be defined in more detail in Chapters 14 and 15.

Other researchers may assess whether someone is an effective leader by using survey items that measure perceptions of leader-member exchange relationship, or LMX for short (Dansereau, Graen, & Haga, 1975; Graen, 1976; Graen & Cashman, 1975; Graen & Scandura, 1987). The research on leader-member exchange will be covered in a later chapter. However, briefly put, *leader-member exchange scales measure whether or not the leader has a high quality relationship with each individual subordinate.* Liden and Maslyn (1998) found that leader-member exchange relationships have four dimensions: contribution (work performance, especially voluntary performance of tasks above the normal work duties); affect (liking and friendship); loyalty (fulfilling mutual obligations); and professional respect (respect for each others' abilities). The leader-member exchange model states that leaders have to treat followers as individuals. As the next study demonstrates, employees want their leaders to treat them like individuals and to show genuine concern for their welfare.

What Do We Want From Leaders? Genuine Concern

An impressive study surveyed over 3,400 leaders and professionals (chief executives and top, senior, and middle managers) employed by the United Kingdom National Health Service (NHS) or by local government agencies (Alimo-Metcalfe & Alban-Metcalfe, 2005). This study asked the participants their perceptions about leaders that were near or close to them, in other words, their immediate line manager or supervisor. The researchers used a three-stage process to find out what these mid-to-upper level managers and professionals really thought about what makes someone an effective leader. In the first stage, they asked a representative subset of their sample open-ended questions. The questions were designed to "gain information about the perceptions of individuals who are perceived to possess leadership characteristics, in that they have a particularly powerful effect on others' motivation, self-confidence, self-efficacy, or performance" (Alimo-Metcalfe & Alban-Metcalfe, 2005, p. 57). By using open-ended questions, the researchers avoided forcing the respondents to answer survey items based on the researchers' preconceived notions. The researchers then used the employees' responses to make questionnaires that they distributed to the full sample of 2,013 NHS managers. In the third stage, they verified the results from the study of NHS leaders by administering the questionnaire to their sample of 1,464 local government managers and professionals. The researchers found that they could classify the respondents' survey responses into the following factors:

1. Valuing Individuals (Genuine concern for others' well-being and development)

2. Networking and Achieving (Inspirational communicator, networker, and achiever)

3. Enabling (Empowers, delegates, and develops potential)

4. Acting With Integrity (Integrity, consistency, honesty, and openness)

5. Being Accessible (Accessible, approachable, in touch)

6. Being Decisive (Decisive, risk taking)

(Alimo-Metcalfe & Alban-Metcalfe, 2005, p. 56)

The first factor—***valuing individuals***—*was far and away the most important factor when it came to one's immediate supervisor or leader. It shouldn't be surprising that people want their leaders to show genuine concern for their well-being.* Indeed, some people even go so far as to argue that leaders should be *servants* to their followers (Greenleaf, 1970, 1996). Recent research, discussed in later chapters, provides additional evidence for this perspective. The view that leaders should be most concerned with, the welfare of their followers, is also consistent with one of the older leadership theories, the *Ohio State High-High Model,* covered in the chapter on leadership behaviors. This theory argues that leaders should show **consideration** *to their followers' needs while also focusing on* **initiating structure** *and clarifying work duties.*

> **Applications:** When was the last time your leader or manager showed genuine concern for your well-being? What are the ways that leaders can show genuine concern to their immediate subordinates?

Leaders Matter

Some researchers have argued that there are many environmental and organizational factors that reduce the effects that leaders and managers have on work groups and on the organization. This view is intuitively appealing because many people have encountered obstacles and bureaucratic limitations on their ability to exert leadership and get things done. Dionne, Yammarino, Atwater, and James (2002) tested these types of environmental factors to see if they prevented or reduced the effects of having leaders who used effective leadership styles. Their study included 940 subordinates' ratings of 156 leaders. To measure whether leaders had any effects on subordinates' performance, they asked the subordinates to rate the effectiveness of their work groups.

Results: None of the environmental factors were significantly correlated with group effectiveness (Dionne et al., 2002, Table 3, p. 459). The correlations with group effectiveness were all very close to zero, thus indicating they had no effects on group performance. In contrast, the leader's use of contingent rewards, the quality of the leader-member exchange, and the leader's likeability had important and statistically significant correlations with group effectiveness. These results indicate that differences between supervisors in their leadership behaviors, skills, and likeability are important: Leadership matters.

Conclusion: Leaders matter.

> **Applications:** Have you ever worked at an organization where you could compare two different supervisors or managers? Were they equally effective so that it didn't matter which one was the supervisor, or was there a noticeable difference between them in leadership effectiveness? Do the effective leaders manage to find ways around bureaucratic obstacles that hinder less effective leaders? Does a manager's effectiveness in leading a group depend more upon his or her personal abilities or more upon the organizational environment?

The following case is about two leaders who are trying to solve one of the world's biggest problems. Clearly, their leadership matters both to their organization as well as to the world.

Case: *Spotlight on Sustainable Practices*

Royal Philips Electronics is partnering with 30 leading European companies and academic institutions as part of the ENLIGHT program (http://www.philips.com/newscenter, 2011, July 4).

Philips continues to improve its products' energy efficiency; the bulb on the right is an improvement over the earlier bulb.

The ENLIGHT program is designed to further reduce the energy consumption of LED lights by up to 40%. By supporting the ENLIGHT program, the new president and CEO of Royal Philips Electronics, Frans van Houten, is continuing the prior CEO's commitment to sustainable practices. A year earlier, the prior CEO, Gerard Kleisterlee, won the Outstanding Leadership in Sustainable Practices award at the CNBC European Business Leaders Awards 2010. Kleisterlee was praised for his vision and for being a great European leader. Philips

Source: Wikipedia/Geoffrey A. Landis (CC-BY)

is headquartered in the Netherlands and employs 117,000 people in countries around the globe. Philips is also the global leader in lighting solutions (i.e., light bulbs, lamps). Under Kleisterlee's leadership, Philips developed its ambitious EcoVision5 program, which calls for improving the energy efficiency of Philips' products by 50% in a mere 5 years. Because 19% of the world's electricity use is on lighting, improving energy efficiency for lighting alone would be a tremendous boon to the world. Frans van Houten is continuing the EcoVision5 program, which also calls for doubling the amount of material that Philips collects and recycles worldwide. Every Philips product also undergoes an environmental audit to assess its impact on energy consumption, environmental pollution, weight, long-term reliability, and recycling.

Sources: http://www.ebla2010.com (retrieved 2010, June 15)
http://www.philips.com

People emerge as leaders at Royal Philips because they are willing to tackle the important problems facing the world and their organization. As the following Personal Reflections illustrates, helping your club, community group, or work group solve problems is one of the most important ways you can become a leader. Joining clubs, community groups, and committees while volunteering to do extra also helps you gain the leadership experience necessary to get promoted and be an effective leader.

PERSONAL REFLECTIONS: *IT'S EASY TO BECOME A LEADER!*

I had a keen interest in leadership during my college and graduate student days. Naturally, I thought one of the best ways to learn leadership skills was by becoming an officer in the various student clubs I belonged to. At first, I thought it might be hard to become elected president or vice president of a club. After all, wouldn't everyone want the privilege, power, and prestige of being a leader? But I soon found that in many clubs the other members seemed eager to elect me as president, vice president, or other officer. They were quite happy for me to have the privilege of arriving early and staying late after meetings to get the actual work of the clubs done—it turns out, it's a lot more effort to be a leader than a follower. Some of the organizations I joined were fairly large, but I discovered that if I simply spoke up during the first day I attended and indicated a willingness to take on some responsibilities, that people I didn't even know would nominate me to one of the leadership positions (the presidency of the organization was sometimes hard to get, but there were always other officer positions for anyone who seemed willing to do the work).

Despite the effort required, I found these clubs and community groups were a great way to learn leadership skills while having fun at the same time. When learning any skill, people make mistakes—it's better to learn from these mistakes while an officer in a club than in your first career-oriented job. Being dumped as a club officer is not as bad as being fired from your dream job!

Now that I'm in the work world, I've noticed that much of the administrative work is done by committees. Often the informal leader of the committee is the one who's most willing to put in the work and effort to get the job done. In the short run, these informal leaders may not be paid any more than the slackers on the committee, but in the long run, these informal leaders are more likely to get promoted to management. And once they are in management, their informal leadership experience helps them succeed and get the next promotion.

Many managers, executives, and small business owners give generously of their time to community groups and charities and often serve in leadership roles in these volunteer organizations. Often these leaders claimed they learned valuable lessons about leadership while participating in community groups while in college, graduate school, or even later in their careers.

Your Turn to Reflect: Does participating in clubs and volunteer organizations help you learn leadership skills? What organizations could you join to gain leadership experience? How difficult is it to become a leader in an organization if you are willing to do the extra work involved? Are there committees at work you could join that would give you some experience leading groups or let you observe the more senior leaders in action?

Values, Ethics, and Corporate Social Responsibility

It's pretty sad when the former head of the NASDAQ stock exchange turns out to be running a Ponzi scheme (Bernard Madoff made off with *billions* before being caught). It's even sadder to find that both governmental leaders and private sector mortgage bankers were rolling the dice with the nation's (and world's) financial security. Enron employees probably felt both sad and out-raged when they discovered that the leaders they knew and admired were deceiving them about the security of their pension plans and jobs (Sims & Brinkmann, 2003). With examples like these, it's not surprising that ethics is a big topic in leadership. This book will cover a variety of unethical leader behaviors, including abusive leadership, throughout the book.

Fortunately, there are still good leaders out there. Many leaders have made their careers out of serving others, and this book will showcase role models who feed the hungry; mentor young children, teenagers, and employees; support educational programs; help their followers with their personal problems; and give generously to charities. Corporate social responsibility means much more than simply not breaking the law—it also means taking a proactive stance to solve the world's problems (Bruton, 2010; Quatro & Sims, 2008). Ethics is not a sideline to leadership, and many of the leadership theories in this book make ethics, empathy, trust, and authenticity a key part of their theories. As the research on these theories demonstrates, being ethical isn't a costly disadvantage. Instead, empathic, considerate, and ethical leaders have an advantage when it comes to motivating their employees to achieve outstanding performance. Instead of finishing last, empathic *nice* people are actually more likely to emerge as leaders.

Evidence-Based Leadership

There are thousands of articles and books about leadership. Many of the books and articles are based on the authors' personal opinions. Unfortunately, the advice given in these articles and books doesn't always agree. This textbook is based on research that attempts to verify whether a particular belief about leadership is valid or not. The key evidence, along with the researchers' names, is given to you in this textbook. But don't worry—*you are not responsible for knowing the researchers' names, and the questions in the test bank don't ask you to know the names of the numerous researchers cited in the text*. But if you wish to do further research in an area, the researchers' names and their articles are listed in the bibliography section so you can look up the articles. That way you don't have to take what this textbook says on faith—you can see for yourself how strong the evidence is for any particular study. The test bank does include questions about the cases. The questions will generally mention both the leaders' names and their organizations' names, so it shouldn't be too hard to remember the case. As with any other textbook, the test bank also has questions about the key theories and studies. You should know the key findings from the studies that are featured. There are also questions about definitions. The term being defined is always italicized and boldfaced in the text, while the rest of the definition is italicized. This should help you quickly find the definitions in each chapter.

The Best of Every Theory

There are many different leadership theories. Instead of viewing these theories as rivals, however, it's best to see them as matching pieces of a puzzle. All of the leadership theories that have become prominent have done so because they have identified a key problem and issue that leaders need to address. Leadership is a complex process. Each of the leadership theories is the best at solving one part of the puzzle, but to have the complete picture, we need to fit all the different leadership theories together. Here is how all the theories in the chapters fit together to complete the puzzle. Part I covers this chapter, the introduction to leadership. **Part II: Traits and Characteristics of Leaders** (Chapters 2-4) covers personality traits and abilities that influence leader emergence and performance:

> Chapter 2: *How Personality Traits Influence Leader Emergence and Performance* covers the Big Five Model of Personality, Core Self-Evaluations, and the Myers-Briggs Psychological Types.

Chapter 3: *Cognitive Intelligence, Complex Task Performance, and Decision Making* goes over research that shows that cognitive intelligence is one of the best predictors of leadership emergence and performance. This chapter also shows how leaders perform complex tasks and make key decisions.

Chapter 4: *How Emotional Intelligence, Skills, and Competencies Increase Leader Effectiveness* demonstrates how emotional abilities help leaders improve employee morale and task performance.

Part III: Adaptive Leadership Approaches (Chapters 5–7) goes over research which covers specific behaviors that leaders can be taught to perform. These chapters also categorize the different leadership styles and examine which styles would be most effective in particular environmental situations. Chapter 7 argues that leaders have to adapt their behaviors to form unique, one-on-one relations with each follower.

Chapter 5: *The Behavioral Approach to Leadership; Women and Leadership* makes the case that people can be taught the two major leadership styles (showing consideration, initiating structure) covered in the Ohio State leadership model and covers related models as well. This chapter also examines male and female leadership styles in different cultures around the world.

Chapter 6: *Situational and Path-Goal Models of Leadership* argues that the environment plays a major role in determining which leadership style leaders should use. It also discusses the research that shows that leaders need to consider the skill level of their followers.

Chapter 7: *Leader-Member Exchange and One-On-One Relationships* goes over how leaders can improve their one-on-one relationships with followers by adapting their leadership approach to form unique interactions with each follower. This covers work-based exchanges (e.g., the leader awards extra perks to subordinates who contribute more). It also demonstrates the importance of mutual liking and similar emotional exchanges between leaders and followers.

Part IV: How Leaders Motivate Themselves and Others (Chapters 8–15) covers the wide variety of ways in which leaders motivate both themselves and others.

Chapter 8 describes how leaders influence their subordinates' motivational levels by influencing their moods and emotions, whereas Chapter 9 describes the steps that leaders and team members can take to motivate themselves. Chapter 10 continues the investigation into how leaders motivate themselves by examining the characteristics that help leaders overcome obstacles.

Chapter 8: *The Importance of Affect and Emotions to Leadership* describes how one of the major functions of leaders is to motivate followers by creating positive moods, emotions, and high job satisfaction. This chapter also goes over research which shows that one of the major ways in which leaders improve task performance is by improving their followers' affect and job satisfaction.

Chapter 9: *Self-Leadership, Empowerment, Shared/Distributed Leadership, and Teams* describes how individuals and group members can also demonstrate leadership by leading themselves. It describes steps that individuals and groups can do to increase their own motivation levels.

Chapter 10: *Authentic Leadership Theory, Positive Organizational Scholarship, and Servant Leadership* describes how leaders have greater psychological capital that helps them overcome organizational challenges and behave ethically. Like the following chapter, this chapter is also concerned with how leaders develop their identities and sense of self. This chapter also explains how some leaders seek to serve their followers and other stakeholders.

The next chapter extends the discussion of ethics, values, and identity by examining how leaders motivate employees to have high ethical standards along with high job performance by creating a sense of collective identity.

Chapter 11: *Identity Processes: Individual, Relational, Social, Organizational, and Cultural* examines how leaders form their own identity as a leader and influence their followers and colleagues to also identify with each other and with the organization. It demonstrates that people are motivated to perform well when they identify with their occupational role. It also examines how culture influences leaders' and followers' identities.

The next four chapters cover how leaders influence and motivate their followers either through directly exerting power, by persuasion and communication, by goal setting and rewards, or by creating and inspiring new visions.

Chapter 12: *Authority, Power, and Persuasion* covers the major theories about how leaders use authority or persuasion to influence others.

Chapter 13: *Charisma, Rhetoric, and Impression Management* further describes persuasion tactics and charismatic communication techniques that leaders use to persuade others to follow their vision and to enhance their own image.

Chapter 14: *Transactional Leadership and Goal Setting* describes how leaders influence their followers toward goal attainment by creating reward systems and organizational structures.

Chapter 15: *Transformational Leadership, Change, and Sensemaking Perspectives* covers how transformational leaders motivate others by creating a new vision for their group, organization, or society. In addition, this chapter covers some other theories about how leaders make sense of the world and relates these theories to the ability to develop new visions that guide organizations and societies.

In sum, by the time you finish reading this book, you should know what personality traits best predict leadership emergence and performance, what other abilities help leaders perform, the major leadership styles used by leaders, what environmental factors you need to take into account when deciding which leadership style to use, various ways to motivate yourself and others, how to develop your own leader identity as well as build group and organizational identification, how to persuade others and use power wisely, how to create organizational structures and goal setting programs, and finally, how to develop new visions and strategies to guide organizations and societies to meet current and future challenges.

The following case study is about two leaders who dramatically increased Wal-Mart's support for environmental sustainability. It also shows how leaders often seek to solve the most important functional problems facing their group, organization, or society. In addition, it shows how leadership can take place across organizational boundaries and at every level of an organization.

Case: *Jib Ellison (Environmentalist) and Lee Scott (Former CEO, Wal-Mart): Sustainability Saves Money and the Environment*

Pulitzer Prize winner Edward Humes' book on Wal-Mart is called *Force of Nature: The Unlikely Story of Wal-Mart's Green Revolution* (2011). As the title suggests, many environmentalists thought it would be unlikely that Wal-Mart would support the green revolution. At one time, environmentalists would be more likely to protest Wal-Mart with picket signs rather than praise Wal-Mart. But environmental advocate Jib Ellison took another route. He invited Wal-Mart executives and environmental activists to take a white-water rafting trip. They would have to paddle together or sink. The trip also let the Wal-Mart executives see what the environmen-

The Palmdale, California Sam's Club has wind turbines to generate environmentally sustainable energy (Sam's Clubs are a division of Wal-Mart).

Source: Wal-Mart

talists were trying to save—the beauty and majesty of nature. The team-building experience worked and the two groups began engaging in earnest conversations about how Wal-Mart could go green.

Lee Scott, Wal-Mart's CEO at the time, had fond memories of fishing trips with his dad. Rob Walton, son of Wal-Mart's founder Sam Walton, was also an avid environmental supporter and outdoor enthusiast. They wanted to save the environment, but like many business leaders they had concerns. Weren't *go green* programs awfully expensive, with little returns either for businesses or the environment? Wal-Mart also took pride in providing low-cost products to its customers. Aren't green products considerably more expensive? Instead of costing Wal-Mart and customers more money, Jib argued that going green could produce significant cost savings. Going green meant being more efficient: using less fuel, less packaging, less electricity, and less waste.

Lee worked with Jib to find a quick and easy ecological and cost saving project that would demonstrate that going green is good for both customers and Wal-Mart. They started with a toy: a car and truck set for toddlers. The truck set came in display boxes that were several inches larger than necessary. A simple change, shrinking the box size, produced big dividends. Smaller boxes meant more boxes per shipping container, more boxes per foot of store shelf (a huge factor in retail), and less cardboard packaging that had to be paid for. The results: Wal-Mart saved $2.4 million per year, 4,000 fewer trees were used for cardboard, and roughly a million gallons of fuel oil was saved. Going green was a win all the way around. And this was just for a single product—the potential savings across the hundreds of thousands of items Wal-Mart sold was huge.

Soon, Wal-Mart was requiring its suppliers to reduce waste in packaging for a large number of products. Wal-Mart is the world's largest retailer by a large margin. When Wal-Mart speaks, other companies listen. Wal-Mart's sustainability requirements hit the world's manufacturers like a force of nature—an irresistible wave promoting efficiency in packaging and shipping.

Wal-Mart began exploring other eco-cost measures. Scott allocated a half-billion dollar annual budget to researching ways Wal-Mart could become more sustainable—an unparalleled budget for going green. Scott also devoted a considerable amount of his own time to the green initiatives. Sustainability became a part of every employee's mission—it wasn't something relegated to an obscure and unimportant department. Because of Wal-Mart's size, even small changes could produce big savings. Vending machines are often lit up like Las Vegas—after all, the vending machine companies don't pay for the electricity they use. Just turning off the lights in the vending machines in employee break rooms saved Wal-Mart $1.5 million in electricity costs. Wal-Mart also discovered that many store counter display lights stayed on regardless of whether customers were nearby—installing motion detectors that

(Continued)

(Continued)

activated the lights saved Wal-Mart money. Wal-Mart was also paying big bucks to have its 9,000 tons of trash per day hauled away. Jib and his team showed that recycling could make money for Wal-Mart. Wal-Mart also began experimenting with selling garments made with organically grown cotton. Wal-Mart became the world's biggest buyer of organic cotton, and as a result fewer toxic chemicals are being released into the environment.

By 2010, Wal-Mart had achieved some impressive results (see Humes, 2011, p. 230–232). Here are just a few of its accomplishments: Wal-Mart had an overall 16% decrease in carbon emissions per $1 million in sales (compared to 2008). The efficiency of its trucks increased by 60% in terms of miles per case delivered: It delivered 77 million more cases, yet drove 100 million fewer miles compared to 2005. It donated 127 million pounds of food that would have previously been thrown away. Its recycling rate increased to 64% of its garbage. It also increased its sales of responsibly sourced wood products (25% of wood furniture), and 55% of its wild caught seafood now comes from sustainable sources, along with 100% of its farmed shrimp.

Go Green. Save Money. Live Better.

Applications: Why do you think Jib was successful in motivating Wal-Mart to become more sustainable when many other environmental activists were unsuccessful? Which works better: protests or cooperation? Manufacturers saved money by using smaller packages for their products. How important do you think Lee Scott and Wal-Mart's leadership was in motivating the manufacturers to save money while supporting the environment? Jib started exerting leadership over Wal-Mart while he was still an outsider, and Lee Scott exerted leadership over many companies besides Wal-Mart. How often does leadership take place outside of organizational boundaries?

Put It in Practice

1. Work your way up the corporate ladder by establishing mentor relationships with senior leaders.

2. Know when you should exert your influence to persuade others and when to act as your group's representative and key problem solver.

3. Respect cultural differences in power distance and assertiveness and understand how your own behaviors will be interpreted by members of different cultures.

4. Lead at the right level by knowing when to focus on individual, group, or organizational level problems. Don't forget to recognize individual differences among your followers.

5. Don't be egotistical—lower-level managers and front-line workers can have good ideas and can demonstrate leadership if given a chance.

6. Value individuals and demonstrate genuine concern for their well-being.

7. Don't pay attention to the naysayers—leaders really do make a difference.

8. Leadership development: You can develop your leadership skills. Learn leadership skills by joining clubs, community groups, and workplace committees and by volunteering to take on leadership roles.

9. Be ethical: Avoid jail and financial collapse; do good deeds instead.

10. Base your choice of leadership tactics on solid research and evidence.

11. Lead by using team building and a cooperative attitude. Find win-win opportunities (like saving the environment while saving money).

Exercises

1. Perceptions of Leaders

Suppose you were in a study like the one done with the UK's National Health System that surveyed mid-to-upper level leaders and managers. How would you have responded when the researchers asked you questions designed to "gain information about the perceptions of individuals who are perceived to possess leadership characteristics, in that they have a particularly powerful effect on others' motivation, self-confidence, self-efficacy, or performance" (Alimo-Metcalfe & Alban-Metcalfe, 2005, p. 57)? What factors would be particularly important to you? Make a list of your top six factors. How does your list compare to the six factors the researchers found?

2. Leaders as Role Models

Make a list of the top leadership skills or managerial skills you want to learn. These could be things like communication skills, networking and social skills, negotiating, motivating others, or even managing your work-life balance. Then, for each skill, list a leader who would be a good role model for that particular activity. You should not worry if you can't find a leader for every skill—by the time you finish this book, you'll have a role model for every skill you need. Your instructor might ask you to share your lists with a group and make a group list or to share some of your role models with the class.

> Visit the Student Study Site at **www.sagepub.com/humphreyel** for these additional tools:
>
> - Learning Goals
> - Leader's Book Case Articles
> - Web Resources
> - Student Self Assessments

References

Alimo-Metcalfe, B., & Alban-Metcalfe, J. (2005). Leadership: Time for a new direction? *Leadership, 1*(51).

Atwater, L., Wang, M., Smither, J. W., & Fleenor, J. W. (2009). Are cultural characteristics associated with the relationship between self and others' ratings of leadership? *Journal of Applied Psychology, 94*(4), 876–886. doi: 10.1037/a0014561

Avolio, B. J. (2011). *Full range leadership development* (2nd ed.). Thousand Oaks, CA: Sage.

Bass, B. M. (1990). *Bass and Stogdill's handbook of leadership: A survey of theory and research.* New York, NY: Free Press.

Bass, B. M., & Avolio, B. J. (1994*). Improving organizational effectiveness through transformational leadership.* Thousand Oaks, CA: Sage.

Bass, B. M., & Riggio, R. E. (2006/2007). *Transformational leadership* (2nd ed.) [Kindle edition]. Mahwah, NJ: Lawrence Erlbaum.

Bourne, L. (2011, February). Most powerful moms in STEM. In H. Jonsen (Ed.), *Working Mother.* Retrieved from http://www.workingmother.com/BestCompanies/most-powerful-moms/2011/02/most-powerful-moms-in-stem

Bruton, G. D. (2010, August). Business and the world's poorest billion—The need for an expanded examination by management scholars. *Academy of Management Perspectives,* 6–10.

Bryant, A. (2010, February 21). Xerox's new chief tries to redefine its culture. *The New York Times.* Retrieved from http://www.nytimes.com/2010/02/21/business/21xerox.html?_r=1

Dansereau, E., Graen, G., & Haga, W. J. (1975). A vertical dyad linkage approach to leadership within formal organizations: A longitudinal investigation of the role making process. *Organizational Behavior and Human Performance, 13,* 46–78.

Dansereau, F., Yammarino, F. J., & Markham, S. E. (1995). Leadership: The multiple levels approach. *Leadership Quarterly, 6,* 251–263.

Day, D. V. (2000). Leadership development: A review in context. *The Leadership Quarterly, 11,* 581–613.

Day, D. V. (2011). Leadership development. In A. Bryman, D. Collinson, K. Grint, B. Jackson, & M. Uhl-Bien (Eds.), *Sage handbook of leadership* (pp. 37–50). London, UK: Sage Publications.

Den Hartog, D. (2004). Assertiveness. In R. House, P. Hanges, M. Javidan, P. Dorfman, & V. Gupta (Eds.), *Culture, leadership, and organizations* (pp. 395–436). Thousand Oaks, CA: Sage.

Dionne, S. D., Yammarino, F. J., Atwater, L. E., & James, L. R. (2002). Neutralizing substitutes for leadership theory: Leadership effects and common-source bias. *Journal of Applied Psychology, 87*(3), 454–464. doi: 10.1037//0021-9010.87.3.454

Eby, L. T., Allen, T. D., Evans, S. C., Ng, T., & DuBois, D. L. (2008). Does mentoring matter? A multidisciplinary meta-analysis comparing mentored and non-mentored individuals. *Journal of Vocational Behavior, 72,* 254–267.

Graen, G. B. (1976). Role-making processes within complex organizations. In M. D. Dunnette (Ed.), *Handbook of industrial and organizational psychology* (pp. 1201–1245). Chicago, IL: Rand McNally.

Graen, G. B., & Cashman, J. (1975). A role-making model of leadership in formal organizations: A development approach. In J. G. Hunt & L. L. Larson (Eds.), *Leadership frontiers* (pp. 143–165). Kent, OH: Kent State University.

Graen, G. B., & Scandura, T. A. (1987). Toward a psychology of dyadic organizing. *Research in Organizational Behavior, 9,* 175–208.

Greenleaf, R. K. (1970). *The servant as leader.* San Francisco, CA: Jossey-Bass.

Greenleaf, R. K. (1996). *On becoming a servant leader.* San Francisco, CA: Jossey-Bass.

The Hay Group. (2011, January 25). *Sixth annual Hay Group study identifies best companies for leadership.* Retrieved from http://www.haygroup.com/ww/Press/Details.aspx?ID=28838

Hofstede, G. (2001). *Culture's consequences: Comparing values, behaviors, institutions and organizations across nations* (2nd ed.). Thousand Oaks, CA: Sage.

House, R., Hanges, P., Javidan, M., Dorfman, P., & Gupta, V. (2004). *Culture, leadership, and organizations.* Thousand Oaks, CA: Sage.

Humes, E. (2011). *Force of nature: The unlikely story of Wal-Mart's green revolution.* New York, NY: HarperCollins.

Kammeyer-Mueller, J. D., & Judge, T. A. (2008). A quantitative review of mentoring research: Test of a model. *Journal of Vocational Behavior, 72,* 269–283.

Liden, R. C., & Maslyn, J. M. (1998). Multidimensionality of leader–member exchange: An empirical assessment through scale development. *Journal of Management, 24,* 43–72.

Northouse, P. G. (2007). *Leadership: Theory and practice.* Thousand Oaks, CA: Sage.

NPR Staff. (2012, May 23). *Xerox CEO: 'If you don't transform, you're stuck'.* Retrieved from http://www.npr.org/2012/05/23/153302563/xerox-ceo-if-you-don-t-transform-you-re-stuck

O'Brien, K. E., Biga, A., Kessler, S. R., & Allen, T. D. (2010). A meta-analytic investigation of gender differences in mentoring. *Journal of Management, 36,* 537–554.

Quatro, S. A., & Sims, R. R., (Eds). (2008). *Executive ethics: Ethical dilemmas and challenges for the C Suite.* Charlotte, NC: Information Age Publishing.

Sims, R. R., & Brinkmann, J. (2003). Enron ethics (or: Culture matters more than codes). *Journal of Business Ethics, 45,* 243–256.

Van Velsor, E., & McCauley, C. D. (2004). Our view of leadership development. In C. D. McCauley & E. Van Velsor (Eds.), *The Center for Creative Leadership handbook of leadership development* (2nd ed., pp. 1–22). San Francisco, CA: Jossey-Bass.

Yammarino, F. J., & Dansereau, F. (2008). Multi-level nature of and multi-level approaches to leadership. *The Leadership Quarterly, 19,* 135–141.

Yammarino, F. J., Dionne, S. D., Chun, J. U., & Dansereau, F. (2005). Leadership and levels of analysis: A state-of-the-science review. *Leadership Quarterly, 16,* 879–919.

PART II

TRAITS AND CHARACTERISTICS OF LEADERS

2

How Personality Traits Influence Leader Emergence and Performance

Chapter Road Map

Case: *James Parker, Southwest Airlines: Not the Best People but the Right People*

James Parker, as former CEO of Southwest Airlines, has a pretty impressive resume as a leader. While he was CEO, Southwest Airlines was one of America's three most admired companies, ranked among the best corporate citizens in America, was one of the most socially responsible in the world, and was worldwide airline of the year. His proudest accomplishment as CEO was protecting the jobs of all of Southwest's employees (the only major airline to do so) and remaining profitable after 9/11. As Parker (2008) explains in his book, *Do the Right Thing*, it's the people that Southwest Airlines has hired over the

Southwest shows its creative side by having special designs on some of its jets, like the Arizona One (depicted below) or the playful Shamu whale design (not shown).

Source: Flickr/StuSeeger (CC-BY)

years that have made the difference. As one of his chapter titles indicates, "Great Organizations Have Great Leaders at Every Level" (p. 83). So how have Parker and Southwest gone about hiring these leaders at every level? As he explains in a chapter provokingly called "Who Wants the 'Best' People?" (p. 105), Southwest doesn't always want the *best* people; instead, it wants the *right* people. If *best* is defined as the candidates with the highest GPAs and the most job experience, that doesn't guarantee getting hired at Southwest. Instead, Parker wants the *right* candidates—leaders whose personalities and attitudes make them a good fit for Southwest Airlines' fun, team-based culture. Southwest's hiring motto is "We hire for attitude and train for skills" (p. 105). True, they hire many people with outstanding GPAs from top colleges and with valuable work experience—and since they hire only 1 to 2 percent of the 100,000 applicants they receive every year, they can and are choosy about their hires. But what sets the successful applicants apart from those with similar qualifications are their personalities and attitudes.

In many companies, managers don't want to spend much time interviewing and selecting new hires—this is likely to be especially true in high turnover companies. But what Southwest Airlines and other great companies have learned is that people are less likely to quit if they are the right fit for the job. When you hire everyone to be leaders, hiring the right person is especially important. New hires either improve your team or drag it down. As Parker puts it, "The better you do at selecting new employees, the less time you will waste down the road dealing with performance, discipline, and discharge issues. Selecting poorly can make your future very stressful. Selecting the right people can make your future a joy" (Parker, 2008, p. 106).

Because Southwest is a customer service-oriented company, it values employees who can interact pleasantly with customers and with each other. Parker prefers people with positive attitudes:

> We used to say that we took our jobs seriously, but not ourselves. In other words, we were looking for people who could laugh, savor life, and enjoy being around other people. We didn't want self-absorbed prima donnas. We wanted other-oriented people who genuinely cared about and respected others. (Parker, 2008, p. 110)

Parker gives a great example of this hiring philosophy. Once they interviewed a pilot with an outstanding flying record, with experience flying a wide variety of aircraft, and with leading people—he truly had a superstar resume, yet he was not hired. Why? He had been rude to the receptionist (Parker, 2008, p. 124).

Parker also realizes that people want to be able to express their personalities at work. His book is full of references about Southwest Airlines being a place where employees "were allowed to be themselves and have fun" (Parker, 2008, p. 111). The best employees want more than just money from their jobs—they want to be able to be open and authentic about themselves and be able to express their individuality at work. He gives an example of a time he recruited a lawyer named Cindy away from a major law firm. While visiting Southwest Airlines, Cindy noticed that one of the paralegals was wearing a toe ring and open sandals. Years later, she confessed to Parker that seeing the paralegal have the freedom to wear toe rings was what made her decide to work at Southwest Airlines. Although most corporations throw the occasional office party, Parker says office parties are not the key to having a fun workplace (although Southwest does have a strong tradition of holding parties every Friday after work and of going all out for Halloween and other holidays). Instead, when listing 15 ways to make people enjoy their work, he lists this as his third point: "People feel they can be themselves and express their personalities." Interestingly, number 1 is "People find their work fulfilling" and 2 is "People feel appreciated" (p. 170).

(Continued)

(Continued)

Applications: Should companies always hire people with the best objective records in terms of experience, test scores, GPAs, and college records, or should they take people's personalities into account? Is it fair to hire people based on their attitudes? Are there some types of work where having a positive outlook should not be important? How important to you would it be to work in a place where you can express your personality?

As the Southwest Airlines case demonstrates, companies hire people based on their personal characteristics and traits. In particular, Southwest Airlines and other corporations want to hire people that have the characteristics and personalities that make them leaders. In order to do so, they have to know what traits make someone an effective leader, as opposed to an ineffective leader or a follower. Thus, this chapter examines research on the personality traits of effective leaders. In particular, this chapter addresses the following questions:

- How do trait theorists view leadership? Does everyone agree with the trait perspective?
- What are the major dimensions that leadership traits can be grouped into?
- How well do personality traits predict leadership emergence and leadership performance? Which specific traits predict best?
- What is the utility of the Myers-Briggs Type Indicator® for understanding leadership?

There are a variety of ways in which individuals differ from each other. People can differ in their personality traits; they can differ in their abilities (cognitive, emotional, physical, etc.); and they can differ in their values, attitudes, and beliefs. This chapter covers dispositional traits such as extraversion, agreeableness, and Core Self-Evaluations, whereas cognitive intelligence and emotional intelligence will be covered in the next two chapters. The effects of values and attitudes on leadership are covered throughout the book.

Two Fundamental Dimensions of Leadership

From the Southwest Airlines example of the pilot with the star resume but who was rude to the receptionist, we can imagine at least two dimensions that are important to leaders. One is the technical competence dimension, as evidenced by the pilot's knowledge of aviation, while the other is the social and interpersonal dimension. In fact, some researchers argue that these are the *two fundamental dimensions that underlie all traits and judgments about people* (for a review of this literature, see Judd, James-Hawkins, Yzerbyt, & Kashima, 2005). Judd and his colleagues refer to the first dimension as the *competency dimension,* which consists of *traits like intelligent, energetic, and motivated,* whereas the second is the *warmth dimension,* which refers to *traits related to being sociable, friendly, and caring.* As we will see in the following chapters, many leadership theories describe leaders along similar dimensions, with some leader types focusing more on the competency dimension and others on the warmth dimension.

The Trait Theory of Leadership and the Value of Personality Traits

Early leadership theories were based on the premise that outstanding leaders differed in important ways from average people due to their extraordinary personalities. As the historian Thomas Carlyle stated, "The history of the world was the biography of great men" (Carlyle, 1907, p. 18; quote taken from Judge, Bono, Ilies, & Gerhardt, 2002, p. 765). According to the *Great Leader trait theory, leaders such as Julius Caesar, Napoleon, Joan of Arc, Washington, Roosevelt, and Queen Elizabeth awed their followers through the force of their personalities and shaped the course of history through their personalities and the decisions they made.* In the business world, leaders like Rockefeller, Carnegie, and Ford also personified the industries they dominated, while Florence Nightingale revolutionized health care and created modern nursing. Thomas Edison and Alexander Graham Bell embodied the spirit of scientist entrepreneurs. With these great leaders as examples, it is easy to see why early scholars were fascinated by personality traits. This approach focused on studying core personality traits that separated leaders from nonleaders and grew to consider typical leaders in businesses and organizations, not just the world changers. This perspective dominated leadership research for the first half of the 20th century.

Skepticism about leadership traits began when some influential reviews claimed that leadership traits did not explain very much, and measures of personality traits were only slightly or moderately correlated with either leadership emergence or performance (Mann, 1959; Stogdill, 1948). After these reviews came out, the number of researchers studying leadership traits plummeted. Some researchers focused on exploring models that linked specific combinations of leader traits with the environment and with the situations that best matched their particular leadership style and traits—we will go over these models in a later chapter. Others argued even more forcefully that traits had nothing to do with leadership, and instead, behaviors were more important—these leadership behaviors were learned behaviors that could be improved by training programs and by experience. We will cover this approach later as well. Some even went so far as to claim that leaders were not important at all. Instead, the environment was all important, and leaders of organizations were merely reflections of the economic, cultural, and social conditions of the times. Scholars still think the environment is important, but beginning in the 1980s, scholars began to accumulate evidence that personality traits also influence leaders' behaviors (Lord, De Vader, & Alliger, 1986).

Applications: Do personality traits make a difference to leadership? Do you think history would have turned out considerably different if Washington, Queen Elizabeth, Martin Luther King, Henry Ford, and Thomas Edison had never been born, or do you think very similar people would have taken their place and the world would have gone on pretty much in the same way? Think about the leaders in the organizations you participate in as an employee or member. Do the leaders' personalities make a difference in their effectiveness, or is it just their job knowledge and skills that determine how effective they are?

Distal and Proximal Attributes

Zaccaro, Kemp and Bader (2004; see also Zaccaro, 2007) have developed a conceptual model that links leaders' personality traits to their leadership behaviors and from there to leadership outcomes. The *distal attributes* in their model are *the personality traits, cognitive abilities, values, and motives of the leaders*. They referred to them as distal because they are the most distant from the leadership outcomes. These innate abilities and motivations give people the chance to develop the more *proximal attributes,* such as *problem solving skills, social appraisal skills, and expertise or knowledge.* These proximal skills are influenced by the operating environment the leader is in; for example, does the leader have a mentor who can sharpen his leadership skills, or does the leader work for an organization with excellent training programs? Support for the distal and proximal model comes from Van Iddekinge, Ferris, and Heffner (2009) and Hirschfeld, Jordan, Thomas, and Field (2008).

A meta-analysis examined 16 personality traits that could be considered to be distal attributes, along with nine more proximal or state-like attributes that represent developed skills (Hoffman, Woehr, Maldagen-Youngjohn, & Lyons, 2011). With regard to personality traits, the meta-analysis summarized

498 studies with a combined sample size of 115,327 participants; for proximal state-like attributes, the meta-analysis summarized 165 studies with 31,524 participants. The 16 personality traits were Achievement Motivation, Initiative, Ambition, Energy, Need for Power, Dominance, Extraversion, Conscientiousness, Honesty/Integrity, Self-Confidence, Adjustment (i.e., social adjustment), Creativity, Flexibility, Self-Monitoring, Charisma, and Cognitive Ability. Of these, *the ones that best predicted leadership effectiveness were Achievement Motivation, Energy, Dominance, Honesty/Integrity, Self-Confidence, Creativity, and Charisma.* Like its name suggests, Achievement Motivation refers to the motivation to achieve, and this concept will be formally defined and examined in greater detail in a later chapter. The meaning of the other traits should also be self-evident from their common definitions and meanings and thus don't need to be technically defined. For example, Energy refers to the degree to which someone is active and energetic, while Dominance refers to the degree to which someone is assertive and strives for dominance in a group.

The nine proximal or state-like skills were Technical Knowledge, Past Experience, Interpersonal Skills, Oral Communication, Written Communication, Management Skills, Problem-Solving Skills, Decision Making, and Organizing and Planning (Hoffman et al., 2011). *The skills that best explained leadership effectiveness were Interpersonal Skills, Oral Communication, Written Communication, Management Skills, Problem-Solving Skills, and Decision Making.* Interestingly, the study found that personality traits and distal traits were roughly equal in the size of their correlations with leader effectiveness. The next two chapters, on cognitive intelligence/complex task performance and on emotional intelligence/competencies, go over these types of skills in more detail.

The Leader's Bookcase: Go to the textbook website to download this article on how leaders' personality traits vary by culture: Casimir, G., & Waldman, D. A. (2007). A cross cultural comparison of the importance of leadership traits for effective low-level and high-level leaders: Australia and China. *International Journal of Cross Cultural Management, 7*(1), 47–60.

The Big Five Model of Personality

Although there are hundreds of personality traits, these different traits can be grouped together into smaller clusters or factors of traits that are related to each other. One of the best known and accepted models is the Five Factor Model of Personality (Goldberg, 1990), also referred to as the Big Five Model. The dimensions of the Big Five are Neuroticism, Extraversion, Openness to

Experience, Agreeableness, and Conscientiousness. Some researchers use the other name for the first dimension, Emotional Stability, to highlight the positive pole of the Neurotic-Emotionally Stable dimension. People high on *Neuroticism tend to be anxious, worried, and depressed, and may have other problems like obsessive-compulsive behaviors.* Conversely, people high on *Emotional Stability tend to be relaxed, calm, happy, and free of neurotic thoughts and behaviors.* Researchers also consider two important lower-order personality traits—self-confidence and self-esteem—to belong to this dimension. As this illustrates, The Big Five groups traits that often—but not always—go together, such as self-confidence and relaxed, into a single dimension.

The Extraversion-Introversion dimension is the second cluster in the Big Five. As you are probably aware, *Extraverts like to socialize with others, but they are also more likely to be energetic, active, and assertive.* In contrast, *Introverts like to spend more time alone, prefer more solitary activities, and draw much of their energy and inspiration from self-reflection.* Leaders almost by definition spend time with others, so it is natural to think that Extraverts would be more likely to emerge as leaders. Extraverts may emerge as leaders more often in part because they are more likely to want the job of leader. For example, a study of a related trait, that of social potency, found that people high on social potency were more likely to occupy leadership roles 6 years later, and thus have higher career earnings (Zhang & Arvey, 2009).

Case: *Oprah Winfrey and J. K. Rowling: One Extravert, One Introvert—Both Successful*

In 2007, *Forbes* declared Oprah Winfrey and J. K. Rowling the two richest women in entertainment, just ahead of Martha Stewart and Madonna. Together, they are a good example of how you can be successful no matter what your personality type. The key is to pick the occupation or industry that matches your personality and skills. Oprah is an Extravert. Her extraverted personality comes into play in her role as a talk show host. She also manages her own magazine and other businesses, as well as her TV show—all of which require her to supervise and interact with numerous people every day. In contrast, J. K. is an Introvert. She achieves success by writing alone. Her successful Harry Potter books and movies have become a billion dollar industry, although as a writer she does not have

Oprah Winfrey celebrates her 50th birthday in 2004 at a party at the Hotel Bel Air.

Source: Flickr/Alan Light (CC-BY)

to supervise the many people who have worked on her movies and related businesses (there are, of course, introverted managers and leaders—the correlation between Extraversion and leadership is only moderate).

Both Oprah and J. K. have used their celebrity to inspire others to overcome the obstacles in their lives. Rowling, for example, has been very forthcoming in describing the bouts of depression she used to feel and has publicly attributed the creation of the Dementors in her novels to her own dark feelings.

J. K. Rowling displays her magic at a White House Easter Egg Roll.

Applications: Do you think Introverts can be just as successful as Extraverts when it comes to leadership? Do you know any Introverts who occupy leadership positions? If so, how effective are they? Does the type of occupation make a difference in whether Introverts or Extraverts make good leaders (or can they be successful on their own)?

Sources: Goldman L., & Blakeley K. (2007, January 18). *Forbes.* Retrieved from http://www.forbes.com/2007/01/17/richest-women-entertainment-tech-media-cz_lg_richwomen07_0118womenstars_lander_print.html

Openness refers to *originality, creativity, and the willingness to try new experiences.* Because leadership in many fields requires adaption to change, willingness to try new strategies, and the need to be innovative, it makes sense that Openness should be a component of effective leadership.

Agreeableness consists of *lower-order traits related to cooperation, altruism, interpersonal sensitivity, and the need to be liked.* Although cooperation is generally a good thing, some scholars suggest that being too concerned with cooperating with others and with being liked by others makes one vulnerable to more assertive people.

Conscientiousness refers to *being punctual, persistent, a willingness to work hard, and the desire to complete tasks correctly.* All of these traits are positive so it is natural to assume that leaders would be more conscientious than others.

Because the personality variables are correlated with each other, researchers use multiple regression to see which variables are responsible for outcomes such as leadership emergence and performance (multiple regression is a statistical method to determine which variables are most important when considered together). Table 2.1 displays the results of a meta-analysis when all five factors are entered into a multiple regression equation (Judge et al., 2002). *For leadership effectiveness, the only two important traits in the multiple regression were Openness and Extraversion—the other three were not statistically significant.* Openness had the largest effect, although the effect for Extraversion was close enough to be essentially tied with Openness. However, Extraversion was somewhat more important than Openness when predicting to leadership emergence, so its overall effect was slightly greater. This suggests that leaders need to be open to new ideas in order to develop plans and effective strategies and extraverted enough to emerge as the leader and to get others to go along with the plans.

In terms of leadership emergence, Agreeableness was *negatively* related to emerging as a leader, demonstrating that it takes some assertiveness to emerge as a leader. However, those low on Agreeableness were *not* more effective as leaders than those high on Agreeableness. Thus, while being low on agreeableness helps one emerge as a leader, it doesn't help one perform better, and organizations may not want to hire people simply because they are low on Agreeableness.

Conscientiousness helped people emerge as leaders, but it is interesting that it didn't help leaders perform more effectively once Openness and Extraversion were taken into account. Perhaps this is because even ineffective leaders can be hard working, and what separates effective leaders most from ineffective ones is the quality of their decisions and their ability to work

Table 2.1   The Effects of the Big Five Personality Measures on Leadership Emergence and Effectiveness

	Leadership Emergence	Leadership Effectiveness
Neuroticism	No significant effect	No significant effect
Extraversion	Positively related	Positively related
Openness	Positively related	Positively related
Agreeableness	Negatively related	No significant effect
Conscientiousness	Positively related	No significant effect

Source: This table is based on data from: Judge, T. A., Bono, J. E., Ilies, R., & Gerhardt, M. W. (2002). Personality and leadership: A qualitative and quantitative review. *Journal of Applied Psychology, 87,* 765–780. Data source used with permission of the American Psychological Association.

with others. Nonetheless, Conscientiousness still shows an important positive correlation with leadership emergence, so potential leaders need to work hard enough to get the promotion.

Neuroticism was not significantly related to either leader emergence or performance when taking into account the effects of the other variables. This is because of Neuroticism's overlap with the other personality variables—when the other variables are not taken into account, Neuroticism is negatively correlated with both leadership emergence and effectiveness.

> **Self-Assessment:** See the textbook website if you want to rate yourself on the Big Five personality traits.

Core Self-Evaluations

Core Self-Evaluations is a relatively new personality trait concept; however, it is composed of four of the oldest and most frequently studied personality traits: Emotional Stability, Self-Esteem, Locus of Control, and Generalized Self-Efficacy (Judge, Locke, & Durham, 1997; Judge, Van Vianen, & De Pater, 2004). Thus, it is a broad measure that includes the key features of these four traits, which are normally correlated with each other. Emotional Stability is one of the Big Five personality factors and was defined earlier in this chapter. *Self-Esteem refers to the degree of approval and sense of self-worth that people have for themselves.* Locus of Control, by the way, refers to the belief that you control what happens to you. People with an *External Locus of Control believe that outside forces—chance, fate, luck, other people—determine what happens to them;* conversely, people with an *Internal Locus of Control believe that they determine their own destiny through their own actions and efforts.* People with high *Generalized Self-Efficacy believe they are generally successful at performing a wide range of tasks and activities* (generalized efficacy is different from task specific efficacy—you may think, for example, that you are good at most types of work tasks but recognize that there are some specific tasks that you can't do).

Judge et al. defined Core Self-Evaluations this way:

> *Core Self-Evaluations is a higher-order concept representing the fundamental evaluations that people make about themselves and their functioning in the environment. Individuals with positive Core Self-Evaluations appraise themselves in a consistently positive manner across situations; such individuals see themselves as capable, worthy, and in control of their lives.* (2004, pp. 326–327) [boldface and italics added]

Judge, Erez, Bono, and Thorensen (2003) were the first to develop a scale to directly measure this concept, called the Core Self-Evaluation Scale; later, this scale was also validated in Spanish and Dutch samples by Judge et al. (2004). Core Self-Evaluations are related to job performance and career earnings (Judge, 2009).

Leaders need to take into account how their subordinates rate on the components of Core Self-Evaluations. For example, De Hoogh and Den Hartog (2009) demonstrated that charismatic leaders can help subordinates with a low Internal Locus of Control, in particular by helping them have lower levels of burnout. In contrast, autocratic leaders increased subordinates' feelings of burnout, especially for subordinates high on Neuroticism. There are many people who are talented and have the potential to perform, yet lack the self-confidence necessary to perform well. Thus, it is the duty of leaders to find ways to motivate and inspire employees to believe in themselves.

> **Applications:** What can managers and leaders do to boost the confidence of their team members?

1. How can you know if others have low self-esteem and low confidence at work? What are the signs and symptoms?

2. What are some suggestions about how you can boost team members' beliefs that they can get the job done and perform well?

CEO Core Self-Evaluations at the Ball Park

Can high Core Self-Evaluations help CEOs have a winning team? According to a study of 75 CEOs of major league baseball teams, it certainly can (Resick, Whitman, Weingarden, and Hiller, 2009). This study examined how the personalities of the baseball CEOs influenced their leadership styles and the performance of their teams. The CEOs with high Core Self-Evaluations were more likely to use two effective leadership styles (transformational leadership and contingent rewards). As a result, these CEOs

–had higher team winning percentages

–had higher fan attendance

–were more likely to be included in the rankings of baseball's greatest executives

–had lower manager turnover

Applications: Think about some of the coaches and sports leaders that you have worked with (this can include recreational leagues and volunteer coaches, organizers, etc). If you want, you can substitute leaders of other extracurricular type activities. How would you rate your different coaches on their self-confidence and Core Self-Evaluations? Did the ones with the best winning percentages seem to have the best Core Self-Evaluations at the beginning of each season? Which coaches and leaders made you feel more self-confident, both as a player and as a person? In recreational leagues, not all players are equally talented—how did the coaches with the highest self-evaluations treat the players with the least initial ability?

PERSONAL REFLECTIONS: *INTERNAL LOCUS OF CONTROL AND THE AMERICAN DREAM*

When I was in high school, I read a number of biographies about business leaders with an internal locus of control philosophy that you can succeed if you try. These books made business seem exciting, with fortunes lost and won based on the skill and insight of the rival leaders. I also admired inventors like Thomas Edison and Alexander Graham Bell who became rich and successful as a result of their own ideas and hard work. The American Dream seemed alive and well. But then I read a number of articles that suggested that dreams of success and upward mobility were nothing but illusions. The mass media was very skeptical about business opportunities. If you did come up with a new idea or product, the media implied big corporations would steal your ideas and put you out of business. And forget about working your way to the top of the corporate hierarchy—the top slots are reserved for the sons and daughters of the already wealthy. And in politics, if you weren't a member of the Kennedy or Rockefellers, or of similarly rich and well connected families, forget about high office. And of course, you had to attend an elite private university (affordable only to the rich) to make connections with other rich and famous families. As a result of all of this negative publicity, I became more skeptical about the chances to become a successful entrepreneur and decided to focus on academics.

I attended one of the nation's elite private universities—The University of Chicago—on a generous full scholarship. Surprisingly, most of the other students there were just like me, from middle class and professional backgrounds. The few ones from mega-rich families still had to work just as hard as the rest of us to get good grades—no one was giving them a free ride grade-wise just because they had rich relatives. And in the next few years, I watched as the seemingly invincible Big Blue—IBM—became humbled by a pair of upstart kids with barely a dime between them. Over and over again, I read about how people from average backgrounds triumphed over the Fortune 500 with their new business ventures. And Sam Walton, who had lived briefly in my hometown (Springfield, MO) as a child, became the richest man in the world through his own efforts (another local boy, Brad Pitt, became one of the world's biggest movie stars). The biggest corporations in the world were also picking people like Jack Welch—whose father was a train conductor—as their CEOs. And in the political realm, the Republicans picked as their star president Ronald Reagan, a man whose father had been a governmental employee during the Great Depression, and the Democrats picked the Man from Hope, Arkansas, Bill Clinton, whose mother was a nurse.

Now there's a *New York Times* top ten bestselling book, *Outliers: The Story of Success*, by Malcolm Gladwell (2008) which casts doubt on people's ability to become successful through their own efforts. According to *Outliers*, it's not enough to be smart or hard working to achieve great success. Instead, you have to be born in the right time periods (narrowed down to a few years each century) and in the right locations. For example, Gladwell argues that Apple cofounders Steve Jobs and Steve Wozniak would never have been successful if they hadn't been born in Silicon Valley, which created a local culture that made scientific breakthroughs more likely. As Malcolm puts it, you could find spare computer parts for sale in every local garage sale. And according to *Outliers*, the window for starting computer manufacturing companies like Apple and software companies like Microsoft was a small band of a few years. After that, you would face too much competition from the early entries in the field to succeed.

Your Turn to Reflect: Do you think that you can be a success starting out from any location and during any time period? Certainly, if you had started a business in the summer of 1929, your chances for success over the next 2 decades would be substantially less than if you had started a business during the mid-1980s. The world economy is not doing too well right now. Do you think you still have plenty of opportunities to make your own destiny?

Leaders with an Internal Locus of Control demonstrate initiative because they believe they can successfully solve problems and obtain goals. The following section covers a related set of personality traits that also concern people's willingness to take initiative and be proactive.

Proactive Leaders Take Charge

Have you ever worked with a manager or coworker who seemed too passive to solve problems? Perhaps the manager or coworker would let work accumulate to an overwhelming level. Perhaps he or she postponed decisions, waited until the last minute to start work on key tasks, or never saw problems coming until they were knocking loudly on the door. Contrast that with a manager or coworker who always seemed to be one step ahead of the game, who solved tasks before they became problems, or who took initiative to improve the workplace instead of being satisfied with the status quo. This latter type of leader has a proactive personality.

A recent meta-analysis has examined the extent to which having a proactive personality influenced performance (Thomas, Whitman, & Viswesvaran, 2010). As defined in this study, "***Proactive personality*** *reflects a relatively stable dispositional tendency for individuals to control situational forces and actively incite change in their environments*" (p. 276; e.g., Bateman & Crant, 1993) [italics and boldface added]. A proactive orientation may be especially important during turbulent times: "Proactive employees who succeed within these dynamic environments do so by realizing that they do not have to play the hand they were dealt. Rather, top performers tend to proactively create circumstances that facilitate personal and organizational success" (Bateman & Crant, 2010, p. 276). The study summarized research that used four different labels for different types of proactive behavior: (1) proactive personality (e.g., Bateman & Crant, 1993), (2) personal initiative (e.g., Frese, Kring, Soose, & Zempel, 1996), (3) voice (e.g., Van Dyne & LePine, 1998), and (4) taking charge (e.g., Morrison & Phelps, 1999). Voice refers to the willingness to speak up with constructive suggestions about problems, and you probably already know what personal initiative and taking charge means—both reflect constructive efforts to improve the organization. The study summarized 25 separate samples with a combined number of 5,045 participants. As expected, *people with all four types of proactive personality had higher performance.*

What's Your Type?

One of the more popular psychological scales is the Myers-Briggs Type Indicator® (MBTI), which is based on the theories of Carl Jung (1971). The MBTI determines people's problem-solving styles according to how they make decisions and gather information. The MBTI measures people's preferences or type according to four dimensions: Sensing vs. iNtuition, Thinking vs. Feeling, Extraversion vs. Introversion, and Judging vs. Perceiving (Myers, 1998; Myers, McCaulley, Quenk, & Hammer, 1998). How do you gather information? *If you gather specific facts and prefer concrete details about things you can see, hear, and touch, you are a **Sensor**. If you prefer abstract data and concepts, you are an **iNtuitive**.* How do you make decisions? *If you make decisions based on impersonal, objective facts, and logical principles,* *you are a **Thinker**. If you make decisions based on people's feelings and values, you are a **Feeler**.* Where do you draw your energy? *If you gain energy and excitement from the external world and from people, then you are an **Extravert**. If you renew your energy and enthusiasm from inward introspection, your own thoughts, and from reading and similar activities, then you're an **Introvert**.* What are your planning processes like? *If you prefer orderly, well structured and scheduled activities, you are a **Judger**. If you are easy going, take things as they come, and prefer to be more spontaneous, you are a **Perceiver**.* The makers of the MBTI claim that the different types are all valid, and that one type is not better than another. Instead, they argue knowing your type can help you find the right occupational match and also help you learn how to communicate with people who have a different type.

Table 2.2 gives an overview of each dimension as it relates to leadership. There are 16 different combinations of these types; for example, one combination typical of many corporate top executives is ENTJ (Extravert, iNtuitive, Thinker, Judger). A book, *Type Talk at Work*, by Kroeger, Thuesen, and Rutledge (2002), explains the 16 different combinations in detail.

Capraro and Capraro (2002) performed a meta-analysis of the research on the reliability of the MBTI, and they concluded that the scales had generally acceptable scale properties. Gardner and Martinko (1996) reviewed the research on the MBTI scales in terms of their overall validity and usefulness for management and leadership. They concluded that the literature generally supports the validity of the scales. However, they noted that the four dimensions may not be bipolar. Bipolar classifications assume most people are at the ends of the range from one pole to the other, with few people in the middle. Because some research indicates many people fall in the middle of the MBTI categories, Gardner and Martinko recommend using continuous scales to measure the dimensions.

Gardner and Martinko (1996) found support for the existence of the Thinking vs. Feeling dimension. People's self-descriptions and even their choice of words are highly correlated with their Thinking vs. Feeling type. *The Thinking and Judging combination is prevalent among managers and administrators at a considerably higher rate than in the general population* (Gardner & Martinko, 1996; Kroeger et al., 2002). It is likely that people high on the Thinking and Judging dimensions are attracted to administration because of their logical decision-making style and willingness to judge and control others. Kroeger et al. (2002) found that the percentage of people with a Thinking style went up as the level increased from middle management to the executive level. They reasoned that this could be due to Thinkers overselecting other Thinkers for promotion; they recommended including more Feeling types in the executive team to achieve a more balanced decision-making process. Gardner and

Table 2.2   Leadership Styles of the Myers-Briggs Psychological Types

Sensors: time-line oriented, focuses on practical details, implementation and action, uses a directive leadership style
iNtuitives: good at seeing patterns, future possibilities, and the *big picture*, leads others by developing visions that guide change
Thinkers: use logic and analysis to make decisions, they focus on problems and are relatively objective, may focus more on giving constructive feedback than on subordinates' feelings
Feelers: empathic focus on people, they make subjective decisions based on their values and make exceptions to policies, they exert influence through their relationships and friendships
Extraverts: are action-oriented, they influence others by talking and interacting with people and developing networks, they tend to be open with others about their feelings and attitudes
Introverts: when they exert leadership, they do it through communicating plans and ideas, or by expressing values; they sometimes communicate in writing
Judgers: they seek control, and they develop schedules, goals, and organizational structures to influence others, they are decisive when making decisions and prefer closure
Perceivers: they may appear to be unfocused, but they are flexible and adaptable, good at generating ideas, and are open to new opportunities, they are curious, easygoing, and fun loving

Source: Adapted from: Kroeger, O., Thuesen, J., & Rutledge, H. (2002). *Type talk at work (revised): How the 16 personality styles determine your success on the job.* New York, NY: Dell.

Martinko found only a few peer reviewed research studies which examined whether Thinking or Feeling managers were more effective, and these studies had inconsistent results.

The limited research on Judging vs. Perceiving and leadership effectiveness also showed inconsistent results. It is possible that task characteristics make a difference, such that leaders who are high on Perceiving perform better on creative tasks, whereas those high on Judging perform more effectively on structured tasks (Gardner & Martinko, 1996).

Gardner and Martinko's (1996) review concluded that *the relative proportion of iNtuitive types increases as one goes from lower to middle to upper management.* This makes sense, because upper managers are the ones who have to develop the vision for the organization, while lower-level managers have to deal with all of the gritty details. Gardner and Martinko found that iNtuitive managers, especially those with a Perceiving style, were more creative. However, they noted that there was a wide range in study findings about whether iNtuitive or Sensing types were more effective managers. They speculated that organizational level and the type of work tasks performed (routine and detailed vs. nonroutine and creative) determined which type of leader would be more effective.

Interestingly, Gardner and Martinko (1996) also found no differences between Extraverts and Introverts in managerial effectiveness. They noted that there was wide variability in the percentage of Introverts and Extraverts according to the study setting; this suggests that occupational differences may be important with regard to Extraversion vs. Introversion. *Thus, the key to leadership success might be to find the occupation that matches one's Extraversion or Introversion type.*

A study of 1,040 Norwegian adults working in a wide variety of industries found support for the notion of matching psychological type to occupational work tasks (Nordvik & Brovold, 1998). They found that scores on the MBTI matched, as expected, with preferences for performing leadership tasks related to production, administration, enterprising, and integration.

A large-scale study in the United States of America examined 6,124 managers working in 16 different industry types and in 1,889 different companies (Gentry, Mondore, & Cox, 2007). This study measured supervisors' and subordinates' perceptions that the managers had *derailment characteristics* that could jeopardize their careers. The study found virtually no difference between Extraverts and Introverts on overall derailment characteristics and negligible mean differences (on a scale from 1 to 5) of 0.04 between Sensors and iNtuitives, of 0.08 between Feelers and Thinkers, and of 0.03 between Judgers and Perceivers (because of the large sample size, these differences were still statistically significant). These results certainly support the concept that no one MBTI type is better than another.

Bottom Line: (1) There is good evidence that the frequency of the MBTI psychological types varies by occupation and organizational level. (2) Managers and administrators are more likely to be Thinkers and Judgers, and the proportion of iNtuitives increases with higher levels. (3) There is little solid research evidence that leader performance overall varies by MBTI type; it is possible that task characteristics may influence which type is most effective.

Many entrepreneurs are high on the traits studied in this chapter, such as Openness. For example, Robert Johnson is the African American cofounder (with his then wife, Sheila) of Black Entertainment Television (BET), a television channel that targets African Americans. His openness to new ideals enabled him to see the possibilities of starting BET, and his proactive personality gave him the initiative to do so. After selling BET and becoming a billionaire, he invested in a wide range of other businesses, including real estate, hospitality, professional sports, media and entertainment, and gaming (Johnson, 2012). The following case is about two business leaders who have also invested in a wide variety of businesses. They have different values but similar personality traits; they are a good example of the difference between beliefs and traits.

Case: *Tom Monaghan vs. Ted Turner: Alike or Different?*

Ted Turner and Jane Fonda at the 1990 Academy Awards

The young Tom Monaghan shows his skill at making pizza

Source: Flickr/Alan Light (CC-BY)   *Source:* Wikipedia/Anthjay

Tom Monaghan founded Domino's Pizza. Ted Turner founded Turner Broadcasting Systems. Many people may think that the conservative Monaghan and the independent to liberal Turner are opposites. But could it be that when it comes to comes to Core Self-Evaluations and the Big Five personality traits that they are basically identical? In particular, both may be extremely high on Openness. Tom's Openness helped him recognize the potential of the pizza business at a time when few people in America ate pizza; it also helped him recognize the importance of delivery when few restaurants made delivery a key part of their strategy. He also made a number of innovations, including new pizza recipes, dough pans, better pizza boxes, insulated carrying bags, conveyer ovens, and a franchising system that enabled supervisors and managers to become franchise owners. Ted's Openness led him to expand from the billboard industry to radio and television. His ability to consider new ideas helped him see cable operators as potential partners instead of competitors the way the other TV broadcasters did. It also helped him see the potential in 24 hour news channels (Cable News Network), all movie channels, and other original hits. Although Ted wasn't looking to own a sports team, his willingness to try new things led him to accept an offer to buy the *Atlanta Braves*.

(Continued)

(Continued)

It is clear that Monaghan and Turner are high on Internal Locus of Control, and both had early lives marked by the struggle to gain independence while in regimented environments. Monaghan and Turner were conscientious at work. Tom often worked 18 hours a day and rarely took a day off. Ted often worked late into the night, and although he spent months every year yachting, he put the same energy and drive into sailing as he did into his businesses. They both have extraverted, active approaches to life, although both also value introspection.

Monaghan and Turner have inspiring life stories. Tom's father died while he was 4 years old, and his mother later gave him and his brother up to an orphanage because she said she couldn't afford to raise them anymore. Yet Tom still managed to start Domino's Pizza and become a self-made billionaire. He's truly a rags-to-riches success story. Ted Turner was sent to a boarding school when he was only 4 years old, and his sister died as a teenager, so he also had some abandonment issues and a complicated relationship with his father. Ted learned many business lessons from his father while working in his father's company during summers and after college. Although Ted inherited a billboard business worth roughly a million dollars when his father committed suicide (when Ted was 24), Ted started and founded the Turner Broadcasting company that made him a multibillionaire.

Education: Tom entered seminary school to become a priest, but he was expelled for disciplinary problems. Later, he enrolled at the University of Michigan to study architecture but left to start Domino's Pizza. Ted went to boarding schools and then entered Brown University as a Classics major before switching to Economics. He was expelled from Brown for having a female student in his dorm room (Ted went wild when his father refused to pay for college).

Military Service: Tom served in the Marines; Ted in the United States Coast Guard.

Speech and Debate: Tom was active in *Toastmasters*, a public speaking organization, and he started a chapter at his corporate headquarters. Ted won his state debate championship in high school. He was vice-president of the Brown Debating Union, and he currently sponsors the Public Forum Debate of the *National Forensic League*. Ted was later known as the Mouth of the South due to his controversial statements. Both used their speaking skills to motivate employees, persuade others, negotiate, do public relations, and express their views and ideology.

Transportation: Tom loves classic cars and once owned 250 antique automobiles. Ted loves yachting, and as skipper of the *Courageous,* he won the *America's Cup* for the United States of America and was inducted into the *America's Cup Hall of Fame* for his racing skills.

Sports: Tom owned the *Detroit Tigers* baseball team, which won the *World Series* under his ownership. He supports physical education programs and built a first class fitness center for the employees at Domino's Headquarters. Ted's team, the *Atlanta Braves*, also won the *World Series*. In addition, Ted owned the National Basketball Association *Atlanta Hawks*. Turner founded the *Goodwill Games*, and he bought a wrestling company and turned it into the *World Championship Wrestling*.

Other Wide Range of Interests: Tom loved the architecture of Frank Lloyd Wright and modeled the Domino's World Headquarters on Wright's principles. Monaghan also developed an intense curiosity about theology. He has an interest in higher education and he funded the development of a new Catholic university and a law school. He is developing a planned community of 11,000 homes in Florida based around the new university. Tom plans to eventually give away his fortune to charity, and he has already donated hundreds of millions of dollars. Turner sponsored a literary award for fiction (how many people like both professional wrestling and classic and modern literature?). He has a strong interest in classic movies, and he's also a Civil War buff; he produced two movies about the Civil War (both of which he appeared in). He has a keen interest in the environment and in controlling population growth, and he created a TV series with an environmental superhero. He has the largest Bison herd in the world and is the largest private land owner in the United States. Ted pledged to donate a billion dollars to the United Nations, and he has already contributed $600 million.

Applications: Do you think Tom Monaghan and Ted Turner are mostly alike in their basic personalities or mostly different? How could Openness and having a wide range of interests help Tom Monaghan or Ted Turner be successful in their businesses? How important is creativity to running a pizza store or a billboard advertising company? Which of their other personality traits might have contributed to their successes?

Source: Turner, T., & Burke, B. (2008). *Call me Ted*. New York, NY: Grand Central Publishing (Hatchette Book Group).

Put It in Practice

1. Hire people whose personalities and attitudes match your organizational culture.

2. When evaluating potential hires or current employees, pay attention to both the competency dimension and the warmth dimension.

3. Don't be a skeptic—personality traits do predict leadership, although not perfectly.

4. Build on your personality traits to develop your proximal skills and attributes such as interpersonal skills, communication skills, and problem solving. Remember that both personality traits and skills predict leadership effectiveness.

5. Realize that Introverts and Extraverts can both be successful; find the path to success that matches your personality.

6. When selecting leaders based on the Big Five, remember that only Openness and Extraversion predicted leadership effectiveness (when controlling for all five personality traits).

7. Develop your own positive Core Self-Evaluations and help your teammates and followers believe in themselves as well. Take control of your life by adopting Internal Locus of Control attitudes.

8. Pay no attention to the naysayers—you can succeed even if you are not born rich or politically connected.

9. Take charge by becoming proactive—change your environment to facilitate your own success and to achieve your organization's goals.

10. Take into account your Myers-Briggs Type Indicator® problem-solving style when choosing your occupation; you should consider occupations that are compatible with your MBTI leadership style.

11. Be open to new experiences—this will help you develop new entrepreneurial approaches.

Exercises

1. Who Am I?

On a separate sheet of paper, write down 10 words that you feel best describe yourself.

For additional fun, the instructor may call for volunteers to bring their sheets up to the instructor's podium. If you want to volunteer, write your name at the top of your sheet before you hand it in *(if you are not volunteering, then you don't have to hand in your sheet)*. Then, stand in the front of the class. After all the volunteers have come forward, the instructor will shuffle the list and then number each list. The volunteers or *contestants* should then introduce themselves to the class by name. The instructor will then read each list to the class, only giving the number instead of the name of the person who wrote it. After reading all of the contestants' lists to the class, the instructor will then go back to list number 1 and reread it to the class. The class will then vote on which class member wrote the list. The instructor will then repeat the process for each remaining list. The instructors should not tell who actually wrote the list until the class has voted on all the lists.

2. **Celebrity Personalities**

For each of the Big Five personality traits, think of a famous leader or a famous person who is high on that trait. Also, try to think of famous people who are low on those traits. Is it easier to think of famous people and leaders in some categories than it is in others? For example, is it easier to think of extraverted leaders than it is introverted ones? If the person is a leader—i.e., someone who supervises and leads groups of others, put an *L* for leader in the appropriate column and row that describes that person. If the person is famous but not a leader (for example, a writer who works alone or an athlete who does not coach or supervise others), then put an *F* in the right spot. Do the leaders tend to concentrate in certain traits?

	High	Low
Neuroticism	_____	_____
Extraversion	_____	_____
Openness	_____	_____
Agreeableness	_____	_____
Conscientiousness	_____	_____

Visit the Student Study Site at **www.sagepub.com/humphreyel** for these additional tools:

- Learning Goals
- Leader's Book Case Articles
- Web Resources
- Student Self Assessments

References

Bateman, T. S., & Crant, M. J. (1993). The proactive component of organizational behavior: A measure and correlates. *Journal of Organizational Behavior, 14,* 103–118.

Capraro, R. M., & Capraro, M. M. (2002). Myers-Briggs Type Indicator score reliability across studies: A meta-analytic reliability generalization study. *Educational and Psychological Measurement, 62,* 590–602.

Carlyle, T. (1907). *The works of Thomas Carlyle in 30 volumes,* (ed. H. D. Traill). London, UK: Chapman and Hall.

Casimir, G., & Waldman, D. A. (2007). A cross cultural comparison of the importance of leadership traits for effective low-level and high-level leaders: Australia and China. *International Journal of Cross Cultural Management, 7*(1), 47–60.

De Hoogh, A. H. B., & Den Hartog, D. N. (2009). Neuroticism and locus of control as moderators of the relationships of charismatic and autocratic leadership with burnout. *Journal of Applied Psychology, 94,* 1058–1057.

Frese, M., Kring, W., Soose, A., & Zempel, J. (1996). Personal initiative at work: Differences between East and West Germany. *Academy of Management Journal, 1,* 37–63.

Gardner, W. L., & Martinko, M. J. (1996). Using the Myers-Briggs Type Indicator to study managers: A literature review and research agenda. *Journal of Management, 22,* 45–83.

Gentry, W. A., Mondore, S. P., & Cox, B. D. (2007). A study of managerial derailment characteristics and personality preferences. *Journal of Management Development, 26,* 857–873.

Gladwell, M. (2008). *Outliers: The story of success.* New York, NY: Little, Brown and Company.

Goldberg, L. R. (1990). Personality processes and individual differences. An alternative "description of personality": The big-five factor structure. *Journal of Personality and Social Psychology, 59,* 1216–1229.

Goldman L., & Blakeley K. (2007, January 18). *Forbes.* Retrieved from http://www .forbes.com/2007/01/17/richest-women-entertainment-tech-media-cz_lg_ richwomen07_0118womenstars_lander_print.html

Hirschfeld, R. R., Jordan, M. H., Thomas, C. H., & Field, H. S. (2008). Observed leadership potential of personnel in a training setting: Big five traits and proximal factors as predictors. *International Journal of Selection and Assessment, 16*(4), 385–402.

Hoffman, B. J., Woehr, D. J., Maldagen-Youngjohn, R., & Lyons, B. D. (2011). Great man or great myth? A quantitative review of the relationship between individual differences and leader effectiveness. *Journal of Occupational and Organizational Psychology, 84,* 347–381.

Johnson, Robert L. (2012, June 13). Retrieved from http://en.wikipedia.org/wiki/ Robert_Johnson

Judd, C. M., James-Hawkins, L., Yzerbyt, V., & Kashima, Y. (2005). Fundamental dimensions of social judgment: Understanding the relations between judgments of competence and warmth. *Journal of Personality and Social Psychology, 89*(6), 899–913.

Judge, T. A. (2009). Core self-evaluations and work success. *Current Directions in Psychological Science, 18*(1), 58–62.

Judge, T. A., Bono, J. E., Ilies, R., & Gerhardt, M. W. (2002). Personality and leadership: A qualitative and quantitative review. *Journal of Applied Psychology, 87,* 765–780.

Judge, T. A., Erez, A., Bono, J. E., & Thorensen, C. J. (2003). The core self-evaluation scale: Development of a measure. *Personnel Psychology, 56,* 303–331.

Judge, T. A., Locke, E. A., & Durham, C. C. (1997). The dispositional causes of job satisfaction: A core evaluations approach. *Research in Organizational Behavior, 19,* 151–188.

Judge, T. A., Van Vianen, A. E. M., & De Pater, I. E. (2004). Emotional stability, core self-evaluations, and job outcomes: A review of the evidence and an agenda for future research. *Human Performance, 17*(3), 325–346.

Jung, C. G. (1971). *Psychological Types. Collected works of C. G. Jung* (Vol. 6). Princeton, NJ: Princeton University Press. Original work published 1923.

Kroeger, O., Thuesen, J., & Rutledge, H. (2002). *Type talk at work (revised): How the 16 personality styles determine your success on the job.* New York, NY: Dell.

Lord, R. G., De Vader, C. L., & Alliger, G. M. (1986). A meta-analysis of the relation between personality traits and leadership perceptions: An application of validity generalization procedures. *Journal of Applied Psychology, 71,* 402–410.

Mann, R. D. (1959). A review of the relationships between personality and performance in small groups. *Psychological Bulletin, 56,* 241–270.

Morrison, E. W., & Phelps, C. C. (1999). Taking charge at work: Extrarole efforts to initiate workplace change. *Academy of Management Journal, 42,* 403–419.

Myers, I. B. (1998). *Introduction to type: A guide to understanding your results on the Myers-Briggs Type Indicato*r (6th ed.). Palo Alto, CA: Consulting Psychologists Press.

Myers, I., McCaulley, M., Quenk, N. L., & Hammer, A. L. (1998). *Manual: A Guide to the development and use of the Myers-Briggs Type Indicator* (3rd ed.). Palo Alto, CA: Consulting Psychologists Press.

Nordvik, H., & Brovold, H. (1998). Personality traits in leadership tasks. *Scandinavian Journal of Psychology, 39,* 61–64.

Parker, J. F. (2008). *Do the right thing.* Upper Saddle River, NJ: Wharton School Publishing.

Resick, C. J., Whitman, D. S., Weingarden, S. M., & Hiller, N. J. (2009). The bright-side and the dark-side of CEO personality: Examining core self-evaluations, narcissism, transformational leadership, and strategic influence. *Journal of Applied Psychology, 94,* 1365–1381.

Stogdill, R. M. (1948). Personal factors associated with leadership: A survey of the literature. *Journal of Psychology, 25,* 35–71.

Thomas, J. P., Whitman, D. S., & Viswesvaran, C. (2010). Employee proactivity in organizations: A comparative meta-analysis of emergent proactive constructs. *Journal of Occupational and Organizational Psychology, 83,* 275–300.

Turner, T., & Burke, B. (2008). *Call me Ted.* New York, NY: Grand Central Publishing (Hatchette Book Group).

Van Dyne, L., & LePine, J. A. (1998). Helping and voice extra-role behaviors: Evidence of construct and predictive validity. *Academy of Management Journal, 41,* 108–119.

Van Iddekinge, C. H., Ferris, G. R., & Heffner, T. S. (2009). Test of a multistage model of distal and proximal antecedents of leader performance. *Personnel Psychology, 62,* 463–469.

Zaccaro, S. J. (2007). Trait-based perspectives of leadership. *American Psychologist, 62*(1), 6–16.

Zaccaro, S. J., Kemp, C., & Bader, P. (2004). Leader traits and attributes. In J. Antonakis, A. T. Cianciolo, & R. J. Sternberg (Eds.), *The nature of leadership* (pp. 101–124). Thousand Oaks, CA: Sage.

Zhang, Z., & Arvey, R. D. (2009). Effects of personality on individual earnings: Leadership role occupancy as a mediator. *Journal of Business Psychology, 24,* 271–280.

3

Cognitive Intelligence, Complex Task Performance, and Decision Making

༚

Chapter Road Map

Case: *Mark Zuckerberg, Facebook: Intelligence or Social Skills?*
Intelligence and Leadership Emergence
Intelligence and Leadership Effectiveness
Education and Entrepreneurial Leadership
Leadership and Complex Task Performance
Personal Reflections: *Demonstrate Your Talents*
Knowledge and Leadership Skills
Case: *Esther Takeuchi, Padmasree Warrior, and Mary Meeker: Brainiacs May Save Your Life or Your Investments*
How Charismatic, Ideological, and Pragmatic Leaders Make Decisions
Improving Leader Intellectual Performance
Think Like a Chess Master: Checkmate Your Corporate Opponent
Think Like a Scientist: Test Your Theories
Decision Making and Crisis Leadership
Why Good Leaders Make Bad Decisions
Case: *Think Like a Billionaire: Warren Buffett—Invest in What You Understand*
Case: *Alcoa and Paul O'Neill's Life Saving Habits*
Put It in Practice
Exercises: (1) Brainstorming Exercise and (2) Think Like a Logical Thinker

༚

Case: *Mark Zuckerberg, Facebook: Intelligence or Social Skills?*

Facebook has become a social networking phenomenon. It has hundreds of millions of members. Not bad for an organization founded as recently as 2004. And it made its key founder, Mark Zuckerberg, rich. With the successful initial public offering of stock (IPO) in May 2012, he's now worth over $19 billion. So what skills and traits enabled Mark to make Facebook such a success? Because Facebook is a social networking site, you might think that its founder had outstanding social skills. Perhaps a keen social awareness helped Mark recognize the need for a social networking site and understand what features would promote social interactions. But according to *The Accidental Billionaires* (Mezrich, 2009), Mark was a shy Harvard computer geek who would stand alone in a corner during parties and social networking events. And Mark's social awareness may not have been particularly keen: He gained infamy (and a disciplinary hearing resulting in probation) by creating a website that allowed people to compare and rate Harvard coeds on attractiveness. As Mezrich (2009) observed, this didn't help Mark's chances of ever getting a date with a Harvard coed.

Mark Zuckerberg dressed casually for the press conference on Facebook's new messaging system

On the other hand, Mark was a computer genius of the highest order. While still in high school, he invented a program called Synapse that enabled MP3 players to know a person's musical tastes and to create tailored playlists. At Harvard, he created a program called Course Match that let Harvard students check what classes other students were enrolled in. And it was Mark's technical knowledge and genius that allowed him to triumph over the dozens of other competitors that were also trying to create social networking sites. Some of these competitors were at Harvard at the same time as Mark. For example, identical twins Tyler and Cameron Winklevoss were at the top of the social hierarchy at Harvard as popular athletes from a rich family (they later competed as rowers in the Olympics and finished sixth), and at six feet five inches, they were literally *big men* on campus. They wanted to start a social networking site at Harvard, and although they had some computer skills, they didn't have the programming brilliance necessary to finish their site. Consequently, they had tried to get Mark Zuckerberg to join them as their programmer (they later sued Mark by claiming that he had stolen their ideas and delayed the start of their website by pretending to be working with them when he was really creating his own competing website—they won around $65 million).

Mark's genius also gave him the upper hand in dealing with his former friend and cofounder of Facebook, Eduardo Saverin. Eduardo had the social skills necessary to gain admittance to one of the most prestigious social clubs at Harvard, the Phoenix, which hosted the best parties, whereas Mark, alas, was not invited to join. Eduardo joined in the creation of Facebook as its business manager in charge of raising advertising dollars and handling business issues; he also contributed the initial several thousand dollars necessary to start the company. However, because Mark's programming genius was the key to success, he had the majority of the company's initial stock, with Eduardo holding 30% (some other cofounders also owned some stock). When Mark and Eduardo argued over business decisions and investment strategies, Mark and the other cofounders removed Eduardo from the management team and diluted his share of ownership of the company to about 5% through some legal maneuvers and by issuing more stock. Result: another lawsuit with at least a partial victory for Eduardo (dollar amounts not revealed). But Mark still retained firm control of the company. Eduardo made about $2 billion in the Facebook IPO, so he's still a winner.

It is possible that *The Accidental Billionaires* (Mezrich, 2009) underestimated Mark's social skills and interpersonal leadership ability. Mark had a large network of friends and fellow computer hackers that he communicated with over the internet before he founded Facebook. Mark also knew how to generate excitement among his fellow programmers. When interviewing potential interns at Harvard for Facebook, Mark threw a big party with drinking contests and shouting spectators. The contests? Solving computer problems in between taking shots. If you've seen the TV series *Chuck*, you've witnessed members of the NerdHerd staging similar contests to celebrate their technical prowess. Why should the jocks have all the fun? And Mark was able to convince a core group of Harvard students to journey with him across the country to Palo Alto, where they lived together in a rented house while they worked around the clock doing programming tasks. For fun, they had run a zip line from the chimney on the roof down to a wading pool in the yard, and they would zip down for a splash during programming breaks (result: another lawsuit over damages to the chimney). And apparently once Facebook became popular, Mark's romantic life improved as well. Moreover, in September 2010, Mark donated $100 million to a school system in New Jersey, and he's shown other signs of increasing maturity and social responsibility as well. Mark was married in 2012.

(Continued)

Applications: How important is intelligence compared to social skills in most organizations? Do you think this varies by the type of business or organization? Who usually ends up on top: the partner with the social skills or the one with the technical know-how? Mark sometimes worked 20 hours straight doing programming, so was his success accidental? If Mark had been higher on ethical awareness and empathy, do you think he could have avoided the disciplinary hearing and the three lawsuits?

Sources: Antunes, A. (2012, May 27). Eduardo Saverin Finally Opens Up: 'No Hard Feelings Between Me And Mark Zuckerberg'. *Forbes.* Retrieved from http://www.forbes.com/sites/andersonantunes/2012/05/27/eduardo-saverin-finally-opens-up-no-hard-feelings-between-me-and-mark-zuckerberg/

Mezrich, B. (2009). *The accidental billionaires: The founding of Facebook: A tale of sex, money, genius, and betrayal.* New York, NY: Doubleday.

Ortutay, B. (2012, May 18). Facebook stock closes nearly flat in debut. *The Associated Press.* Retrieved from http://entertainment.verizon.com/news/read.php?id=19080445&ps=915&cat=&cps=0&lang=en

As the founding of Facebook illustrates, many leaders succeed by solving complex problems, often problems that their competitors can't solve. This requires intelligence and knowledge. Mark Zuckerberg also made a number of good decisions about features to include in Facebook, the best place for the company headquarters, and so forth. Good decision making is a crucial part of leadership (Finkelstein, Whitehead, & Campbell, 2009). Not all leaders make decisions in the same way. For example, one leadership model classifies leaders into three different types according to how they make decisions. Our ability to make good leadership decisions is not fixed, and there are things that we can do to improve our decision making. Good decision making may be especially difficult during crisis situations or when the stakes are high. Thus, in this chapter, we will explore the answers to the following questions:

- How important is intelligence to leadership emergence and to leadership effectiveness?
- Is performing complex tasks a crucial part of leadership? Are you more likely to be seen as a leader if you perform complex tasks?
- How important is knowledge, gained either from educational experiences or life experiences, to the development of leadership skills?
- What are the differences among charismatic, ideological, and pragmatic leaders in how they make decisions?

- How can we improve our decision making to think more like the way outstanding leaders think?
- How do crisis situations or high stakes investments influence leaders' decision making?
- Why do even bright leaders sometimes make obvious cognitive blunders?

Intelligence and Leadership Emergence

Judge, Colbert, and Ilies (2004) performed a meta-analysis of the research on leadership emergence. Most of the studies on leadership emergence have strangers meet in small groups while discussing a topic or while performing some work tasks. At the end of the meeting, they separate the group members and have them rate each other on leadership and on other traits like intelligence. The researchers then correlate the perceived leadership ratings with the perceived intelligence ratings. In their meta-analysis, Judge et al. (2004) *found that perceived intelligence correlated strongly with perceived leadership emergence.*

The high correlation between leadership emergence and perceived intelligence makes sense because we are likely to support as leaders people that we think are making smart decisions during group activities. However, it would also be useful to know if leadership emergence correlates with intelligence as measured by traditional pen-and-paper intelligence tests. Judge et al. (2004) found that *when intelligence is measured by IQ tests, it correlates positively with leadership emergence* (when corrected for measurement error and range restrictions, the correlation is 0.25). Although the correlation is smaller than the correlation with perceived intelligence, it is still an important correlation. However, the size of the correlation suggests that other factors in addition to intelligence may also be important in explaining leadership emergence.

Intelligence and Leadership Effectiveness

Intelligence may help people in their struggle to obtain leadership positions. Once they are in the leadership position, it may also help them perform better as leaders. Fortunately, this commonsense assumption is supported by the Judge et al. (2004) meta-analysis; they found that *when intelligence is measured by IQ tests, it correlates positively with perceived effectiveness and with objective effectiveness* (corrected correlations: 0.17 and 0.33). These correlations indicate that intelligence is one of the key traits that make leaders effective. However, the sizes of the correlations suggest that personality factors and leadership styles also play a role in leadership effectiveness.

Intelligence helps leaders in part because it helps them learn and gain knowledge about their industry. On-the-job learning is important, but formal education is also important to most leaders, as the following section demonstrates.

Education and Entrepreneurial Leadership

After reading about how college dropouts like Bill Gates and Mark Zuckerberg have made billions, you might not think that you need a college degree. However, Bill Gates and Mark Zuckerberg became successful because they read ahead of the rest of the class. Rather than skipping assigned readings in their computer classes (as most college dropouts would do), they had read during their own free time college level and graduate level materials on high technology (starting in high school). Although many undergraduates regard Friday and Saturday nights as prime party time, Zuckerberg often used those nights as prime programming time. In other words, both of these billionaires had studied on their own to gain the equivalent of a college degree in their chosen areas of study. For most of us mere mortals, however, it helps to have some instruction and a structured program of study when it comes to mastering the mysteries of science, finance, or marketing.

A study done by Duke University and the Kauffman Foundation examined the educational backgrounds of 549 successful company founders from a wide variety of industries (Wadhwa, Aggarwal, Holly, & Salkever, 2009). They found that these entrepreneurial leaders are far better educated than the general public:

95% had bachelor degrees

47% had advanced graduate degrees

11% had PhDs

1% had MDs

These founders also did very well in school: Over half of them ranked themselves in the top 10% of their high school class, and almost as many, 37.5%, ranked themselves in the top 10% of their college class. Less than 5% of them put themselves in the bottom 30% of their college class.

In addition, most of these entrepreneurs founded their businesses after first getting valuable work experience in their industry. The founders were on average forty years old when they started their companies. The vast majority also grew up in middle-class families, and only 6% came from wealthy families.

Leadership and Complex Task Performance

Intelligence may help leaders succeed because it allows them to perform highly complex tasks better than their followers. In the work world, groups are usually formed to solve problems or to accomplish work tasks. Thus, those who work on the most functionally important tasks are more likely to be seen as leaders.

A series of studies by Humphrey and his colleagues demonstrate the powerful influence that performing complex tasks has on leadership perceptions. Humphrey (1985) created an assessment center and a simulated corporate office that had five-person work groups. The college students drew cards to see if they would be one of the three clerks or one of the two managers in each group. The random assignment assured that, on average, the people assigned to be clerks would be as talented as those assigned to be managers. The managers performed a number of complex and functionally important tasks and in addition, gave instructions to the clerks; in contrast, the clerks worked on simple and highly repetitive tasks such as alphabetizing names and adding up payroll hours. *The managers' greater task complexity gave them an advantage in demonstrating their talents*—observers, including the group members, could see that the managers had the abilities to write reports, perform complex calculations, and give directions to the clerks, but they had no information about how well the clerks could perform these complex tasks. In addition, the managers responded to their more interesting work with enthusiasm and vigor, while the clerks responded to their dull tasks with boredom. *Thus, the managers had an advantage in terms of emotional displays because their natural emotional reactions made them seem enthusiastic and motivated, whereas the emotional displays of the clerks made them seem bored and unmotivated.* As a result, even the clerks rated their two coworker clerks lower on leadership-related traits than they rated the two managers. This was true even when the clerks were asked to rate the other group members on how successful they would be in their future careers and on how well they would make a good executive. Here's a sample of how the clerks rated each other and the managers on a 1 to 9 scale (the differences are statistically significant at p < .01 or greater):

	Managers	Other Clerks
Leadership	6.7	5.9
Assertiveness	6.9	6.2
Successful careers	7.1	6.6
Executive	6.5	5.7

In two later studies, people were *not* assigned to be either managers or clerks. Instead, participants were given their choice of tasks to perform during the first round of an assessment center (Kellett, Humphrey, & Sleeth, 2002, 2006). Some participants decided to work on complex, important tasks, whereas others picked simple, clerical tasks to perform (all the participants in each group were seated together around a common table and thus could observe each others' work). In round 2, the participants worked together on a joint decision-making task. In the 2002 study, college grade point average (GPA) was used as an indicator of the person's cognitive ability, while the 2006 study used the Wonderlic Scale—a measure of cognitive ability commonly used by researchers as well as by corporations (for hiring and promotion decisions). In the 2002 study, the college GPA predicted directly to leadership perceptions and emergence. The results were very similar to that of the meta-analysis discussed earlier in terms of the size of the influence of intelligence on leadership emergence. However, *the number of complex tasks that people performed had an even bigger effect on leadership emergence.* The overall pattern of results was the same when the Wonderlic Scale was used in the 2006 study. Interestingly, in both of these studies, some people worked very hard at performing the simple tasks, but performing a large number of simple tasks did not help them become a leader. Instead, it was the number of complex and challenging tasks they performed that predicted leadership emergence. These studies show that it is not enough to be intelligent—people must use their intelligence to perform the more cognitively demanding and important tasks if they want to be the leader.

PERSONAL REFLECTIONS: *DEMONSTRATE YOUR TALENTS*

It's not always easy to demonstrate your talents and rise to the top. For one thing, where do you start out after you graduate from college or graduate school?—often at the bottom, doing bottom-level, unsophisticated stuff. Even a degree from Harvard may not guarantee you'll get noticed. Tony Hsieh (CEO of Zappos.com) graduated from Harvard and landed what he thought was his dream job at Oracle (Hsieh, 2010). He was stuck doing routine statistical reports that used little of his talents. His position was so unimportant that his boss didn't even notice when he took long breaks, came in late, and left early. After a couple of months, Tony quit because he couldn't stand the boredom and lack of attention. Hicks Waldron had it even worse (Kleinfield, 1987). He graduated at the top of his class with an engineering degree from the University of Minnesota. He thought he would be designing engines when he joined GE. Instead, he was assigned to count drops that leaked from a hydraulic braking system—week after week, drip, drip, drip. He complained and asked for a more challenging assignment, so they assigned him to the night shift. Waldron eventually obtained the more challenging assignments that proved his worth, and he became a GE VP before becoming Avon's CEO. While many employees would appreciate having well-paid, easy jobs, Hsieh and Waldron realized that if they wanted to rise to the top, they needed to demonstrate their talents by working on complex, functionally important tasks.

The other lesson that's really important to take away from the studies on job complexity and leadership perceptions is that we shouldn't judge people too much by the type of work that they do, because our impressions are likely to be inaccurate. In the biographies of the great leaders that I've read, I've seen how these leaders try to avoid making these mistaken judgments. They talk to people, regardless of their level in the company, and really try to find out what they are like. They don't assume that someone has no ideas or skills simply because of their job title, the work they do, or the clothes they are wearing.

Your Turn to Reflect: Think of some of the organizations, workplaces, clubs, etc., that you've been in. Do the people who do the most difficult and challenging tasks get credit for their accomplishments and emerge as the leader most often? When you are hired as an entry level worker, how difficult is it to prove that you have the skills and abilities to handle the more complex jobs?

Knowledge and Leadership Skills

As Mumford and his colleagues point out, in order to be effective, leaders need to develop their leadership skills (Mumford, Marks, Connelly, Zaccaro, & Reiter-Palmon, 2000; Mumford, Zaccaro, Connelly, & Marks, 2000; Mumford, Zaccaro, Harding, Jacobs, & Fleishman, 2000). Many leadership theories talk about leadership styles in terms of the leader's preference for being either task oriented or relationship oriented. However, Mumford and his coauthors argued that *leaders with the same style can differ greatly in their leadership skills. These differences can be traced in part to the sophistication of the leaders' knowledge structures* (Lord & Emrich, 2000). For example, two people may both desire to be relationship-oriented leaders, but one may have a much more sophisticated understanding of ways to motivate people.

We are used to thinking about knowledge with regard to the sort of complex computer tasks and analytical tasks that Mark Zuckerberg solves so successfully. And the model developed by Mumford and his colleagues highlights the importance of solving these sorts of complex problems to leadership (Mumford, Zaccaro, Connelly, et al., 2000). As they point out, intelligence and experience help leaders develop the *solution construction skills* necessary to solve group and organizational problems. As they argue, *solving complex technical and organizational problems is a major, not a minor, part of leadership.*

Many leadership models define leadership solely in terms of a leader's ability to influence others. In other words, these models see leadership solely in interpersonal terms. Yet, Thomas Edison, Henry Ford, Mark Zuckerberg, Bill Gates, Larry Page, Sergey Brin, Tony Hsieh, and many other industrial and hi-tech leaders became leaders of large organizations because of their ability to solve complex technical problems. These leaders illustrate how solving complex technical problems is a major route to leadership in today's world. The following case features three other leaders who obtained influential leadership positions because of their ability to solve complex technical problems.

Case: *Esther Takeuchi, Padmasree Warrior, and Mary Meeker: Brainiacs May Save Your Life or Your Investments*

A FastCompany.com article (2009) on the most influential women in technology lists Esther Takeuchi as one of the top five female brainiacs. And for good reason—she holds the record for the most number of patents given to an American woman. Among her many inventions is a battery used in implantable defibrillators. Perhaps you or someone you know depends on this battery as a life-saving device. Esther spent 23 years at GreatBatch, and she now leads an academic research center at the University of Buffalo. She's a great example of how complex task performance can save lives and help intelligent people emerge as leaders.

Padmasree Warrior, Cisco Chief Technology Officer and Senior Vice President

Another example is Padmasree Warrior; her engineering expertise helped her advance up the ranks to become Chief Technology Officer at Motorola. She left Motorola in 2007 to join Cisco as its Chief Technology Officer and Senior Vice President and General Manager of the Enterprise,

Commercial, and Small Business group, where she supervises 10,000 engineers. Padmasree has been recognized by *Fast Company Magazine* as among the 10 most creative women in business (Evans, 2010).

Fortune magazine has its own list of the smartest people in tech. It awarded the Smartest Analyst title to Mary Meeker, a managing director at Morgan Stanley and head of its global technology research team (Hempel & Kowitt, 2010). In the 1990s, Meeker was dubbed *Queen of the Net* and one of her predictions concerned the long-term value of Amazon. com. She turned out to be right on that as well as on the majority of her recommended buys.

Applications: Do you think solving complex technical problems is one route to leadership success in fields such as engineering, computer programming, manufacturing, medicine, accounting, and finance? Are there some fields where technical problem solving would not be important to leadership success? Do you know anyone who has risen to a leadership position because of his or her technical problem-solving skills? How effective was he or she as a leader?

In addition, just as leaders have knowledge about programming, accounting, engineering, etc., leaders also develop social judgment skills (Connelly, Gilbert, Zaccaro, Threlfall, Marks, & Mumford, 2000). *The development of these **social judgment skills** also requires the development of sophisticated and organized knowledge structures.* Again, experience and innate intelligence helps with the development of this type of knowledge, which eventually people experience as wisdom. Leaders learn specific skills, such as what are the best ways to begin a speech, how to give performance appraisals, and so forth. Together, the ability of leaders to develop their knowledge structures about work tasks and about social situations enables them to engage in planning, solve complex tasks, and lead diverse and socially complex groups (Marta, Leritz, & Mumford, 2005).

Although traditional intelligence tests measure math and verbal skills, there are some tests that measure people's knowledge about social situations. ***Situational judgment tests*** (e.g., McDaniel, Hartman, Whetzel, & Grubb, 2007; McDaniel & Nguyen, 2001) *ask people to make judgments about the specific social situations that leaders or others might encounter. A meta-analysis found that situational judgment test scores are positively correlated with interpersonal skills, teamwork skills, and leadership* (Christian, Edwards, & Bradley, 2010).

The Leader's Bookcase: For an article that includes interesting quotes from leaders and employees in a hi-tech company in Sweden, download from the textbook website: Larsson, M., Segerstéen, S., & Svensson, C. (2011). Information and informality: Leaders as knowledge brokers in a high-tech firm. *Journal of Leadership & Organizational Studies, 18,* 175–191. This study shows that knowledge about both technical information and organizational issues is important to leadership.

The next section covers how three different types of leaders make decisions. Of the three types, pragmatic leaders are likely to be most concerned with solving complex technical problems and with taking a problem-solving approach to organizational issues.

How Charismatic, Ideological, and Pragmatic Leaders Make Decisions

Although charismatic leaders often get the most press and the most glory, Mike Mumford and his colleagues argued that pragmatic leaders may sometimes be the most effective (Hunter, Bedell-Avers, & Mumford, 2009; Mumford, 2006; Mumford & Van Doorn, 2001; Strange & Mumford, 2002). Mumford and Van Doorn (2001), for example, argued that Benjamin Franklin was effective due to his problem-solving approach, which led him to advocate for things like paved roads, paper currency, the building of hospitals, etc. Mumford and his colleagues' *CIP model classify leaders into three types: charismatic, who use a vision-based approach; ideological, who value existing traditions;* and *pragmatic, who focus on rational problem solving.* Mumford (2006) argued that these three types of leaders use different mental models of the world to guide them while making decisions and choosing courses of action. For example, charismatic leaders focus on future outcomes, change, and a promise of a better future. Ideological leaders focus on the past and on preexisting ways of doing things, and they pay close attention to their internal sense of values. Pragmatic leaders focus on the present and on solving specific problems. According to the CIP model, all three types of leaders may produce outstanding results. However, the environment may determine which leader type is most effective in any particular circumstance.

Although the CIP considers seven different factors that influence leader effectiveness (Hunter et al., 2009), let's focus in this section on one particular factor: the degree of environmental complexity. Although many leadership models implicitly assume that the environment is relatively stable, researchers are now arguing that the effects of a complex, dynamic, and rapidly changing environment need to be taken into account (Uhl-Bien, Marion, & McKelvey, 2008). Hunter et al. (2009) reasoned that pragmatic leaders would show a consistent level of performance across both high and low environmental conditions. Their emphasis on problem solving would allow them to be flexible and be able to adapt to changes, whereas ideological leaders tend to be more rigid. However, ideological leaders' adherence to a core set of values may help them at times filter out excessive information and guide them during chaotic times. Because charismatic leaders often pursue multiple goals, too much environmental complexity may overwhelm them and overload their information processing capacity. Hunter et al. (2009) used a computerized leadership simulation that allowed them to vary the environmental complexity that faced the three different types of leaders. College students answered a questionnaire that allowed the researchers to classify them according to their leadership type. In addition, they created environmental situations that represented the preferred environment for each of the three different leadership styles.

What's interesting is that there was no main effect for type of leader; in other words, *the three types of leaders did not differ in their overall effectiveness* (Hunter et al., 2009). So if you have a more pragmatic style or an ideological style, you can hold your head up just as high as those with a charismatic style. Instead, *what is important is the interaction between the leader style, the environmental complexity, and the type of situation.* The studies on the CIP model demonstrate that ideological and pragmatic leadership styles exist, and that they are just as valid and effective as the charismatic style, depending upon the situation.

Improving Leader Intellectual Performance

So far, we've learned that more intelligent people are more likely to emerge as leaders. This certainly helps in selection and hiring, but it would also be useful to know how to improve our intellectual performance as leaders. Fortunately, there are several things that we can do to improve our intellectual performance. Reading from a wide variety of sources is one of the best things you can do to improve your verbal skills and vocabulary. It is fun, and it could help you score a few more questions right on the verbal section of personnel selection tests—perhaps enough to put you on the fast track instead of the subordinate track. Many people also think that playing puzzle games and memory games can improve your mental abilities. The next few sections will go over some specific strategies to improve your mental performance.

Think Like a Chess Master:
Checkmate Your Corporate Opponent

Some of the world's greatest thinkers have advocated playing chess as a way to improve one's mental performance and leadership skills. Benjamin Franklin, for example, was a strong believer in the value of playing chess, and he wrote and published the first book on chess in America. He credited chess playing not only with improving his scientific skills but also with helping him devise successful strategies for negotiating with the French for their support during the American Revolution (Blumer & Hoyde & Meyer, 2002, *Benjamin Franklin*, episode called "The Chessmaster"). According to Franklin, playing chess helps one learn to plan ahead, see the relationship among different pieces (or parts of a problem), anticipate danger and the opponents' moves, and persevere in the face of obstacles (chess players can sometimes win even when down substantially in pieces). Another great scientist, architect, diplomat, and politician, Thomas Jefferson, also recommended chess playing. In his autobiography, Arnold Schwarzenegger (with Peter Petre, 2012) frequently mentioned how much he loved playing chess, and his wife even featured a chess set in a poster she made for him of his favorite things. Could playing chess have helped him develop his successful strategies to become a world champion bodybuilder, a multimillionaire entrepreneur and real estate investor, a world famous movie star, and governor of California? Eduardo Saverin, the Facebook cofounder, is also a chess player; when he was only 13 he made international news by beating a chess grand master (Antunes, 2012). Even world heavyweight boxing champions like Lennox Lewis have claimed that playing chess helped them anticipate their boxing opponents' moves and win matches.

So why does playing a game make such a difference? One reason may be because it encourages people to practice over and over again, hours at a time, several key steps necessary to rational decision making. In particular, *it encourages people to generate alternatives and to think in a logical, orderly fashion.* When most people are presented with a problem, usually one answer or potential solution pops into their head as a response. People usually go with this solution right away or possibly spend a little time evaluating the first option that occurred to them. Only if that solution seems unsatisfying do most people go on to think up another possible alternative. However, grand master chess players know that *you should first think up your alternatives before you start evaluating them.* This way, you don't spend all of your time and energy evaluating a single move (Kotov, 2003). Moreover, they know that the generation of alternatives is where creativity comes in. The first solution or option that presents itself is likely to be the same old solution that everyone uses. Sometimes, of course, this makes sense—you don't always need to reinvent the wheel. But if you want to make better decisions than most people do, you need to come up with better options. By generating your alternatives first, you are more likely to come up with a winning move in chess and in business.

In addition, *brilliant moves often look stupid at first glance—if they didn't, everyone would think of them, and they would just be average, commonplace moves.* This is why brainstorming experts recommend withholding judgment (and ridicule) during the alternative generation phase. Most major new inventions have in fact been laughed at by at least some people: Mark Twain ridiculed the telephone as too expensive to ever become popular (he invested instead in a failed printing press invention), and Bill Gates once thought the Internet had no potential.

When evaluating each alternative, assign each option a point on a 1 to 10 scale. This will help you compare your choices when you are finished evaluating the last alternative. Otherwise, you'll exhaust yourself mentally and emotionally by bouncing back and forth between each option in a haphazard fashion. Then take a fresh look at your top candidate move before making the actual move. This helps you avoid making obvious blunders—sometimes moves that look stupid at first glance really are stupid.

Chess also helps because it forces you to consider what the other person will do. In most human interactions, people spend the majority of their time thinking about what they want out of the interaction. Only infrequently do people think about what the other person wants or will say next. In contrast, in chess you spend half your time waiting for the other player to move, and *successful players consider their opponents' potential moves as carefully as they plan their own moves.* In your next committee meeting, try anticipating how people will react to the various proposals and arguments that are being made. Keep score!

When most people talk about brainstorming and generating alternatives, they are usually talking about something they do relatively infrequently— perhaps once a year or once a quarter during planning sessions. But Robert W. Galvin, former Chairman and CEO of Motorola, *made generating alternatives a way of life. For him, it was something he did every day when he helped Motorola grow from a small electronics firm to a Fortune 500 company.* Galvin also made sure that every employee at Motorola received a book on brainstorming (Creative Education Foundation [2013]). If you have a decision to make, generate those alternatives!

Self-Assessment: Visit the textbook website to do a fun exercise that tests your creativity and logical thinking.

Think Like a Scientist: Test Your Theories

The scientific method has brought mankind out of the Dark Ages and into the modern world and produced technological wonders that have dramatically improved life expectancy and our standard of living. You too can use the power of the scientific method to improve your leadership effectiveness and managerial decision making. There are several basic steps to the scientific model. *First, observe; second, develop a theory to explain your observations; third, predict what will happen according to your theory; fourth, test your theory; five, reformulate your theory; and repeat the process if necessary.* You can use this process to help you understand and improve your interactions with others in the work world and in your private life as well. For example, suppose you are having trouble establishing a connection with some of the influential members of a committee you are on. Observe the people—what things do they tend to respond negatively to? What things get a positive reaction? What type of communication style do they use? How do they respond to people with different communication styles? Then, test your theory by making some statements that match the committee members' preferred styles. Was your hypothesis correct? If not, try again. You can use a similar approach to help you motivate your coworkers—what do you think will motivate them? Test it—if your theory doesn't work try something else. The same processes works for testing your business strategies—observe your competitors and test your theories about what makes them successful. Unfortunately, many people persist in trying the same approach over and over again even if they obtain poor results.

The following section shows the importance of generating alternatives and thinking clearly while responding to crisis situations.

Decision Making and Crisis Leadership

It can be hard to think in a crisis, yet that is when leaders need to think most clearly (Hannah, Avolio, Luthans, & Harms, 2008; Hannah, Uhl-Bien, Avolio, & Cavarretta, 2009). As Hadley and her colleagues state, "During any public health and safety crisis, whether it is an airplane crash, hurricane, infectious disease pandemic, or terrorist act, there is a tremendous need for effective leadership. Good decisions must be made quickly, despite the uncertainty, time pressure, and high stakes associated with such a crisis" (Hadley, Pittinsky, Sommer, & Zhu, 2011, p. 633). Hadley and her colleagues developed a scale to assess how well leaders think during these crisis situations: the Crisis Leader Efficacy in Assessing and Deciding scale (C-LEAD). As the scale title suggests, *the C-LEAD scale is concerned with leaders' beliefs in their ability to assess information and make decisions.*

In a series of three studies, Hadley and her coauthors (2011) surveyed a wide variety of public and private leaders who had responded to a wide range of emergency situations, including fires, epidemics, and other catastrophes. For example, they surveyed and interviewed the senior fire official who handled the infamous nightclub fire in Rhode Island in which 100 people died and many more were injured. The official pointed out how crisis leaders have to keep making decisions even in the face of limited or incomplete information: "You have to be much more focused on what it is you've got to do now and use the sort of iterative process of saying, 'We've made that decision, now what are the consequences that we didn't predict?' I think it's quite a different leadership function largely because of the need to act in the absence of a lot of information" (Hadley et al., 2011, p. 638).

The urgency of crisis situations tends to narrow people's focus, thus reducing the generation of alternatives. It takes a clear-headed leader to be able to rapidly consider various responses and pick the best one when the stakes are high and time is limited. Not surprisingly, the study found that intelligence was positively related to the leaders' C-LEAD scores and to their ability to make correct decisions as crisis leaders (Hadley et al., 2011).

> **Applications:** Can you think of a crisis situation you witnessed? How did the leaders respond? Was it easy to assess information and make decisions, or was there something about the crisis that made decision making more difficult?

The high stakes involved in crisis situations can make it difficult to think clearly. There are many other situations that are not a crisis but that also involve high stakes. For example, many investment decisions also involve major stakes, whether it is your own pension plan or a major business acquisition. The next section illustrates how even good leaders can make poor decisions.

Why Good Leaders Make Bad Decisions

To understand how leaders make decisions, read *Think Again: Why Good Leaders Make Bad Decisions and How to Keep It From Happening to You*, by Finkelstein et al. (2009). They analyzed 83 cases in which leaders made bad decisions, ranging from bad acquisitions and bad business strategies to governmental and military blunders. Their book highlights the importance of pattern recognition to both good and bad decision making. *Pattern recognition allows leaders to handle complex situations by recognizing key features of the situation that match previously learned patterns.* Most of our perceptual processes operate by pattern recognition; for example, we can recognize drawings of a face even when only a few facial features are depicted. Pattern recognition operates on the basis of gap filling. For instance, we imagine facial features even when they are not shown. In most cases, gap filling aids pattern recognition, but it can produce erroneous decisions when the current situation does not match prior patterns in important ways. Thus, *misleading experiences can cause mistaken pattern recognition.* Finkelstein and his colleagues (2009) demonstrated that this can happen when leaders make business decisions. For example, Quaker had been successfully led by its CEO, William Smithburg, for over a dozen years before misleading experiences led him astray. Early in his reign as CEO, he had bought Gatorade, which turned out to be a huge hit for Quaker. So when he had the opportunity to buy another drink company, Snapple, his pattern recognition lit up the opportunity as a big win. Unfortunately for Smithburg and Quaker, Snapple's market and organizational culture was quite different from both Gatorade's and Quaker's. Yet as Finkelstein and his colleagues argued, gap-filling processes probably caused Smithburg to perceive Snapple as more similar to Gatorade than what it really was.

In addition, our pattern recognition is usually aided by emotional tagging. *Emotional tagging occurs when the memories that form the basis for pattern recognition are tagged with emotions.* Finkelstein et al. (2009) argue that "Emotions are essential to decision making" (p. 9). Emotional tags let us know whether something is important or not—a memory with a neutral emotional tag lets us know that something is probably not that important, while a memory with a strong emotional tag alerts us to the importance of the memory and the role that it plays in the pattern being observed. Thus, emotional tags focus our attention on key aspects of the situation and in most cases, aid effective decision making. Emotions also prompt us to take action—they are the motivating force in the decision-making process. *Problems occur, however, when emotions are tagged to misleading experiences.* In the Quaker case, for example, Smithburg's memories of his huge success with Gatorade labeled buying a drink company with a strong positive emotional tag. The disastrous results—Quaker lost $1.4 billion when it sold Snapple just 3 years after buying it, Smithburg lost his job as CEO, and Quaker itself was taken over by PepsiCo.

Finkelstein and his colleagues recommend four safeguards to prevent leaders from making bad decisions. First, the organization should have a decision-making culture based on data gathering and analysis, and where necessary, the leader should also be exposed to new personal experiences that will form the basis of new pattern formations. Consequently, the leader will not have to rely on old and outdated pattern recognition. Second, the leader should encourage group debate and the challenging of assumptions. This could help expose inaccuracies in assumptions due to misleading prior experiences. Third, organizations should have governance structures that separate idea proposal from idea approval. For example, CEOs should have their plans approved by independent chairs and boards of directors. This prevents too great of a reliance on any one leader's possibly flawed decision making. Fourth, organizations and leaders should require the active monitoring of the progress of the decision's outcomes. As the authors note, when leaders know the outcomes of their decisions will be publicly monitored, they are likely to *think again* about the wisdom of their decisions.

The following two cases illustrate effective decision making. The first is about a business leader who learned how to avoid making bad business decisions. As a result, he became the world's richest man. The second is about a business leader who knew how habits influence our thoughts and behaviors; he saved lives and increased profits by developing good organizational habits and routines.

Case: *Think Like a Billionaire: Warren Buffett—Invest in What You Understand*

In 2008, *Forbes* listed Warren Buffett as the richest man in the world, although his rank dropped to third in 2012 after he gave away over $17 billion dollars to charity. What's impressive is that his wealth is entirely self-made as a result of his outstanding decision making in the field of investments. Buffett grew up in Omaha, Nebraska where his grandfather owned a grocery store. Later, he moved to Washington, DC when his father was elected to Congress and where Warren attended high school. He started (with a friend) his first business as a high school freshman by buying three coin-operated pinball machines. He enrolled in college and enjoyed the frat life at the Wharton School, but he returned to his home state to graduate with a degree in economics at the University of Nebraska.

Warren Buffett

Source: Wikipedia/Mark Hirschey (CC BY-SA)

(Continued)

(Continued)

Later, Buffett attended Columbia University's graduate business school because he wanted to study with Benjamin Graham, who had written *The Intelligent Investor* in 1949. Graham had become rich as a stockbroker and investor during the 1920s, but he lost his fortune during the stock market crash of 1929. Graham learned from his mistakes, and he passed his advice on to Buffett about how to avoid financial disasters and even profit from them. After Buffett graduated in 1951, he used these principles to guide him in his investments, and they helped him avoid the losses due to the numerous bubbles in various industries over the last half century. Like a scientist, Buffett used abstract, theoretical principles to guide his investment strategy. *Graham taught Warren to use the market fluctuations to his own advantage and to only buy when there was a margin of safety.* **A margin of safety** *exists when stocks and bonds are trading at substantially less than their intrinsic value based on assets, current earnings, and so forth.* Since Graham had personally lost a fortune in 1929, you can understand why he thought a margin of safety was important. Unfortunately, although millions of investors have read about the stock market collapse and the Great Depression, most people seem unable to learn from the lessons of the past if they have only read about them in books. Buffett was smart enough to learn from his mentor's personal experiences and to value his advice (learning from others' experiences is good advice in every field, not just in investing). A good example of how Buffett used this strategy was when a scandal (in the early 1960s) lowered American Express's stock price from $65 to $35. Even now, investors often overreact to bad news, headlines in papers, etc., instead of considering the real assets and cash flow of a company. Buffett and his partners invested 40% of their portfolio ($13 million) in American Express stock and made a $20 million profit in 2 years.

Buffett also believes in investing in what he can understand. Thus, he prefers buying stock from companies that make products that he can understand and even use and from which he can calculate future earnings based on current earnings. Thus, some of his best investments were in Coca-Cola and in Gillette. Although again, this seems like commonsense advice, many investors in the last 2 decades became infatuated with hi-tech stocks that made products that they didn't really understand and that often were not making any profit. Many of these companies had few real assets. Investors bought these products on promises of growth and future earnings. For example, The AOL-Time Warner merger was the largest merger in history. Time Warner's revenues were 5 times greater than AOL's, yet market hysteria over hi-tech companies resulted in AOL having almost twice the market value of Time Warner. Result: Over 40,000 people lost their jobs after the AOL-Time Warner merger, and Time Warner stock holders like Ted Turner lost up to 80% of their investment value. By sticking to his two principles of buying only when he can calculate a margin of safety based on current assets and earnings and only buying stock in companies that make products he understands, Buffett avoided making bad investments like in AOL.

Buffett is also a great philanthropist, and he has pledged 99% of his wealth to charity. He is a major contributor to the Gates Foundation established by another former richest person, Bill Gates.

Applications: Not all billionaires agree with Buffett about how much you need to understand something or research something before making a decision. Some argue that you can never get all of the information that you would like, and that you have to move on new ideas before others do. They worry more about paralysis by analysis. And totally new products, like Facebook in its first year, may in fact have strong potential earnings although little current cash flow. Which approach do you prefer?

Sources: Buffett, Warren. Retrieved June 10, 2012 from http://en.wikipedia.org/wiki/Warren_Buffett

Forbes.com (2009, March 11). The world's billionaires: #2 Warren Buffett. Retrieved January 20, 2013 from http://www.forbes.com/2009/03/11/worlds-richest-people-billionaires-2009-billionaires_land.html and http://www.forbes.com/profile/warren-buffett/

Hagstrom, R. G. (2005). *The Warren Buffett way* (2nd ed.). Hoboken, NJ: Wiley.

Turner, T., & Burke, B. (2008). *Call me Ted.* New York, NY: Hatchette Book Group.

Case: *Alcoa and Paul O'Neill's Life Saving Habits*

Charles Duhigg's brilliant book is entitled, *The Power of Habit: Why We Do What We Do in Life and Business* (2012). Charles argued that "Most of the choices we make each day may feel like the products of well-considered decision making, but they're not. They're habits" (2012, location 126). Charles cited studies that show that "40% of the actions people perform each day weren't actual decisions, but habits" (2012, "Prologue," location 130). Moreover, he argued that "When a habit emerges, the brain stops fully participating in decision making" (2012, "The Habit Loop: How Habits Work," location 459). When habits are formed, people respond to cues that trigger the habit with automatic routines. Following these well-learned behavioral patterns requires little mental

(Continued)

(Continued)

effort, so as a result, the brain stops thinking much about what the person is doing. Like people, organizations can also have habits and routines which guide their behaviors and decisions. Charles described how a leader, Paul O'Neill, saved lives and improved performance by changing organizational habits and routines.

When Paul took office as Alcoa's (Aluminum Corporation of America) new CEO in 1987, he knew that there was a lot of hostility between workers and management. The prior CEO was hated so much that workers burned effigies of him in the parking lot. The workers also resisted efforts to improve productivity and reduce waste and defects. Paul stated that "you can't *order* people to change. That's not how the brain works. So I decided I was going to start by focusing on one thing. If I could start disrupting the habits around one thing, it would spread throughout the entire company" (2012, "Keystone Habits, or the Ballad of Paul O'Neill: Which Habits Matter Most," location 1722). Paul got workers and management working together by focusing on safety—something that workers were deeply concerned about. Paul knew that changing safety habits would trigger a whole range of other habit changes that would improve efficiency and ultimately profits.

Alcoa employees handle metal that's 1,500 degrees hot and operate machines "that can rip a man's arm off" (2012, "Keystone Habits, or the Ballad of Paul O'Neill: Which Habits Matter Most," location 1685). When an employee was killed because he jumped over a safety barrier to repair a broken piece of equipment, O'Neill called an emergency meeting so he could personally investigate what happened. Less than 7 days later, safety rails at all Alcoa facilities were painted a bright yellow, and workers and managers received additional training about how to handle needed repairs to equipment. Paul knew that accidents happened when the manufacturing process went wrong—something bad for both workers and Alcoa. Whenever an accident happened, Paul encouraged workers and quality control experts to work together to figure out what went wrong. It turned out that worn out and poorly maintained equipment was a major cause of both accidents and poor quality aluminum. Workers were empowered to report equipment that needed replacing, and as a result, accidents declined dramatically and profits soared.

To keep track of accidents and to improve safety, Paul instituted reporting procedures that dramatically increased communication throughout the organization. Every accident had to be reported within 24 hours to Paul, along with a plan to prevent similar future accidents from happening. This created a chain of communication from the bottom to the top. Once people developed the habit of communicating about safety, the communication habit also spread to other things. For example, for several years, a worker had an idea about a more efficient way to respond to changes in customer demands for colors in aluminum siding, but he never told management about his idea. But "then he figures, since we keep on asking for safety recommendations, why not tell them about this *other* idea?" (2012, "Keystone Habits, or the Ballad of Paul O'Neill: Which Habits Matter Most," location 2013). The employee's idea doubled Alcoa's profits on aluminum siding.

Paul instilled habits that saved lives while doubling the stock price value of Alcoa. The great thing about routines and habits is that they can continue long after they are started. Paul retired from Alcoa in 2000, but Alcoa's injuries continued to decline. In "2010, 82 percent of Alcoa locations didn't lose one employee day due to injury," and "on average, workers are more likely to get injured at a software company, animating cartoons for movie studios, or doing taxes as an accountant than handling molten aluminum at Alcoa" (2012, "Keystone Habits, or the Ballad of Paul O'Neill: Which Habits Matter Most," location 2142). Overall, this is another great example of how doing the ethical thing is good for both society and businesses.

Applications: How many actions do you carry out each day out of habit? How hard is it to change a habit? Can you describe any organizational routines that act like habits? Could most companies profit by focusing on safety and ethics?

Put It in Practice

1. You don't have to be the life of the party—rise to a leadership position by demonstrating your technical skills and complex problem-solving abilities.

2. Use your intelligence to emerge as a leader. Team members really do select smart people to be leaders.

3. Use your intellectual skills to perform more effectively as a leader.

4. Don't be a dropout: 95% of successful entrepreneurial leaders have college degrees and half have advanced degrees.

5. Demonstrate your leadership ability by choosing to work on important and complex tasks.

6. Don't be a snob, and don't judge others by their work assignments—if given a chance, lower-level employees might surprise you by what they can do.

7. Improve your leadership skills by expanding your knowledge about how to solve complex technical and organizational problems—a key duty of leaders. Don't forget to improve your social judgment skills as well.

8. Realize that charismatic, ideological, and pragmatic leaders can all make effective decisions—what is important is how their decision-making style matches the environment.

9. Improve your leadership abilities by reading, playing mentally stimulating games, practicing the rational decision-making process by playing chess, and by thinking like a scientist.

10. In a crisis, become an effective leader by assessing the available information, rapidly evaluating different response options, and making decisive decisions even when the information is limited. Adjust your plans as new developments occur.

11. Guard against making decisions based on misleading recognition of prior patterns by gathering data, encouraging debate and the challenging of assumptions, separating idea proposal from idea approval, and by monitoring the outcomes of decisions.

12. To think like a billionaire, use clear principles to guide your business strategy, calculate your margins of safety, and make investments and other decisions about things that you understand. Learn from others' mistakes and life experiences.

13. Change habits, save lives, and double your profits.

Exercises

1. Brainstorming Exercise

Prior Preparation Required: Before coming to class, students (or the instructor) need to bring in photos from magazines or newspapers. Half of the photos need to be of standard commercial products, such as cars, computers, soap, food products, etc. The other half should be creative pictures unrelated to the products. For example, they could be pictures of the moon, forests, animals, people doing interesting things, or artwork. The product photos should be placed in one pile and the creative pictures in another.

Students should form groups. One member of the group should select two pictures from the pile of product photos, while a second member should pick two creative pictures. By having two people pick from the different piles, it minimizes the chance that the product photos and the creative photos will be closely related. However, if by chance the creative photo is closely related to the product photo, the team members may pick new photos (e.g., if the product consists of a cereal, don't choose a picture of a cereal bowl as the creative picture).

After picking the photos, the students should use the creative photos to inspire them to develop marketing slogans about the two products. Feel free to develop an entire commercial based on the slogan. Try to develop as many slogans or commercials as possible.

2. Think Like a Logical Thinker

On a sheet of paper, number 10 lines from 1 to 10. Your instructor will read 10 words to you. As each word is read, write down the first word that comes to mind. The instructor will then tell you how to code your answers.

Visit the Student Study Site at **www.sagepub.com/humphreyel** for these additional tools:

- Learning Goals
- Leader's Book Case Articles
- Web Resources
- Student Self Assessments

References

Antunes, A. (2012, May 27). Eduardo Saverin finally opens up: 'No hard feelings between me and Mark Zuckerberg'. *Forbes*. Retrieved from http://www.forbes.com/sites/andersonantunes/2012/05/27/eduardo-saverin-finally-opens-up-no-hard-feelings-between-me-and-mark-zuckerberg/

Blumer, R. (Writer), & Hoyde, E., & Meyer, M. (Directors). (2002). The Chess Master. [Television series episode]. In C. Allan (Executive Producer), *Benjamin Franklin*. Arlington, VA: PBS.

Christian, M. S., Edwards, B. D., & Bradley, J. C. (2010). Situational judgment tests: Constructs assessed and a meta-analysis of their criterion-related validities. *Personnel Psychology, 63*, 83–117.

Connelly, M. S., Gilbert, J. A., Zaccaro, S. J., Threlfall, K. V., Marks, M. A., & Mumford, M. D. (2000). Predicting organizational leadership: The impact of problem solving skills, social judgment skills, and knowledge. *The Leadership Quarterly, 11*, 65–86.

Creative Education Foundation (2013, January). Retrieved from http://www.creativeeducationfoundation.org/taxonomy/term/35

Duhigg, C. (2012). *The power of habit: Why we do what we do in life and business* [Kindle edition]. New York, NY: Random House.

Evans, S. (2010, May 20). The 10 most creative women in business. *FastCompany*. Retrieved from http://www.fastcompany.com/pics/10-most-creative-women-business?slide=7#8

FastCompany.Com (2009, January 14). Women in tech: The brainiacs. Retrieved from http://www.fastcompany.com/magazine/132/the-most-influential-women-in-technology-the-brainiacs.html

Finkelstein, S., Whitehead, J., & Campbell, A. (2009). *Think again: Why good leaders make bad decisions and how to keep it from happening to you*. [Kindle edition]. Cambridge, MA: Harvard Business Press.

Forbes.com (2009, March 11). The world's billionaires: #2 Warren Buffett. Retrieved from http://www.forbes.com/2009/03/11/worlds-richest-people-billionaires-2009-billionaires_land.html

Hadley, C. N., Pittinsky, T. L., Sommer, S. A., & Zhu, W. (2011). Measuring the efficacy of leaders to assess information and make decisions in a crisis: The C-LEAD scale. *The Leadership Quarterly, 22,* 633–648.

Hagstrom, R. G. (2005). *The Warren Buffett way* (2nd ed.). Hoboken, NJ: Wiley.

Hannah, S. T., Avolio, B. J., Luthans, F., & Harms, P. D. (2008). Leadership efficacy: Review and future directions. *The Leadership Quarterly, 19,* 669–692.

Hannah, S., Uhl-Bien, M., Avolio, B. J., & Cavarretta, F. (2009). A framework for examining leadership in extreme contexts. *The Leadership Quarterly, 20,* 897–919.

Hempel, J., & Kowitt, B. (2010, July 26). Smartest people in tech. *Fortune*, 82–94.

Hsieh, T. (2010). *Delivering happiness: A path to profits, passion, and purpose*. New York, NY: Business Plus (Hachette Book Group).

Humphrey, R. H. (1985). How work roles influence perceptions: Structural-cognitive processes and organizational behavior. *American Sociological Review, 50,* 242–252.

Hunter, S. T., Bedell-Avers, K. E., & Mumford, M. D. (2009). Impact of situational framing and complexity on charismatic, ideological and pragmatic leaders: Investigating using a computer simulation. *The Leadership Quarterly, 20,* 383–404.

Judge, T. A., Colbert, A. E., & Ilies, R. (2004). Intelligence and leadership: A quantitative review and test of theoretical propositions. *Journal of Applied Psychology, 89,* 542–555.

Kellett, J. B., Humphrey, R. H., & Sleeth, R. G. (2002). Empathy and complex task performance: Two routes to leadership. *The Leadership Quarterly, 13,* 523–544.

Kellett, J. B., Humphrey, R. H., & Sleeth, R. G. (2006). Empathy and the emergence of task and relations leaders. *The Leadership Quarterly, 17,* 146–162.

Kleinfield, S. (1987). *Staying at the top*. New York, NY: Signet.

Kotov, A. (2003). *Think like a grandmaster: Algebraic edition*. London, UK: Batsford.

Larsson, M., Segersteen, S., & Svensson, C. (2011). Information and informality: Leaders as knowledge brokers in a high-tech firm. *Journal of Leadership & Organizational Studies, 18,* 175–191.

Lord, R. G., & Emrich, C. G. (2000). Thinking outside the box by looking inside the box: Extending the cognitive revolution in leadership research. *The Leadership Quarterly, 11,* 551–579.

Marta, S., Leritz, L. E., & Mumford, M. D. (2005). Leadership skills and the group performance: Situational demands, behavioral requirements, and planning. *The Leadership Quarterly, 16,* 97–120.

McDaniel, M. A., Hartman, N. S., Whetzel, D. L., & Grubb, W. L. (2007). Situational judgment tests, response instructions, and validity: A meta-analysis. *Personnel Psychology, 60,* 63–91.

McDaniel, M. A, & Nguyen, N. T. (2001). Situational judgment tests: A review of practice and constructs assessed. *International Journal of Selection and Assessment, 9,* 103–113.

Mezrich, B. (2009). *The accidental billionaires: The founding of Facebook: A tale of sex, money, genius, and betrayal.* New York, NY: Doubleday.

Mumford, M. D. (2006). *Pathways to outstanding leadership: A comparative analysis of charismatic, ideological and pragmatic leaders.* Mahwah, NJ: Erlbaum.

Mumford, M. D., Marks, M. A., Connelly, M. S., Zaccaro, S. J., & Reiter-Palmon, R. (2000). Development of leadership skills: Experience, timing, and growth. *The Leadership Quarterly, 11,* 87–114.

Mumford, M. D., & Van Doorn, J. R. (2001). The leadership of pragmatism: Reconsidering Franklin in the age of charisma. *The Leadership Quarterly, 12,* 274–309.

Mumford, M. D., Zaccaro, S. J., Connelly, M. S., & Marks, M. A. (2000). Leadership skills: Conclusions and future directions. *The Leadership Quarterly, 11,* 155–170.

Mumford, M. D., Zaccaro, S. J., Harding, F. D., Jacobs, T. O., & Fleishman, E. A. (2000). Leadership skills for a changing world: Solving complex social problems. *The Leadership Quarterly, 11,* 11–35.

Ortutay, B. (2012, May 18). Facebook stock closes nearly flat in debut. *The Associated Press.* Retrieved from http://entertainment.verizon.com/news/read.php?id=19080445&ps=915&cat=&cps=0&lang=en

Schwarzenegger, A., & Petre, P. (2012). *Total recall.* New York, NY: Simon & Schuster.

Strange, J. M., & Mumford, M. D. (2002). The origins of vision: Charismatic versus ideological leadership. *The Leadership Quarterly, 13,* 343–377.

Turner, T., & Burke, B. (2008). *Call me Ted.* New York, NY: Hatchette Book Group.

Uhl-Bien, M., Marion, R., & McKelvey, B. (2008). Complexity Leadership Theory: Shifting leadership from the industrial age to the knowledge era. *The Leadership Quarterly, 18,* 298–318.

Wadhwa, V., Aggarwal, K., Holly, R., & Salkever, A. (2009). *Anatomy of an entrepreneur: Family background and motivation.* Retrieved from the Kaufman Foundation Small Research Projects Research website: http://ssrn.com/abstracts=1431263

4

How Emotional Intelligence, Skills, and Competencies Increase Leader Effectiveness

Chapter Road Map

(1) Hiring the Disabled and (2) Empathic Leaders
Case: *Pick Your Coach: Mike Krzyzewski vs. John Wooden*
Put It in Practice
**Exercises: (1) Emotional Intelligence Charades and (2) The Importance of Body
    Language and Facial Expressions**

ॐ

Case: *Sergey Brin and Larry Page, Google: How IQ Plus EQ Equals Phenomenal Success*

Google has become one of the fastest grow-ing companies in history, and within 10 years, had advertising revenues of $16 billion a year—almost as much revenue as the four largest television networks combined. Its two 38-year-old cofounders, Sergey Brin and Larry Page, were each ranked 24th on the *Forbes'* 2012 list of the world's richest peo-ple ($18.7 billion each). Both had college professors for parents and neither one had inherited wealth—indeed, Sergey lived his first 6 years in Moscow with his parents and his grandmother in a 350 square foot apart-ment. It's not surprising that this phenome-nal success was achieved by partners high on two of the most important

Left to right: Eric E. Schmidt, Sergey Brin, and Larry Page of Google

leadership traits: cognitive intelligence and emotional intelligence. A math prodigy, Sergey quit high school after his junior year so he could attend the University of Maryland full time, and he graduated college in 3 years. Larry graduated with honors from the University of Michigan's engineering school, where he helped build the 1993 national champion Maize & Blue solar car. Larry also took part in the LeaderShape program at the University of Michigan, where he was an honor society president, and he credits these experiences with helping him develop the leadership skills he needed to start Google. Sergey and Larry entered PhD programs at Stanford, where they created the innovative algorithm behind Google's search engine.

But in order to become the leaders of an organization that grew to have 20,000 employees, they needed more than just intellectual brilliance; they needed the emotional intelligence and competencies that would allow them to persuade, attract, and motivate these thousands of talented and experienced employees. History is full of geniuses who were not able to profit greatly from their own creations. Just look at Larry Page's boyhood hero, Tesla. Tesla invented a few little things that you might think would have made him wealthy, like AC current, the AC engine, and radio (apparently before Marconi), yet he died penniless—a fate Larry wanted to avoid. And the hi-tech field is full of people whose inventions led to a business start-up, only to be forced out of the companies they created because they lacked the management skills needed for a big organization—like Cisco, for example. But as Janet Lowe (2009) argues, Brin and Page had extraordinary entrepreneurial personalities and the ability to lead others. As she puts it, "Their regal demeanors have shown forth in the way they initially marketed their company, as they dealt with venture capitalists, in the way they chose a chief executive officer.... They invariably acted independently and with self-assurance" (p. 5).

Brin and Page were not the first to invent web search engines or many of the other Google services, such as email (Gmail) or internet maps (Google Earth). Instead, they improved on existing services offered by competitors. In Google's early days, these competitors had vastly superior financial resources and large existing market shares. Yet Larry and Sergey were able to hire people from their often better-funded competitors and motivate their employees to be more productive and innovative than the competition. Both Larry and Sergey have traits typical of those with high emotional intelligence and competencies (EQ): They value emotional expressiveness, they show empathy toward both their employees and society at large, and they have outstanding relationship management skills. Their exceptional emotional skills enabled them to create an organization that has been ranked as the best place to work for by *Fortune* magazine, as well as numerous other publications.

The extent to which they value emotional expression is shown by their pick of an experienced CEO to help them run Google: Dr. Eric Schmidt. Schmidt won their approval in part because he—like Larry and Sergey—attended the Burning Man festivals. These festivals combine art, music, and freewheeling behavior and are "an outpost for radical personal expression" (Lowe, 2009, p. 43). Together, these three created a culture at Google that encouraged emotional expression and creativity (in January 2011, Larry took over the CEO role). In addition to allowing employees considerable freedom to decorate their workspaces as they liked, dress as they liked, etc., they also gave their employees freedom to use 20% of their work time on projects of their own choosing. During this 20% time, employees came up with some of Google's most profitable ideas and products.

(Continued)

(Continued)

Larry and Sergey also showed considerable empathy toward their employees' needs with high salaries, stock options, and luxury benefits. For example, they provide free food for all employees at the Googleplex headquarters—not just standard cafeteria food but gourmet quality meals (Google spends $7,530 per year per employee for food). Although many billionaires wait until near the end of their careers to become major contributors to charity, Brin and Page created their charity, Google.org, at the same time as they held their initial public stock options, and they are leaders in researching and using green technology.

Applications: How rare is it for people to be high on both cognitive and emotional intelligence? How could being empathic help Larry and Sergey succeed?

Sources: Lowe, J. (2009). *Google Speaks.* Hoboken, NJ: Wiley.

Google. Retrieved June 18, 2012 from http://en.wikipedia.org/wiki/Google

The World's Billionaires. Retrieved January 21, 2013 from http://www.forbes.com/billionaires/list/

Most people would probably feel anxious while negotiating deals that had the potential to transform them from relatively poor students into billionaires; after all, what if the venture capitalists said no or demanded a greater share of the profits? Yet Larry Page and Sergey Brin managed to control their emotions enough during these negotiations to appear calm, even regal. This suggests they are high on one of the key emotional intelligence dimensions, the ability to regulate their own emotions. Their ability to understand others' needs, their empathy, their support of open emotional expression, and other behaviors suggest they are high on emotional intelligence and related emotional competencies. We will define these emotional intelligence dimensions and related competencies in this chapter while addressing these questions:

- What are the major dimensions of emotional intelligence?
- What are the three major types of emotional intelligence and emotional competencies measures that organizations can use to select and assess leaders?
- How important is emotional intelligence to job performance and leadership effectiveness?
- Can leaders balance both intellect and emotions while leading others?

- Why is it important for leaders to regulate their own emotions to prevent emotional hijacking and to generate feelings of enthusiasm?
- How important is empathy and emotional expressiveness to leadership?

Emotional Intelligence: Perceiving and Managing Emotions

Have you ever wondered what someone else was feeling or thinking? Most likely, yes—we've probably all wondered at some time or another whether someone really likes us, or perhaps we've wondered if a friend is really in a good mood or just faking it so as not to put a damper on the evening. And in the workplace, knowing what our boss feels about us and about various issues can be important. Being able to sense others' feelings and thoughts is essential to everyday life, both in our social life and in the work world. And if you've ever had to make some major life decisions, you might have found out that it's not always easy to know your own feelings. Do you want to accept the job offer with the biggest paycheck or the one with the best working conditions and the friendliest people? The ability to understand other people's feelings, as well as your own emotions, is one of the key components of emotional intelligence.

Another part of emotional intelligence involves the ability to control our own emotions. Have you ever become angry and shouted at someone when you know you should have remained calm? Practically everyone has. People high on emotional intelligence are better at controlling their own emotional reactions. They are also better at creating positive emotions, such as enthusiasm for the task at hand. Moreover, they are also able to influence other people's moods and emotions—perhaps you've had a coach who knew how to keep the team's spirit up even when the team was behind. *Emotional intelligence researchers refer to controlling one's emotions either as* **regulating emotions** *or as* **managing emotions.**

Ashkanasy and Daus (2005) classify the types of emotional intelligence measures that organizations can use to select leaders into three streams. The first two streams use the same definition of emotional intelligence but use different ways to measure and assess emotional intelligence. The third stream uses a somewhat broader definition of emotional competencies that includes related social skills in addition to the ability to perceive and regulate emotions. Because of this broader range, some advocates of this tradition have switched from using the term *emotional intelligence* to using the broader term *emotional competencies.*

In the following sections, we'll cover the formal definitions of emotional intelligence and go over the different ways to measure emotional intelligence and related competencies.

Stream 1: Ability-Based Emotional Intelligence Measures

The first stream uses Salovey and Mayer's theoretical model of emotional intelligence *and* their ability-based method to measure emotional intelligence. Salovey and Mayer (1990) were the first to use the term emotional intelligence in its modern and most widely used form today. Their definition of **emotional intelligence** *emphasized the ability to perceive and understand emotions and to regulate emotions, both with regards to oneself and others.* In their original model, (p. 194) they also emphasized how empathy was a crucial part of emotional intelligence: *"Empathy may be a central characteristic of emotionally intelligent behavior,"* and they defined **empathy** *as "the ability to comprehend another's feelings and to re-experience them oneself"* [boldface and italics added]. Their latest measure of emotional intelligence is the MSCEIT V2.0 (Mayer, Salovey, Caruso, & Sitarenous, 2003), which is an updated version of the Mayer–Salovey–Caruso Emotional Intelligence Test (MSCEIT) (Mayer, Salovey, & Caruso, 2002). The MSCEIT V2.0 divides emotional intelligence into four branches (Mayer, Salovey, Caruso, & Sitarenous, 2003, p. 97):

a. *perceiving emotion accurately—assesses the ability to decode emotions in facial expressions, vocal tones, and even artistic expressions*

b. *using emotion to facilitate thought—assesses the ability to use feelings to aid decision making, problem solving and creative thinking*

c. *understanding emotion—this further measures the ability to label emotions and to match appropriate emotions to the situation*

d. *managing emotion—this dimension concerns the ability to regulate emotions, to think about one's feelings, and to assess the effect different emotions would have on others*

The MSCEIT uses items that can be scored as either right or wrong—just like a traditional cognitive intelligence test. For example, test takers are shown pictures of facial expressions, and they have to rate on a 5 point scale how much a particular emotion is being expressed. The researchers determined which answers are correct by using consensus scoring. In other words, if the majority of people think the facial expression shows a 4 on anger, then 4 would be counted as a right answer. The researchers have also used a panel of experts to judge the correct answers; the expert and consensus scores are very highly correlated. The advantage of the ability-based approach to measuring emotional intelligence is that it doesn't require people to self-rate themselves on emotional intelligence. Thus, it could help diagnose whether someone does in fact have a problem with recognizing emotions, which could be useful in psychological counseling and in giving feedback to people. It also helps in selection and hiring where people might be tempted to give inflated self-ratings of their personality traits and strengths. In order to do well on the MSCEIT, people actually have to have the ability to read facial expressions and perform the other tasks on the MSCEIT.

The first dimension of the MSCEIT, the ability to recognize emotions, may be particularly important. The MSCEIT is not the only method that has been used to study people's ability to recognize emotions in facial expressions, vocal tone, and body language. As the next two sections demonstrate, there are other approaches as well.

The Ability to Recognize Emotions and Workplace Effectiveness

One of the most popular methods to measure people's ability to recognize emotions accurately is the Profile of Nonverbal Sensitivity (PONS) developed by Rosenthal, Hall, DiMatteo, Rogers, & Archer (1979). This measure has people watch or listen to sound clips and videos (with and without sound). Another test is Nowicki and Duke's (1994) Diagnostic Analysis of Nonverbal Accuracy (DANVA), which also uses sound clips; however, it uses still photos instead of videos to measure the ability to recognize facial expressions. A meta-analysis summarized 18 studies (with 1,232 participants) that tested these and other types of emotion recognition measures to see if they were correlated with workplace effectiveness and job performance (Elfenbein, Foo, White, Tan, & Aik, 2007). *This meta-analysis found that the ability to recognize emotions correlated positively with workplace effectiveness.* The authors also conducted an additional study, using students from a university in Singapore, that found that the ability to recognize emotions is especially important during buying-selling negotiations—a situation in which people might try to hide their true emotions. As the next section demonstrates, the ability to recognize emotions is particularly important when people might be lying or hiding their emotions.

Detecting Lies in the Workplace

Do you hate it when people lie to you? Most people do. Unfortunately, leaders often find themselves in situations where they wonder if someone is lying to them or not. Why is there some missing inventory? The employees claim they don't know; are they lying? The vendors claim to be able to meet your quality demands—are they fudging the truth? Your department heads tell you your strategic plan is great, but why do they look so worried?

Fortunately, leaders can turn to Paul Ekman for help in determining the truth (Ekman & Friesen, 2003). Ekman is the world's foremost expert in decoding facial expressions to detect lies and other hidden emotions. On his website, Ekman explains how *to read all seven universal emotional expressions: anger, fear, sadness, disgust, contempt, surprise, and happiness*—even when they are hidden in microexpressions that last one twenty-fifth of a second. Now you too can learn his secrets by going to his website: http://www.paulekman.com.

In addition, David Lieberman's (2007) book, *You Can Read Anyone*, explains how to make accurate S.N.A.P. (Strategic Noninvasive Analysis and Profile) decisions about your coworkers, clients, bosses, and subordinates. Lieberman's method (also used by the FBI) relies on analysis of people's motives and of the social situation. Thus, whereas Ekman's methods draw upon the first emotional intelligence dimension (perceiving others' emotions accurately through facial expressions and body language), Lieberman's methods draw upon the next two emotional intelligence abilities, in particular the understanding of emotions. When people's expressed emotions do not match what they should be if they were telling the truth, they might be lying. His methods can help leaders understand whether people are allies or not, whether colleagues really like them and will provide support, and whether potential employees have the right personality traits for the job (emotional stability, self-esteem, etc.).

Stream 2: Self-Report Measures That Use the Mayer and Salovey Theoretical Model

Some researchers accept Mayer and Salovey's definition and model of emotional intelligence but do not feel that the ability-based approach is the best way to measure emotional intelligence (Ashkanasy & Daus, 2005). *Most personality traits are usually measured by self-reports*—you've probably taken a number of personality measures in which you rate yourself on traits like extraversion. In addition, *peer reports may also be a good way to assess how someone behaves in group settings*. Ashton-James (2003), for instance, believes that emotional intelligence measures should assess how people are actually behaving in particular contexts like work settings or other settings where people experience the emotions they are rating.

Jordan, Ashkanasy, Hartel, and Hooper (2002) developed the **Workgroup** **Emotional Intelligence Profile,** *version 3 (WEIP-3), which has people rate themselves and their peers on emotional intelligence.* They administered the WEIP scales to Australian university students involved in semester-long project teams. They found that groups that had higher average levels of emotional intelligence were better performers during the initial few weeks of the project. This makes sense because people higher on emotional intelligence are able to more quickly assess each other's personalities, moods, needs, etc., and thus are able to more quickly form effective teams. In a later study, Jordan and Lawrence (2009) developed a short form of the WEIP with only 16 items; they found support for the short form of the WEIP in an Australian national sample of working adults.

Wong and Law (2002) and Law, Wong, and Song (2004) have also developed *a self-report measure of emotional intelligence in the Stream 2 category:* **Wong and Law Emotional Intelligence Scale (WLEIS).** Wong and Law, for example, found that the emotional intelligence of both followers and leaders is important. In their study, the followers' emotional intelligence influenced both their job satisfaction and their job performance. In addition, leaders high on emotional intelligence were able to influence the job satisfaction of their followers, as well as their organizational citizenship behavior (i.e., voluntary helping behaviors that were optional). A study of managers and their subordinates in Crete, Greece, found that managers' emotional intelligence (self-rated WLEIS) predicted how they were rated on emotional intelligence by their subordinates, which in turn predicted their subordinates' job satisfaction (Zampetakis & Moustakis, 2011).

Stream 3: Mixed Models of Emotional Competencies and Related Social Skills

Daniel Goleman was inspired by Salovey and Mayer's (1990) initial work on emotional intelligence. His book, *Emotional Intelligence: Why It Can Matter More Than IQ* (Goleman, 1995), became a national bestseller and introduced the concept of emotional intelligence to the general public. Goleman's model included a broader range of emotion-related variables than the four branches of the MSCEIT V2.0 (Mayer, Salovey, Caruso, & Sitarenous, 2003), and Goleman and his coauthors (Boyatzis & Goleman, 2002) later began referring to emotional competencies instead of emotional intelligence to reflect this broader conceptualization. Although Goleman's first book focused on educational settings and overall success in life, Goleman coauthored, along with Richard Boyatzis and Annie McKee, another bestselling book: *Primal Leadership: Learning to Lead with Emotional Intelligence* (2004). A key concept in *Primal Leadership* is resonance. **Resonance** *occurs when leaders "are attuned to people's feelings" and create the sense that they "are on the same wavelength emotionally"; resonant leaders use this emotional synchronization to move "people in a positive emotional direction"* (Goleman, Boyatzis, & McKee, 2004, pp. 19-20) [italics added]. Although resonant leaders normally create positive emotional climates, they are sensitive to the feelings of their team members. If a sad event has occurred, they express this sadness for the group, and by expressing sympathy, they eventually help the group members recover from their sadness.

Boyatzis and Goleman (2002) developed the Emotional Competency Inventory (ECI), which has four main dimensions: self-awareness, self-management, social awareness, and relationship management (each dimension also has subscales) (Wolff, 2006). Researchers who have used the ECI have used the items for both self-ratings and for peer evaluations (often as part of a 360 degree evaluation). Other scales in the Stream 3 category have also become popular, including the Bar-On EQi (Bar-On, 2002); in addition, Bar-On now has a model of emotional-social intelligence (ESI) (Bar-On, 2006). More recently, Goleman and Boyatzis (2008) have expanded their concept of emotional intelligence, which they regarded as grounded in individual psychology and are now studying social intelligence. They argue that *"A more relationship-based construct for assessing leadership is* **social intelligence,** *which we define as a set of interpersonal competencies built on specific neural circuits (and related endocrine systems) that inspire others to be effective"* (p. 3) [boldface and italics added]. As Goleman and Boyatzis point out, there is biological evidence behind the theories of emotional and social intelligence: Scientists have even discovered *mirror neurons* that mimic the emotions that people observe. Goleman and Boyatzis argue that emotional displays operate on and stimulate the mirror neurons in a way that is hard for the observer to resist. Goleman and Boyatzis reasoned that socially intelligent leaders show empathy, attunement, organizational awareness, influence, developing others, inspiration, and teamwork. They developed a 360-degree evaluation tool, the Emotional and Social Competency Inventory, to help leaders improve their social intelligence.

Emotional Intelligence/Competency and Job Performance

Are people higher in emotional intelligence/competency better than average at performing most jobs? In particular, leaders want to know if emotional intelligence helps people perform better when taking into account other personality factors that are related to performance, such as cognitive intelligence and the Big Five personality factors. A meta-analytical summary of research studies in work settings (43 different studies, with a total of 5,795 participants) found that emotional intelligence/competency is an important predictor of job performance when controlling for personality and cognitive intelligence (O'Boyle, Humphrey, Pollack, Hawver, & Story, 2011). The researchers used a new statistical technique called *dominance analyses* that allowed them to determine the relative importance of each variable. Here are the rankings in order of importance when predicting job performance:

Stream 1: 1st, cognitive intelligence; 2nd, conscientiousness; 3rd, emotional intelligence

Stream 2: 1st, cognitive intelligence, 2nd, emotional intelligence; 3rd, conscientiousness

Stream 3: 1st, cognitive intelligence, 2nd, emotional competency; 3rd, conscientiousness

Thus, the three most important predictors of job performance are cognitive intelligence, emotional intelligence/competency, and conscientiousness.

Emotional Intelligence/Competencies and Leadership Outcomes

Walter, Cole, and Humphrey (2011) reviewed the studies on emotional intelligence/competency and leadership. They classified the studies according to whether they studied leadership emergence, looked at the type of leadership styles and behaviors the leaders used, or measured overall leader effectiveness and performance. They found the following results:

Leadership Emergence: 100% of the studies on emergence supported the premise that emotional intelligence/competencies were positively related to leadership emergence.

Leadership Behaviors: 81% of the studies on behaviors fully or partially supported the theory that emotionally intelligent/competent leaders were more likely to use effective leadership behaviors (such as transformational leadership behaviors).

Leadership Effectiveness: 87.5% of the studies fully or partially supported the hypothesis that emotionally intelligent/competent leaders were more effective.

Conclusion: **The available research paints a consistent picture showing that emotional intelligence and emotional competency are important to leadership emergence, to performing effective leadership behaviors, and to overall leadership effectiveness.**

It is likely that emotional intelligence/competencies may help leaders in other ways as well. For example, a meta-analysis examined emotional intelligence/competencies and health outcomes (35 studies with 44 separate samples with a total sample of 7,898) (Schutte, Malouff, Thorsteinsson, Bhullar, & Rooke, 2007). This study found that emotionally intelligent/competent individuals had better physical, mental, and psychosomatic health. Although not directly on leaders, it does suggest that emotionally intelligent leaders would be better able to handle the stresses and strains of leadership.

> **The Leader's Bookcase:** To see how religious leaders' emotional competencies improve their parishioners' satisfaction, download from the textbook website: Boyatzis, R., Brizz, T., & Godwin, L. (2011). The effect of religious leaders' emotional and social competencies on improving parish vibrancy. *Journal of Leadership & Organizational Studies, 18,* 192–206.

Emotional Competencies and Intelligence in the Classroom

Emotional competencies may also help people do well in school, especially when it comes to leading teams. Offerman, Bailey, Vasilopoulos, Seal, and Sass (2004) studied which is more important to classroom performance: cognitive intelligence or emotional competency. They found that which is most important depends on the class assignment. They used the ECI-U (Boyatzis & Goleman, 2002) to measure emotional competencies and SAT scores to assess cognitive ability. Interestingly, the total SAT scores predicted the individual exam grades, but the ECI scores did not. In contrast, the ECI score was a good predictor of the team project grade, but the SAT was not significantly related to the team project grade. Moreover, the ECI predicted both leadership effectiveness ratings and leadership rankings. Interestingly, the total SAT scores did not correlate significantly with either leadership scale. However, SAT math scores were *negatively* related to leadership effectiveness scores, while SAT verbal scores were positively related to leadership effectiveness and also were correlated with rankings. These results suggest that *for solitary activities that are primarily cognitive in nature—like studying for exams—cognitive intelligence is the best predictor. For group projects and activities that require leadership skills, however, emotional competency may be of equal or greater importance.*

Other researchers also found that emotional intelligence was important in student project teams (Côté, Lopes, Salovey, & Miners, 2010). These researchers found that emotional intelligence (as measured by the MSCEIT) was a better predictor of leadership emergence than cognitive intelligence or any of the Big Five personality measures.

> **Applications:** How would emotional competency help with team performance and cognitive intelligence help with taking exams? Think of the type of career you want to enter after you graduate. Would your job have you use the same sort of skills you use when taking exams, or would your work activities be more similar to those you do as part of group project teams?

PERSONAL REFLECTIONS: *BALANCING EMOTIONS AND INTELLECT IN THE CLASSROOM*

When I was a graduate student at the University of Michigan, my officemate, Jack, a senior graduate student, told me, "Don't pay any attention to your first set of teaching evaluations, because they'll be lousy." "Maybe for you," I thought, "but not me." I had spent practically my whole life in classrooms, so I thought I knew the ropes. I pretended to listen while Jack explained that it took a few semesters to become a good teacher, so I shouldn't worry if the first semester went poorly—which it would, he assured me. Unfortunately, Jack was right—students gave me horrible ratings during my first semester as a teaching assistant—ratings which I fully deserved. As a young graduate student, barely older than most of the other students, my first concern was to prove to the students that I knew enough to be in front of them. Thus, I asked very tough discussion questions that were too hard to generate good discussion. I realized this when I asked one of these questions, and I was surprised when a student—the best one in the class—answered it correctly right away. And since I wanted to be a serious scholar, I didn't do any of the fun classroom activities that Jack had suggested—these were beneath a brilliant scientist like me. As a result, the students rated me as very knowledgeable but gave me low overall evaluations. And I hadn't enjoyed the class all that much either—did I really want to be a teacher?

In following semesters, I tried introducing fun exercises. I focused on introducing more of an emotional component into the classroom. Eventually, I had some classes with lively, free flowing discussions and lots of causal chitchat. Students started saying how much they enjoyed the class, but some made comments on the evaluations that they hadn't learned as much as they thought they would, and that it was hard to take notes and to know what was important. So in some classes, I started focusing on organization and task instruction. I found that I could either have a classroom that was lively and fun, but not too challenging intellectually, or I would have a task-oriented class in which we covered a lot of material but had fewer genuine interactions. I found it hard to do both at once. Finally, after a few semesters of teaching, I was able to find ways to simultaneously be intellectually and emotionally engaged with the students, and my teaching ratings skyrocketed.

Your Turn to Reflect: Do most people lead with either the heart or the mind, but not both? How difficult is it to do both at once?

Emotional Competency in the Military

Emotional competency is not just for college teachers or Silicon Valley types; it's also useful for rough and ready military teams as well. This is shown by some excellent work by Koman and Wolff (2008) in the U.S. military. They studied 81 aircrew and maintenance teams with a total of 422 servicemen as respondents. Team leaders had worked with their teams for an average of 10.6 months. The team leaders were assessed on the Emotional Competency Inventory (ECI-2). According to the model developed by Koman and Wolff, the leaders' emotional intelligence would determine the degree to which the teams developed emotionally competent team norms. These team norms would in turn influence the team's performance. Basically, their model looks like this:

Leader Emotional Competency → Emotionally Competent
Team Norms→ Team Performance

They found support for both parts of the model: *Leaders' emotional competency influenced the development of emotionally competent team norms, and the norms influenced performance.*

America's allies across the Big Pond found similar results with regard to emotional intelligence in the British Royal Navy (Young & Dulewicz, 2007). This study examined the performance of 261 officers. *The officers higher on emotional self-awareness had higher performance ratings.* The study also suggests that accurately perceiving how others see you is important to performance—something that people high on the emotional competencies of perceiving others' emotions should be good at. This is consistent with prior research on the importance of self-other agreement to leadership (Atwater, Ostroff, Yammarino, & Fleenor, 1998; Atwater & Yammarino, 1992).

Emotional Hijacking vs. Enthusiasm

As Goleman, Boyatzis and McKee (2004) observed, sometimes we let our emotions hijack our reasoning processes. We become so afraid, angry, or upset that we can't think clearly. Have you ever been in an argument with a friend, parent, spouse, coworker, or boss, where you said some things in anger, only the next day to ask yourself, "How could I have said something that stupid?" There is a reason why this happens. When we perceive threats, stress hormones start pumping through our brain, preparing us to either fight or flee. Fighting and fleeing are not contemplative, deep thinking activities. Instead, they require fast action and reflexes. As a result, stress hormones divert activity from the parts of the brain most responsible for our higher reasoning processes and instead stimulate the more primitive parts of our brain responsible for physical action. Brain scans which monitor which parts of the brain are most active reveal that the frontal cortex becomes less active when people are too upset—we literally do become more stupid when we're angry!

Leaders high on emotion management are better able to resist emotional hijacking. One of the big myths about emotional intelligence is that it's all about putting on happy faces and acting emotional all of the time. *In fact, during times of crisis, people high on emotional intelligence become less emotional than others lower on emotion management skills.*

On the flip side, during routine times, when many people become bored or unmotivated, people high on emotional intelligence are better able to generate enthusiasm and excitement about performing the tasks they are working on. Biographies of great leaders reveal how these leaders feel excitement and passion about tasks that many people regard as boring chores at best. How many of us get energized about inventory management? Sam Walton did. Or does making pizzas in front of a hot pizza oven seem thrilling? Tom Monaghan thought it was.

In their autobiographies, great leaders often mention childhood experiences where they had to learn to control their emotions, and they point out how these experiences—unpleasant at the time—helped them develop the emotional regulation abilities that contributed to their leadership effectiveness later in life. The following case about a successful military and business leader is a good example of how leaders learn self-control and use it to be successful.

Case: *Guts: Combat, H***-Raising, Cancer, Business Start-Ups, and Undying Love (Note: *** substituted for real letters in title)*

In his book, *Guts* (2009), Robert Nylen goes through just about every possible scenario that would require a man raised in the 1950s and 1960s to display courage, to control fear, and to avoid emotional hijacking. Boys in his generation, raised, coached, and mentored by WWII veterans, were taught not to get upset by trivial things like broken bones during football practice. As his coach explained rather unsympathetically, if Nylen had taken the hit (from a charging future state champion athlete) instead of backing up half a step, he wouldn't have broken his leg. During most of these life events, Nylen was able to control his fears and emotions enough to pull through with honor. But Nylen is honest enough to admit that—like all of us at one time or another—he was paralyzed with fear or slunk off out of embarrassment or anxiety at various times as well. Here are some of the challenges to his emotional self-control that he faced during his life:

High School Bullies—it's bad enough when they pick on us—even worse when they mock someone we love. Although 8 years old, Robert was still ashamed that he didn't come to the defense of a crippled older sibling.

School Plays—during one play, he's the sole star speaking every line with pride; in the next play, he has stage fright, and he can't speak his single line.

Injured Father—his father was strong, confident, charming and witty, and successful in his career, yet he accidently fell down some stairs and suffered permanent brain damage that affected his mood and personality. Robert is mortified that he wasn't able to help.

College—Robert felt compelled to prove his courage by partying hard and getting in fights.

Combat—Robert was paralyzed with fear when the man in front of him was blown to bits; but during other battles, he was calm enough to be a leader and take charge. He initiated flanking movements while coming under fire, he helped the wounded man in front of him despite his own shrapnel injuries (blood was squirting from his leg like water from a water pistol), and he returned to combat after having been shot in earlier battles—still eager to lead others on patrol.

Public Speaking, Job Interviews, and Cold Calling—after combat, you might think these would be a breeze, but Robert found they took almost as much courage. He hung up with embarrassment and mental paralysis when asked a simple question during his first sales call.

Business Start-Ups—Robert found that costarting his own magazines, *The New England Monthly* and *Beliefnet.com*, was a *cringing* experience. Fortunately, Robert was later able to enjoy running the magazines, and he and his partners made a good profit.

Cancer—Four years of cancer treatments and multiple operations (plus broken bones from ATV and auto accidents) is enough to try anyone's emotional management skills. Nylen maintained his courage, humor, and leadership abilities while facing his own death.

Applications: What are some of the times where you've had the toughest time controlling your emotions? Have there been any events at work where it was hard to control your emotions? Have you witnessed any one at work *losing it*? Have you seen anyone get stage fright? Are good leaders better at controlling their emotions and helping others stay calm?

Empathy, Emotional Expression, Intelligence, and Leadership

Although many researchers focus on either emotional intelligence or cognitive intelligence, Humphrey and his colleagues argued that both are important to leadership (Humphrey, 2002; Kellett, Humphrey, & Sleeth, 2002, 2006). Their model emphasizes empathy, emotional expression, intelligence, and complex task performance. In their studies, the authors developed a measure of *Interactive Empathy that measures whether leaders take initiative in creating a two-way emotional bond in which they influence others' emotions as well as feel others' emotions.* In contrast, many traditional definitions of empathy describe a one-way process in which the receiver feels what others are feeling—this may help in understanding someone but could result in the receiver feeling sad (if the others are sad) and in being unduly influenced by others, as opposed to leading others. Figure 4.1 shows the results from their 2006 study.

Interactive Empathy was the best predictor of leadership emergence in the study (Kellett, Humphrey, & Sleeth, 2006). Interestingly, it predicted both relations leadership (leadership that supports subordinates' needs) and task leadership (leadership that focuses on task completion). This shows that empathy is not just another form of relations leadership, and that it has important benefits for task leaders as well. Wolff, Pescosolido, and Druskat (2002) also argued on theoretical grounds that empathy could help with task activities.

The study also shows that the *ability to express one's own emotions* can work through empathy—for example, one could express sympathetic or supportive emotions. However, it also has a direct effect on task leadership.

Figure 4.1   How Emotional and Cognitive Factors Predict Relations and Task Leadership Emergence

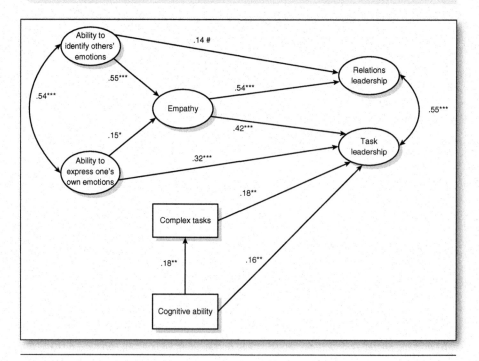

# p < .10 * p < .05 ** p < .01 *** p < .001

Source: Adapted from Kellett, Humphrey, & Sleeth, 2006. Used with permission from Elsevier.

People could, for example, express their emotions quite clearly but in a task-oriented, nonempathic way: Get to work! Van Kleef et al. (2009) and Lindebaum and Fielden (forthcoming), for example, demonstrate how some leaders use displays of anger to signal the need to improve performance. Other scholars, such as Riggio and Reichard (2008), also argue for the importance of social expressiveness to leaders.

The other key emotional intelligence ability in the study (Kellett et al., 2006), *the ability to identify others' emotions, worked mostly through Interactive Empathy.* Another study that examined perspective taking (which involves the ability to understand others' attitudes) in call centers had very similar results, in that the effects of perspective taking were partially mediated by empathy (i.e., worked through empathy) (Axtell, Parker, Holman, & Totterdell, 2007). Both of these studies show the central importance of empathy to other emotional intelligence abilities and to organizational outcomes.

Another study found that empathic leaders help their followers experience less stress and physical symptoms, and followers with empathic leaders showed a stronger relationship between positive affect and daily goal progress than did followers with less empathic leaders (Scott, Colquitt, Paddock, & Judge, 2010). A further study found that empathic leaders (as rated by their subordinates) were also rated higher in performance by their own supervisors in a study of leaders in 38 countries (Sadri, Weber, & Gentry, 2011). Together, these studies demonstrate that empathy is important to leader emergence as well as to leader and follower performance.

> **Self-Assessment:** Visit the textbook website to assess yourself on Interactive Empathy and on related abilities, traits, and competencies.

The following case is an example of a leader who was motivated by empathy to help others, intelligent enough to figure out how to help, and emotionally expressive enough to persuade others to do the right thing.

Case: *Florence Nightingale: Empathic, Smart, and Emotionally Expressive*

Julie Rehmeyer (2008) entitled her article about the founder of modern nursing "Florence Nightingale: The Passionate Statistician." Her title captures how Nightingale changed the world by being both empathic and smart. Florence

(Continued)

(Continued)

Florence Nightingale, circa 1850s

Source: Wikipedia/H. Lenthall

was born into a wealthy family and grew up in a palatial estate (*Florence Nightingale: An Introduction to Her Life and Family*, edited by McDonald, 2002). She could have spent her life traveling the globe in ease and luxury. Instead, she spent her life serving the sick and injured and witnessed the horrors of the Crimean War firsthand. She almost died herself from Crimean fever (which killed more soldiers than battle did), but she remained dedicated to nursing the sick and dying in the military hospitals, often late at night when the other staff had left. Her empathic treatment of the sick earned her the nickname The Lady With the Lamp because of her late night rounds.

Florence's empathic nature made her worry about soldiers even after the war was over. She collected data which demonstrated that English soldiers died even in peace time at rates twice that of the average civilian. She pioneered the use of applied statistics to understand the causes of their higher mortality. She knew she had to use empathic, emotional expressions to win public support for the reforms she advocated, and her letters and writings combine passion and intellect (McDonald, 2002). Her personal experiences as a nurse in the Crimean War allowed her to tell vivid, emotionally appealing stories to persuade others, and she knew she had to present her research the same way. Her mentor told her to present statistics in an emotionally neutral, dry manner. "Statistics should be the dryest [sic] of all reading" (Rehmeyer, 2008). But Florence knew that to persuade Queen Victoria she needed a way to bring the data to life. Nightingale pioneered the use of graphs in public policy documents, and she developed an early form of the modern pie chart designed "to affect thro' the Eyes what we fail to convey to the public through their word-proof ears" (Rehmeyer, 2008). Nightingale's reforms were approved and resulted in dramatically lower mortality rates for soldiers and for millions of others.

(1) Hiring the Disabled and (2) Empathic Leaders

The Positive Vibes Café's main mission is to hire and train disabled people so that they can obtain jobs in the food industry (Lohmann, 2009). Kelley Narowski is one of the employees at the Positive Vibe Café. She became a paraplegic as a result of a traffic accident when she was 25. Now 36 years old, she maneuvers her wheelchair with finesse around the café, serving wine and food to the customers. After her crash, she realized she had a choice to make: "You can lie in bed the rest of your life, or you can get up and make things happen and be independent" (2009, p. B1). Pretty good advice for everyone. Her result: a new boyfriend, a new car, a new job, and an active lifestyle. She's been to Paris, and she travels around America as well. Kelley praises the Positive Vibe's founder, Garth Larcen, for creating opportunities for people with disabilities to be independent and to be treated with equality. Garth has managed to find a way to make empathy a key part of his career and workplace.

Garth is not alone in desiring to have a career that allows him to express the empathic side of his personality. Millions of people have chosen jobs that give them the chance to show care and concern for others (e.g., social workers, teachers, doctors and other health care workers). And many high paying executives list the chance to mentor others and to give back to society as one of the things they like best about their careers. A good example is Kimberly Davis; after she earned her degree in Economics/Finance from Spelman College in Atlanta, Georgia, she spent 30 years in finance (FastCompany.com, 2012). She worked her way up to become Senior Vice President & Director of Recruiting, Training & Development for Chase Manhattan's Global Banking organization. As an African American woman, she knows how important it is to give back to the community. She is now Managing Director of Global Philanthropy and President of the charitable JPMorgan Chase Foundation (JPMorgan.com, 2012). She also worked with her alma mater to develop the Spelman LEADS program, which aims to help women of color become leaders.

You don't have to work for a charity to demonstrate empathy or other forms of emotional competency. Good coaches, for instance, should also care about their players. For example, National Football League coach Tony Dungy had a record 10 straight playoff appearances, and he also led his Indianapolis Colts to a Super Bowl title in 2007 (he was the first African American head coach to win the Super Bowl). As he explains in his *New York Times* bestselling book (Dungy & Whitaker, 2007), *Quiet Strength: The Principles, Practices, and Priorities of a Winning Life,* Tony believes that coaches should be teachers who care about their players. Tony understands the benefits of emotion management, and he recommends that coaches remain calm when things go badly instead of yelling and screaming. Tony is actively involved with many charities, and he serves as the national spokesperson for the fatherhood program All Pro Dad. The following case is about two other leaders who cared deeply about their players but had different ways of expressing their care and concern.

Case: *Pick Your Coach: Mike Krzyzewski vs. John Wooden*

Tournament: Emotional Expression vs. Emotional Control

Mike Krzyzewski (Coach K) and the late John Wooden are two of the greatest basketball coaches in the history of the sport, or in any sport for that matter. Under his leadership, Duke's Blue Devils won 13 ACC Championships and 4 NCAA Tournament National Championships. And let's not forget the 2008 Summer Olympic Gold Medal the USA's men's Redeem team won under his coaching, the 2010 FIBA World Championship, and another Olympic Gold Medal winning team in 2012. John Wooden coached the UCLA basketball team to 10 NCAA National Championships in 12 years—a record unmatched by any other coach. Wooden also had four 30-0 seasons—no other coach has more than one. Both Mike and John have written best-

Coach K talks to children of service members at the Pentagon as part of the Hoops for Troops program.

Source: Department of Defense/ William D. Moss

selling leadership books—let's see how their advice stacks up. Coach K is a fan of emotional expression—his book is called *Leading with the Heart* (Krzyzewski & Phillips, 2004). In contrast, Coach Wooden, in his book, *Wooden on Leadership* (with Steve Jamison), emphasizes emotional control and regulation and a stoic expression.

Coach K gives numerous examples throughout his book of the value of being able to identify others' emotions. This lets him know when he needs to reassure nervous players before they make crucial free throws, get the players to start thinking like a team instead of individuals, or to get them to stop acting too cocky and to start focusing on the game. In his Coach K's Tips section (Krzyzewski & Phillips, 2004, p. 115), he states, "As a leader, you must be able to read your players" and "People talk to you in different ways— through facial expressions, moods, mannerisms, body language, the tone of their voice, the look in their eyes." He believes that the team members should be "at a high level emotionally before every contest" (p. 132). How does he accomplish this? Through emotional expression. He explains his philosophy (p. 157) this way: "A leader also has to show the face his team needs to see. Because, before he ever utters a word, they see his face. They also see his eyes, even his walk." Coach K gives a good example of how Interactive

Empathy can create positive moods in team members—he understands his players' moods, but he also transfers his sense of confidence to them as well. As he puts it (p. 157), "A good leader presents an image that gives confidence to his team. And I make it a point to transform that image to the players by encouraging them to walk right, to stand right, to look good." Coach K believes in using a variety of emotional expressions: "Portray an image that can give your team whatever they may need at that moment: a smile, a frown, emotion, anger, a joke" (p. 158).

Coach Wooden had quite a different philosophy about emotional expression. His approach emphasized emotional control and avoiding emotional hijacking. He gave an example early in his career where he let his emotions get out of control. When he was coaching high school, the coach of the losing team starting cussing Wooden out in front of all of the players and parents, and Wooden responded by knocking him to the ground (Wooden, 2005, p. 111). Wooden learned from his mistakes, and he became determined to adopt a stoic, emotionless expression during games. Even his wife couldn't tell from his expressions whether his team had won or lost. When instructing his players, Wooden kept the same calm demeanor on his face, regardless of whether the team was winning or losing. He never berated players for mistakes—he simply told them what they should be doing right. In his *Rules to Live By*, Wooden stated, "Control Emotion or Emotion Will Control You" (p. 114). He explained this rule by stating, "Uncontrolled emotion or mercurial displays of temperament erode a leader's stature, lessen respect from others, and will undermine your team's efforts." Wooden also avoided pep talks and the *ups* of emotional enthusiasm because he felt these would be followed by emotional downs. Instead, he focused on the details of the game and developing consistency in play. He argued that "emotional control is a primary component of consistency" (p. 108).

Although he argued for emotional control, Coach Wooden, like Coach K, believed in empathic concern for his players. Indeed, Wooden has a whole chapter devoted to loving his players. Wooden stated (2005, p. 80), "Although it may sound out of place in the rough-and-tumble context of sports or corporate competition, I believe you must have love in your heart for the people under your leadership. I did." It is easy to be skeptical when you hear about famous people talking about how much they care for their players or employees, but consider this: Both Wooden and Krzyzewski turned down very lucrative deals from professional sports teams so they could continue to coach the teams they loved. Coach K reportedly turned down a $40 million 5 year deal

(Continued)

(Continued)

with part ownership, and Wooden never asked for a raise on his $35,000 a year salary (his salary in 1975 after winning 10 national championships), and he turned down an offer for 10 times as much.

Applications: Who would you rather have as your coach? Why? Can leaders be high on both emotional control and emotional expression? Have you witnessed coaches or players losing control?

Sources: Krzyzewski, M., & Phillips, D. T. (2004). *Leading with the Heart.* New York, NY: Business Plus Publishers.

Wooden, J., & Jamison, S. (2005). *Wooden on leadership.* New York, NY: McGraw-Hill.

Sources for win-loss records and salary data: Krzyzewski, Mike. Retrieved January 21, 2013 from http://en.wikipedia.org/wiki/Mike_Krzyzewski

Wooden, John. Retrieved October 6, 2009 from http://en.wikipedia.org/wiki/John_Wooden

Put It in Practice

1. For phenomenal success, lead with both your heart and your head.

2. To be an effective leader, you need to be able to both (a) perceive emotions and (b) regulate emotions. In addition, you need to (c) understand the appropriate emotions for different situations and (d) use emotions to facilitate your thinking.

3. The ability to recognize others' emotions can help you perform your job more effectively and also help you during negotiations.

4. The ability to read others' emotions can help you detect lies, judge your level of support from coworkers and other people, and figure out if people have the right personalities for various jobs.

5. You can also use self- and peer-evaluations to help assess people on emotional intelligence and leadership.

6. As a leader, you should strive to create resonance with others; also, you can use measures of emotional competencies or social intelligence to assess a broader range of emotion related leadership skills and relationship management abilities.

7. Remember that the three most important predictors of job performance are cognitive intelligence, emotional intelligence/competency, and conscientiousness.

8. Emotional intelligence and emotional competencies are important to leadership emergence, to performing effective leadership behaviors, and to overall leadership effectiveness.

9. For solitary educational activities, draw most upon your cognitive skills; for group activities, use your emotional intelligence/competencies and verbal skills to emerge as a leader.

10. Don't forget to balance your intellectual and emotional sides when leading others.

11. When leading groups, boost performance by helping the groups develop emotionally competent team norms.

12. Manage your emotions to prevent emotional hijacking and to create feelings of enthusiasm for your leadership responsibilities and work duties.

13. Continue to develop your emotional management skills throughout your life by taking on emotionally challenging responsibilities.

14. Use Interactive Empathy: Effective leaders take the initiative to create two-way empathic bonds with others. Don't be afraid to express assertive nonempathic emotions if the situation requires it.

15. Like Florence Nightingale, Garth Larcen, and Kimberly Davis, you can change the world for the better by combining empathy, intelligence, and emotionally expressive communication.

16. Regardless of whether you focus on emotional control or emotional expression, you should still care about your followers and lead with your heart.

Exercises

1. Emotional Intelligence Charades

A volunteer will come up to the front of the class and silently read a word describing a particular emotion or facial expression. The volunteer then acts out or expresses the emotion through facial expressions and body language. The class will try to guess. Whoever guesses gets to perform the next clue. Some expressions, like being happy, may not be too difficult—feel free to try more challenging ones, like quizzical or whimsical.

2. The Importance of Body Language and Facial Expressions

Form partners and tell one of your favorite, most exciting stories to your partner without using facial expressions, hand movements, or other body language. While you are speaking, your partner should keep track of how many times you slip up and use facial expressions, body language, etc.

Because much of our body language is unconscious, it's often hard to control. Then switch roles with your partner. How exciting did your story seem when you couldn't use your normal body language?

Visit the Student Study Site at **www.sagepub.com/humphreyel** for these additional tools:

- Learning Goals
- Leader's Book Case Articles
- Web Resources
- Student Self Assessments

References

Ashkanasy, N. M., & Daus, C. S. (2005). Rumors of the death of emotional intelligence in organizational behavior are vastly exaggerated. *Journal of Organizational Behavior, 26*, 441–452.

Ashton-James, C. E. (2003). *Is emotional intelligence a viable construct?* Unpublished manuscript. UQ Business School, Brisbane, Australia.

Atwater, L. E., Ostroff, C., Yammarino, F. J., & Fleenor, J. W. (1998). Self-other agreement: Does it really matter? *Personnel Psychology, 51*, 577–598.

Atwater, L., & Yammarino, F. (1992). Does self-other agreement on leadership perceptions moderate the validity of leadership and performance predictions? *Personnel Psychology, 45*, 141–164.

Axtel, C. M., Parker, S. K., Holman, D., & Totterdell, P. (2007). Enhancing customer service: Perspective taking in a call centre. *European Journal of Work and Organizational Psychology, 16*, 141–168.

Bar-On, R. (2002). *BarOn emotional quotient short form (EQ-i:Short): Technical manual.* Toronto, CA: Multi-Health Systems.

Bar-On, R. (2006). The Bar-On Model of Emotional-Social Intelligence (ESI). *Psicothema, 18*, 13–25.

Boyatzis, R., Brizz, T., & Godwin, L. (2011). The effect of religious leaders' emotional and social competencies on improving parish vibrancy. *Journal of Leadership & Organizational Studies, 18*, 192–206.

Boyatzis, R. E., & Goleman, D. (2002). *The emotional competency inventory.* Boston, MA: The Hay Group.

Côté, S., Lopes, P. N., Salovey, P., & Miners, C. T. H. (2010). Emotional intelligence and leadership emergence in small groups. *The Leadership Quarterly, 21*, 496–508.

Dungy, T., & Whitaker, N. (2007). *Quiet strength: The principles, practices, and priorities of a winning life.* Carol Stream, IL: Tyndale House.

Ekman, P., & Friesen, W. V. (2003). *Unmasking the face: A guide to recognizing emotions from facial expressions.* Cambridge, MA: Malor Books.

Elfenbein, H. A., Foo, M. D., White, J., Tan, H. H., & Aik, V. C. (2007). Reading your counterpart: The benefit of emotion recognition accuracy for effectiveness in negotiation. *Journal of Nonverbal Behavior, 31,* 205–223.

FastCompany.com. (2012, March 3). *30 second interview.* Retrieved from http://www.30secondmba.com/user/kimberly-davis

Goleman, D. (1995). *Emotional Intelligence: Why It Can Matter More Than IQ.* New York, NY: Bantam Books.

Goleman, D., & Boyatzis, R. (2008). Social intelligence and the biology of leadership. *Harvard Business Review, 86,* 74–81.

Goleman, D., Boyatzis, R., & McKee, A. (2004). *Primal leadership: Learning to lead with emotional intelligence.* Boston, MA: Harvard Business School Press.

Google. Retrieved June 18, 2012 from http://en.wikipedia.org/wiki/Google

Humphrey, R. H. (2002). The many faces of emotional leadership. *The Leadership Quarterly, 13,* 493–504.

Jordan, P. J., Ashkanasy, N. M., Hartel, C. E. J., & Hooper, G. S. (2002). Workgroup emotional intelligence: Scale development and relationship to team process effectiveness and goal focus. *Human Resource Management Review, 12,* 195–214.

Jordan, P. J., & Lawrence, S. A. (2009). Emotional intelligence in teams: Development and initial validation of the short version of the Workgroup Emotional Intelligence Profile (WEIP-S). *Journal of Management & Organization, 15,* 452–469.

JPMorgan.com (2012, June 18). *Kimberly Davis.* Retrieved from http://www.jpmorganchase.com/corporate/Corporate-Responsibility/company-culture-profiles.htm

Kellett, J. B., Humphrey, R. H., & Sleeth, R. G. (2002). Empathy and complex task performance: Two routes to leadership. *The Leadership Quarterly, 13,* 523–544.

Kellett, J. B., Humphrey, R. H., & Sleeth, R. G. (2006). Empathy and the emergence of task and relations leaders. *The Leadership Quarterly, 17,* 146–162.

Koman, E. S., & Wolff, S. B. (2008). Emotional intelligence competencies in the team and team leader. *Journal of Management Development, 27,* 55–75.

Krzyzewski, Mike. Retrieved January 21, 2013 from http://en.wikipedia.org/wiki/Mike_Krzyzewski

Krzyzewski, M., & Phillips, D. T. (2004). *Leading With the Heart,* New York, NY: Business Plus Publishers.

Law, K. S., Wong, C., & Song, L. J. (2004). The construct and criterion validity of emotional intelligence and its potential utility in management research. *Journal of Applied Psychology, 87*(3), 483–496.

Lieberman, D. J. (2007). *You can read anyone.* New York, NY: MJF Books.

Lindebaum, D., & Fielden, S. (forthcoming). It's good to be angry: Enacting anger in construction project management to achieve perceived leader effectiveness. *Human Relations.*

Lohmann, B. (2009, October 2). After car crash, paraplegic woman 'kept doing things'. *Richmond Times-Dispatch,* pp. B1–B6.

Lowe, J. (2009). *Google Speaks*. Hoboken, NJ: Wiley

Mayer, J. D., Salovey, P., & Caruso, D. R. (2002). *Mayer-Salovey-Caruso Emotional Intelligence Test (MSCEIT) user's manual*. Toronto, Ontario, Canada: Multi-Health Systems.

Mayer, J. D., Salovey, P., Caruso, D. R., & Sitarenous, G. (2003). Measuring emotional intelligence with the MSCEIT V2.0, *Emotion, 3*, 97–105.

McDonald, L. (Ed.). (2002). *Florence Nightingale: An Introduction to Her Life and Family*. Waterloo, Ontario, Canada: Wilfrid Laurier University Press.

Nowicki, S. Jr., & Duke, M. P. (1994). Individual differences in the nonverbal communication of affect: The diagnostic analysis of nonverbal accuracy scale. *Journal of Nonverbal Behavior, 19*, 9–35.

Nylen, R. (2009). *Guts: Combat, hell-raising, cancer, business start-ups, and undying love: One American guy's reckless, lucky life*. New York, NY: Random House.

O'Boyle, E., Humphrey, R. H., Pollack, J. M., Hawver, T. H., & Story, P. (2011). The relation between emotional intelligence and job performance: A meta-analysis. *Journal of Organizational Behavior, 32*, 788–818.

Offermann, L., Bailey, J. R., Vasilopoulos, N. L., Seal, C. & Sass, M. (2004). EQ versus IQ: The relative contribution of emotional intelligence and cognitive ability to individual and team performance. *Human Performance, 17*, 219–243.

Rehmeyer, J. (2008, November 26). Florence Nightingale: The passionate statistician. *Science News*. Retrieved from www.sciencenews.org/index/generic/activity/view/id/38937/title/Florence_Nightingale_The_passionate_statistician

Riggio, R. E., & Reichard, R. J. (2008). The emotional and social intelligences of effective leadership: An emotional and social skill approach. *Journal of Managerial Psychology, 23*, 169–185.

Rosenthal, R., Hall, J. A., DiMatteo, M. R., Rogers, P. L., & Archer, D. (1979). *Sensitivity to nonverbal communication: The PONS test*. Baltimore, MD: Johns Hopkins University Press.

Sadri, G., Weber, T. J., & Gentry, W. A. (2011). Empathic emotion and leadership performance: An empirical analysis across 38 countries. *The Leadership Quarterly, 22*, 818–830.

Salovey, P., & Mayer, J. D. (1990). Emotional intelligence. *Imagination, Cognition, and Personality, 9*, 185–211.

Schutte, N. S., Malouff, J. M., Thorsteinsson, E. B., Bhullar, N., & Rooke, S. E. (2007). A meta-analytic investigation of the relationship between emotional intelligence and health. *Personality and Individual Differences, 42*, 921–933.

Scott, B. A., Colquitt, J. A., Paddock, E. L., & Judge, T. A. (2010). A daily investigation of the role of manager empathy on employee well-being. *Organizational Behavior and Human Decision Processes, 113*, 127–140.

Van Kleef, G. A., Homan, A. C., Beersma, B., van Knippenberg, D., van Knippenberg, B., & Damen, F. (2009). Searing sentiment or cold calculation? The effects of leader emotional displays on team performance depend on follower epistemic motivation. *Academy of Management Journal, 52,* 562–580.

Walter, F., Cole, M. S., & Humphrey, R. H. (2011). Leadership and emotional intelligence: Past findings, current criticisms, and future directions. Emotional Intelligence: Sine Qua Non of leadership or folderol? *The Academy of Management Perspectives, 25,* 45–59.

Wolff, S. B. (2006). *Emotional Competence Inventory (ECI), Technical Manual,* Hay Group, McClelland Center for Research and Innovation, Boston, MA.

Wolff, S. B., Pescosolido, A. T., & Druskat, V. U. (2002). Emotional intelligence as the basis of leadership emergence in self-managing teams. *The Leadership Quarterly, 13,* 505–522.

Wong, C. S., & Law, K. S. (2002). The effects of leader and follower emotional intelligence on performance and attitude: An exploratory study. *The Leadership Quarterly, 13,* 243–274.

Wooden, John. Retrieved October 6, 2009 from http://en.wikipedia.org/wiki/John_Wooden

Wooden, J., & Jamison, S. (2005). *Wooden on leadership.* New York, NY: McGraw-Hill.

The World's Billionaires. Retrieved January 21, 2013 from http://www.forbes.com/billionaires/list/

Young, M., & Dulewicz, V. (2007). Relationships between emotional and congruent self-awareness and performance in the British Royal Navy. *Journal of Managerial Psychology, 22,* 465–478.

Zampetakis, L. A., & Moustakis, V. (2011). Managers' trait emotional intelligence and group outcomes: The case of group job satisfaction. *Small Group Research, 42,* 77–102.

PART III

ADAPTIVE LEADERSHIP APPROACHES

5

The Behavioral Approach to Leadership; Women and Leadership

Chapter Road Map

Case: *Margaret Thatcher—the Iron Lady*
Put It in Practice
Exercises: (1) High-High Leader Behaviors and (2) Reducing Stress Through
  Consideration and Initiating Structure

&oæ&

Case: *It Pays to Be Nice*

In their book, *The Power of Nice: How to Conquer the Business World With Kindness* (2006), Linda Kaplan Thaler and Robin Koval argue that nice guys and gals can finish first. They should know: They built from scratch The Kaplan Thaler Group, one of the fastest-growing advertising firms in the United States of America, which now has a billion dollars in billings. To a cynic, their advice might sound like sentimental platitudes—the sort of stuff that you'll tell elementary school children but that you wouldn't use yourself in the cutthroat competitive world of business. One of their chapters is entitled "Tell the Truth," and another one is even called "Help Your Enemies." But they back up each of their *power of nice principles* with real life business examples where being nice helped them win clients and motivate employees. They believe their "growth is the result not of fear and intimidation, but of smiles and compliments" (p. 3). They cite research that backs up their claims that nice people do better in almost all areas of life. Genial people are lucky in love, with one half the average divorce rate (Sanders, 2005). Nice people are healthier: Older Americans who are friendly, helpful, and supportive have a 60% lower rate of premature death. And nice people make better employees: For every 2% increase in service employees' helpfulness and cheerfulness, revenue rises 1% (Goleman, Boyatzis, & McKee, 2004).

Tennessee Celeste Claflin (Tennie) and her sister, Victoria, opened the first female-owned Wall Street stock brokerage in 1870. Tennie also published a newspaper that promoted women's rights, sexual freedom, and less prudish and restrictive women's clothing—she even dared to bare her ankles in public. For more on this fascinating woman, see http:// en.wikipedia.org/wiki/ Tennessee_Celeste_Claflin

MRS TENNIE C. CLAFLIN. BROKER.

Source: Geo. Stinson & Co., publishers, Portland, ME

Linda and Robin back up the research with lessons from their own business careers. They believe that "It is often the small kindnesses—the smiles, gestures, compliments, favors—that make our day and can even change our lives" (Thaler & Koval, 2006, p. 4). One of their power of nice principles is that *positive impressions are like seeds* that grow and expand. Just like a tiny seed can grow into an enormous tree that bears tremendous amounts of fruit, our kind words and gestures can later pay big dividends in terms of positive relationships with others and new business opportunities. Business people often feel they should be nice to their clients and bosses, and of course, this makes sense. Linda and Robin describe how they were friendly to Donald Trump's wife, Melania, while she was an actress in an Aflac commercial for them. Their seeds of kindness led to Linda being invited to be a judge on Trump's *The Apprentice* show, where Trump gave a glowing endorsement of the advertising firm on national TV free of charge. But Linda and Robin emphasize that you need to be friendly to everyone—even subordinates and strangers. You can never tell how these widely distributed seeds can later bear fruit.

As they observe in their power of nice principle number 3, *people change*. Someone who is a stranger, subordinate, or an apparently unimportant person can later become an important business contact or even your boss. They give an example where they received a call from a woman who wanted to meet with them—they thought perhaps she wanted to apply for a job. They met with her just to be nice. It turned out the woman had been a junior employee who had worked with Linda 25 years earlier and still remembered the kind way Linda had treated her when she was only a low-level rookie. The woman repaid Linda's kindness 25 years later by giving her two big advertising contracts worth $40 million.

In another power of nice principle, Kaplan Thaler and Koval state that "Nice must be automatic" (Thaler & Koval, 2006, p. 10). If you are habitually nice to everyone you meet, you don't have to fake being nice on those important occasions when you want to make a good impression. Being nice would be an automatic habit, and you wouldn't have to remind yourself to adopt an unfamiliar way of behaving while in front of the VIPS. Your friendly behaviors would be natural and sincere—and would look that way to others as well. They give an example of how a consulting firm lost a bid for a very large contract. The consultants had spent a considerable amount of time preparing the bid, and they did a terrific job with their presentation. Unfortunately for them, all their efforts were for naught, because their executive who had picked up the potential client at the airport had neglected to offer to help her with her bags. This lack of common courtesy created such a negative impression that they lost the contract.

(Continued)

(Continued)

Being nice isn't something you do just for clients—employees need to be treated with respect as well. As they explain in their chapter "Put Your Head on Their Shoulders," you need to harness the power of empathy. That's why they celebrate the successes of all their employees—not just those who win million dollar contracts. All their employees, from security guards on up, are doing work that is important and that deserves to be recognized. During brainstorming sessions to develop ad campaigns for clients, even an apparently dumb idea needs to be treated with respect. Quickly dismissing the other person's proposal will make that person feel bad. Instead, by asking questions about how they came up with that concept, they can make the other person feel appreciated even if they don't use the idea. And sometimes these questions discover a really terrific underlying thought.

Linda and Robin found that the friendly camaraderie among their employees helped them land one of their first big contracts. Coldwell Banker picked them because they liked the way the Kaplan Thaler employees joked around with each other and genuinely seemed to like each other. Robin and Linda were surprised by this: Don't most ad agency employees like each other? Not so, said the Coldwell Banker executives: The employees in the other agencies seemed to be jockeying for position with their coworkers rather than working together.

Applications: How important is being considerate and nice in the workplace? Who gets ahead: the team member who is always jockeying for position or the team member who is always kind and considerate to other team members? Which teams are more productive: those with friendly and considerate members or those with competitive members?

Source: Goleman, D., Boyatzis, R., & McKee, A. (2004). *Primal leadership: Realizing the power of emotional intelligence.* Boston, MA: Harvard Business School Press.

Sanders, T. (2005). *The likeability factor: How to boost your L-factor & achieve your life's dreams.* New York, NY: Crown.

Thaler, L. K., & Koval, R. (2006). *The power of nice: How to conquer the business world with kindness.* New York, NY: Broadway Business.

The above case demonstrates that being considerate can help in the business world. As the research in this chapter demonstrates, showing consideration for employees' needs is one of the two major categories of leadership behaviors, according to the Ohio State model of leadership. The other category is called initiating structure and consists of task-oriented type behaviors (e.g., organizing work, scheduling production, explaining work tasks). This leadership type of behavior is illustrated by the concluding case. Although this chapter covers both types of behaviors, this chapter gives somewhat more attention to the benefits of showing consideration. A later chapter, on contingent rewards and transactional leadership, goes over additional ways leaders can initiate structure and take a task-oriented approach to leadership. This chapter begins by giving an overview of the behavioral approach to leadership, which assumes that leadership can be taught, and that leadership is not a function of personality traits. After covering some of the early behavioral approaches, the chapter goes into more detail into the Ohio State model, which has gained increasing attention and empirical support in recent years. In addition, this chapter also has a focus on women in leadership. The opening and closing cases demonstrate that women can effectively use both types of leadership behaviors. The chapter also covers a comprehensive worldwide study that examined male and female leadership styles around the world. In this chapter, you'll learn the answers to the following questions:

- Can you learn leader behaviors?
- Which is more important: initiating structure or showing consideration? How are these two styles related to follower job satisfaction, satisfaction with the leader, and group and organizational performance?
- How does the type of occupation, business, or organizational setting influence which leadership style is most effective?
- How does initiating structure and showing consideration influence employee stress levels and organizational commitment?
- Do male and female leaders around the world differ in their use of consideration and initiating structure?

You Can Learn to Be a Leader!

Many of the leadership approaches we have discussed so far assume that your leadership ability depends upon your traits. In other words, you were born to be either a leader or a follower. Although most trait researchers today recognize that the environment plays a role in determining our behaviors, the overall focus of many trait theorists is on how traits determine our leadership styles and outcomes. (This is somewhat less true of emotion researchers, who often argue that emotional competencies can be taught). In contrast to the trait approach, the theories covered in this chapter were developed by researchers who argued that what counts most are your behaviors, and that you can be taught various leadership skills. These researchers believe that people can make major changes in their leadership style as a result of experience, training, and mentoring.

These researchers still needed to know what behaviors made leaders effective. It is interesting that the early leader behavioral theorists classified leader behaviors into two broad categories that correspond closely to the two fundamental dimensions of traits (competency and warmth) that we discussed in the personality chapter (Judd, James-Hawkins, Yzerbyt, & Kashima, 2005). The different behavioral theorists have their own names for task-oriented behaviors and for relationship-oriented behaviors, but most have categories that correspond to these two broad groupings. This agreement between the trait theorists and behavioral theorists is reassuring and strongly suggests that these are two important areas for leadership. Although most behavioral theorists agree about the two basic dimensions, there are still important differences that distinguish the various behavioral models from each other.

> **Applications:** Can people change their basic leadership approach through training and experience? Have you witnessed anyone making a big change in how he or she leads people or interacts with others? How hard is it to make these changes?

The Good, the Bad, and the Organized

Many early management scholars and behavioral theorists took a rather negative view of task-oriented leaders who focused on getting the job done instead of focusing on supporting employee needs. However, other scholars described task leaders more in terms of their ability to organize the work and get the job done; these scholars recognized that task leadership plays an important role in the success of the work group and organization. It is possible that task leadership may even improve job satisfaction because people do not like working in disorganized, inefficient, and confusing workplaces without clear instructions or procedures.

One of the early scholars who described task leaders in a rather negative light was Douglas McGregor. He argued that managers subscribe to either a positive set of beliefs about workers, which he called Theory Y, or to a negative set of beliefs, which he called Theory X. *Managers who believe **Theory X** assume that workers are basically lazy, irresponsible, and incapable of taking initiative or making decisions; thus, workers need to be closely monitored and even coerced to get them to perform their jobs.* In contrast, *managers who believe **Theory Y** think that workers will be intrinsically motivated if given the chance to take pride in their work and achievements.* McGregor (1960) strongly argued that Theory Y was the correct approach to take in his influential book about managerial philosophy, *The Human Side of Enterprise.* However, McGregor did not test his philosophy empirically, and there have been relatively few studies that have tested his theory using scales that directly measure Theory X and Theory Y orientations. Although his theories are among the most widely known management theories, the popularity of his theory is due mostly to its intuitive appeal. However, there is some good evidence that leaders who hold more positive views about subordinates get better results than those who hold negative attitudes toward workers. Hall and Donnell (1979) summarized the results of *five studies with over 12,000 managers and found that managers who held negative, Theory X type attitudes were more likely to be lower-achieving managers.* More recently, Kopelman and his colleagues have developed some new scales to directly measure Theory Y and Theory X beliefs and behaviors, and these scales may spur some new research into this older topic (Kopelman, Prottas, & Davis, 2008; Kopelman, Prottas, & Falk, 2010).

A series of studies done at the University of Michigan also classified task leaders in a way that suggested they were not concerned with employee needs. *The University of Michigan studies classified leaders on a single dimension that ranged from employee centered at one end to job centered at the other* (Bowers & Seashore, 1966; Likert, 1961). In other words, leaders were *either* employee centered or job centered—there was no category for leaders high on both task focus and employee support.

In contrast to the above perspectives, researchers at Ohio State argued that leaders could be high on both of their two dimensions: consideration and initiating structure (Hemphill & Coons, 1957; Fleishman, 1973). *The Ohio State researchers argue that leaders show consideration when they support employees' needs by being friendly, caring about the employees' personal welfare, and listening to their suggestions and concerns. Leaders are high in initiating structure when they explain work roles, specify how to do the work, assign tasks and schedule production, and set high performance standards.* Their model suggests that consideration increases job satisfaction and commitment, whereas initiating structure improves task performance. This model is sometimes called the High-High Model because these researchers recommend that leaders should do high amounts of both consideration and initiating structure. However, although the Ohio State researchers generally recommend being high on both dimensions, many leaders and corporate cultures tend to be high on only one dimension.

Blake and his colleagues developed a model, first called the **Managerial Grid** (Blake & Mouton, 1964) and later the **Leadership Grid** (Blake & McCanse, 1991), that classifies leadership along two dimensions similar to those in the Ohio State model. Blake and his colleagues refer to the *first dimension as Concern for People* and the *second as Concern for Results (or Production).* The Grid became very widely used in textbooks and in corporate training programs because it does a good job illustrating five different combinations of the two dimensions:

> *Impoverished Management*: When managers are low on both concern for people and concern for results, the managers are not really doing their job as managers. In other words, they are simply collecting their paychecks while providing little leadership, direction, or support.

> *Authority-Compliance Management*: Managers with this style have high concern for results but little concern for people. Leaders who use this style are demanding and controlling, but at least they try to organize the work place efficiently.

> *Country Club Management*: Leaders who use this style have a high concern for people but are low on concern for results. They are friendly and supportive to employees, but they may not push them to be as productive as needed when competition increases. Leaders with this style tend to have low voluntary turnover among their employees. Country Club Management can be an effective style according to some studies.

> *Middle-of-the-Road Management*: These leaders are moderate on both dimensions. This can lead to adequate performance in many environments. These leaders tend to balance the need to be productive with the need to show concern for their employees.

> *Team Management*: These leaders have a high concern for people while also having a high concern for results and production. Obviously, it is difficult to be high on both of these dimensions at once. These leaders succeed by getting their team members' input and participation in achieving the team goals. They are excellent communicators and problem solvers. They often use group rewards and incentives based on productivity to motivate their employees while simultaneously taking care of their financial needs. Blake and his colleagues generally advocate Team Management as the best overall approach.

The Forgotten Ones

For roughly 3 decades, various behavioral approaches based on the Ohio State and Michigan models dominated leadership research. However, a variety of new approaches began to emerge in the late 1970s, and the more traditional behavioral theories went out of style and began to seem old-fashioned. This neglect led Judge, Piccolo, and Ilies (2004) to refer to these older behavioral models as the *forgotten ones*. However, these forgotten models might still be valid, so Judge and his two colleagues decided to summarize the studies on initiating structure and consideration using modern meta-analysis techniques. When they corrected for measurement errors and summarized across various leadership criteria (such as follower satisfaction with the leader, leader perfor-mance, and leader effectiveness), here is what they found:

1. *The correlation between consideration and overall leadership is impressive—clearly leaders who support their subordinates and team members and look out for their welfare are more effective leaders.*

2. *The correlation for consideration with leadership is considerably larger than is the correlation for initiating structure and leadership.*

3. *However, initiating structure is still an important predictor of leadership effectiveness.*

The researchers also examined whether the relative importance of initiat-ing structure and consideration varied by four industry types: business, col-lege, military, and public sector (Judge et al., 2004). Consideration had its strongest effects in the college setting; interestingly, this was also the setting where initiating structure was least important (compared to the other three settings, initiating structure still had a positive effect on leadership in college environments). Across the four settings, consideration behaviors had their least impact in the military setting; however, the impact of consideration was still strong in the military setting. Interestingly, initiating structure had its largest effect in the military—the only setting in which the effects of initiat-ing structure were larger than the effects of consideration on leadership. Thus, in the military, both initiating structure and showing consideration are highly important and are roughly equal in importance. In the business and public sector segments, the effects are very similar to those presented above for the overall findings, with the effects of consideration being substantially higher than the (still important) effects for initiating structure.

Judge et al. (2004) also examined consideration and initiating structure with regard to specific leadership criteria related to either follower satisfac-tion or job performance. As expected, *consideration is much more strongly related to follower job satisfaction compared to initiating structure. Consideration is even more strongly correlated with follower satisfaction with the leader* and is also bigger than the correlation for initiating structure and follower satisfaction with the leader. Nevertheless, initiating structure's correlations with follower job satisfaction and satisfaction with the leader are still positive and large enough to be of practical importance. *Thus, contrary to the early perspective that task leaders most likely decrease employee satis-faction, leaders high on initiating structure generally improve job satisfaction, and they are respected by their subordinates and team members.* After all, who wants to work in a messy, disorganized, and inefficient workplace?

Although consideration has its largest effects on employee job satisfaction, it also helps with performance and effectiveness. *For group-organization performance, Judge et al. (2004) found that consideration and initiating structure were equally effective.* Thus, leaders need to perform behaviors related to both consideration and initiating structure if they want to have high performance. These results strongly support the High-High model—leaders should be high on both dimensions if they want to maximize performance and minimize turnover.

> **Self-Assessment:** Go to the textbook website to assess yourself on initiating structure and showing consideration.

Although it is intuitively appealing to think that consideration-type leadership might be most related to ethical leadership, the above study found that task-oriented leadership high on initiating structure can improve employee satisfaction and thus have beneficial effects on employees. Indeed, studies of ethical leaders like Martin Luther King find that these leaders often have characteristics associated with task-oriented leaders, such as courage, while also having empathy and compassion for others and a strong sense of community (Fluker, 2009). The next section illustrates how leaders who are typically high in initiating structure risk their lives to save others; this section is followed by a case on Paula Deen which illustrates how leaders high in consideration save lives in their own way.

Brave, Tough, and . . . Considerate: Aviation Rescue Fire Fighters

You have to be brave to jump out of a perfectly good airplane—and even braver to jump out of one into a raging forest fire. Traditionally, people who work in dangerous jobs such as fire fighters, SWAT team members, and military units are trained using a tough, task-oriented approach. This task-oriented approach can help people focus on their responsibilities and retain control of their emotions during crisis situations that would cause many people to panic. However, fire fighters and other rescue workers also depend for their lives on their leaders and teammates. In these situations, it might be a good thing to have leaders high on consideration, i.e., leaders who look out for the welfare and best interests of their teammates and subordinates. People in these occupations often spend long hours together as well, even living together for days or months at a time. Leaders high on consideration may be able to help these workers handle the normal stresses and interpersonal tensions that come from such close contact.

The Australian aviation fire service had studied the leadership styles used by their supervisors and had determined that they predominantly used initiating structure. Their surveys revealed that job satisfaction was a problem and that there was a need for leadership development and training. As a result, they implemented training programs to teach leaders how to use more consideration-type leader behaviors. Two researchers, Bartolo and Furlonger (2000), studied the aviation fire service workers and leaders after this training program was put into place. After the training, they found that satisfaction with the supervision was high. Moreover, they found that both consideration and initiating structure were positively related to satisfaction with the leader.

The aviation fire fighter study has two important findings. First, it supports the overall premise that *leaders can be trained to adopt behaviors related to showing consideration and initiating structure*. Second, it shows that *both types of leader behaviors are important even in occupations that are often stereotyped as being exclusively task oriented*. It really shouldn't come as any surprise that rescue workers and their leaders can be high in consideration-type behaviors: After all, they are risking their lives for the welfare of others.

Case: *Paula Deen, Flying Hams, and Smithfield's Foods Helping Hungry Homes*

You don't have to be a fireman or a member of another dangerous occupation to save lives and show true consideration—you can save lives by feeding the hungry. However, as celebrity chef Paula Deen learned when she was hit by a flying ham, even feeding the hungry can carry certain risks. Although the accident with the flying ham seemed to gain the most news attention, the giving away of millions of servings of protein (i.e., meat, fish and fowl) is more noteworthy. Paula Deen, her husband, and her two sons helped Smithfield Foods deliver a million servings of meat during their 10 city tour. This tour was part of the company's larger Helping Hungry Homes program. As Smithfield points out on its website, there are 35 million people in *food insecure* households in the United States of America. Paula Deen, Smithfield Foods, and their additional

Paula Deen opened her first restaurant with her two sons and named it Lady and Sons.

Source: Flickr/greenbob16
(CC-BY)

(Continued)

(Continued)

partners, Safeway, Inc., The United Food and Commercial Workers Union, and Food Network, are showing true leadership by publicizing this pressing need and by their own food contributions. The Helping Hungry Homes program plans to donate 20 million servings of protein during the next 3 years. Interestingly, the announcements from Smithfield's and Safeway didn't even mention their Chairmen's or CEOs' names—perhaps they are more concerned with feeding the hungry than in glorifying themselves: consideration leadership at its best.

Applications: Would leaders known for their charity work have an easier time recruiting good employees? Do you think the personality traits that would motivate someone to contribute to charity would also motivate that person to use consideration-type leadership at the workplace? Can task leadership also help with charity programs? Do businesses have an obligation to help with social problems like hunger?

Source: Smithfield Foods' Helping Hungry Homes (2010). Retrieved from www.smithfield foods.com/responsibility/helping.aspx

A Manufacturing Example

Increase Organizational Commitment and Reduce Stress by Initiating Structure and Showing Consideration

According to a study by Dale and Fox (2008), the two leader behaviors of initiating structure and showing consideration may improve organizational commitment because they reduce stress at work. The view that task leaders are only concerned about production and are not concerned about people would suggest that these leaders would increase stress with relentless demands for ever greater productivity. When done right, however, task leadership may actually reduce stress. There are many aspects of initiating structure that should reduce role ambiguity and role conflict. As Dale and Fox argue, leaders high on initiating structure may provide useful rules and policies for employees to follow, and employees may appreciate knowing what to do. These procedures may also increase perceptions that the leaders and the organization are dependable. Dale and Fox argue that leaders high on initiating structure are likely to provide needed information to employees about how to do the job and perform at higher levels. Again, this should increase commitment and reduce stress.

It is perhaps even easier to see how leaders who perform consideration-type behaviors increase commitment and reduce stress. Leaders show consideration when they listen to employees' problems and suggestions. This reduces stress by allowing employees to blow off steam and express their emotional tensions, as well as solve the stressful problems. Leaders high on consideration are also likely to become friends with their subordinates and team members. Considerable research has found that friendly social interaction increases commitment while reducing stress and turnover.

Dale and Fox (2008) tested their theories by surveying 147 employees in a Midwestern (U.S.A.) manufacturing facility. The employees averaged 36 years of age, almost all had high school degrees, and 39% had college degrees or better. Consistent with their expectations, both initiating structure and consideration increased commitment and reduced stress, with consideration having the larger effects. They also tested a sequential model:

Leader behaviors (initiating structure, consideration) →
stress → organizational commitment

Initiating structure worked entirely through reducing stress. In other words, initiating structure increased organizational commitment only because it reduced stress. In contrast, leaders high on consideration behaviors reduced stress, which increased commitment, but consideration also increased commitment directly as well. Leaders high on consideration may increase commitment in a wide variety of ways, and employees are more likely to want to stay with a leader and a company that provides a friendly and supportive atmosphere. Wouldn't you stick around longer at a company where you were friends with your manager and coworkers?

> **Applications:** How should leaders respond when employees are having a stressful day? Should they focus on initiating structure to eliminate problems and confusion, or should they focus on listening to employees and expressing support? Think of some of the times you and your coworkers experienced stress at work—what did your leaders do?

Keep on Rolling: Leadership in Public Transportation

Zimmerman, Mount, and Goff (2008) examined whether initiating structure and showing consideration helped public transportation leaders improve their goal performance. They studied 396 leaders working for a large passenger train organization in the eastern United States. Roughly three quarters of the leaders were in their 40s and 50s and had over 10 years of tenure with the company. Almost all had either a bachelor's degree or higher (43%) or at least some college (45%). The leaders were first line supervisors (40%), middle managers (48%), and senior managers (12%). The study began when the company first set performance goals for the leaders in five areas (financial, safety, employee satisfaction, customer satisfaction, and diversity). A month later, the company administered multisource feedback instruments where the leaders were rated by (1) their supervisors, (2) themselves, and (3) others (peers and subordinates). The first time this was done for developmental purposes to help the leaders improve their performance. Eight months later, the multisource forms were filled out again for administrative purposes as part of the performance appraisal process for pay raises and promotions. A month after this, the leaders were evaluated by their supervisors on how they had achieved the five performance goals.

Zimmerman et al. (2008) found that *when supervisors evaluated leaders on leadership style, consideration was over 6 times greater than initiating structure in improving goal performance.* However, somewhat surprisingly, when the leaders evaluated themselves on leadership style, consideration actually had small negative effects on performance, whereas initiating structure had a positive impact on goal performance. The pattern for other ratings was similar to self-ratings. The authors argue that the supervisors' ratings may actually be more accurate than self-ratings or other ratings: When we rate ourselves, we may be judging ourselves compared to our internal standards, our desire to improve, and so forth, while the supervisors might be comparing each leader to the other leaders and thus have a better basis of comparison. Zimmerman (personal communication, March 25, 2010) provided *a great example of how one of the leaders showed consideration leadership: When she had received a plaque and a bonus for improving efficiency in her department, she replaced her name on the plaque with the names of the employees in her department, and she split her bonus equally among the employees.*

Shopping for Consideration

Some evidence that it pays off financially to use consideration-style leadership comes from a study by another group of Dutch researchers: Koene, Vogelaar, and Soeters, (2002). These researchers examined the leadership style of 50 managers of supermarkets in the Netherlands. Instead of measuring perceived leadership effectiveness, they used some objective store performance data: (1) net profit as a percentage of total sales and (2) controllable costs as a percentage of total store sales (controllable costs included such things as stock losses, personnel costs, and packaging costs). The net profit varied considerably by store, from a low of 0.98% to a high of 8.72% (clearly it pays to get the right manager!). They also had 2,156 store employees rate the store managers on leadership. The employees assessed their leaders on consideration leadership, initiating structure, and also on charismatic leadership. The results: When using a multiple regression to control for store size and similar factors, initiating structure had no effect on net profit or on controllable costs. In contrast, *both consideration and charisma influenced the two objective performance variables.* Consequently, it pays to be considerate to your employees.

> **Applications:** Have you ever witnessed employees wasting supplies or being careless about controlling costs? Are employees more likely to be negligent about controlling costs when they think their managers are treating them inconsiderately?

PERSONAL REFLECTIONS: *HIGH-HIGH MENTORS*

I've been fortunate to have several High-High mentors during the start of my career. These mentors taught me the research craft by initiating structure and giving me some great instruction, and they've also motivated me by showing personal consideration. When I was a doctoral student at the University of Michigan, my faculty mentor was Howard Schuman. He was Director of the Institute for Social Research, the largest university survey research center in the world, and thus was very busy. But he still took time out to give me some very useful advice about how to write journal articles; even today, after years of writing experience, I find myself recalling his words of advice and applying them to my current projects. Howard also looked out for my personal welfare by making sure that I had summer support (i.e., summer employment) and teaching or research assistantships during the academic year. Howard's support took away much of the anxiety that comes from being a student in a highly competitive program.

A few years later, when I was an assistant professor, a senior faculty member, Dick Osborn, took on the mentorship role for me. Dick was also very busy and was in the process of publishing his way to the Academy of Management's Wall of Fame (when this award was created a few years later, Dick was one of the 30 members around the world so honored, based on an objective measure of the number of articles he had published in Academy-sponsored journals). Dick took time out from his own ambitious agenda to give me some detailed advice on my plans for a new research project. Based on his comments, I made a major change to my research design, and as a result, I was able to publish my research. I've found it interesting that many of the most prominent leaders I know, the ones working the hardest to be the most productive in their field, are the ones who take the most time out to support others.

Your Turn to Reflect: How difficult is it to give specific task advice while still coming across as friendly and supportive? Are people at the top of their game better at initiating structure and showing support? Have you had any High-High leaders?

Men and Women Around the World: Do They Use Different Leadership Behaviors?

Van Emmerik, Euwema, and Wendt (2008), researchers from the Netherlands and Belgium, published a fascinating study on leadership around the world. First, they looked at whether leaders in different cultures used the same amounts of initiating structure and showing consideration. Second, they wanted to know if men and women differed in how frequently they used these two leader behaviors in each country. The authors had access to an impressive database collected by the worldwide consulting firm, the Hay Group. Their data set had 64,038 subordinates rating the leadership behaviors of 13,595 managers in 42 countries. The employees worked for 473 organizations both public and private. Roughly three quarters (73%) of the managers were men—this figure by itself is informative about the degree to which women occupy leadership roles around the world: 27% in their sample. When the type of culture was correlated with the percentage of females in the managerial sample, women were more likely to be managers in the Anglo, English speaking cultures like the United States and the United Kingdom compared to the global average. Eastern European cultures also had a slight positive correlation for the percentages of women leaders. The correlations were negative for the percentages of women managers in Germanic European cultures, Latin American, sub-Saharan, and Arab cultures, thus indicating that in these cultures, compared to the global average, women were less likely to be leaders.

Because of socialization processes, men and women may differ in their use of consideration and initiating structure (Carless, 1998; Eagly & Johnson, 1990). Women are often socialized to perform nurturing and care-giving roles, such as raising children, so it is possible these experiences would pre-dispose women to use higher amounts of consideration-type behaviors when they are leaders. In contrast, men are often taught to be tough, to engage in aggressive sports, and to focus on problem solving instead of emotional support. As a result, male leaders may use higher amounts of initiating structure. The researchers tested whether women would score higher on consideration across all cultures. For their total sample, they found a moderately small correlation which indicated that women were rated higher on consideration by their subordinates. Interestingly, women were also rated higher on initiating structure, although in this case, the correlation was very small.

Because of differences in culture, it is likely that how often leaders perform consideration-type behaviors or initiate structure would vary a great deal. The researchers grouped their 42 countries into 10 cultural clusters according to the GLOBE study results (Dorfman & House, 2004; House, Hanges, Javidan, Dorfman, & Gupta, 2004). Figure 5.1 illustrates how the leaders in the different cultural clusters are rated by their subordinates on these two leader behaviors.

Although there were cultural differences in the degree to which leaders used consideration, these cultural differences were fairly small. In contrast, there were fairly important differences in the degree to which leaders initiated

Figure 5.1   Mean Scores on Consideration (Panel A) and Initiating Structure (Panel B) for the 10 Globe Clusters as Rated by the Subordinates of Male and Female Managers

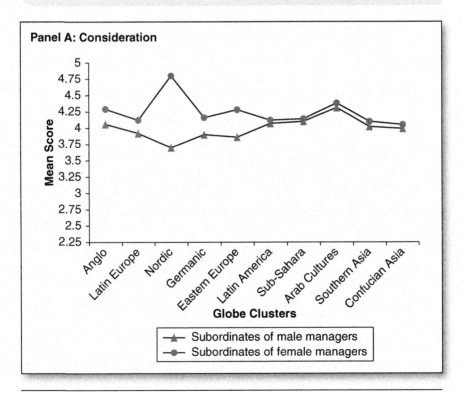

(Continued)

Figure 5.1 (Continued)

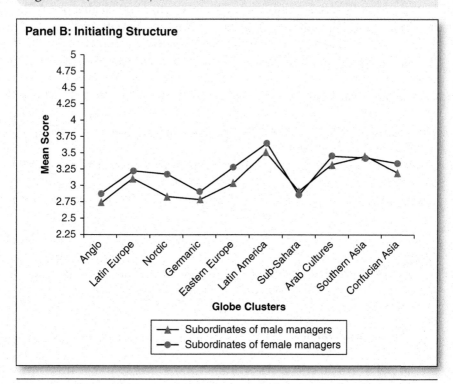

Panel B: Initiating Structure

Source: Used with permission from: Van Emmerik, I. J. H., Euwema, M. C., & Wendt, H., (2008). Leadership behaviors around the world: The relative importance of gender versus cultural background. *International Journal of Cross Cultural Management, 8*, 297–315.

structure according to culture. From Figure 5.1, we can see that some of the cultures with the longest histories of democracy and freedom are lower on initiating structure, such as the Anglo cultures and the various European cultures. Leaders in these cultures may believe that employees should be consulted about decisions and should have some autonomy in deciding how tasks should be done.

From Figure 5.1, we can also see that there are some cross-cultural differences in the gap between how often men and women use consideration-leadership behaviors. The gap is especially large for the Nordic cultures, but there are some differences in the Anglo cluster and in the other European cultures as well. The other cultures did not show the gender gap for consideration. In contrast, cross-cultural differences seemed to be relatively unimportant in explaining the small gender differences between men and women in initiating structure: Only one culture differed from the others in its pattern of male-female differences in initiating structure.

The Big Picture: (1) The authors concluded, "**In this large worldwide sample, gender differences in managerial behavior appear to be rather limited,**" and male and female managers "do not differ much in leadership behaviors" (Van Emmerik et al., 2008, p. 310) [boldface added]. (2) In addition, **cultural differences (but not gender differences) in initiating structure are important: The Anglo and European cultures are lower in initiating structure.**

> **Applications:** Are women more considerate in Western cultures? What impact would the cultural differences in initiating structure have on how you would lead people in Anglo and European cultures versus other cultures? What can be done to increase the number of women in leadership positions around the world?

> **The Leader's Bookcase:** Visit the textbook website to download the article on gender and cross-cultural leadership: Van Emmerik, I. J. H., Euwema, M. C., & Wendt, H., (2008). Leadership behaviors around the world: The relative importance of gender versus cultural background. *International Journal of Cross Cultural Management, 8*, 297–315.

Developmental Opportunities for Men and Women

As the preceding worldwide study indicated, only 27% of the world's managerial leaders are women. Given that men and women use similar leadership styles, why is there such a big difference in the proportions of men and women in leadership roles? One reason may be the number of developmental opportunities seized by men and women early in their careers. A fascinating study by Irene De Pater and her colleagues shows the importance of negotiating for career-developing tasks (De Pater et al., 2009). The researchers assigned 85 male and 85 female business students (at a U.S. university) to work together in mixed-sex teams of two. The participants were on average 24 years old and 95% had work experience, so they were representative of people in the early stages of their careers where gaining developmental opportunities would be important to skill development and future promotions opportunities. In the first session, the participants were individually given a list of complex and simple tasks that they could perform during the second session. The participants were asked to rate their preferences for performing the tasks. At this stage, men and women were equally likely to express preferences for performing the career-enhancing complex tasks. In the second session, however, each pair had to decide how they would allocate performing the three complex tasks and the three simple tasks. After the pairs of men and women negotiated with each other for the tasks they would work on, the men ended up with 1.75 of the complex tasks and the women with only 1.25 of the complex tasks. This also meant that the women got stuck performing more of the simple tasks. In many committees and other work settings, team members have to divide up the work, and as a result, some employees get to perform career and skill enhancing assignments while others get stuck with the routine grunt work. This study suggests that women need to be given more developmental opportunities to help them move up the organizational hierarchy.

Women, Innovation, and Top Management Team Performance

Although roughly a quarter of the world's managerial leaders are women, the proportion at the very top is even smaller. Dezso and Ross (2012) examined the top management teams of the S&P 1,500 firms. In 1992, less than 10% of these firms had a female member of the top management team; however, by 2001, roughly 30% had at least one woman on the top team. Although there was a steady increase from 1992 through 2001, the number of women in top management roles leveled off from 2001 to 2006. Dezso and Ross also wanted to see if having women in the top management team influenced firm performance. They reasoned that female middle managers would be more motivated by seeing top female role models and that this would contribute to overall firm performance. Moreover, they reasoned that women on the top management team would contribute to innovation by offering differing viewpoints and additional information. Although the presence of women on top management teams had no effect of firm performance for the total sample of firms, the researchers found that *firms that had a high intensity innovation strategy benefited from having women in the top team and were more profitable as a result.* Their study suggests that women top team members can provide useful information and differing perspectives that can boost innovation and firm performance. The studies reviewed in this chapter generally support the relative importance of consideration-type leadership over initiating structure. However, there may be circumstances where initiating structure is more useful. Although Goleman et al. (2002) in *Primal Leadership* do not recommend a *Commanding* leadership style (similar in some ways to initiating structure) for most circumstances, they do recommend it for crisis and emergency situations. As mentioned earlier, military settings also call for an initiating style of leadership. The following case illustrates how Margaret Thatcher used a directive leadership style to combat the economic crisis facing the United Kingdom. As with all of the political leader profiles, the focus is on describing the personality traits and leadership styles of the leaders, rather than on the correctness of their political, economic, and foreign policies.

Case: *Margaret Thatcher—the Iron Lady*

When a prime minister's nickname is the Iron Lady, you know her primary leadership style is likely to be high on task orientation and initiating structure. Thatcher served as the United Kingdom's Prime Minister from 1979 to 1990—longer than Churchill or any other leader in the 20th century. She was also the only woman to serve as the UK's Prime Minister.

Former British Prime Minister Margaret Thatcher

In her autobiography, Thatcher (1995) describes her close relationship with her father. Her father grew up in a working class family, and he worked his way up to a store manager position. By being thrifty and saving money, he was able to make the down payment on a loan to buy his own grocery store with an apartment above it for his wife and daughters. Margaret and her mother and sister would help out in the grocery store, and eventually, her father was able to open some other small grocery stores as well.

Source: Margaret Thatcher Foundation/Chris Collin (CC-BY-SA)

Margaret was born in 1925, so she spent most of her youth enduring the hardships of the Great Depression and the rationings and shortages imposed by World War II. Her father was also very active in charity organizations such as the Rotary Club and in Conservative politics, and eventually, he was elected the Mayor of Grantham. It is easy to see how Thatcher's early life shaped her political philosophy. Because she was from a working-class and middle-class background, she had sympathy for the problems of the poor. However, she believed that the solutions for poverty would be for people to follow her family's example and to practice thrift, work hard, save money, and get an education (her first cabinet appointment was as Secretary of State for Education and Science). She made this apparent by her *Good Housekeeping* campaign based on prudent government spending. During the 1930s, she was keenly aware of the atrocities committed by the National Socialists (i.e., Nazis) in Germany (her family took in a Jewish teenage refugee shortly after Hitler marched into Austria), and she was also aware of the horrors inflicted on Russia by the communists (and later on Eastern Europe as well). Thus, she opposed big governments—whether Fascist or Socialist—that could take control over people's lives in the guise of providing them public services.

Thatcher (1995, pp. 569–579) describes the four components of her economic program. First, she controlled the monetary supply to bring down inflation from

(Continued)

(Continued)

21.9% in May 1980 to a low of 2.4 percent in the summer of 1986, with rates around 5% in the mid-80s. Second, she took charge of public finances. Public sector borrowing had reached 9.25% of GDP in 1975/1976. She began paying back government debt and reduced government debt as a percentage of national income to levels not seen since before WWI. Controlling public expenditures allowed the lowering of the basic income tax rate from 33% to 25% and the top rate from 83% to 40% (some indirect taxes were increased). Third, she privatized many state-owned businesses and reduced the state-owned portion of the economy by 60%. She supported a program that helped tenants in 1.5 million governmental housing units buy their residences. Fourth, she made a number of structural changes to promote a *supply-side revolution*. Britain's gross domestic product (GDP) grew less than 1% annually from 1973 to 1979 but grew at 2.25% during the 1980s, thus substantially increasing the standard of living. Thatcher's policies were controversial and strongly opposed by many. To make the changes Thatcher did, perhaps it takes someone with a nickname like The Iron Lady.

Applications: How important do you think people's early home lives are on the development of their leadership style? During times of economic or military crisis, is the initiating structure style more useful than the consideration style?

Source: Thatcher, M. (1995). *The path to power* (U.S.A. ed.). New York, NY: HarperCollins.

Blema Steinberg (2008) analyzes Thatcher in her book *Women in Power: The Personalities and Leadership Styles of Indira Gandhi, Golda Meir, and Margaret Thatcher*. According to Steinberg, Thatcher has a dominant personality backed up by conscientiousness and a strong work ethic. Female leaders can be as tough as male leaders (Steinberg, 2008, p. 303): Thatcher, Gandhi, and Meir all score higher on dominance than Presidents Clinton and George W. Bush. Steinberg (2008) quotes Thatcher as saying, "I don't mind how much my ministers talk—as long as they do what I say (p. 270). Interestingly enough, Thatcher (1995) entitled her autobiography *The Path to Power*, which is certainly a dominating title.

Steinberg (2008) classifies Thatcher as primarily motivated by ideology and secondarily by pragmatism and power. However, Ligon, Hunter, and Mumford (2008) classify Thatcher as a charismatic leader (as opposed to an ideological one) who is motivated by socialized power (i.e., uses authority for the good of others), as opposed to personalized power (power for self-aggrandizement). The differences between the two studies are likely due to differences in their coding systems. Ligon, Hunter, and Mumford distinguish between ideological leaders whose values are based on preserving past traditions from charismatic leaders who are guided by visions of a radically different future. Sternberg does not include the charismatic leadership style in her system, so it is likely that she collapses value or vision-oriented leaders into the ideological category regardless of whether they are past oriented or future oriented. Thatcher (1995) gives considerable attention in her autobiography to books analyzing future trends and possibilities, and she strove to bring her own vision of the United Kingdom's future into existence. Thatcher's effect on the United Kingdom has often been termed the *Thatcher Revolution*, so it's clear that she meets the major change requirement specified by Ligon, Hunter, and Mumford. Thatcher seems to have been motivated to use her authority in a way that she believed would benefit society and thus fits the socialized power definition. Sternberg also had several measures of leader involvement with personnel, cabinet members, her own party members, opposition party members, and so forth, and Thatcher scored extremely high on all measures of involvement—she definitely exerted leadership and was a hands-on leader.

Put It in Practice

1. Increase your power by being nice and considerate to everyone.

2. You can learn to be a better leader.

3. For best results, focus on both people and work tasks, for example, by showing both consideration and initiating structure.

4. Use the High-High Approach: Although consideration is much more strongly related to follower job satisfaction compared to initiating structure, initiating structure still improves follower job satisfaction. Initiating structure and showing consideration are equally effective in improving group-organization effectiveness. To maximize performance and minimize turnover, be high on both showing consideration and initiating structure.

5. Even in occupations with a high-task oriented culture, organizations can improve followers' satisfaction with their leaders by teaching the leaders to show more consideration.

6. Leaders can demonstrate consideration leadership by feeding the hungry or supporting other forms of charity.

7. Reduce your followers' stress levels by showing consideration and initiating structure.

8. Show consideration by sharing your awards, honors, and even bonuses with your followers; remember that in one study showing consideration was 6 times more important than initiating structure in improving goal performance.

9. Boost profits and reduce waste by using charismatic, considerate leadership.

10. As a mentor, motivate your protégés by giving them task instructions and by showing consideration for their personal welfare.

11. Remember that gender differences in managerial behavior appear to be rather limited, but there are significant cultural differences in the degree to which leaders initiate structure.

12. Give everyone a chance: Women as well as men need developmental opportunities to learn new skills and demonstrate their abilities to perform complex tasks.

13. Be innovative: Include both men and women on your team.

14. During times of crisis, a commanding and dominant leadership style that emphasizes initiating structure may be needed to bring about major changes. Don't forget that female leaders can also use a dominant leadership style.

Exercises

1. High-High Leader Behaviors

Form groups of about five people. Most people are best at either showing consideration or initiating structure—this exercise will help team members learn how to do both. Group members should make a list of five specific behaviors that managers can do to show consideration and five behaviors that initiate structure. If possible, give examples of actual managers or leaders and describe how they perform these behaviors. List specific behaviors such as "holding birthday parties for employees on their birthdays" rather than more general advice like "be nice."

2. Reducing Stress Through Consideration and Initiating Structure

Form groups of about five people. Each group member should describe a specific stressful event encountered at work (or in a club, sports team, etc.). Were the problems caused by a lack of structure (unclear rules, lack of instructions about how to do the work) or by inconsiderate behaviors? For each event, the team members should brainstorm about possible leader behaviors related to showing either consideration or initiating structure that could reduce the stress. For each event, which type of leader behaviors would be most effective?

Visit the Student Study Site at **www.sagepub.com/humphreyel** for these additional tools:

- Learning Goals
- Leader's Book Case Articles
- Web Resources
- Student Self Assessments

References

Bartolo, K., & Furlonger, B. (2000). Leadership and job satisfaction among aviation fire fighters in Australia. *Journal of Managerial Psychology, 15,* 87–97.

Blake, R. R., & McCanse, A. A. (1991). *Leadership dilemmas: Grid solutions.* Houston, TX: Gulf Publishing Company.

Blake, R. R., & Mouton, J. S. (1964). *The managerial grid.* Houston, TX: Gulf Publishing Company.

Bowers, D. G., & Seashore, S. E. (1966). Predicting organizational effectiveness with a four-factor theory of leadership. *Administrative Sciences Quarterly, 11,* 238–263.

Carless, S. A. (1998). Gender differences in transformational leadership: An examination of superior, leader, and subordinate perspectives. *Sex Roles, 39,* 887–902.

Dale, K., & Fox, M. L. (2008). Leadership style and organizational commitment: Mediating effect of role stress. *Journal of Managerial Issues, 20,* 109–130.

De Pater, I. E., Van Vianen, A. E. M., Humphrey, R. H., Sleeth, R. G., Hartman, N. S., & Fischer, A. H. (2009). Task choice and the division of challenging tasks between men and women. *Group and Organization Management, 34,* 563–589.

Dezso, C. L., & Ross, D. G. (2012). Does female representation in top management improve firm performance? A panel data investigation. *Strategic Management Journal, 33,* 1072–1089.

Dorfman, P. W., & House, R. J. (2004). Cultural influences on organizational leadership: Literature review, theoretical rationale, and GLOBE project goals. In R. J. House, P. J. Hanges, M. Javidan, P. W. Dorfman, & V. Gupta (Eds.), *Culture, leadership, and organizations. The GLOBE study of 62 societies,* pp. 51–73. London, UK: Sage.

Eagly, A. H., & Johnson, B. T. (1990). Gender and leadership style: A meta-analysis. *Psychological Bulletin, 108,* 233–56.

Fleishman, E. A. (1973). Twenty years of consideration and structure. In E. A. Fleishman & J. G. Hunt (Eds.), *Current developments in the study of leadership* (pp. 1–40). Carbondale, IL: Southern Illinois University Press.

Fluker, W. E. (2009). *Ethical leadership: The quest for character, civility, and community.* Minneapolis, MN: Augsburg Fortress.

Goleman, D., Boyatzis, R., & McKee, A. (2004*). Primal leadership: Realizing the power of emotional intelligence.* Boston, MA: Harvard Business School Press.

Hall, J., & Donnell, S. M. (1979). Managerial achievement: The personal side of behavioral theory. *Human Relations, 32,* 77–101.

Hemphill, J. K., & Coons, A. E. (1957). Development of the Leader Behavior Description Questionnaire. In R. M. Stodgill & A. E. Coons (Eds.), *Leader behavior: Its description and measurement* (Research Monograph No. 88). Columbus, OH: Ohio State University, Bureau of Business Research.

House, R. J., Hanges, P. J., Javidan, M., Dorfman, P. W., & Gupta, V. (2004) *Culture, leadership, and organizations. The GLOBE study of 62 societies.* London, UK: Sage.

Judd, C. M., James-Hawkins, L., Yzerbyt, V., & Kashima, Y. (2005). Fundamental dimensions of social judgment: Understanding the relations between judgments of competence and warmth. *Journal of Personality and Social Psychology, 89*(6), 899–913.

Judge, T. A., Piccolo, R. F., & Ilies, R. (2004). The forgotten ones? The validity of consideration and initiating structure in leadership research. *Journal of Applied Psychology, 89,* 36–51.

Koene, B. A. S., Vogelaar, A. L. W., & Soeters, J. L. (2002). Leadership effects on organizational climate and financial performance: Local leadership effect in chain organizations. *The Leadership Quarterly, 13,* 193–215.

Kopelman, R. E., Prottas, D. J., & Davis, A. L. (2008). Douglas McGregor's theory X and Y: Toward a construct-valid measure. *Journal of Managerial Issues, 20,* 255–271.

Kopelman, R. E., Prottas, D. J., & Falk, D. W. (2010). Construct validation of a theory x/y behavior scale. *Leadership & Organization Development Journal, 31,* 120–135.

Ligon, G. S., Hunter, S. T., & Mumford, M. D. (2008). Development of outstanding leadership: A life narrative approach. *The Leadership Quarterly, 19,* 312–334.

Likert, R. (1961*). New patterns of management.* New York, NY: McGraw-Hill.

McGregor, D. (1960). *The human side of enterprise.* New York, NY: McGraw-Hill.

Sanders, T. (2005). *The likeability factor: How to boost your L-factor & achieve your life's dreams.* New York, NY: Crown.

Smithfield Foods' Helping Hungry Homes (2010). Retrieved from www.smithfieldfoods.com/responsibility/helping.aspx

Steinberg, B. S. (2008). *Women in power: The personalities and leadership styles of Indira Gandhi, Golda Meir, and Margaret Thatcher.* Montreal, Canada: McGill-Queen's University Press.

Thaler, L. K., & Koval, R. (2006). *The power of nice: How to conquer the business world with kindness.* New York, NY: Broadway Business.

Thatcher, M. (1995). *The path to power* (U.S.A. ed.). New York, NY: HarperCollins.

Van Emmerik, I. J. H., Euwema, M. C., & Wendt, H., (2008). Leadership behaviors around the world: The relative importance of gender versus cultural background. *International Journal of Cross Cultural Management, 8,* 297–315.

Zimmerman, R. D., Mount, M. K., & Goff, M. III. (2008). Multisource feedback and leaders' goal performance: Moderating effects of rating purpose, rater perspective, and performance dimension. *International Journal of Selection and Assessment, 16,* 121–133.

6

Situational and Path-Goal Models of Leadership

Chapter Road Map

Case: *Battle for the Caribbean*
Fiedler's Contingency Theory
The Hersey-Blanchard Situational Leadership® Model
Path-Goal Models of Leadership
Case: *The Mary Kay Way: Make People Feel Important*
Team Players Need Structure
Why Should You Be the Boss? The Importance of Relative Task Complexity
Personal Reflections: *The Need to Give Orders*
Clarifying Rewards for Extra Effort in Law Enforcement
Case: *Jack Welch, former CEO, General Electric*
Put It in Practice
Exercises: (1) Applying Fiedler's Model and (2) Apply Path-Goal Theory

Case: *Battle for the Caribbean*

No, this isn't about battling pirates, but it does have sinking ships, mutineers, plagues and deaths with corpses piling up in freezers, military coups, smugglers, shipboard romance, plenty of treasure hunters, and cutthroat, back-stabbing competition (Wall Street style). Garin (2006) describes all of this in *Devils on the Deep Blue Sea: The Dreams, Schemes and Showdowns That Built America's Cruise-Ship Empires*). Sailing along the way, we can also learn the leadership principles that helped the three main rivals start a whole new industry and vanquish their 28 other contenders to the bottom of the Caribbean (figuratively speaking).

The Carnival cruise ship named Destiny at port in St. Lucia, April 2007.

Source: Wikipedia/WikiEK

Ted Arison, an international entrepreneur temporarily working in the United States of America, made a small fortune when he sold his airfreight shipping company to his partner. Instead of retiring young and wealthy, Arison plunked his whole fortune down on a lease for a cruise ship. He sold out bookings for cruises from Miami while waiting for the leased ship to arrive. Unfortunately, Arison lost his entire fortune before the cruises even began when Israel seized the ship from its owner during bankruptcy proceedings. Ever the optimist, the destitute Arison had to borrow a friend's phone to make a long distance call to a Norwegian shipping magnate with a spare ship. Fortunately, Knut Kloster was a visionary leader as well, and he flew from Oslo 2 days later to meet Arison. Together, they became known as the fathers of the modern cruise industry. Kloster and his Norwegian backers owned the ships and supervised the maritime personnel, while Arison acted as their agent responsible for running the onboard hotels and obtaining bookings for the Norwegian Caribbean Lines (NCL). Their partnership worked well for years until an acrimonious lawsuit over who had rights to the *float* split the partnership. Arison was investing the money that customers paid in advance (the float) for cruise tickets (sometimes as much as a year in advance) in his private businesses before turning over the cash to NCL. Arison started his own cruise line, Carnival, in part with money he had *borrowed* from the float.

Arison, the visionary master salesman with the *good guy* demeanor, was assisted during his career by his loyal associate, Zonis. Zonis was the detail-minded task leader who kept track of every penny and played the *bad guy* enforcer who implemented Ted's ideas. Micky Arison grew up watching his father and Zonis work, and he learned both his father's visionary skills and Zonis's hard-headed management style. The third major industry competitor was also formed by a similar pair of a visionary and a detailed, task-oriented leader: the Americans Edwin Stephan and Pete Whelpton. Edwin was the visionary leader with ideas for a whole new type of cruise ship designed for entertaining passengers as opposed to simply transporting them. His big plans were literally big: His blueprints covered the floors and walls of his home. Whelpton was the tough *brawler* who supervised and trained the staff.

Stephan showed his plans to another group of Norwegian shipping tycoons headed by Sigurd Skaugen and Anders Wilhelmsen. The Norwegians hired Stephan to be president (without equity ownership) of the new company, Royal Caribbean Cruise Lines, and built his dream ships. Both the Norwegians and Whelpton used highly directive, telling styles of leadership to prepare the new company employees well in advance of the first cruise. The Norwegian sailors and officers were used to working on cargo ships and not with customers. They were sent to charm boot camps to learn the courtly skills that Americans would expect from luxury liner officers, such as table manners, knowledge of wine and food, and various other social niceties, including dancing. Whelpton built a mock cruise ship replica of the hotel and dining room areas in a warehouse. He drilled his staff for weeks practicing basic maneuvers. He timed them to the second as they carried trays around corners at full speed and loaded and unloaded luggage. Not everyone could handle the pressure, and when Whelpton "got mad, guys got fired" (Garin, 2006, p. 63).

High efficiency is crucial to the success of cruise ships. Modern cruise ships are like small cities—cities that must be emptied and then replenished during the 8 hour window between trips. For example, Voyager of the Seas holds 3,800 passengers plus the employees. It serves 160,000 meals a week. Meals must be prepared, dishes washed, rooms cleaned, supplies loaded, and baggage transported according to very tight schedules. Passengers have to be serviced quickly. To make this happen, employees need detailed instructions. The high efficiency means cruises are great bargains for passengers.

Zonis's tough, highly directed leadership style was met with some resistance shortly after the 30-year-old Micky was made president of Carnival in 1979. Roughly 300 workers spontaneously seized two of the Carnival ships. Frightened passengers on the Carnival Fun Ships were hustled off the ships. Micky worried the workers would destroy the ships; he sent in private security

(Continued)

(Continued)

SWAT teams. Micky, a self-proclaimed hippy who wore love beads and long hair, fired the protestors. He resolved to treat the new hires better. Zonis, who felt betrayed by the workers he had known for years, also wept years later describing the firings. He pointed out that the workers made substantially more at Carnival than at their prior jobs and eagerly recruited their family members and friends to work at Carnival—would they do that for a bad job?

And the winner of the Battle for the Caribbean? Industry observers proclaimed Micky Arison the Emperor of the Waves after another successful takeover in 2003. Half of all the cruise ship travelers in the world now ride on Carnival ships. Micky and his sister are two of the 100 richest billionaires in the world. Micky also owns the Miami Heat basketball team.

Applications: Do visionary leaders usually need task-oriented leaders to assist them, or are most visionary leaders usually good at task leadership as well? Do some employees need highly directive leaders and need to be told exactly what to do? Does making more money make up for putting up with directive bosses and poor working conditions? Would the strike have been avoided if Zonis had used both consideration and task leadership?

As the cruise ship case demonstrates, many jobs require leaders to give very specific, detailed-oriented instructions to employees and to *run a tight ship*. The 2012 wreck of the Costa Concordia, in which 32 people are assumed to have died, shows that following orders and standard protocols are still important in the cruise ship industry. The tragedy demonstrates that rules about safe distances from reefs, crew training for emergencies, and evacuation procedures need to be followed precisely. Captains also need to set the proper example by following established rules as well with regard to who gets evacuated first (the captain, or the passengers).

As the sections below demonstrate, there are some leadership theorists who argue that the type of leadership style you should use depends on the type of work that people are doing and on their skill level. With highly structured jobs done by unskilled labor, some theories call for directive, task-oriented *telling* styles of leadership similar to what Zonis and Whelpton practiced. With other types of workers and jobs, however, they recommend more relationship-oriented styles or delegation and achievement-oriented leadership. One approach, the path-goal model, also calls for leaders to motivate employees by boosting their confidence that they can perform the

tasks and by rewarding task completion. These approach
ent from the High-High model from Chapter 5, which
should use consideration and initiating structure for
chapter addresses the following questions:

- What are the key environmental situations that leaders need to take ...
- What are the characteristics of followers that leaders need to consider?
- How can leaders create positive expectations for followers about their ability
  to achieve goals and receive rewards?
- When should leaders use high rates of giving orders to subordinates, and when
  should they use participation?

Fiedler's Contingency Theory

Fred Fiedler (1967) was one of the first scholars to develop a model of how
the environment influences leadership effectiveness. According to Fiedler,
leaders are either task motivated or relationship motivated. Fiedler's two
leader types are similar to the two main leader types in the Ohio State model
discussed in earlier chapters: Task leaders focus on initiating structure and
getting the job done, whereas relationship-oriented leaders focus on establishing positive relationships with others and showing consideration. In
order to be effective, leaders need to be in situations that match their preferred leadership style (Fiedler & Chemers, 1984). Fiedler didn't believe that
leaders could successfully change their style, so he recommended changing
the environment to match the leader's style or reassigning the leader to the
appropriate situation for his or her style.

Fiedler classified the environment according to three situational factors
(Fiedler, 1967). The first is leader-member relations, which he classifies as
either good or poor. *If the members like the leader, trust the leader, have
confidence in the leader, and generally have positive feelings about the leader,
then **leader-member relations** are good; otherwise, they are poor.* The second
situational factor is **task structure:** *When tasks are clearly defined and the
work procedures are clearly understood by the group members, then the task
is structured; when the tasks are ambiguous and there are multiple ways the
group members might seek to achieve the goals, then the task is unstructured.* The third factor is **position power:** *The leader's position power is
strong if the leader has the authority to hire and fire group members, make
pay raises, give bonuses or other financial rewards, and distribute various
perks, status symbols, and desirable work assignments; otherwise, it is weak.*
Table 6.1 outlines the eight combinations in which these three situational

rs can be combined. The three situational factors combine to determine
degree of situational favorableness, ranging from highly favorable (good
leader-member relations, structured tasks, and strong position power) to
highly unfavorable (poor leader-member relations, unstructured tasks, weak
position power).

Fiedler developed his model inductively by spotting the patterns that
emerged when he classified his study results according to his two leadership
styles and the eight combinations of situational factors. Based on his empirical
results, he formulated his theory, which he and his followers then tested
in later studies. This theory argued that under the three most favorable
situations (rows 1-3), that task-motivated leaders achieve the best results.
Task leaders can take advantage of the positive situation to encourage the
group members to perform at their best. Because these leaders are the ones
most motivated by the task, they would push the group members to higher
levels of performance than would more relationship-oriented leaders.

Table 6.1 Fiedler's Contingency Model and Meta-Analytical Results

Situational Variables			Meta-Analysis		
Leader-Member Relations	Task Structure	Position Power	Fiedler	Lab	Field
Good	Structured	Strong	Task	Task	Task
Good	Structured	Weak	Task	Relations	Task
Good	Unstructured	Strong	Task	Task	Task
Good	Unstructured	Weak	Relations	Relations	Relations
Poor	Structured	Strong	Relations	Zero	Relations
Poor	Structured	Weak	Relations	Relations	Zero
Poor	Unstructured	Strong	Relations	Relations	Relations
Poor	Unstructured	Weak	Task	Task	Task

The contingency model was adapted from F. E. Fiedler (1967). *A theory of leadership
effectiveness*. New York, NY: McGraw-Hill. The meta-analysis was adapted from Peters,
L. H., Hartke, D. D., & Pohlmann, J. T. (1985). Fiedler's contingency theory of leadership: An
application of the meta-analysis procedures of Schmidt and Hunter. *Psychological Bulletin, 97,*
274–285.

However, when the situation is only moderate in terms of favorableness (rows 4-7), then leaders need to win over the group members in order to obtain their cooperation, and relationship-motivated leaders are best at this. Under these circumstances, the group members are united in their poor relationship with the leader (rows 5-7), or they have the upper hand on two out of the three situational factors (row 4). A relationship-motivated leader thus would be the best at repairing the poor leader-member relations and getting the team motivated again. Fiedler's recommendation for the least favorable situation (row 8) is interesting because he recommends returning to the task-motivated leadership style. Under these conditions, it takes a strong leader to hold the group together and to keep the members focused on the task.

Peters, Hartke, and Pohlmann (1985) conducted a meta-analysis to see if the available evidence supported Fiedler's model. Table 6.1 under the Fiedler column lists the results of their meta-analysis of the studies that Fiedler used to induce his model. For example, in row 1, the induced studies showed that task leadership was found to be the most successful. Peters and his colleagues found that Fiedler's model did correctly summarize the results of the studies that Fiedler used to develop his model. After Fiedler developed his model, other studies were performed to test the validity of the model, and Table 6.1 shows the meta-analysis of these studies broken down by whether they were lab studies or field studies. *The lab studies differed in two of the rows from Fiedler's model.* In row 2, the lab studies found that relationship-motivated leaders, not task leaders, were actually more effective. In row 5, Fiedler's model specified that relationship-motivated leaders would be more effective, but the zero correlation in the lab studies indicated that relationship leaders would be neither more, nor less, effective than task leaders. *The field studies only differed from Fiedler's model for row 6 with the zero correlation again indicating no difference between the two styles.*

Fiedler's method of measuring leadership style does not allow leaders to be rated as high on both task and relationship leadership. He developed a Least Preferred Coworker Measure to assess leaders' styles (Fiedler & Chemers, 1984). According to this measure, task leaders rate their least preferred coworkers relatively negatively, whereas relationship leaders are still relatively accepting of their least preferred coworkers. This is a rather indirect way of measuring leadership style, and it is also one that puts somewhat of a negative spin on task leaders. As discussed in the chapter on the behavioral approach to leadership, leaders can be high on both initiating structure and showing consideration. Thus, while Fiedler's model and supporting research indicate that under certain conditions, leaders should focus on either task leadership or relationship leadership, it says nothing about whether they should back up the dominant focus with a supporting role from the other style. For example, under the highly favorable conditions in row 1, the meta-analysis supports Fiedler's model in showing that task leadership produces better results than relationship leadership, but it is possible that task leaders, who in addition perform consideration-type behaviors, might do even better. There has been almost no research using Fiedler's contingency model since the 1980s. Although the meta-analysis provided fairly good support for this model, it is possible that cultural changes and the empowerment movement might change how employees would react to purely task-oriented leadership.

The Hersey-Blanchard Situational Leadership® Model

The Hersey-Blanchard Situational Leadership®[1] Model (Hersey & Blanchard, 1969) allows leaders to be high on both task and relationship leadership. However, like the Fiedler model, it also argues that under certain circumstances leaders should focus on either one or the other style. It argues that subordinates can vary on maturity, ranging from immature subordinates who are both psychologically unmotivated and lacking in experience, to highly motivated and skilled employees. Later, Hersey and his colleagues (Hersey, Blanchard, & Johnson, 1996) used the term *follower readiness* instead of maturity—it's probably not good PR to describe some of your employees as immature. Also, the later version emphasizes how readiness refers to ability to do the specific task or job, as opposed to the employee's personality traits or character. This model has four environmental situations that call for four different leadership styles:

> S1 (*high task, low relationship*): The **telling style** *consists of highly directive, low-supportive leadership in which leaders give detailed instructions and use close monitoring with relatively little emotional support.* This style should be used for employees who have (1) low task skills and (2) a negative, unwilling attitude or are insecure and lacking confidence in their ability to do the job without detailed instructions.
>
> S2 (*high task, high relationship*): The **selling style** *consists of highly directive, highly supportive leadership in which the leader focuses on setting goals and giving*

---

[1]Situational Leadership® is a registered trademark of Leadership Studies, Inc.

instructions while also giving encouragement. Although the leader solicits some input from the followers during coaching, the leader still makes the key decisions about goals and processes. Subordinates in this category have more competence than in S1, but they need encouragement to gain a deeper commitment to the goal and to the organization.

*S3 (high relationship, low task): The **participating style** has leaders encourage participation from subordinates in determining how the job is done, and the leaders focus on listening to subordinates, giving praise and recognition, facilitating problem solving, and obtaining resources.* Subordinates in this category have moderate to high expertise but still need some support and help from their leaders.

*S4 (low relationship, low task): When using the **delegating style**, leaders set the overall goals but turn day-to-day decision making over to the employees.* Leaders have to provide relatively little task instruction because of the employees' expertise and little relationship leadership because of their high level of commitment and interest in their jobs.

Although the theory has been widely published, the evidence in support of the Hersey and Blanchard model is mixed at best and very limited in quantity. Vecchio and his colleagues have been among the most active in testing the model. In their latest article, Vecchio, Bullis, and Brazil (2006) tested the model using 860 participants from 86 squads in the U.S. Military Academy. They did not find the predicted relationship among follower attributes and leadership style. They concluded that **"the theory may have little practical utility"** (p. 407) [boldface added]. In another study, Fernandez and Vecchio (1997) surveyed 332 university employees and their 32 supervisors. They reasoned that the Hersey and Blanchard model may be more accurate for comparisons across jobs than within a single occupation because follower readiness/maturity may not vary much within one job category. Thus, their study sampled a wide range of occupations including custodians, staff members, faculty, and administrators. They found that *only 16.9% of the cases would be correctly matched according to the four quadrants recommended by the theory.* Although they did find that supervisory monitoring increased job satisfaction for lower-level employees, while consideration-type behaviors helped most for mid- and upper-level managers, this does not fit the pattern in the model, although it is consistent with some of the underlying principles. They concluded that the theory is not descriptively accurate.

Other researchers reached the same conclusions about the Hersey and Blanchard model. Goodson, McGee, and Cashman (1986) surveyed 85 store managers, 56 assistant managers, and 318 sales clerks working for a national retail chain. They examined five outcome variables: role ambiguity, overall job satisfaction, satisfaction with supervision, satisfaction with communication, and organizational commitment. *They found virtually no support for the pattern recommended by Hersey and Blanchard. Instead, they found support for the simpler model advocated by the High-High model, which recommends that leaders perform both initiating structure and showing consideration.* In their study, both of these variables were positively related to satisfaction with supervision and satisfaction with communication, although only consideration was related to overall job satisfaction and organizational commitment.

> **The Leader's Bookcase:** Make your own judgment about how strong the evidence is by downloading this article from the textbook website: Vecchio, R. P., Bullis, R. C., & Brazil, D. M. (2006). The utility of situational leadership theory: A replication in a military setting. *Small Group Research, 37*, 407–424.

Path-Goal Models of Leadership

What do people want from a leader? Often, people want a leader who can show them the money. In other words, people want a leader who can show them how to get bonuses, pay raises, promotions, and any other perks that they want. Of course, organizations don't pass out pay raises like candy; usually they give them only for getting the job done right. Thus, people want leaders who can show them how to achieve the challenging goals that will justify their big bonuses and promotions. In other words, people want a leader who can show them the path to success. In addition, people may want a leader who can make the job more fun and satisfying.

Path-goal theory is based on the expectancy theory of motivation. Expectancy theory (Georgopoulos, Mahoney, & Jones, 1957; Vroom, 1964) basically states that people ask themselves three questions when deciding how much effort they are going to put into a task. First, they ask, "How likely is it that I can achieve this task—get it done—if I try?" Second, they ask, "If I get the job done, what is the likelihood that I'll get a reward or benefit?" Third, "How much do I value the reward or benefit that I'll get?" Expectancy theory argues that people answer these questions with probability estimates. For example, one person may think there's a 90% chance that he or she could increase productivity to meet the new company goals, whereas another

employee may estimate there is only a 50% chance. Lower probability estimates act as nagging doubts that lower one's will to persevere or continue
working. If you can't ever achieve it, you might as well give up now. People
may also be skeptical about the odds of being rewarded. Some may think
there's an 80% chance that the company will follow through on its promise
to give bonuses, but others may think the odds are much less. For example,
they may believe politics, being friends with the boss, or overall company
profitability play a role in determining bonuses—not goal achievement.
Again, these nagging doubts sap one's will to perform. People may also vary
in how much they value the rewards being offered. Some may place a high
value on the bonus, while others may want more vacation time. Expectancy
theory also argues that people take into account the costs associated with
achievement, like the extra effort involved, less time with family, and so forth.
The anticipated rewards have to outweigh the anticipated costs.

According to path-goal theory, it's the job of the leader to banish these
nagging doubts from the minds of their followers and make them confident
they can get the job done and receive the rewards they deserve (Evans, 1970;
House, 1971; House & Mitchell, 1974). *Leaders engage in* **path clarification**
*to let followers know what behaviors will be rewarded, to teach them how
to achieve the task, and to remove other obstacles in the way of achievement.*
One of the more interesting concepts from path-goal theory concerns advice
about when to give orders and be directive. New employees often find their
jobs confusing and ambiguous, and even experienced employees may find
certain aspects of their job confusing or unclear. Path-goal theory argues that
employees appreciate directive behavior when it removes ambiguity and
clarifies confusing situations. Under these circumstances, order giving and
directive behavior reduces stress and increases satisfaction with the leader.
On the other hand, telling people what to do when they already know what
to do breeds resentment. The orders serve no useful purpose other than
reminding employees who's the boss.

Leaders can also engage in path clarification by providing emotional support. Leaders who provide emotional support can boost the confidence of
employees that they can achieve the challenging goals or learn the new job.
Emotional support also helps employees believe that the leader is looking
out for them and will reward them fairly. In other words, supportive leader
behaviors boost employees' probability estimates that they can accomplish
the task and will be rewarded. Supportive leaders may also help by making
an otherwise boring job more fun by having office parties and other morale
boosting activities. The following case illustrates a leader recognized for her
outstanding supportive and participative leadership.

Case: *The Mary Kay Way: Make People Feel Important*

As the title of her book suggests, *The Mary Kay Way: Timeless Principles From America's Greatest Woman Entrepreneur* (2008), Mary Kay Ash was a great entrepreneur. Indeed, an academic study by Baylor University declared her the "Greatest Female Entrepreneur in American History" (p. xv). How did she become so successful? She made her employees feel important, she boosted their confidence, and she made their jobs fun. Mary Kay believed that "You Build with People" and that "A Company is Only as Good as its People" (p. 15). Mary Kay also believed that

Mary Kay rewards its top agents with the lease of Pink Cadillacs like this one. The Pink Cadillacs are also good advertising.

Source: Flickr/Bruce Turner (CC-BY)

Every person is special! I sincerely believe this. Each of us wants to feel good about himself or herself, but to me it is just as important to make others feel the same way. Whenever I meet someone, I try to imagine him or her wearing an invisible sign that says: MAKE ME FEEL IMPORTANT! I respond to this sign immediately, and it works wonders. (p. 21)

People would tell Mary Kay that she didn't need to make her employees feel important—after all, she was paying them. But she thought they were wrong and said, "Making people feel important is precisely what a leader is paid for—because making people feel important motivates them to do better work" (Ash, 2008, p. 23).

You've probably walked by cosmetic counters at department stores and seen bored looking clerks behind the counters. Maybe you've even seen anxious and uncertain customers trying on the products—would their friends and family members like the way the makeup made them look? Mary Kay found a way to make selling cosmetics an ego-lifting, fun experience for both employees and customers. Her Beauty Consultants would host classes on skin care and other cosmetic issues, and after each class, the Beauty Consultants would encourage the guests to comment on each others' improvement—naturally everyone would praise each other. The fun atmosphere and fulsome praise would even motivate many of the customers to join the Mary Kay sales force. Mary Kay realized that people especially need praise when learning new skills. She believed that leaders need to praise people to success and that "little successes pave the way to bigger successes" (Ash, 2008, p. 31). Mary Kay also believed that tangible rewards—like bonuses and gifts—are most effective when given with praise, recognition, and public applause. She would hold parties and large-scale celebrations to recognize her top sales people. At these events, she would give away jewelry, trips, and her famous Pink Cadillacs to recognize and reward top performers.

Applications: When was the last time (a) your manager, (b) a coworker, or (c) a friend or family member praised you and made you feel important? How much does praise and recognition improve motivation (if any)? How often do managers need to give praise?

Source: Ash, M. K. (2008). *The Mary Kay way: Timeless principles from America's greatest woman entrepreneur.* Hoboken, NJ: Wiley.

House (1971) and House and Mitchell (1974) took a behavioral approach to leadership and argued that leaders should vary their leadership behaviors according to the situation and the characteristics of the employees. They claimed that leaders should use one of four styles according to the situation: directive, supportive, participative, and achievement leadership. According to path-goal theory, leaders should be able to use all four leadership styles to meet the unique needs of each employee. There were 120 studies on the path-goal model as summarized in a meta-analysis by Wofford and Liska in 1993 (the last year a meta-analysis was performed; relatively few studies have directly tested the path-goal model since then). These studies had 83,105 participants. The meta-analysis examined directive and supportive leadership, but there were not enough studies at the time to examine participative and achievement leadership. The meta-analysis only found partial support for the view that leaders should vary how much directive or supportive leadership they provide according to the situation; thus in most situations, leaders should continue to initiate structure and show consideration. The four styles are described below along with the key meta-analysis findings:

Directive Leadership: An initiating structure style of leadership in which leaders give clear instructions about how to do the job, make rules, and set performance standards. Leaders should use this to reduce ambiguity, role confusion, and anxiety about how to do the job. Thus, leaders should use this style more frequently when employees are inexperienced or otherwise are low in ability (this is supported by the meta-analysis results). According to the theory, leaders should also use this more often when the tasks are unstructured and complex and the employees do not have the skills necessary to engage in participative decision making. Leaders should be clear about goals and the associated rewards.

Supportive Leadership: Similar to consideration leadership, leaders use this type of leadership to boost the confidence of their employees and to reduce boredom and increase job satisfaction. Leaders are friendly, approachable and helpful, and they may use office parties or other activities to make the workplace environment more exciting. According to the results of the path-goal theory meta-analysis, this style is especially useful for simple and highly structured jobs to boost satisfaction with the leader and for complex unstructured tasks to reduce anxiety and boost performance.

Participative Leadership: Leaders draw upon the expertise of their followers by inviting them to share their knowledge and opinions with the leader and to participate in decision making. By sharing information with followers, leaders reduce task uncertainty and boost followers' confidence. Thus, this style is useful when the task is complex and unstructured, provided the team members have the skills necessary to contribute to the decision-making process. According to path-goal theory, this style is *not* useful when tasks are highly structured.

Achievement Leadership: Here the leaders set challenging goals for their followers while expressing confidence in their abilities. Leaders should use this with highly skilled followers performing complex, unstructured tasks. Leaders use this style to encourage their followers to take responsibility and to do their very best.

House later developed some further theoretical propositions about path-goal theory (House, 1996; also see Evans, 1996 for a review). However, Schriesheim, Castro, Zhou, and DeChurch (2006) tested one of the new path-goal propositions which stated that emphasizing contingent rewards has a *negative* effect on efforts to emphasize values (e.g., doing the work because you believe in the values and mission of the organization). In contrast, the researchers found that contingent rewards and values augment each other (have *positive* and additive effects) as theorized by transformational leadership models. In other words, people appreciate being well paid to provide a socially valuable service or product, and the promise of extra money doesn't reduce people's belief in the value of their work.

The research on path-goal theory found that when employees perform highly structured jobs or jobs with low job scope, such as simple, highly repetitive jobs, considerate, supportive leadership is especially helpful. Supportive leadership may help in these situations because it reduces boredom and increases morale.

Team Players Need Structure

There are likely to be a large number of situational factors that leaders need to take into account when deciding how much to focus on initiating structure versus showing consideration. One factor is *task interdependence: the degree to which people must interact in a coordinated way to achieve goals.* With high

Mia Hamm of the United States playing against Germany in 1997 at St. Louis, MO, USA. Team sports like soccer require high levels of task interdependence.

Source: Wikipedia/Johnmaxmena (CC-BY)

task interdependence, each group member must coordinate his or her activities with the activities of other group members; with low task interdependence, the employee or group member operates independently of the others. Fry, Kerr, and Lee (1986) reasoned that in team sports, coaches would need to be high on initiating structure to ensure that all of the players coordinate their moves with each other. This would be especially true if they are supervising relatively inexperienced high school players. In contrast, in individual sports such as golf, team members work largely independently and might benefit instead from consideration leadership. They surveyed players from eight different sports on 22 teams, with a total of 419 athletes. The high interdependence sports consisted of football, basketball, ice hockey, and volleyball; the low interdependence sports were tennis, swimming, track, golf, and wrestling. Consistent with their hypothesis, among sports that required high interdependence, the winning coaches were higher on initiating structure compared to the losing coaches. As expected, the winning coaches in high interdependence sports were higher on initiating structure than were the winning coaches in low interdependence sports. This demonstrates that initiating structure is not as important to winning in low interdependence sports. Also, the winning coaches in low interdependence sports were considerably more likely to use consideration leadership than were the winning coaches in high interdependence sports. This study supports the general premise that leaders need to vary the relative proportions of initiating structure and showing consideration according to situational factors like task interdependence.

> **Applications:** How hard is it to get players in team sports like basketball to coordinate their efforts? Do you need coaches high in initiating structure to tell players who will get the ball, what tactic they will use, and so forth? Is this more important for relatively inexperienced players like high school athletes?

Why Should You Be the Boss? The Importance of Relative Task Complexity

Have you ever had your manager or committee chair, coworker, etc., ask you to do something, and think to yourself, "Why should he (or she) be giving the orders around here?" You are especially likely to think this if the person giving the orders is lower than you on important status characteristics like education, experience, seniority, or age (Ridgeway & Berger, 1986). According to Humphrey and Berthiaume (1993a, 1993b), relative task complexity is also an important factor that people use when deciding who should be giving the orders. People are less likely to resent taking orders from someone if they believe that person has the experience, knowledge, and capacity to know what should be done. Moreover, if the leader is performing the more challenging and difficult work, then followers may believe the leader is earning the right to be in charge, and that the orders contribute to group performance. Thus, Humphrey and Berthiaume reasoned that when leaders perform more complex work than followers do, subordinates may view orders from managers as further evidence of leadership ability. However, when managers and their followers are performing equally complex work (or equally simple work), then managers do not have any advantage over their subordinates in terms of knowledge. In these cases, subordinates may feel that leaders should use participative or consultative styles instead of directive styles, and higher rates of order giving by the leaders should not increase perceptions of leadership. When leaders perform work that is less complex than that of their followers, however, then followers may believe that the leader's main role is to direct the group member's activities, and order giving will increase perceptions of the leader's ability.

Humphrey and Berthiaume (1993a) tested these hypotheses by randomly assigning 216 upper-level undergraduate students to 72 three-person groups in which one person was randomly assigned to be the manager.

Relative complexity influenced subordinates' ratings of the leaders: *The managers were rated highest on leadership when they performed more complex work than subordinates, followed by the two equal complexity conditions (both complex or both simple), and managers had the worst ratings when they supervised people performing more complex work than they themselves performed.* The job characteristics and work procedures also influenced how often the leaders gave orders or made requests to the subordinates. As hypothesized, *higher rates of order giving increased perceptions of leadership ability when the managers performed either relatively more complex work or relatively less complex work.* Order giving had no effect when managers and subordinates performed equally complex work. These results were replicated in a study using MBA students who were asked to list the traits that characterized leaders in different work settings (Humphrey & Berthiaume, 1993b). Subjects listed more directive traits when leaders performed relatively more complex work than their subordinates but listed few directive traits in the equal complexity conditions. When managers performed less complex work, subjects listed participatory as well as directive traits.

Self-Assessment: Visit the textbook website to see how you would rate leaders under various conditions. How comfortable are you giving orders to others?

PERSONAL REFLECTIONS: *THE NEED TO GIVE ORDERS*

Many people seem to get a real thrill out of being in charge—they love giving orders and telling others what to do. Personally, I've never received any pleasure from giving orders to other people. In fact, it always makes me feel a little uncomfortable. I don't like receiving orders and I'm pretty high on the need for autonomy. So I always imagine that other people would resent any orders I gave them too. However, I don't mind cooperating with others on work tasks, and I also don't mind it when someone more knowledgeable than me instructs me in how to do something. I usually appreciate their advice. When I am in charge, I prefer to use a more collegial approach that emphasizes participation and achievement rather than power.

Leaders of major organizations have to be comfortable directing other people's activities. Also, many people admire leaders such as General Patton and CEO Jack Welch who are known for their tough, directive leadership style. Personally, I prefer leaders such as Eisenhower—he managed to win the largest war in history while still acting like a gentlemen. He gave many orders but never in an abusive way. Nonetheless, many of the leadership theorists in this chapter recommend directive leadership under certain circumstances. Thus, I was curious about whether I could create conditions in which subordinates—the ones receiving the orders—rated their leaders more favorably when the leaders gave them more orders. As the above study with my former PhD student, Ruth Berthiaume, demonstrates, subordinates did rate their leaders higher when they gave more orders under certain circumstances. Perhaps the participants understand that effective leaders have to make requests of others to get the job done. It's also true that *good leaders make good followers*. In other words, effective leaders don't resent taking orders from their superiors. In large organizations, almost everyone has at least one superior.

Your Turn to Reflect: Does a willingness to give orders show someone has leadership ability? How should leaders make requests, issue orders, direct others, etc.? Do you have to act tough to give orders, or can you give orders in a more polite way? Are the people who rise to the top in organizations those who respect authority figures and accept their requests as just and fair?

Clarifying Rewards for Extra Effort in Law Enforcement

Densten (2006) argues that leaders have to negotiate extra effort from their employees, and in order to negotiate successfully, leaders have to clarify for subordinates the rewards they can expect to receive. Densten links several concepts in House's (1996) reformulated path-goal theory to the literature on negotiations. Densten tested his theories in a survey of 480 Australian law enforcement senior managers. He developed a sequential model in which the leaders first define the boundaries of the transaction in terms of what tasks should be done. Then, leaders need to acknowledge involvement and *specify rewards*. And thirdly, leaders need to *clarify* the agreement and make clear the mutual outcomes expected. Densten found that while defining the boundaries and specifying rewards influenced clarification, only clarification had a direct effect on the subordinate's production of extra effort. Densten speculates that clarification comes after rewarding behaviors because subordinates use the leaders' history of rewarding extra work to form their perceptions of the current deal—if past promises of rewards have not been kept, then the clarification level in the current negotiation is likely to be low.

The following case about Jack Welch is a good example of how leaders can apply the basic principles of path-goal theory and other situational leadership models to achieve outstanding results. Notice in the case how Welch clarifies the path to success, specifies rewards, and uses a variety of leadership styles.

Case: *Jack Welch, former CEO, General Electric*

Fortune magazine named Jack Welch Manager of the Century (the 20th century). Not bad for someone whose father was a train conductor. Jack earned a PhD in chemical engineering from the University of Illinois and worked his way up GE's ranks. GE was America's 10th largest corporation by market value when Jack became CEO and Chair in 1981, with a market value of $14 billion. By the time he retired in 2001, GE's market value had increased to over $410 billion, making it the most valuable business in the world. How did he achieve this impressive feat? Jack made the rewards of working at GE extremely clear. He pushed the level at which bonuses and stock options were offered considerably further down the ranks of managers and employees.

Jack Welch, former CEO of General Electric

Source: Wikipedia/Hamilton83 (CC-BY)

Eventually, almost one third of GE employees became eligible for stock options. Before he took over, these perks were offered mostly to VPs and other top executives. Under his leadership, even people like Bill Lane, his speech writer and head of communications, were pulling down total annual compensation packages in the seven figures (Lane, 2008). For many managers, the majority of their compensation came in the form of bonuses or stock options. These bonuses and options were highly contingent on the performance of the department they supervised and the overall performance of GE. Bill Lane commented that his base salary was such an insignificant portion of his compensation that he couldn't even remember what it was to the nearest $25,000.

What happened at the other end of the performance scale was also extremely clear: Low performers, or even many slightly below average performers, were fired. For several years, Welch had a forced distribution performance appraisal system that resulted in the bottom 10% of managers being fired (Welch, 2003). Welch personally fired many managers that he felt were not passionate enough about their jobs. However, Welch's policy of firing the bottom 10% eventually became unworkable and he was forced to abandon it. By 1986, *Neutron Jack* had reduced the number of GE employees by 112,000 (over one quarter of the workforce). Of these, 36,000 were in businesses that were sold; the rest were eliminated from the remaining business divisions. He was

(Continued)

(Continued)

criticized for firing so many employees when GE was doing well financially, but he argued that many laid off GE workers received generous severance packages and job retraining. He maintained that rival companies, which waited until times were bad to lay off people, were not able to afford such benefits to workers who were let go.

Welch (2003) placed a strong emphasis on showing people how to succeed. He greatly expanded the role of GE's management education and training programs at Crotonville, and to show the importance of these programs, he would personally greet incoming classes. He also attended sessions when they were on new topics. Lane (2008) gives an example of how he and Welch attended a session on a new concept called *best practices*. The best practices strategy called for businesses to examine other corporations that were leaders in particular areas and to adopt their techniques. Welch became an early adopter of the best practices strategy and aggressively implemented it soon after hearing about it. Much of the success of GE was due to the best practices programs. GE also developed its own Work Out program that enabled thousands of GE employees to make suggestions for improvements. Welch campaigned to eliminate bureaucracy at GE, and he believed in quickly implementing new ideas and programs.

Welch transformed the communication patterns at GE to make GE a learning organization (Lane, 2008). Before Welch, many corporate talks were boring, routine presentations that conveyed little that was new or useful. Jack transformed the communication culture so that speakers celebrated their work unit's recent successes while also conveying useful ideas about how to improve GE's performance. Jack also wanted to see leaders express a passion and enthusiasm for their job. Welch developed his own 4Es leadership model that clearly demonstrated his belief that leaders should energize their followers (Krames, 2005). The four E's mean that leaders have energy, they energize others, they have a competitive edge and make tough decisions, and they execute and achieve measureable results.

Welch was also a great business strategist. He demanded that every business unit of GE be either number 1 or 2 in its industry or be sold off. He reduced GE's holdings in manufacturing and greatly expanded its holdings in financial services. Welch made a good call as the manufacturing segment of the American economy lost value while financial services blossomed. Eventually, GEs financial services division accounted for 40% of its value.

Jack could both terrify and inspire others (Lane, 2008). His voice could clearly be heard through the halls of the GE headquarters as he gave what was known as *spankings*. Even his top executives received these spankings—apparently these chewing outs were frequent events. On the other hand, Jack was very social, and employees had genuine good times at the frequent GE parties and social events. Jack introduced a lively and informal culture into what had been a rather staid company.

Applications: Which do you think best characterizes your opinion of Welch: Neutron Jack or Manager of the Century? Why? Many other business leaders assumed that GE's success was due to Jack's tough leadership style, and they tried to imitate him without much success. However, Jack's downsizing of GE occurred mostly during the first quarter of his reign as CEO, and he had to abandon his policy of firing the bottom 10%. In contrast, his policies of generous bonuses and stock options continued throughout his career, as did his emphasis on best practices and on making GE a learning organization. What do you think contributed most to his success?

Sources: Krames, J. A. (2005). *Jack Welch and the 4 E's of leadership: How to put GE's leadership formula to work in your organization.* New York, NY: McGraw-Hill.

Lane, B. (2008). *Jacked up: The inside story of how Jack Welch talked GE into becoming the world's greatest company.* New York, NY: McGraw-Hill.

Welch, J. (2003). *Straight from the gut.* New York, NY: Business Plus.

Put It in Practice

1. Cruise to success by travelling with partners: If you are a friendly, visionary leader, bring along a task-oriented partner to keep you under budget and on schedule.

2. Who's behind the wheel? Your ability to take charge and be directive depends on your relative influence. Use task leadership if you get along with your junior officers and crew (have good leader-member relations), know where you are going (have high task structure), and own the ship (have high position power). If relatively low on these, use your relationship leadership skills to persuade the others to go where you want to go. In the worst case scenario (low on all three), be directive. Pick the travel locale or environment that matches your leadership style.

3. Treat even the lowest skilled squad members with consideration: Although there are some situational models that recommend a telling style low on support, these models may have little practical utility.

4. Map out the route: Clarify the path to success by teaching followers how to achieve the goal and by rewarding them along the way with things they value (i.e., use path clarification). Give people instructions only when they are anxious and don't know where to go—no one likes backseat drivers who give unnecessary directions.

5. Consider your crew when choosing your leadership style: Pick directive, supportive, participative, or achievement leadership styles based on the experience and skill levels of your sailors. Let them take the wheel if they have the right experience and know the reefs.

6. Make every crew member feel important: Praise people to success and give public recognition when passing out treasure.

7. Take command when tasks are interdependent: When playing shipboard sports, use relatively more initiating structure leadership when the sport requires high task interdependence; use relatively more consideration leadership when the athletes are playing individual sports.

8. Avoid mutiny: Demonstrate your right to command by issuing orders when you perform more complex tasks and have more knowledge and experience than your crew; when the crew does the more complex work, demonstrate you have at least some value by directing the group activities. A high rate of issuing orders does not help you gain respect when you and the crew do equally complex (or simple) work.

9. When you're the junior officer on board, don't resent the captain just because he (or she) is giving the orders. Remember that good leaders also make good followers. When you are in charge, give orders to get the job done, not just to show others who's boss.

10. Lay down the law: Define the boundaries of the work to be done, specify the rewards, and clarify the agreement by making clear the mutual outcomes expected. Don't use vague *pirates' codes*.

11. Like Captain Neutron Jack, sell off the clunker ships, train the officers on best practices, and share the treasure (i.e., sell business units not in the top 2 in their industry, and give bonuses and stock options).

Exercises

1. Apply Fiedler's Model

Apply Fiedler's Contingency Model of Leadership to the cruise ship industry case at the beginning of the chapter. How would you classify the situational factors at Carnival before the workers seized the two ships? What leadership style would Fiedler's model recommend for that situation? Zonis thought he had good leader-member relations with the workers—what leadership style would Fiedler recommend if that were true? With bad leader-member relations, what style would he recommend?

2. **Apply Path-Goal Theory**

Apply path-goal theory to Welch's leadership of GE. What did he do in terms of path clarification? Which of the four leadership styles did he use?

Multimedia: See Jack in action: Visit the textbook website to find links for the following talks:

October 16, 2001—Jack Welch at University of Chicago Graduate School of Business

Jack Welch Talks About Leadership and the State of Corporate America at UCLA Anderson School of Management

Jack Welch on Leadership

Visit the Student Study Site at **www.sagepub.com/humphreyel** for these additional tools:

- Learning Goals
- Leader's Book Case Articles
- Web Resources
- Student Self Assessments

References

Ash, M. K. (2008). *The Mary Kay way: Timeless principles from America's greatest woman entrepreneur.* Hoboken, NJ: Wiley.

Densten, I. (2006). Negotiating extra effort through contingent rewards. *Leadership & Organization Development Journal, 2006, 27,* 38–49.

Evans, M. G. (1970). The effects of supervisory behavior on the path-goal relationship. *Organizational Behavior and Human Performance, 5,* 277–298.

Evans, M. G. (1996). R. J. House's "a path-goal theory of leader effectiveness." *The Leadership Quarterly, 7,* 305–309.

Fernandez, C. F., & Vecchio, R. P. (1997). Situational leadership theory revisited: A test of an across-jobs perspective. *Leadership Quarterly, 8,* 67–84.

Fiedler, F. E. (1967). *A theory of leadership effectiveness.* New York, NY: McGraw-Hill.

Fiedler, F. E., & Chemers, M. M. (1984). *Improving leadership effectiveness: The LEADER MATCH concept* (2nd ed.). New York, NY: Wiley.

Fry, L. W., Kerr, S., & Lee, C. (1986). Effects of different leader behaviors under different levels of task interdependence. *Human Relations, 39,* 1067–1082.

Garin, K. A. (2006). *Devils on the deep blue sea: The dreams, schemes and show-downs that built America's cruise-ship empires.* New York, NY: PLUME (Penguin Group).

Georgopoulos, B. S., Mahoney, T. M., & Jones, L. W. (1957). A path-goal approach to productivity. *Journal of Applied Psychology, 41,* 345–353.

Goodson, J. R., McGee, G. W., & Cashman, J. F. (1989). Situational leadership theory: A test of leader prescriptions. *Group and Organizational Studies, 14,* 446–461.

Hersey, P., & Blanchard, K. H. (1969). Life cycle theory of leadership. *Training and Development Journal, 23,* 26–34.

Hersey, P., Blanchard, K. H., & Johnson, D. (1996). *Management of organizational behavior: Utilizing human resources* (7th ed.). Engelwood Cliffs, NJ: Prentice Hall.

House, R. J. (1971). A path-goal theory of leader effectiveness. *Administrative Science Quarterly, 16,* 321–338.

House, R. J. (1996). Path-goal theory of leadership: Lessons, legacy, and a reformulated theory. *The Leadership Quarterly, 7,* 323–352.

House, R. J., & Mitchell, T. R. (1974). Path-goal theory of leadership. *Journal of Contemporary Business, 3,* 81–97.

Humphrey, R. H., & Berthiaume, R. D. (1993a). Job characteristics and biases in subordinates' appraisals of managers. *Basic and Applied Social Psychology, 14,* 401–420.

Humphrey, R. H., & Berthiaume, R. D. (1993b). The use of trait listings to measure recommendations for managerial behavior under different levels of task complexity. *Journal of Social Psychology, 133,* 279–292.

Krames, J. A. (2005). *Jack Welch and the 4 E's of leadership: How to put GE's leadership formula to work in your organization.* New York, NY: McGraw-Hill.

Lane, B. (2008). *Jacked up: The inside story of how Jack Welch talked GE into becoming the world's greatest company.* New York, NY: McGraw-Hill.

Peters, L. H., Hartke, D. D., & Pohlmann, J. T. (1985). Fiedler's contingency theory of leadership: An application of the meta-analysis procedures of Schmidt and Hunter. *Psychological Bulletin, 97,* 274–285.

Ridgeway, C. L., & Berger, J. (1986). Expectations, legitimation, and dominance behavior in task groups. *American Sociological Review, 51,* 603–617.

Schriesheim, C. A., Castro, S. L., Zhou, X., & DeChurch, L. A. (2006). An investigation of path-goal and transformational leadership theory predictions at the individual level of analysis. *The Leadership Quarterly, 17,* 21–38.

Vecchio, R. P., Bullis, R. C., & Brazil, D. M. (2006). The utility of situational leadership theory: A replication in a military setting. *Small Group Research, 37,* 407–424.

Vroom, V. H. (1964). *Work and motivation.* New York, NY: Wiley.

Welch, J. (2003). *Straight from the gut.* New York, NY: Business Plus.

Wofford, J. C., & Liska, L. Z. (1993). Path-goal theories of leadership: A meta-analysis. *Journal of Management, 19,* 857–876.

7

Leader-Member Exchange and One-on-One Relationships

Chapter Road Map

Case: *Work With Friends: Tony Hsieh and Zappos.com*

In *Delivering Happiness: A Path to Profits, Passion, and Purpose*, Tony Hsieh (2010) shows us how to make friends *and* succeed in business. And how does Tony define success? Not by the money he's made by selling Zappos.com for $1.2 billion to Amazon.com. Instead, Tony has always defined success and happiness in terms of his friendships and the life experiences he's had. To a cynic, this may sound like a meaningless PR statement. But time and time again, Tony gave up money to pursue his interests and work with his friends. And Tony's willingness to put people and experiences first—over money—is what ultimately led to the biggest financial returns for him and his friends.

Tony Hsieh, CEO of Zappos

Tony and his good friend, Sanjay, thought they had hit the jackpot when they graduated from Harvard with great job offers from Oracle: At $40,000 a year (good money in 1995), they would be making more than their other friends from Harvard. But soon, Tony found that his job—running routine statistical tests—was pretty boring. Moreover, no one seemed to even know who he was or care. He felt isolated. Sanjay was bored as well. So they started their own business—doing web design—on the side just to keep from getting bored. After a few months, they had some paying clients, but their income from web designing was still far less than they made at Oracle. Nevertheless, Tony and Sanjay decided to quit Oracle (a nerve-racking decision for Tony) and devote their time to their web design business.

Tony and Sanjay came up with the idea for LinkExchange, and in a couple of days, they developed a test program. LinkExchange allowed web sites to advertise on other participating web sites for free: If a web site showed a thousand banner ads, they would get 500 free ads posted on other sites, and LinkExchange would be able to sell the remaining 500 slots to advertisers. The site grew rapidly, and they were offered a million dollars for the site after only 5 months. People interested primarily in money might have taken the easy cash, but Tony and Sanjay enjoyed what they were doing and turned down the offer. A few friends who had stopped by to visit began working with them on LinkExchange. Soon, 25 people, mostly friends, were working with them. Not long after, Yahoo's founder, Jerry Wang, offered them $20 million, but Tony and Sanjay were still having fun working together and running the site. Why sell when they were having a great time? They turned Jerry down but accepted $3 million from another investor (for a 20% stake) so they could grow the business. Tony didn't mind working long hours because he was working with his friends.

Eventually, Tony ran out of friends to hire, and he had to hire strangers. LinkExchange grew to about 100 employees. The new employees were smart but connived and bickered over stock options and money. The friendly atmosphere was gone, and Tony knew it was time to sell when he found himself repeatedly hitting the snooze button in the morning. Microsoft bought LinkExchange for $265 million, with Tony's share being $32 million plus another $8 million if he agreed to stay for another year as a mostly figurehead officer. Although at first Tony agreed to stay on for the $8 million, he found that the excitement was gone—what he wanted was some new experiences—and he gave up the extra cash. Tony realized that the happiest times in his life involved being creative and connecting with others—making money wasn't the key.

Tony and some of his friends became venture capitalists (fund name: Venture Frogs) so they could help other people make their own dreams come true. They funded 20 entrepreneurial plans, most of which went bankrupt or were barely profitable. But one of the businesses was Zappos.com. Tony invested in Zappos.com because he liked the passion and excitement that Nick Swinmurn had for the idea of selling shoes over the Internet. Tony began investing more and more of his own money in Zappos and began to take on more of the hands-on leadership responsibilities. His advisors urged him to limit his investments in Zappos.com, but Tony risked his own financial future because he felt committed to the people he knew at Zappos.com. Tony had to sell a loft he used for parties (a 40% loss over his purchase price) to help Zappos.com survive. Tony believed in Nick, Fred, and the many other people he had gotten to know at Zappos.com. After 10 years of struggle, Zappos.com finally became big enough to be profitable.

Zappos.com became profitable because Tony learned his lessons from LinkExchange about the importance of friendly interpersonal exchanges at work. Zappos.com became one of *Fortune's* 100 Best Places to Work For because Tony encouraged everyone to know each other and to form friends at work. When employees logged on, they would be shown pictures of other employees and asked their names and some questions about them. Zappos.com had a long list of parties and social activities that employees could

(Continued)

(Continued)

participate in. To weed out new recruits only interested in money, Zappos.com offered new employees $2,000 if they decided to quit within the first few weeks—few accepted the offer. Zappos.com's turnover was unusually low because people didn't want to leave their coworkers—people who were like family to them. Also, Zappos.com didn't offshore its call center. Tony knew that friendly customer service was actually Zappos's core competency. Highly satisfied call center employees were able to provide friendly service to customers and boost sales through word-of-mouth recommendations and repeat business. When you're happy and enjoy your job, you don't have to fake being cheerful to customers.

Applications: How important is it to work with friends? Are groups more productive when everyone is friends? Tony proved his commitment to LinkExchange and Zappos by investing his own money and by working hard—do you think his commitment spurred others to be equally committed? How could having parties and working with friends make call center employees better at providing customer service?

As the Zappos.com case illustrates, great leaders often succeed by creating effective interpersonal relationships with others. This chapter explores how leaders create effective one-on-one relationships with others. In particular, it examines the leader-member exchange (LMX) approach to interpersonal relationships between leaders and followers. Many traditional leadership approaches argue that most people have one particular leadership style that they use with everyone. In contrast, LMX theorists argue that leaders develop unique, one-on-one relationships with each follower and thus use different leadership approaches with different followers. This chapter also discusses what it is that leaders exchange with each other as part of their leader-follower relationships. Although early models assumed that these exchanges were closely related to workplace contributions and rewards for performance, later scholars explored the important role that liking and friendships play in LMX relationships. In addition, researchers have examined how often followers and leaders agree about what makes for a good relationship. These scholars have discovered that leaders and followers do not always see eye to eye when judging their relationship. Although the opening case demonstrates how workplace friendships can benefit leaders and followers, the closing case demonstrates that business failures can endanger workplace friendships. When reading this chapter, consider the following questions:

- Do leaders use the same leadership style with everyone?
- How is the quality of leader-member relationships related to performance and organizational commitment?
- What role do extrinsic exchanges (task completion, perks, and bonuses), personality traits, and affect play in forming leader-member relationships?
- How come subordinates and leaders do not always agree about the quality of their relationship? Can better communication techniques improve agreement and relationship quality?
- How can leaders form trusting, loyal, and committed relationships with their followers?

Do Leaders Use the Same Approach With Everyone?

Do you treat everyone the same, or do you treat your friends and favorite coworkers differently than you treat casual acquaintances or other coworkers? Perhaps you are more open, relaxed, and friendly with your favorite coworkers, perhaps even joke around a little with them and discuss personal issues. Perhaps with other coworkers you are polite, but your interactions are briefer and revolve more closely around specific work tasks. In the same way, leaders may have close, friendly, and personal relationships with some coworkers and subordinates and more formal, impersonal relationships with other teammates or subordinates.

Some leadership models assume that leaders have a specific leadership style, for example, a task leadership style, which they use with everyone. In contrast, *leader-member exchange (LMX) theorists argue that leaders have individualized, personal relationships with each member of their group* (Dansereau, Graen, & Haga, 1975; Graen, 1976; Graen & Cashman, 1975; Graen & Scandura, 1987). For example, with one group member, the leader may have a very friendly, relationship-oriented relationship. With a second member, the leader may have a moderately friendly connection. And with a third person, the leader may have purely task-oriented interactions. Consequently, leaders use a variety of leadership styles according to the type of relationship they have with each person. LMX researchers use the term *dyadic relationship* to refer to *the one-on-one relationship between a follower and a leader* (a dyad consists of two people who are linked in some way).

Although leader-member exchange theory focuses on individualized relationships, researchers often collapse the relationships into high and low relationship quality groups. *The high quality relationships* are often referred to as the *in-group or cadre;* whereas *the low quality relationship groups* are referred to as the *out-group or hired hands.* The members of the in-group are treated with a more considerate, friendly, and personal manner, whereas the out-group members are supervised in a more impersonal manner that focuses more closely on work tasks. However, more recently, scholars have renewed their interest in the individualized relationship aspect of leader-member exchange (Wallis, Yammarino, & Feyerherm, in press). These scholars have found evidence that leaders' effects on performance operates on one-to-one relationships with subordinates rather than at the subgroup (i.e., in-group vs. out-group) level (Markham, Yammarino, Murry, & Palanski, 2010).

Leader-member exchange scholars include the word *exchange* in the name of their theory because of the exchanges that take place between leaders and followers. Although the members of the in-group receive more friendly treatment, the early leader-member exchange scholars assumed that followers join the in-group by contributing more in the way of performance. In other words, *in exchange for the privilege of being a member of the in-group, the in-group members produce higher quality work.* In turn, the leader reciprocates by granting in-group membership and various perks and benefits.

> **Applications:** Are there in-groups and out-groups at work, or do you think every relationship is different in some important way? Do leaders use different leadership styles with different people, or do they use the same basic style with everyone?

Leader-Member Exchange and Performance Outcomes

A meta-analysis by Gerstner and Day (1997) provides good support for the notion that higher quality leader-member exchange relationships result in higher performance and other positive outcomes. They summarized 79 separate studies with a total sample size of 13,885. They found that *leader-member exchange quality was positively related to subordinate performance* as rated subjectively by the supervisor and also when measured by more objective measures. In addition, the *leader-member exchange quality was related to the subordinate's satisfaction with the supervisor, the subordinate's level of organizational commitment, and the subordinate's overall job satisfaction.*

A more recent meta-analysis examined the degree to which positive leader-member exchanges encouraged subordinates to perform more organizational citizenship behaviors (Ilies, Nahrgang, & Morgeson, 2007). *Organizational citizenship behaviors involve the voluntary behaviors that are not part of one's specific job duties,* such as helping out a coworker that needs help, joining optional committees, making suggestions for improvement, mentoring new employees, and so forth. Because of their voluntary nature, organizational citizenship behaviors should be influenced by the overall attitudes employees have about their leaders and their organization. After all, when your boss is treating you right, you might want to pass on the good treatment to the new recruit. Ilies and his colleagues (2007) summarized the research from 50 independent samples of workers with a total sample size of 9,324. *They found a positive, moderately strong relationship between leader-member exchange quality and organizational citizenship behavior.*

Job Performance or Friendship?

How do you think people form in-groups at work? Does the boss always include the hardest workers in the in-group? Or does the manager sometimes include in the in-group people simply because he or she likes them? Can you get into the in-group simply by flattering the person in charge? In other words, do you get into the in-group more by being buddies with the boss or more by working hard? Or does your boss value hard workers and reward them with respect and friendship as well as work-related perks? After all, if subordinates are responsible, hardworking, and reliable, they deserve some positive affect and friendly feelings.

The early LMX researchers focused on exchanges related to task performance and rewards such as desirable work assignments. These researchers developed a 7-item scale, the LMX7, which became widely used (Graen, Novak, & Sommerkamp, 1982). However, some researchers argued for a broader conceptualization of leader-member relationships (Schriesheim, Castro, & Cogliser, 1999). Liden and Maslyn (1998) developed scales that had dimensions related to affect and liking. The four dimensions they developed are

Contribution: This dimension measures work performance, especially with regard to extra chores that are not part of the standard job description.

Affect: This dimension assesses the degree of friendship and liking.

Loyalty: This measures the fulfilling of mutual obligations and demonstrations of loyalty.

Professional Respect: The degree to which the interacting parties demonstrate respect for each others' abilities.

Other studies have since found support for these four dimensions of leader-member exchange, although the LMX7 continues to be widely used as well.

> **Self-Assessment:** Go to the textbook web site to rate your LMX relationships.

Does Everyone Want to Be in the In-Group?

How come the leader doesn't include everyone in the in-group? Perhaps it is because not everyone really wants to be in the leader's in-group. If being in the in-group means going above and beyond the normal work duties, some employees might say, "Count me out!" To some employees, simply doing the regular job is work enough. Perhaps they only intend to keep the job for a year or two, so they are not looking for a promotion or outstanding performance appraisals. Or if being in the in-group means hanging out with the boss after work, perhaps some employees would rather spend their free time with other people.

Although most leadership theories focus on the leader, Maslyn and Uhl-Bien (2001) reasoned that the quality of the leader-member relationship depends upon the effort put into it by both the leader and the follower. Perhaps you've put some effort into a group project (either at school or work) only to have a group member respond by showing up late for meetings, being unprepared, and so forth. Or perhaps someone wanted to become a close friend, but you only wanted to remain acquaintances? Maslyn and Uhl-Bien (2001) found that the same dynamics happen with managers and subordinates: The success of the dyadic relationship depends upon the effort put into the relationship by both partners.

Sometimes leaders have trouble motivating subordinates to work hard enough to deserve to be in the in-group. Part of the problem may be that many organizations do not give their frontline and midlevel leaders enough perks, bonuses, and other incentives that they can use to reward employees for doing outstanding work. In other words, leaders have to have something they can exchange to followers for doing above average work.

> **Applications:** What are some perks or other benefits that leaders could give people to be part of the hard working in-group? Do you think most employees want to be in the in-group?

Loyalty and Turnover

An excellent study by Ballinger, Lehman, and Schoorman (2010) demonstrated that positive leader-member relationships can increase loyalty and prevent turnover. They studied turnover in 45 veterinary hospitals and examined 330 leader-member exchange relationships. Over a 640 day period, employees with positive leader-member exchange relationships were less likely to experience turnover than were the employees who had poor leader-member relationships. In addition, nine of the hospitals had succession events that resulted in new leadership. After the succession events, the employees who had strong leader-member exchange relationships with the departing leaders were more likely to leave compared to those employees who had low leader-member exchange quality. Clearly, some employees are loyal to their leaders—not just to the company—and their interpersonal relationships can make a difference in whether they stay or go.

> **Applications:** What would make you feel loyal to a leader? Do you feel more loyalty to organizations or to specific people in the organizations?

Disrespect: It's a Killer

Professional respect is one of the four dimensions of the leader-member exchange scale developed by Liden and Maslyn (1998). So how important is it to show respect to your subordinates, peers, and supervisors? Consider this: Hardly a week goes by without a story in the newspapers about someone who was killed because they disrespected someone. Often, these slights are almost unbelievable in their insignificance: a disdainful comment about shoes or clothing, a put-down about a jump shot, an accidental shove without an apology. Certainly nothing that would seem worth killing someone over or going to prison for.

And it's not just street killings that are caused by disrespect; divorces and break-ups are also caused by a lack of respect. Psychologists who study dating, marriage,

The Radical's Arms (1819) painted by George Cruikshank. This English cartoon was about the Reign of Terror in France.

Source: Wikipedia/George Cruikshank

and divorce know that one of the surest signs of an impending breakup is when people start rolling their eyes or in other ways express disgust and disrespect to their partners.

Great historical events may also have been influenced by a lack of respect. Although there were plenty of economic reasons for the Thirteen Colonies to break away from the British Crown, it is interesting how often the leaders of the American Revolution cite specific instances of disrespect shown to them by British governors and noblemen (Phillips, 1998). Both George Washington and Ben Franklin cite instances of being treated with disdain by their British rulers as causes of their change in attitudes toward the Crown. Being kept waiting, obvious inattention on the part of the nobles who should have been listening, and being dismissed with a casual, negligent wave of the hand were some of the slights that infuriated Washington and Franklin. In addition, some nobles made disparaging comments about a jacket that Franklin wore. Franklin made sure he wore the same jacket when he returned to England as part of the victorious American delegation to conclude the war.

Lack of respect may also have played a role in starting the French Revolution. Contrary to what many people think, the decades preceding the French Revolution were marked by prosperity and a growing middle class, not by starvation and increasing poverty. So why rebel? One reason may be the Cascade of Disdain (Markham, 1966). Higher ranking nobles would let their disdain cascade down on the lower ranked nobles, who in turn would pass on the disdain to nonnobles. The growing and increasingly powerful middle class found that they were still snubbed at parties and official events by the ruling nobles. A fashion trend may have played a role as well: A form of sarcastic humor—directed at servants and commoners—became the rage among witty nobles, resulting in a different sort of rage among the commoners.

Many managers and leaders think they can get away with minor signs of disrespect toward their subordinates: After all, they are the bosses. But if you don't want to start a rebellion in the workplace, perhaps you should refrain from that witty sarcastic remark. The following case is about a leader who understands the importance of respect to building strong leader-member relationships.

Case: *Charlotte Beers, CEO and Teacher: Work Is All About Relationships*

Charlotte Beers' book is entitled *I'd Rather Be in Charge: A Legendary Business Leader's Roadmap for Achieving Pride, Power, and Joy at Work* (2012). Charlotte's had plenty of experience being in charge. She served as CEO of Tatham-Laird

& Kudner before becoming Chair and CEO of Ogilvy & Mather Worldwide, a multi-national advertising agency. She also served as Colin Powell's Undersecretary of State. Now, she lists "teacher" as her job description. She gives seminars on how women can become leaders. She emphasizes the importance of building relation-ships. She states, "And work is, finally, all about our relationships: with ourselves, our peers, and our superiors" ("Introduction," location 124). She starts with our relationships to ourselves because she believes that you need to be your authentic self if you want to inspire and lead others. You have to understand your authentic self—your values, your beliefs, your causes, and what it is that you are striving to achieve. When you truly know yourself, you can present your self-portrait to others. This self-portrait lets others know who you are and what you can do.

According to Charlotte, the three relationship Rs are respect, reputation, and recognition. Beers defines respect this way: "Respect is acknowledging that there's a whole amazing range of talents, approaches, responses, and qualities others have that may not be at all like yours" (Beers, 2012, "6 Relationships," p. 139, location 2237). Charlotte describes a woman, Sam, who had trouble establishing relationships with her coworkers and her boss. Sam came from a family that valued intellectual achievement, and she had trouble respecting others in her company who were not as brainy as she was. Sam's self-portrait was, "I am a brain in a jar" ("6 Relationships," p. 140, location 2251). As Charlotte put it, "Sam felt encased in a transparent prison; she could see out but was not fully engaged with others. Brain on, relationships off" (p. 140, location 2252). Sam felt that she was missing out and needed to respect others more if she was going to establish relationships at work. Her new self-portrait became "I am a brain in a jar ... with feet" (p. 141, location 2257). Her feet represented the relationships she hoped to make. As Sam stated, "I don't think I can change the brain in a jar, but I can offer to travel around more, investigate the qualities of others" (p. 141, location 2260). Sam began learning more about her boss's talents. Respect runs both ways—when Sam began respecting her boss, she was able to show him that she had more to offer than he realized. As a result, Sam gained new opportunities at work.

Charlotte is also quite clear that you need to be proactive in building your reputation and gaining recognition if you want to rise to the top and be the one in charge. She states that you have to use your self-portrait to reveal to others your best qualities—the ones "you want to be known for" (Beers, 2012, "6 Relationships," p. 141, location 2268). Charlotte emphasizes that "Building a reputation for your own qualities supersedes all other forms of engaging" (p. 141, location 2274).

(Continued)

(Continued)

Applications: How often do people observe their coworkers and managers without establishing real relationships with them? Have you ever felt like there was a transparent barrier preventing you from interacting with others? What can you do to break the glass? What part of your self-portrait would you want to broadcast to others as a way of building your reputation?

In addition to treating subordinates with respect, leaders should support their subordinates when they encounter problems. The following section demonstrates the importance of supporting employees during stressful times.

Source: Beers, C. (2012). *I'd rather be in charge: A legendary business leader's roadmap for achieving pride, power, and joy at work* [Kindle edition]. New York, NY: Vanguard Press.

Supervisor Interactions in the Social Services

The need for supportive supervision and leadership is especially important in the social services field. In fields such as child welfare, mental health, and other social service fields, employees help their clients cope with major life problems—problems that may not be easy to solve. Social service employees deal with heavy case loads, governmental regulations, and administrative burdens. Sometimes they have to handle clients who cannot control their own behaviors and who have violent behavioral tendencies. Consequently, social service work can be stressful and emotionally draining.

A meta-analysis by Mor Barak, Travis, Pyun, and Xie (2009) demonstrated the importance of effective leadership and supervision to social service workers. They summarized the research published in 27 articles. The articles had a combined sample of 10,867 employees from the fields of child welfare, social work, and mental health. They examined three ways in which supervisors could have positive effects on performance and commitment and reduce the negative effects of job stress on social service workers. The three methods they examined were

Task assistance: This includes tangible help with activities, training and instruction in how to accomplish tasks, advice, and help in solving work-related problems.

Social and emotional supervisory support: This consists of listening to workers and helping them cope with their job stresses and emotional needs.

Supervisory interpersonal interaction: This measures the workers' perceptions of their relationship with their supervisors and their satisfaction with their supervisors (some of the studies used LMX scales, but others used related scales).

The meta-analysis clearly showed the importance of good supervision to the service workers. All three methods in which supervisors could support service workers improved employees' positive outcomes in terms of job performance, organizational commitment, and turnover intentions. Although the meta-analysis had no studies on the effects of task assistance on reducing negative outcomes, the studies on the other two dimensions demonstrated that providing social and emotional support and creating positive supervisory interactions reduced stress and burnout.

Conclusions: Emotionally supportive and interpersonally effective leaders can boost social service employees' performance and commitment while reducing their stress and burnout. Task assistance clearly helps with job performance and commitment as well.

In addition to supporting employees, leaders should also work to establish trust. As the following section demonstrates, trust is important to both followers and leaders.

The Importance of Trust and Performance to Leader-Member Exchanges

In any interpersonal relationship, trust is undoubtedly important. Trust is especially important in the workplace and to our exchanges with leaders (Whitener, Brodt, Korsgaard, & Werner, 1998). *A meta-analysis by Dirks and Ferrin (2002) found that trust is related to leader-member exchange as well as to job satisfaction and performance.* As Lau and Cobb (2010) argue, the degree of trust among organizational members determines whether they exchange things with each other on low quality negotiated *this for that* type of exchanges versus higher quality, long-term relationships in which the members look out for each others' best interests. Integrity, honesty, and other traits related to ethics are of course important to trust. However, in the work world, competence and job performance are also important to the development of trust (Dirks & Ferrin, 2002). Employees, regardless of whether they are leaders, followers, or coworkers, often have to rely on others to do their share of joint projects and get their work done correctly and on time. It is not enough to have good intentions and ethical desires—both leaders and followers also have to have the competence and ability to follow through on their good intentions and get the job done.

A study by Davis and Bryant (2010) demonstrated the importance of both performance and trust to leader-member exchange relationships. They examined Industry/University Cooperative Research Centers that were supported by U.S.A. National Science Foundation grants. Leader-member exchange relationships may be especially important to research centers because it is likely that high quality leader-member relationships empower people to be innovative (Graen & Scandura, 1987). For example, Scott and Bruce (1994, 1998) studied research and development professions, and they found that positive leader-member exchange relationships did improve innovation. Likewise, Tierney, Farmer, and Graen (1999) found that positive leader-member relations improved employee creativity. Davis and Bryant (2010) surveyed the research center directors and the university administrators that the directors worked most closely with. They found that the quality of the leader-member exchange was strongly related to the performance of the center (as evaluated by the administrators). Moreover, *trust was also related to the center's performance*. In addition, they found that performance was a mediator between the leader-member exchange relationship and the university administrators' commitment to the center. In other words, their model looked like this:

Leader-Member Exchange → Center Performance →
University Commitment

This is certainly a powerful reminder than no matter how much you get along with your boss, client, or sponsor, that if you don't perform, you're history.

Personality traits may also influence how easily people form high quality leader-member relationships. As the following section indicates, empathic and ethical leaders are better at establishing high quality leader-member relationships with others.

Personality Traits and Leader-Member Relationships

Why do some leaders seem to have lots of loyal followers and dedicated workers—subordinates who like them and admire them? The leader's personality undoubtedly plays a role in determining how easy it is to get subordinates, peers, and coworkers to join his or her in-group.

Like Kellett, Humphrey, and Sleeth (2006), Mahsud, Yukl, and Prussia (2010) found that the leader's empathy was a good predictor of relationship-oriented leadership behaviors (their sample included ratings of 218 managers; 60% were frontline managers and 40% were midlevel or executive level). These relationship-oriented behaviors, in turn, predicted the quality of the leader-member exchange relationships. In slightly simplified form, their model looks like this:

Leader Empathy → Relationship Behaviors→ Leader-Member Exchange
Quality

Mahsud et al. (2010) also found that ethical leadership predicted relationship behaviors and the quality of the leader-member exchange. In other words, leaders high on ethical leadership were more likely to have high quality in-group type relationships with their subordinates. In other words, their model looked like this:

Leader Ethical Behavior → Relationship Behaviors → Leader-Member
Exchange Quality

In addition to its influence through relationship behaviors, ethical leadership also had a direct influence on the quality of the leader-member exchange. This shows the importance of fair treatment and ethical behavior to establishing good relations with subordinates.

The subordinate's personality is also important to the establishment of the leader-member exchange relationship. Jordan and Troth (2011) reasoned that subordinates high on emotional intelligence would be better able to establish positive interpersonal relationship with their leaders and thus would have better leader-member exchange relationships with them. As a result of their better leader-member relationships, Jordan and Troth (2011) also expected that the more emotionally intelligent employees would have lower turnover intentions and higher job satisfaction. Their model is

Emotional Intelligence → Leader-Member Exchange → Job Satisfaction,
Turnover Intentions

Jordan and Troth (2011) tested their model with a sample of 579 employees who worked in a private pathology company. They found strong support for their model. Their results suggest that it is often in the best interests of subordinates, as well as leaders, to put effort into developing high quality leader-member exchange relationships.

Another study looked at extraversion and agreeableness among both leaders and followers (Nahrgang, Morgeson, & Ilies, 2009). These researchers assigned 69 Masters of Business Administration (MBA) students to supervise teams of four to six students in undergraduate classes working on a group project (a total of 330 team members, which formed 330 dyads).

The MBA team leaders were responsible for recruiting, training, and supervising the team members throughout the semester-long project. The leaders who were high on agreeableness were more successful at establishing positive leader-member relationships (as measured by the team members) during the initial meeting. In addition, team members high on extraversion also contributed to the initial establishment of positive leader-member relationships (as measured by the leaders). Over time, both parties (leaders and members) reported increases in leader-member exchange quality. In addition, the actual performance levels of both the leaders and the members played a large role in how they were evaluated in terms of the leader-member relations.

A Portuguese Example: Leaders and Subordinates Don't Always Agree

Werbel and Henriques (2009) found that leaders and subordinates don't always agree as to what should be the basis for forming trusting relationships and good leader-member relationships. Supervisors, for example, want to know that they can delegate work to subordinates and have it completed properly. Subordinates, on the other hand, want to know that they will be treated fairly. Werbel and Henriques (2009) examined perceptions of trust and leader-member relationships in surveys of 304 supervisor-subordinate dyads from 33 Portuguese firms in the service, manufacturing, governmental, and agricultural sectors. Roughly three quarters (77%) of the leaders were first-line supervisors. They found that trust is related to leader-member exchange quality for both subordinates and leaders. Below is what they also found:

> **Leaders trust subordinates:** Leaders trust subordinates when they are available and easily observed and when the subordinates seem receptive to input from the leaders.

> **Subordinates trust leaders:** Subordinates trust leaders when the leaders are perceived to be competent, to be open with the subordinates, to have integrity, and to be available.

Seeing Eye to Eye

As the previous study indicates, subordinates and leaders do not always agree as to what is important in establishing trust. This raises the question as to how often leaders and subordinates agree about how good their leader-member relationships are. A meta-analysis by Sin, Nahrgang, and Morgeson (2009) examined this issue. They summarized the research from 64 separate studies with a total of 10,884 dyads. *The meta-analysis found that there was a moderate overall level of agreement between leaders and subordinates about the quality of the leader-member relationship.* Moreover, the agreement increased with increases in tenure and time spent working together.

Other researchers studied 285 matched pairs of leaders and subordinates who worked for a large county library system in the United States (Cogliser, Schriesheim, Scandura, & Gardner, 2009). They classified the agreement between followers and leaders into four categories and calculated the percentage of dyads that belonged to each category. They also looked at the subordinates' performance level (rated on a 1-7 scale) and commitment (1-5 scale):

Balanced/Low Leader-Member Relations: Both leaders and followers perceive the relationships to be poor. Percentage of sample: 29%. Job performance: 4.2. Commitment: 3.4.

Balanced/High Leader-Member Relations: Both leaders and followers perceive the relationships to be good. Percentage of sample: 31%. Job performance: 5.6. Commitment: 3.8.

Follower Overestimation: The followers rate the relationship higher than the leaders do. Percentage of sample: 19%. Job performance: 4.6. Commitment: 3.7.

Follower Underestimation: The followers rate the relationship lower than the leaders do. Percentage of sample: 21%. Job performance: 5.3. Commitment: 3.3.

The researchers found that when the leader and subordinates both agreed that the leader-member relationship quality was poor, the job performance, job satisfaction, and organizational commitment of the followers were also low. Likewise, when they both agreed that the relationship was good, follower performance, satisfaction, and commitment were also high. Almost 1 out of 5 subordinates overestimated their relationships with their leaders. Not surprisingly, these subordinates also had low overall job performance, although still somewhat better than the performance of those employees who agreed with their leaders that they had low leader-member relationships. About one fifth of the followers were underestimators. These underestimators had higher job performance than the overestimators but lower job satisfaction and commitment. *This suggests that the leaders of the underestimators need to do a better job communicating their approval and positive regard if they want to keep these above average performers.*

Applications: Do you know what your manager really thinks of you? What could managers do to make the underestimators feel they are an appreciated part of the in-group? Do managers spend too much time praising and rewarding the outstanding subordinates and not enough time recognizing the average to above average performers?

The Leader's Bookcase: Visit the textbook web site to download another interesting article about perceptions and leader-member relationships: Rosen, C. C., Harris, K. J., & Kacmar, K. M. (2011). LMX, context perceptions, and performance: An uncertainty management perspective. *Journal of Management, 37,* 819–838.

Leader-Member Attributions: Who Gets the Blame, Who Gets the Praise?

Attribution researchers have long studied how people decide whether some-one's behavior is due to his or her personality and characteristics or to the environment (Heider, 1958; Kelley, 1971; Weiner, 1986). *When we think the person's behavior is due to personality traits and characteristics like talent, skill, ability, determination, and effort, we are making an **internal attribution**. When we think the person's behavior is due to a variety of external factors, such as task difficulty (too easy or too hard), obstacles in the environment, help provided by others, etc., we are making an **external attribution**.* Green and Mitchell (1979) argued that leaders' attributions about the causes of followers' poor performance are especially important. When leaders think the poor performance was due to lack of effort, they are likely to respond with criticism, punishment, or other negative reactions. In contrast, when they think the poor performance was due to environmental causes, such as lack of resources, they are likely to respond quite differently, perhaps with sympathy and offers of help. When leaders think that new employees are putting in their full effort but have low ability, they may respond by offering further training and instruction. Research has confirmed that attributions about poor performance are important to leader-member relationships (Ashkanasy, 1989, 1995; Dasborough & Ashkanasy, 2002; Green & Liden, 1980; Martinko, Harvey, & Douglas, 2007).

Unfortunately, our attributional processes are not always accurate. *The actor-observer bias causes observers to overattribute the behavior they see other people perform to their personality traits and characteristics; in contrast, when judging themselves (i.e., they are the actor), people tend to overattribute their behavior to environmental causes* (Jones & Nisbett, 1971). Of course, **self-serving biases** *also exist, so both leaders and followers are quite willing to attribute their successes to their own internal characteristics while attributing their failures to external causes* (Dobbins & Russell, 1986). Martinko and Gardner (1987) argued that these biases can be especially damaging to leader-member relationships. The actor-observer bias means that leaders are likely to overattribute poor performance to followers' personal characteristics and underestimate the extent to which poor working conditions caused the performance problems. This can lead to conflict and poor leader-member relationships. Incorrectly blaming followers can also cause the leaders to take inappropriate actions, such as punishing subordinates instead of fixing machines in poor repair, improving work procedures, etc.

A large number of other biases may influence how leaders and followers evaluate each other. For example, Humphrey (1997) wanted to know what would happen if observers saw three people each perform a mix of complex and simple managerial tasks. For some types of tasks, performing the complex task would mean that you could also perform simpler tasks of that type. For example, if you can perform algebra and complex statistics, you also know how to add and subtract. Thus, once you've watched someone successfully perform higher level math, watching the person perform simple math tasks doesn't tell you anything more about that person's math abilities. However, research on how people make judgments suggests that the brain works by combing pieces of information in a weighted average (Anderson, 1981). *This research also suggests that the brain also averages in nondiagnostic information, e.g., information that isn't useful for making the judgment, thus creating a* **dilution effect** *on the diagnostic information* (Nisbett, Zukier, & Lemley, 1981). The weighted averaging model had not been applied to abilities, but it suggested to Humphrey that if someone does some work tasks that would be rated a 9 on complexity and then some tasks that would be rated a 5, the person would be rated a 7 on ability by observers (the logically correct rating would be a 9). Research on leadership prototypes has also shown that we judge people by comparing their traits to an ideal leadership prototype—the more matches we see, the more likely we are to think they are good leaders (Lord, Foti, & De Vader, 1984). Humphrey reasoned that watching someone perform simple tasks would dilute the overall match with the good leadership prototype. He had observers watch films in which all three actors performed equally complex work, but two of the actors performed some lower level tasks as well. Consistent with the information dilution effect, performing the simple tasks diluted the favorable impression made by performing the complex tasks. The three actors were rated on leadership ability according to the proportions in which they performed complex to simple tasks even though all three had demonstrated their ability to perform the more complex leadership tasks. Thus, if you want to be rated high on ability, try to do high rates of complex tasks in front of others, and do your simple work and routine grunt work while out of sight.

As the following section implies, leaders and followers are more likely to see eye to eye and avoid making attributional mistakes when they both have a chance to speak and express their thoughts in a lively, supportive conversation.

PERSONAL REFLECTIONS: *FAIR-EXCHANGE CONVERSATIONS*

In some conversations, you can see upward spirals in enthusiasm. One person begins with an interesting story or a joke, and the other person responds with moderate enthusiasm. Then when the second person speaks, the first person reciprocates with equal or greater enthusiasm. Laughter, smiles, exclamations of "That's great!" begin to pepper the conversation. Soon, the two are telling more and more stories with ever greater enthusiasm. Even jokes they've heard before are greeted with smiles and exclamations of "That's a classic!" The enthusiasm unleashes the speakers' natural creativity, and ad lib touches to jokes or stories begin to appear—little conversational flourishes abound. The speakers play off of each other's stories and comments. The speakers become more creative and their delivery improves dramatically. Their body language becomes expansive, free flowing, active, and unguarded. Even routine details of their day begin to sound fascinating.

But in other conversations, quite a different story unfolds. Perhaps the first speaker tells a story, and the listener responds with appropriate enthusiasm, say a 7 on the enthusiasm scale. But when the second person tells a story, the first speaker fails to reciprocate and instead, responds with a lower level of enthusiasm, say a 6 or a 5. The first speaker wishes to appear superior to the second speaker and wants to dominate the conversation. If done subtly enough, the first speaker gains the conversational edge—people are laughing or paying attention to his or her jokes and stories while the second speaker begins talking less due to lack of reinforcement. In less subtle cases, the first speaker actually criticizes or puts down the second speakers' jokes and stories as unfunny, stupid, too well known, etc. In both the subtle and unsubtle versions, however, the enthusiasm level is unlikely to rise very much. Most often, the enthusiasm level goes down—people generally don't respond well to people who are not reciprocating with gusto, and the conversation begins to dwindle. Even interesting stories are told with a lack of flair and sound dull.

Leaders often have to speak more than others as part of their job duties—they may have to communicate information, facilitate group discussion, and so forth. However, effective leaders usually try to bring out the best in others by encouraging them to speak and express their opinions. They know that in order to look good, they have to make others look good as well—that's the only way to get the positive upward emotional spiral that will make everyone feel good about the team and its leader. Leaders have to make being in the group a rewarding experience.

Your Turn to Reflect: What makes for a good conversation? How often do people try to gain the edge in conversations versus trying to make everyone look good? Are the people who are good at creating upward spirals in enthusiasm more likely to become leaders?

The following case is about a leader who was good at creating enthusiasm among his employees and business partners. In addition, Lane gives us the inside scoop on how leaders have a variety of interpersonal relationships with their business partners as well as with their subordinates. Some of his relationships were based on friendships and common values, others on purely economic considerations; the worst involved self-serving backstabbers who pretended to be friends.

Case: *Leadership Relationships in the Boom and Bust Years*

Randall Lane's book (2010) is called *The Zeroes: My Misadventures in the Decade Wall Street Went Insane*. As editor of *Trader Monthly*, he had a ring-side seat to the powerful effect that Wall Street's boom and bust years had on people's relationships as well as on their finances. After working for a few years for some of the most prestigious business publications, Lane started a new magazine, *P.O.V.* (for point of view). After spending 18 million dollars of his investors' money, Lane had to shut *P.O.V.* down. However, Randall had built close friendships with his staff. In the boom times in the early 2000s, his staff members went on to find good jobs, some with high paying, stable magazines with excellent job security.

A friend of a friend of a friend told a London stock broker, Magnus Greaves, about Lane, and soon, Magnus was calling up Lane for advice on how to start a magazine for stock market traders. Magnus was an African Canadian who had hit it big as a cofounder of a trading company (MacFutures) headquartered in London's version of Wall Street (London International Financial Futures and Options Exchange, called Life for short). Magnus's parents had met in a bookstore, and they taught him never to be without something to read. Thus, Lane

(Continued)

(Continued)

After the 1929 stock market crash, many people lost their family and friendship ties as they travelled the country looking for work. The 2008 stock market crash was not as bad, but it still disrupted many people's relationships with their coworkers, friends, and family members.

Source: Library of Congress

and Magnus shared the love of the written word as well as an interest in business publications. They also shared a willingness to take risks—risky sports, risky exotic travel, and risky entrepreneurial plans. Magnus referred to his risk tolerance as *unlllliiimmmittted*. Soon, Magnus was calling Lane his buddy and introducing him to his traders and his wild lifestyle. After 18 months of discussions and trips back and forth from New York and London, Magnus decided to invest the few million initial dollars necessary to launch the magazine, and with a handshake, he made Lane an equal partner. Lane would edit and manage the magazine and thus contribute sweat equity. The new company was named Doubledown Media, after a poker term, and its first magazine was called *Trader Monthly* (eventually Doubledown produced five magazines in the United States and the UK).

Lane rehired many of his former *P.O.V.* staffers. Interestingly, they accepted his job offers even when they knew they would be making less money and would have lower job security. After all, they had already been through one failed start-up with Randall. Why would they do this? Undoubtedly, it was the friendly, interpersonal relationships they had established with Lane and with each other. As Lane put it, they were loyal—loyal to him and to each other. Lane and his former P.O.V. all-stars began planning their new magazine while meeting in a venue that reflected their common interests: a Greenwich Village bar that was the former hangout of the poet Dylan Thomas. Later, while working on *Trader Monthly*, Lane's crew would hold elaborate surprise birthday parties for him.

Lane established a different sort of relationship with Jim Dunning, a legend in the publishing world. Whereas Magnus called Randall *Buddy*, Jim played the *tough love* experienced coach. He asked detailed, tough questions and expected answers. Jim began coaching Lane on how to succeed in the publishing world and also on how to court investors. Jim took Lane to the places where deal makers congregated and introduced him to the key players and investors in the publishing world. Personal relationships were still important: As Jim put it, he was investing in Lane (i.e., the person, not just the business).

Lane also tried a partnership with Lenny Dykstra, the former World Series winning baseball star (and alleged steroid user) turned financial advisor. Lenny went from being the lavish-spending pal who would make Lane rich into the paranoid loser who sued Lane and treated him like an enemy. Dykstra epitomized the eccentric millionaire (he would stay up for 5 days in a row and sleep on weekends) who controls others with his wealth: Dykstra admitted hiring his friends. Lenny ended up bankrupt and homeless.

Lane, Magnus, and Jim almost succeeded in making Doubledown Media a success. Investors were willing to loan them $200 million to buy a bigger company, and the deal only failed when the seller became too greedy. Doubledown was assessed in value at between $17 and $24 million (a significant increase over the $10 million that had been invested), and potential buyers were courting them. Success was in their grasp! Then the worldwide financial meltdown hit, and within 6 months, Doubledown plummeted into bankruptcy as advertising revenues dried up (bankruptcy selling price: $55,000). Lane personally lost half a million he had taken from his own retirement fund, and his mother lost a hundred thousand. Jim and Magnus both lost millions but remained rich (Magnus knew to limit his risks after all). In addition, the employees who had left good jobs to work with Randall became unemployed during a major downturn in the job market (500 other magazines also failed, depressing the market for magazine employees). Some Doubledown employees did not take their losses too gracefully. Lane had used his own retirement money to fund payroll, but the unemployed former staffers were still mad. Two of them even launched media campaigns by getting people they knew in the mass media to run negative stories about Lane and Doubledown. Lane's story is a powerful reminder that leadership carries risks: both to our relationships as well as to our careers.

Applications: Where would you rather work: at a place with good job security and pay but where you were treated in an impersonal, formal manner, like just another employee, or in a place with less job security and pay but with good friends and colleagues who treat you like a member of the in-group?

Source: Lane, R. (2010). *The zeroes: My misadventures in the decade Wall Street went insane* [Kindle edition]. New York, NY: Portfolio, Penguin Group.

Put It in Practice

1. Work with friends and you can enjoy your job while still making money. And remember, happy employees provide better customer service and have lower turnover.

2. Treat people as individuals—vary your leadership style to match each group member's unique personality and needs. Reward your in-group members with special perks in exchange for their greater contributions.

3. Boost followers' job performance, organizational commitment, and job satisfaction by establishing positive leader-member exchange relationships with them. Followers with positive LMX relationships with the boss are also more likely to do voluntary organizational citizenship behaviors.

4. Be friendly and likeable. Affect is one of the four dimensions of LMX: Contribution, Affect, Loyalty, and Professional Respect.

5. You can't all be friends: Be realistic in recognizing that not all employees want to be in the in-group—especially if it means working harder or hanging with the boss. Motivate people to join your in-group by offering worthwhile benefits for joining.

6. Loyalty: Establish strong interpersonal ties and your employees will want to stay at the company as long as you do.

7. Avoid rebellion: Don't disrespect your subordinates.

8. Build relationships: Become the one in charge by using the three Rs: respect, reputation, and recognition. Put feet on your glass jar and engage with others.

9. Support the supporters: Even those who provide support to others, such as social workers, can need emotional and interpersonal support. Increase performance and reduce burnout and stress by providing social and emotional support and by creating positive interpersonal interactions.

10. If you don't perform, you're history! Positive leader-member relationships with your administrators can help you perform better, but it is your performance that builds their commitment to you.

11. Be empathic and ethical: Leaders high on empathy and ethical behavior perform more relationship-oriented leadership behaviors and have better LMX relationships. When you are the follower, use your emotional intelligence to establish better LMX relationships with your leader. When you have excellent LMX relationships, you won't need to quit the company!

12. Build subordinate trust: Create trust by being competent and open, showing integrity, and by being available when your subordinates need you. Gain your leader's trust by being available, easily observed, and receptive to your leader's input.

13. See eye to eye with all your good employees—not just the stars—by letting them know how much you appreciate them.

14. Avoid mistaken judgments: Don't fall prey to actor-observers biases and blame your workers for poor performance when it's really the environment's fault. Don't be diluted: Demonstrate your ability to do complex work while in front of others and do the routine simple work out of sight.

15. Engage in fair exchange conversations: Build enthusiasm by reinforcing your partner's conversation and you'll both look good.

16. Entrepreneurial leadership has risks: both to your relationships as well as to your career. Hire loyal staffers, become buddies with investors, seek the advice of tough-love mentors, and avoid eccentric partners.

Exercises

1. **Leader-Member Relationships: In-Group/Out-Groups or Individualized Relationships?**

   Think of a group that you belong to and identify the leader of that group. Rate each member's relationship with the leader on a 1 to 10 scale. Do the ratings fall into two distinct clusters with a big clump for the in-group and another clump for the out-group? For example, you might have four or five relationships rated 8 or 9 and another four or five relationships rated 5 and 6 with a noticeable gap in ratings between the two groups. Or do they fall more into a continuous distribution with some people scattered throughout the rating scale?

2. **Commitment: Good Times, Bad Times**

   Think of some of the activities that you've done with your friends, coworkers, and teammates. Sort these into two categories: (1) fun activities such as listening to music and going to parties or movies and (2) activities like helping each other out with studying or work problems, picking you up when your car breaks down, helping you when you are sick, etc. Now rate each activity (1-10 scale) on how much they make you feel committed and loyal to the other person. Have you ever had any fair weather friends who were the life of the party but who wouldn't help you out during the tough times? What things can leaders do to demonstrate their commitment and loyalty to their team? Which leader gets your commitment: the one who throws great office parties or the one who stays late working side by side with you on your big project?

Visit the Student Study Site at **www.sagepub.com/humphreyel** for these additional tools:

- Learning Goals
- Leader's Book Case Articles
- Web Resources
- Student Self Assessments

References

Anderson, N. H. (1981). *Foundations of information integration theory*. San Diego, CA: Academic Press.

Ashkanasy, N. M. (1989). Causal attributions and supervisors' response to subordinate performance: The Green and Mitchell model revisited. *Journal of Applied Social Psychology, 19*, 309–330.

Ashkanasy, N. M. (1995). Supervisory attributions and evaluative judgments of subordinate performance: A further test of the Green and Mitchell model. In M. J. Martinko (Ed.), *Attribution theory: An organizational perspective* (pp. 211–228). Delray Beach, FL: St. Lucie Press.

Ballinger, G. A., Lehman, D. W., & Schoorman, F. D. (2010). Leader–member exchange and turnover before and after succession events. *Organizational Behavior and Human Decision Processes, 113*, 25–36.

Beers, C. (2012). *I'd rather be in charge: A legendary business leader's roadmap for achieving pride, power, and joy at work* [Kindle edition]. New York, NY: Vanguard Press.

Cogliser, C. C., Schriesheim, C. A., Scandura, T. A., & Gardner, W. L. (2009). Balance in leader and follower perceptions of leader–member exchange: Relationships with performance and work attitudes. *The Leadership Quarterly, 20*, 452–465.

Dansereau, E., Graen, G., & Haga, W. J. (1975). A vertical dyad linkage approach to leadership within formal organizations: A longitudinal investigation of the role making process. *Organizational Behavior and Human Performance, 13*, 46–78.

Dasborough, M. T., & Ashkanasy, N. M. (2002). Emotion and attribution of intentionality in leader–member relationships. *The Leadership Quarterly, 13*, 615–634.

Davis, D. D., & Bryant, J. L. (2010). Leader-member exchange, trust, and performance in national science foundation industry/university cooperative research centers. *Journal of Technology Transfers, 35*, 511–526.

Dirks, K. T., & Ferrin, D. L. (2002). Trust in leadership: Meta-analytic findings and implications for research and practice. *Journal of Applied Psychology, 87*, 611–628.

Dobbins, G. H., & Russell, J. M. (1986). Self-serving biases in leadership: A laboratory experiment. *Journal of Management, 12*, 475–483.

Gerstner, C. R., & Day, D. V. (1997). Meta-analytic review of leader-member exchange theory: Correlates and construct ideas. *Journal of Applied Psychology, 82*, 827–844.

Graen, G. B. (1976). Role-making processes within complex organizations. In M. D. Dunnette (Ed.), *Handbook of industrial and organizational psychology* (pp. 1201–1245). Chicago, IL: Rand McNally.

Graen, G. B., & Cashman, J. (1975). A role-making model of leadership in formal organizations: A development approach. In J. G. Hunt & L. L. Larson (Eds.), *Leadership frontiers* (pp. 143–165). Kent, OH: Kent State University.

Graen, G. B., Novak, M. A., & Sommerkamp, P. (1982). The effects of leader-member exchange and job design on productivity and satisfaction: Testing a dual attachment model. *Organizational Behavior and Human Performance, 30*, 109–131.

Graen, G. B., & Scandura, T. A. (1987). Toward a psychology of dyadic organizing. *Research in Organizational Behavior, 9*, 175–208.

Green, S. G., & Liden, R. C. (1980). Contextual and attributional influences on control decisions. *Journal of Applied Psychology, 65*, 453–458.

Green, S. G., & Mitchell, T. R. (1979). Attributional processes of leaders in leader–member interactions. *Organizational Behavior and Human Performance, 23*, 429–458.

Heider, F. (1958). *The psychology of interpersonal relations.* New York, NY: Wiley.

Hsieh, T. (2010). *Delivering happiness: A path to profits, passion, and purpose* [Kindle edition]. New York, NY: Business Plus.

Humphrey, R. H. (1997). Job characteristics, prototypes, and the information dilution effect. *Journal of Psychology: Interdisciplinary and Applied, 131*, 211–224.

Ilies, R., Nahrgang, J. D., & Morgeson, F. P. (2007). Leader–member exchange and citizenship behaviors: A meta-analysis. *Journal of Applied Psychology, 92*, 269–277.

Jones, E. E., & Nisbett, R. E. (1971). The actor and the observer: Divergent perceptions of the causes of behavior. In E. E. Jones, D. E. Kanouse, H. H. Kelley, R. E. Nisbett, S. Valins, & B. Weiner (Eds.), *Attribution: Perceiving the causes of behavior* (pp. 79–94). Morristown, NJ: General Learning Press.

Jordan, P. J., & Troth, A. (2011). Emotional intelligence and leader member exchange: The relationship with employee turnover intentions and job satisfaction. *Leadership & Organization Development Journal, 32*, 260–280.

Kellett, J. B., Humphrey, R. H., & Sleeth, R. G. (2006). Empathy and the emergence of task and relations leaders. *The Leadership Quarterly, 17*, 146–162.

Kelley, H. H. (1971). *Attributions in social interaction.* New York, NY: General Learning Press.

Lane, R. (2010). *The zeroes: My misadventures in the decade Wall Street went insane* [Kindle edition]. New York, NY: Portfolio, Penguin Group.

Lau, R. S., & Cobb, A. T. (2010). Understanding the connections between relationship conflict and performance: The intervening roles of trust and exchange. *Journal of Organizational Behavior, 31*, 898–917.

Liden, R. C., & Maslyn, J. M. (1998). Multidimensionality of leader–member exchange: An empirical assessment through scale development. *Journal of Management, 24*, 43–72.

Lord, R. G., Foti, R. J., & De Vader, C. L. (1984). A test of leadership categorization theory: Internal structure, information processing, and leadership perceptions. *Organizational Behavior and Human Performance, 34*, 343–378.

Mahsud, R., Yukl, G., & Prussia, G. (2010). Leader empathy, ethical leadership, and relations-oriented behaviors as antecedents of leader-member exchange quality. *Journal of Managerial Psychology, 25*, 561–577.

Markham, F. (1966). *Napoleon.* New York, NY: Mentor.

Markham, S. E., Yammarino, F. J., Murry, W. D., & Palanski, M. E. (2010). Leader–member exchange, shared values, and performance: Agreement and levels of analysis do matter. *The Leadership Quarterly, 21*, 469–480.

Martinko, M. J., & Gardner, W. L. (1987). The leader–member attribution process. *Academy of Management Review, 12*, 235–249.

Martinko, M. J., Harvey, P., & Douglas, S. C. (2007). The role, function, and contribution of attribution theory to leadership: A review. *The Leadership Quarterly, 18*, 561–585.

Maslyn, J. M., & Uhl-Bien, M. (2001). Leader-member exchange and its dimensions: Effects of self-effort and other's effort on relationship quality. *Journal of Applied Psychology, 86,* 697–708.

Mor Barak, M. E., Travis, D. J., Pyun, H., & Xie, B. (2009). The impact of supervision on worker outcomes: A meta-analysis. *Social Service Review (March),* 3–32.

Nahrgang, J. D., Morgeson, F. P., & Ilies, R. (2009). The development of leader-member exchanges: Exploring how personality and performance influence leader and member relationships over time. *Organizational Behavior and Human Decision Processes, 108,* 256–266.

Nisbett, R. E., Zukier, H., & Lemley, R. E. (1981). The dilution effect: Non-diagnostic information weakens the implications of diagnostic information. *Cognitive Psychology, 13,* 248–277.

Phillips, D. T. (1998). *The founding fathers on leadership.* New York, NY: Business Plus.

Rosen, C. C., Harris, K. J., & Kacmar, K. M. (2011). LMX, context perceptions, and performance: An uncertainty management perspective. *Journal of Management, 37,* 819–838.

Schriesheim, C. A., Castro, S., & Cogliser, C. C. (1999). Leader-member exchange research: A comprehensive review of theory, measurement, and data-analytic procedures. *The Leadership Quarterly, 10,* 63–113.

Scott, S. G., & Bruce, R. A. (1994). Determinants of innovative behavior: A path model of individual innovation in the workplace. *Academy of Management Journal, 37,* 580–607.

Scott, S. G., & Bruce, R. A. (1998). Following the leader in R&D: The joint effect of subordinate problem-solving style and leader-member relations on innovative behavior. *IEEE Transactions on Engineering Management, 45,* 3–10.

Sin, H. P., Nahrgang, J. D., & Morgeson, F. P. (2009). Understanding why they don't see eye to eye: An examination of leader–member exchange (lmx) agreement. *Journal of Applied Psychology, 94,* 1048–1057.

Tierney, P., Farmer, S. M., & Graen, G. B. (1999). An examination of leadership and employee creativity: The relevance of traits and relationships. *Personnel Psychology, 52,* 591–619.

Wallis, N. C., Yammarino, F. J., & Feyerherm, A. (in press). Individualized leadership: A qualitative study of senior executive leaders. *The Leadership Quarterly.*

Weiner, B. (1986). *An attributional theory of motivation and emotion.* New York, NY: Springer-Verlag.

Werbel, J. D., & Henriques, P. L. (2009). Different views of trust and relational leadership: Supervisor and subordinate perspectives. *Journal of Managerial Psychology, 24,* 780–796.

Whitener, E. M., Brodt, S. E., Korsgaard, M. A., & Werner, J. M. (1998). Managers as initiators of trust: An exchange relationship framework for understanding managerial trustworthy behavior. *Academy of Management Review, 23,* 513–530.

PART IV

HOW LEADERS MOTIVATE
THEMSELVES AND OTHERS

8

The Importance of Affect and Emotions to Leadership

Chapter Road Map

Case: *Sir Richard Branson: It Must Be Fun*

Sir Richard Branson (taken while he was at the eTalk Festival Party and the Toronto International Film Festival)

Sir Richard Branson's attempts to set hot air balloon records helped create an exciting image for Branson and Virgin. This photo shows Branson, Steve Fossett, and Per Lindstrand being rescued by the U.S. Coast Guard after their balloon crashed north of Oahu in December 1998.

Source: U.S. Coast Guard Visual Information Gallery, AMT2 Marc Alarcon

Sir Richard Branson is one of the world's most successful entrepreneurs, a self-made multibillionaire (worth about $4.2 billion) who pioneered the branded venture capitalism strategy. As head of the Virgin Group, he oversees an astonishing 400 plus set of companies that share the Virgin brand identity. So how does he pick which business proposals he wants to fund and include in the Virgin Group? His first criterion, as listed in a *SUCCESS* magazine interview, is that "Any proposal I like must sound fun" (Vinnedge & Nash, 2009, p. 48). Of course, it is easy to think, "Sure, now that he's a billionaire he can focus on fun, but didn't he have to live a life of drudgery and constant toil when he was a poor young man starting his first few businesses?" Well, if you read Branson's biography, *Losing My Virginity* (2004), you'll see that he summarizes his business philosophy by stating that fun "has informed everything I've done from the outset. More than any other element, fun is the secret of Virgin's success" (p. 342).

So how did having fun make Branson successful? Branson's first business venture was a college magazine called *Student*. Richard demonstrated incredible task persistence, as he had to make an almost unbelievable number of calls soliciting business ads. But his greatest leadership success was due to the fun atmosphere he created for the students working on the magazine. He and some of the other magazine workers lived in a basement apartment owned by a relative of a *Student* staff member. This basement served as the magazine headquarters as well as the scene of frequent parties. By creating a student run club-like atmosphere and a chic image, Branson was able to get students all around the United Kingdom to distribute the magazine while working as unpaid volunteers (the key staff people were paid small salaries).

Branson also took care to make the chain of music stores he opened up fun places to work at. He created a relaxed atmosphere for the stores where people could feel comfortable hanging out talking about music (some stores had cushions on the floor for people to sit on). This was quite a different atmosphere from the formal retail feel of most department music stores at that time, and this undoubtedly helped him attract employees knowledgeable about records as well as die-hard record fans. Later, Branson opened his own recording studio, Virgin Music. How could he get stars to record at his studio instead of at a well-established recording studio? He realized that modern rock stars, unlike the musicians of an earlier age, didn't like the discipline of standard studio hours. They wanted to sleep late and record whenever they felt like it—perhaps even after midnight. So Branson bought a big mansion out in the country where stars could stay for weeks at a time as they recorded songs and had a fun time in between.

Next, Branson started an airline—Virgin Atlantic—much against the advice of his financial advisers. Why? Because he thought it would be fun. Although airlines have to take off on time, be properly maintained, and obey numerous government regulations, Branson manages to create the same positive moods and atmosphere among his employees and customers as he did with his other businesses. He has been successful at running airlines (he started three other airlines in Australia and America), and he has also branched out into a wide variety of other businesses, including Virgin Cola (which outsells Pepsi's diet and regular coke in the United Kingdom; Branson, 2004, p. 12) and a cell phone company, Virgin Mobile.

Applications: Can work be fun? Can leaders create positive moods in other types of retail outlets and businesses? Would you want to work for an organization that values fun at work?

Sources: Branson, R. (2004). *Losing My Virginity: How I've survived, had fun, and made a fortune doing business my way.* New York, NY: Times Business.

Vinnedge, M., & Nash, J. (2009). Virgin entrepereneur: Richard Branson started his first businesses as a youth. Decades later, he's still excited by the next new idea, the next challenge. Success [E-reader version]. Retrieved from http://www.thefreelibrary.com/Virgin+entrepreneur%3a+Richard+Branson+started+his+first+businesses+as...-a0202078557

Branson's story is just one of many that illustrate how leaders succeed by motivating their employees. One way to motivate employees is by creating a positive, fun-filled atmosphere where employees experience positive emotions at work. Branson's motivational strategy is not unique; moreover, his leadership philosophy is backed up by research done in the last 2 decades which demonstrates that leaders can create positive moods and emotions among their followers. This research takes a very different approach to emotions than the traditional bureaucratic approach to management as advocated by Max Weber, as we'll explore in the following section. After discussing the debate over the role of emotions in the workplace, the chapter will show how affect is important to leadership at five different levels. It will also discuss how our daily moods and emotions are an important part of our overall job satisfaction. In addition, this chapter discusses the evidence that job satisfaction is important not only to organizational commitment but to job performance. Because employees' moods and emotions are important to job performance, many scholars are now arguing that leaders need to act as *mood managers* responsible for improving their employees' moods and morale. In this chapter, we'll explore the following questions:

- What are the limitations of Administrative Rationality?
- How can you use emotions to make better decisions and improve performance?
- What is the Five-Level Model of Emotion in Organizations, and how can it be used?
- What is Affective Events Theory, and how can it be applied?
- How can leaders boost performance by managing followers' affect and job satisfaction?

The Myth of Administrative Rationality

About a century ago, Max Weber, a German scholar, developed the theory of the modern bureaucracy. He advocated many useful ideas, such as promotion on merit, rather than on family ties or friendship ties, as was frequently done at the time he was writing. Thus, his ideas carried great weight and his theories came to dominate modern management thought for decades. Unfortunately, he also advocated the elimination of all emotion from the workplace (Ashforth & Humphrey, 1995). Here is a quote from Weber that captures Weber's (1968) views that bureaucracy prospers:

> . . . the more it is "dehumanized," the more completely it succeeds in eliminating from official business love, hatred, and all purely personal, irrational, and emotional elements which escape calculation. (p. 75)

Although undoubtedly brilliant, Weber suffered from manic depression, and his problems coping with his emotions may have tainted his views about emotions. Ironically, Weber also authored an influential theory about charisma which describes the important role that emotional appeals play in charisma. However, he believed that these emotional appeals could persuade the masses to follow demagogues (as we all know, Germany did have a problem with this in the 1930s and 1940s). Fortunately, later scholars realized that democratic and well-meaning leaders also use emotions in their charismatic appeals, and that emotionally arousing language can help leaders achieve beneficial goals and a positive organizational culture (Van Maanen & Kundra, 1989).

Gareth Morgan (1986) was one of the first scholars to critique Weber's overemphasis on banishing emotions. *Morgan brilliantly depicted how administrative rationality became the dominant managerial paradigm, which he aptly described as an overrationalized view of organizational life.* As a result of what Morgan saw as this overrationalized approach, business schools trained future leaders primarily in terms of technical skills, such as accounting and finance. Moreover, organizations tended to devalue jobs that dealt with emotions. Even employees who were supposed to provide emotional support to clients or to other employees were judged more by their performance of routine technical tasks than by the effectiveness of their emotion-related work tasks. For example, nurses and hospice workers might be judged more by the number of technical task they performed (I.V.s given, pills dispensed) than by how well they supported patients' emotional needs. Likewise, elementary school teachers might be judged on completion of paperwork more than on the degree to which they established a positive relationship with their students.

Methods to Control Emotions

As a result of this emphasis on rationality, organizations developed procedures that tried to reduce or control emotional expressions in the workplace (Ashforth & Humphrey, 1995). Four of the more common methods are displayed in Table 8.1. It is true that negative emotions like anger and fear can disrupt the workplace, and even positive emotions like happiness can be disruptive if employees let out enthusiastic cheers and so forth inappropriately. Thus, the procedures in Table 8.1 may help leaders and employees manage disruptive emotions in the workplace. However, as Ashforth and Humphrey (1995) argued, don't overlook the positive role that emotions can play. As you will see in the following sections, research suggests that there are benefits to allowing people to express their emotions in the workplace, and rather than working to suppress emotions, managers should tap into the benefits of emotional expression.

Table 8.1   Organizational Methods for Regulating the Experience and Expression of Emotions in the Workplace

Neutralizing Emotion
Definition: Organizational tactics designed to *prevent the emergence* of emotions through formalized processes and structured interactions between people. The structured role interactions substitute for the development of real interpersonal interactions between people.
Examples: Hospitals use paperwork such as consent forms to focus patients on routine, nonemotionally expressive behavior, while doctors use technical, nonemotionally arousing language and scripted questions that require a neutral task focus.
Buffering Emotion
Definition: Procedures that seek to *compartmentalize* emotions and rationality into separate encounters. Leaders or key employees may perform the positive emotional interactions with clients or subordinates while leaving the task activities with unpleasant emotional connotations or boring routines to others.
Examples: Doctors can appear unmotivated by money in their interactions with patients by leaving the bill collecting to receptionists. Managers can hold office parties and have lunch with subordinates to create positive encounters that are compartmentalized away from frustrating routine work activities.
Prescribing Emotion
Definition: Organizational rules and expectations that regulate which emotions employees *display* to others and the manner in which they display them. This also requires employees to *suppress* emotional displays that are not consistent with the prescribed emotional displays.
Examples: Waiters and waitresses may be told to smile at customers and greet them with scripted phrases, such as "Welcome" or "Have a nice day." Bill collectors may need to display mild irritation, while construction workers may be expected to avoid expressing fear or anxiety while working on rooftops or other dangerous locations.
Normalizing Emotion
Definition: Procedures that restore the emotional equilibrium after the expression of disruptive emotions. The two main methods involve (1) diffusing or lessening the unacceptable emotion and (2) reframing the meaning of the emotional outburst. People who commit the embarrassing outbursts may use humor, apologies, and socially acceptable stock phrases to diffuse the situation. People may also attempt to reframe an emotional reaction in the guise of rationality.

> *Examples:* After expressing anger at his boss, the employee apologizes and adds a stock phrase, "Hey, it's been a long day," to explain the outburst. During a committee meeting, employees who are anxious about their ability to handle new work procedures and technology may attempt to mask their concerns by reframing their opposition in terms of concerns about the cost of the new equipment.

Source: Based on: Ashforth, B. E., & Humphrey, R. H. (1995). Emotion in the workplace: A reappraisal. *Human Relations, 48*(2), 97–125.

Emotions and Decision Making

One of the findings in recent research is that an overemphasis on rationality may *not* be the key to better decision making and innovation. In fact, a study conducted by Pirola-Merlo, Hartel, Mann, and Hirst (2002) illustrates how the emotions conveyed by a leader can potentially have a beneficial impact on employees' emotions and, in turn, strengthen their decision-making processes. Pirola-Merlo et al. (2002) examined the performance of research and development teams. A research lab may seem to be the perfect place to practice Weber's advice to eliminate all emotion from the workplace; after all, research and development seems to be an almost exclusively cognitive task. What the researchers found, however, was that certain leaders of the research and development teams had a major impact on the affective climate of the teams. By helping team members overcome the mood-dampening effects of typical research obstacles, the leaders with facilitative and transformational leadership styles were able to create positive affective climates at work. As one would expect, the bad leaders added to the frustrations and exacerbated the bad moods of the researchers. These mood effects in turn had a strong influence on the performance of the research and development teams. Rather than being a hindrance to good decision making and research, positive emotions have the potential to stimulate creativity, fuel the innovative drive, and power the passionate pursuit of excellence.

> **Applications:** Think of the various emotions you have experienced and witnessed at work. Share a story with the class about a time when someone became emotional (happy, sad, angry, affectionate, frustrated, proud, surprised, embarrassed, etc.). Based on your experiences, do you think the workplace is largely nonemotional, or do you think people experience a wide variety of sometimes very intense emotions? What influence do leaders and managers have on the moods and emotions their followers feel?

The Five-Level Model of Emotion in Organizations

The Five-Level Model of Emotion in Organizations provides a useful overview of the way in which leaders can use knowledge of emotions to improve performance at every level. This model was created by Ashkanasy (2003a, 2003b) and further developed by Ashkanasy and Jordan (2008) and Ashkanasy and Humphrey (2011, forthcoming). Table 8.2 gives the application of this model to leadership as developed by Ashkanasy and Humphrey (forthcoming).

Table 8.2   Attributes of Successful Leaders at the Five Levels of Emotions in Organizations

Level 1: Within-Person
Successful leaders time their peak moods to occur when they need to be their best as a leader. Their greater resiliency and energy levels means they have longer periods of peak positive moods than less successful leaders or followers. They are better able to overcome the mood dampening effects of negative events. They also create positive affective events for followers and they help their followers change feelings of frustration to optimism.
Level 2: Between-Persons (individual differences)
Good leaders tend to have average emotional baselines in the positive range. Moreover, they experience positive emotions more intensely and negative emotions less intensely than unsuccessful leaders or followers. They also have higher empathy and emotional intelligence and they are better at using emotions to help them make decisions.
Level 3: Interpersonal
Successful leaders take the initiative when it comes to expressing their emotions and establishing emotional connections with others. They are good at recognizing others' emotions and they develop trusting, authentic relationships with others.
Level 4: Groups & Teams
At this level, successful leaders work to create shared positive moods among group members. They influence emotional contagion by expressing the appropriate emotions for the situation, which are usually positive ones like enthusiasm, confidence, and support. When forming teams, they select team members with high emotional intelligence.
Level 5: Organization-Wide
Outstanding leaders create their organizations' unique culture by specifying the emotional display rules for organizational members. They recognize the value of high job satisfaction and they work to create positive emotional climates.

Source: Based on Ashkanasy, N. M., & Humphrey, R. H. (forthcoming). Leadership and emotion: A multilevel perspective. In D. V. Day (Ed.), *The Oxford handbook of leadership and organizations.*

Level 1: Within-Person

Level 1 examines how a person experiences different moods and emotions throughout the day. Are you a morning person, or do you feel your best in the afternoon or evening? Research has shown that people have natural rhythms in their moods throughout the day, with some people preferring one time of day, while others prefer different times (Clark, Watson, & Leeka, 1989). Although you may have a natural preference for one time of day, there are steps you can take to shift your peak *feel good* time to the part of the day when you as a leader most need your energy and drive. Shifting when you eat, exercise, and go to sleep can have big returns in helping you feel your best when you need to be at your best.

Leaders, because of their greater investment in their careers and their duties as leaders, may experience more of their peak hours at work, whereas subordinates and those less invested in their careers may save their peak energy for before or after work. Many managers have watched an employee acting sluggish, tired, and exhausted at work, only to see the same employee after work energetically playing sports or being the life of the party. In addition, leaders are likely to have greater stamina and thus have considerably longer peak hours in which they feel energetic and in a mood for work. Leaders such as Napoleon and Margaret Thatcher were known to be able to get by on 4 hours of sleep or less per night while engaging in highly stressful activities like fighting wars or coping with major economic upheavals while at the same time exuding energy and enthusiasm to their exhausted subordinates. Facebook's founder, Mark Zuckerberg, was known to work for 20 hours straight doing programming; Martha Stewart skipped on sleep as well. Note: It is inadvisable to try to sleep less than what your body naturally requires; we can't all be Napoleon or Zuckerberg.

Level 1 is also where affective events have their impact. Weiss and Cropanzano (1996; Weiss, Nichols, & Daus, 1999) developed *Affective Events Theory to explain how workplace events influence our moods and emotions.* Have you ever been in a good mood at work, perhaps chatting with an attractive or amusing coworker, when you spill coffee on yourself? There goes your good mood, replaced by the emotion of embarrassment. Or perhaps you are feeling bored and unmotivated, and the boss stops by and congratulates you on your last project. Sudden mood perk! Or perhaps your emotions swing rapidly due to a mix of good tips (happiness) and pushy and demanding customers (anger, irritation). According to Affective Events Theory, these almost random events that are intermittently boosting or depressing our moods and emotions throughout the day have a big impact on our work attitudes and behaviors.

According to the leaders as mood and emotion managers perspective (e.g., Humphrey, 2002; Pescosolido, 2002), one of the duties of a leader is to create positive affective events for subordinates and to help subordinates cope with the negative events that do occur. Leaders are also likely to be more resistant to the mood dampening effects of negative events (Humphrey, Pollack, & Hawver, 2008) because of their greater resiliency (Hannah & Luthans, 2008; Luthans & Avolio, 2003).

A heavy workload or a series of frustrating events can easily drain our energy at work. When this happens, how can we restore our vitality? Fritz, Lam, and Spreitzer (2011) surveyed 214 knowledge workers who worked for a U.S. software development company. Here is what they found:

> The energy management strategies found to be most positively related to vitality were the following (in order of magnitude): (1) learn something new, (2) focus on what gives me joy in my work, (3) set a new goal, (4) do something that will make a colleague happy, (5) make time to show gratitude to someone I work with, (6) seek feedback, (7) reflect on how I make a difference at work, and (8) reflect on the meaning of my work. (p. 34)

Moods, Emotions, and Affect: What Are the Differences?

> **Moods:** (1) may be longer lasting, (2) are generally weaker in intensity, (3) may not be directly related or caused by a specific event or person (i.e., you might just wake up in a bad mood or feel happy for no particular cause), and (4) are usually classified along two dimensions (a) hedonic tone ranging from positive to negative on pleasantness and (b) arousal/activation.
>
> **Emotions:** (1) are shorter lived, (2) are usually more intensely felt, (3) are directed at and caused by a specific object, event, or person, and (4) although emotions can be grouped into positive and negative emotions, researchers differ as to how many core or basic emotions exist, with most listing between 5 and 10 basic emotions like happiness, love, sadness, anger, fear, surprise, and disgust, and hundreds of words exist to describe more complex emotions.
>
> **Affect:** A broader term that includes both emotions and moods. (Diener, Smith, & Fujita, 1995; Elfenbein & Ambady, 2002; Fisher, 2000; Fridja, 1993; Plutchik, 1994; Watson & Tellegen, 1985; Weiss & Cropanzano, 1996)

Although there are a small number of core emotions, there are many mixed and thus more complex emotions, as the following case indicates. In addition, this case demonstrates that emotions are a key part of our motivational process. The case also demonstrates how people can differ in their emotional reactions to the same object—millions love Thomas Kinkade's dreamy landscapes, but others prefer more realistic landscapes and paintings.

Case: *Thomas Kinkade and the Longing for Success*

It is easy to paint something ugly; it takes a rare genius to paint something that inspires us to feel peaceful, tranquil, and serene. That's why Thomas Kinkade became the most collected American artist of his generation. Kinkade painted beautiful pictures of landscapes and nostalgic-looking cottages. Thomas also had a talent for business and marketing. He knew that in order to share his paintings with millions of people that he would need to create a business. He became a leader by hiring artists to help make reproductions of his artwork and by starting a franchise system. Although Thomas's paintings sell for thousands of dollars, he also created a business that put his artwork on many useful household objects like calendars, coffee mugs, and even wallpaper. He and his business partner also came up with the idea to call Kinkade the Painter of Light—a brilliant marketing title. Some contemporary art critics scorned Kinkade because he commercialized his artwork this way. Yet it is interesting that every major art museum has plenty of coffee mugs and similar items for sale that feature works by the great French Impressionists and other esteemed artists. Perhaps there is nothing wrong with making art both useful and available to the masses.

Nostalgia is an interesting emotion; the Encarta Dictionary defines it as a sentimental recollection, or "a mixed feeling of happiness, sadness, and longing when recalling a person, place, or event from the past, or the past in general." Perhaps Kinkade could paint nostalgic scenes so well because his own life contained both happy and sad memories. He grew up poor in a little town in the mountains. Although poor, he didn't let this stop him from appreciating the beauty of the mountains that he painted so well. He lived in a house so run down that the porch fell off the house, plaster fell down on the dinner table, and a broken window was boarded up with cardboard. He and his brother would stand outside one of the fine Victorian style houses in town and dream of living there. Many of his paintings feature the Victorian homes that he and his brother longed to live in, and once he made it rich, he was able to buy his own Ivy Gate dream house.

Kinkade's paintings reveal a longing for simpler, happier times that are uncomplicated by the complexities of modern life. Unfortunately, Kinkade was apparently beset by the complexities that come with operating a business. Kinkade became quite wealthy from his paintings, and his company ranked in the top 50 licensed brands in the United States of America. The last public report for his company revealed sales of $104 million in 2002 (he bought up the company stock and took it private after that). Unfortunately, the 279 galleries that he franchised to others eventually went bankrupt (he also sold his

(Continued)

(Continued)

paintings through thousands of independent art dealers). Some of his franchise holders filed a million dollar lawsuit against him because they were upset that their franchises went bankrupt while Thomas remained rich. His personal life also began to unravel, and his wife divorced him during the same year that his franchise company went bankrupt (2010). Although Thomas himself denied that the art critics' complaints hurt him, his brother claimed that Thomas was depressed by the critics and by the lawsuit and divorce. Thomas unexpectedly died of natural causes at the relatively young age of 54 in April 2012.

Thomas lived long enough to see that he had won over at least some of the art critics. The year before his death, an edited book was published by a distinguished university press that argued that Kinkade deserves a place among America's great artists. This book is appropriately entitled *Thomas Kinkade: The Artist in the Mall*, (edited by Boylan, 2011).

Applications: Many of Kinkade's paintings evoke a sense of longing; the Encarta Dictionary defines *longing* as yearning, and as "a persistent and strong desire, usually for somebody or something unattainable or not within immediate reach." The dictionary also gives as related words desire, wish, yearning, hunger, craving, ache, pining, and lust. Certainly the unattainable part of the definition sounds like a demotivator, but what about the rest of the definition? Yearning, desire, hunger, and craving certainly sound like strong motivators. Do you think these urges motivated Kinkade to succeed? Do Kinkade's paintings inspire you to leadership success? (You can see many of his paintings by typing his name into Google Images; Google Images.) What type of artwork motivates you?

Sources: Boylan, A. L. (Ed.). (2011). *Thomas Kinkade: The artist in the mall.* Durham, NC: Duke University Press.

Pender, K. (2012, April 10). Kinkade works selling briskly since artist's death. Retrieved from http://www.sfgate.com/cgi-bin/article.cgi?f=/c/a/2012/04/10/BUNK1OOVFQ.DTL&type=printable

Sulek, J. P. (2012, April 16). Personal attacks took toll on Thomas Kinkade. *San Jose Mercury News Monterey County Herald.* Retrieved from http://www.montereyherald.com/state/ci_20386590/personal-attacks-took-toll-thomas-kincade

Level 2: Between-Person

Level 2 in the model focuses on the differences between people in terms of affect-related personality traits. *According to Affective Events Theory (Weiss & Cropanzano, 1996), people differ in their average mood levels and* *affective traits (Watson & Tellegen, 1985). People have an **average emotional baseline**; some people tend to be happy most of the time so their baseline would be in the positive half, whereas others tend to experience negative moods and emotions more frequently and thus have a negative baseline.* Think of Snow White and the Seven Dwarfs: One dwarf was Happy, and another was Grumpy. The Seven Dwarfs also illustrate the activity/arousal dimension of affect, because one Dwarf was Sleepy, while the other more active Dwarfs would whistle while they worked.

One difference between leaders and followers concerns their average emotional baseline. Leaders are more likely to have the appropriate emotional baseline for the situations they are in, which in most leadership situations call for a positive emotional baseline. Leaders are also likely to have more appropriate activity arousal levels—high enough on the positive dimensions to make them energetic and enthusiastic, but not so high on the negative emotions that they would experience intense anger, fear, and frustration.

Affective events, as described in Level 1, can temporarily elevate people's moods and emotions above their normal baseline or lower their emotional state below their average level. Although hassles or uplifts are an important influence upon people's affective state, individual differences are also important. People high on negative affectivity tend to experience negative moods more frequently, have lower job satisfaction, and be more critical about a wide range of issues and subjects.

Although workplace events may elevate or lower people's affective state above or below their baseline, people try to return to their average baseline. Thus, a normally happy person who has experienced an irritating workplace event will usually seek to return to a good mood by talking to a friendly coworker or doing something else positive. Interestingly, this is even true for people who are high on negative affectivity who are temporarily in a more positive mood than usual. Under these occasions, they may do things to lower their mood back to normal. For example, people may be out enjoying a great dinner, laughing and joking together, only to have someone start bringing up negative and depressing stories and topics of conversation.

> **Applications:** What are some ways you can boost your mood while (1) at work and (2) away from work (at home or other places)? What can leaders and managers do to boost moods and create positive emotions at work?

People also differ in their attitudes and values, and this can influence their leadership styles, work behaviors, and decision making. *Ashkanasy and Jordan (2008) observed that leaders are above all decision makers, and as demonstrated by Damasio (1994), people make decisions by accessing their feelings and bodily reactions, what Damasio termed* **somatic markers**. *You and I may better know somatic markers as gut feelings.* Rather than being a separate process from rational decision making, these gut feelings are a crucial part of everyday decision making. People sometimes distrust their gut feelings under the false belief that the rational part of their brain that makes conscious calculations based on numbers will arrive at a better conclusion. Yet these gut feelings may be better at helping us access our true values and attitudes than more controlled conscious processing. Effective leaders are better at accessing their gut feelings and true values, and they use these feelings to guide their decision making. Emotional intelligence, covered in an earlier chapter, also is an important between-person variable that influences leadership and decision making.

As is discussed in a later section in this chapter, people high on negative affectivity do not always perform worse, and there are some occasions where people in a bad mood outperform those in better moods. Even negative emotions like worry or anxiety can sometimes help us make better decisions. We have all of our emotions, even anger, fear, and sadness, for a purpose: They help us survive. The trick is to use these often negative emotions appropriately.

Level 3: Interpersonal Relationships

Ashkanasy and Jordan (2008) classify the emotional components of interpersonal relationships and exchanges primarily in terms of the perception and communication of emotion. Effective leaders are better at accurately perceiving others' emotions and understanding their thoughts, desires, and motivations. In addition, effective leaders are better at communicating their own emotions in a way that has the desired effect on others. As they point out, leader-member exchanges depend on emotional interchanges as well as instrumental ones. Members of the leaders' in-group expect emotional support and personal attention from their leaders. *Moreover, they draw upon Mumby and Putnam's (1992) concept of* **bounded emotionality**, *which refers to the many ways in which organizations restrict, regulate, and control the expression of emotions during everyday encounters.* Likewise, Martin, Knopoff, and Beckman (1998) argued that instead of using bureaucratic impersonality, effective leaders enhance their relationships by using and controlling emotional expressions.

Level 3 is also where emotional labor takes place. *Hochschild (1979, 1983) invented the term* **emotional labor**; *organizations require their employees to perform emotional labor when they specify the emotions that service workers should display to customers and patients.* If you have ever worked as a waiter or waitress, you know what Hochschild is talking about. For most restaurants and retail establishments, *service with a smile* is part of your work duties, whether you feel like smiling or not (Pugh, 2001). Although emotional labor has traditionally been thought of as something performed by service agents, this concept also has important implications for leadership, and we'll cover this approach in more detail in another chapter (Humphrey, 2006; Humphrey et al., 2008).

The development of trust also takes place at this level. Leaders who create trusting relationships with their followers have more productive work groups and organizations.

Level 4: Groups & Teams

Level 4 is where Ashkanasy (2003a) puts the leadership of groups and teams. This is the level in which leaders influence the affective tone and climate of teams and groups. Rather than being a minor aspect of leadership, the "management of group members' emotions is a major leadership function" (Humphrey, 2002, p. 499).

One way in which leaders influence the affective tone of the team is through emotional contagion processes. *Emotional contagion occurs when emotions spread from one person to another, for example, laughter, smiles, and general moods often spread easily from one person to another* (Barsade, 2002; Friedman & Riggio, 1981; Kelly & Barsade, 2001). Barger and Grandey (2006), for example, found that employees' smiles were mimicked by customers and also influenced perceptions of service quality. If you are in a movie theater watching a comedy, you have probably noticed that you laugh more often when audience members around you are laughing as well. The same movie, when watched at home alone, may provoke considerably less laughter. In the workplace as well, these shared emotions can have a strong influence on group members' behaviors (Barsade, 2002). Sy, Côté, and Saavedra (2005) found that leaders' moods were emotionally contagious to group members, and that leaders who created a positive emotional atmosphere had more productive teams. In an experimental study that manipulated leaders' mood while the leaders gave speeches, Johnson (2009) found that leaders' mood influenced the ratings of the leaders, and through mood contagion, the moods and performance of the followers. Tse, Dasborough, and Ashkanasy (2008) also found that a positive affective climate had beneficial effects for leaders—in their study, a positive affective climate helps leaders create more positive exchanges among team members. In addition, groups can vary in their group level of emotional intelligence (Jordan, Ashkanasy, & Hartel, 2002).

Level 5: Organization-Wide

Ashkanasy (2003a) uses as his operational definition of **organization-wide affect** *De Rivera's (1992) colorful definition: "An objective group phenomenon that can be palpably sensed—as when one enters a party or a city and feels an attitude of gaiety or depression, openness or fear"* (p. 197). Organizational leaders, especially their founders, shape the culture and determine the emotional display rules that guide employees' emotional displays. Perhaps the best example of this is the Google headquarters, called the Googleplex—even its name suggests a creative organizational culture that values affective experiences. Google's culture can easily be sensed by a stroll through the Googleplex, where you'll see lava lamps, bean bags for chairs, conference rooms called huddle rooms that use giant exercise balls for participants to sit on, and foosball games and pool tables in the break rooms. Google employees have freedom to decorate their own work areas in creative ways, as is shown by the upside-down umbrella hanging from one employee's office ceiling. If you walk through the Googleplex late at night, you can see another part of the Google culture—dedicated employees still at work. Feel free to verify all this by using the Google search engine to find pictures of the Googleplex.

> **The Leader's Bookcase:** You can learn more about the Five-Level Model by downloading this publication from the textbook website: Ashkanasy, N. M., & Humphrey, R.H. (2011). A multi-level view of leadership and emotions: Leading with emotional labor. In D. Collinson, K. Grint, B. Jackson, and M. Uhl-Bien (Eds.), *Sage handbook of leadership.* London, UK: Sage.

Affect and Job Satisfaction

For years, job satisfaction was seen primarily in terms of people's cognitive evaluation of their pay, benefits, satisfaction with supervision, the work itself, and so forth. These variables are undoubtedly important, as the research on the Job Characteristics Model confirms (Fried & Ferris, 1987). However, *Affective Events theorists believe that our average mood level during the day is another way of looking at job satisfaction* (Fisher, 2000; Weiss et al., 1999). Are you feeling in a good mood most of the time at work or feeling lousy? Perhaps in one job you were in a good mood 80% of the time, whereas in another, you were only in a positive mood 40% of the time. Affective Events researchers use an experience sampling methodology to measure the frequency of moods and emotions that people feel. They give people timers that go off at random points throughout the day; when the timer goes off, the participants jot down their current mood and any emotions they are feeling. *This allows researchers to measure* **state affect,** *which refers to the affect that people are experiencing at that time point, whereas* **trait affect** *refers to the more stable personality trait of positive or negative affectivity discussed earlier.* Fisher (2000) used this method to study 121 employees for 2 weeks. She also asked people to assess their job satisfaction with the various facets of their job such as pay, supervision, promotion opportunities, coworkers, and the work itself. The employees also rated their general job satisfaction in three different ways. She found that the frequency with which the employees experienced positive emotions at work explained overall job satisfaction even when controlling for their satisfaction with the facets of their job such as pay and so forth.

In a meta-analysis of the relationship between state positive affect and job satisfaction, researchers found an impressive correlation between the two: Those with higher state positive affect had higher job satisfaction (Thoresen, Kaplan, Barsky, Warren, & de Chermont, 2003); *moreover, trait positive affect correlated well with job satisfaction.* Thus, the majority of studies clearly show that both state and trait affect influences people's overall satisfaction at work (for an excellent review, see Wagner & Ilies, 2008).

Job satisfaction is an important variable in and of itself. Some people spend the majority of their waking hours at work, and job satisfaction is likely to be a major part of overall life satisfaction even for those with part-time jobs. After all, isn't the point of having a job and making money to find fulfillment and happiness? Many organizational leaders recognize they have a moral obligation to be concerned with the job satisfaction of their employees. Fortunately, as we will see in the next section, job satisfaction also increases productivity and performance. Thus, improving job satisfaction is a win-win situation for employees, leaders, and organizations.

> **Self-Assessment:** Rate how satisfied you are at work by visiting the textbook web site.

Affect, Job Satisfaction, and Performance

A few years ago some researchers published an article that claimed that job satisfaction did not increase performance. This counterintuitive assertion of course made for some great news stories—after all, reporters love controversial and counterintuitive stories. Thus, this assertion was widely carried in the business press and in newspapers. It wasn't hard to imagine how many leaders would respond to this news: "You mean I can mistreat employees all I want, and they will be just as productive? Great! Let's cut benefits, cut pay, lengthen the work day, and increase verbal abuse of employees." Even non-abusive leaders probably began to see job satisfaction as something that was nice but not essential to profits and their bonuses.

Fortunately, *a review was done that examined over 300 studies on job satisfaction and performance (Judge, Thoresen, Bono, & Patton, 2001). This study found that the correlation between job satisfaction and performance is moderately strong,* and the correlation is higher for complex jobs where the employees have the freedom to act on their more positive attitudes. In other words, even on routine jobs such as working on assembly lines or in fast food windows, job satisfaction has a positive impact, and this impact is even greater for professionals, managers, and leaders who have the authority to make decisions or choose how productive they will be. We would not expect the correlation between job satisfaction and productivity to be perfect—after all, ability, experience, training, resources, and a myriad of other factors also influence performance.

A moderately strong correlation between job satisfaction and productivity is still a very important finding, and in today's competitive world, it can make the difference between being a profitable industry leader and bankruptcy. Indeed, a study (Fulmer, Gerhart, & Scott, 2003) compared the profitability of companies that made the 100 Best Companies to Work For list with a set of matching companies (the companies were matched on industry type and size). *For the 1998-2000 time period, the 100 Best companies had an investment return of 82%, whereas the matching companies only had a 37% return.* Not bad for a moderately strong correlation between job satisfaction and productivity.

How Affect Increases Performance

How does increasing positive affect increase performance? Judge and Kammeyer-Muellar (2008) reviewed research on affect and concluded that this research "nearly universally suggests that positive mood states improve performance" (p. 144). They found the following consequences for positive and negative moods:

Positive Affect

Have more cognitive resources—positive moods increase mental resources and flexibility in thinking about problems (Isen, Johnson, Mertz, & Robinson, 1985) and creative problem solving (Isen, Daubman, & Nowicki, 1987).

Be intrinsically motivated—people in positive moods are more intrinsically motivated (Estrada, Isen, & Young, 1994) and find their work tasks more pleasant (Kraiger, Billings, & Isen, 1989).

Negative Affect

Workplace deviance—negative emotions are related to workplace deviance (Glomb, Steel, & Arvey, 2002) and momentary hostile feelings also explain workplace deviance (Judge, Scott, & Ilies, 2006).

Lower reward expectations—people in negative moods are less likely to believe they will be rewarded for performance (Erez & Isen, 2002) and thus are less motivated to perform.

Absence—people in negative moods are significantly more likely to be absent from work (Hardy, Woods, & Wall, 2003).

In their review of the literature on affect and performance, Wagner and Ilies (2008) concluded that affect helped in the following areas:

Task Performance—positive affect increases overall task performance and reduces the depletion of cognitive and emotional resources.

Customer Service Performance—service employees' displays of positive emotions (i.e., smiling) increases customer satisfaction.

Team Performance—positive affect increases group cooperation and performance.

Organizational citizenship and counterproductive behavior—people with positive affect perform more good citizenship behaviors, while those in negative affective states were more likely to commit counterproductive work behaviors.

Creative performance—positive moods generally increase creativity (see studies by Isen, Daubman, & Nowicki, 1987), although in some cases, alternating between good and bad moods may help in being creative while also examining details and being realistic (George & Zhou, 2002).

How Leaders Can Help: Leaders as Mood and Emotion Managers

Leaders can have a powerful influence on the moods and morale of their team members. By influencing the moods, emotions, morale, and job satisfaction of their employees, they can indirectly influence their productivity (Humphrey, 2002; Pescosolido, 2002). A good example is a study done by McColl-Kennedy and Anderson (2002). They surveyed 121 sales representatives in Australia

Washington Crossing the Delaware by Emanuel Leutze, MMA-NYC, 1851. Perhaps Washington's greatest leadership ability was his ability to keep his troop's morale up while they endured hunger, cold, pain, delayed pay, and high death rates. After early military losses, Washington revived the morale of his soldiers by leading them on a daring surprise attack across the Delaware. Later, during the harsh wintry living conditions at Valley Forge, about 3,000 out of 11,000 soldiers died from cold, hunger, and disease. Yet Washington inspired his troops to continue fighting by displaying fortitude and determination while sharing their hardships. He slept in a cold tent while having the troops build wooden huts for each other, and he was one of the last ones to move into a shelter. To learn more, see *The Founding Fathers on Leadership*, by Donald T. Phillips (2008).

Source: Emanuel Leutze, 1851. Metropolitan Museum of Art, New York City.

who worked for an international pharmaceutical firm. In addition, they obtained objective sales data from the company. McColl-Kennedy and Anderson wanted to know how leaders improved the performance of their subordinates—was it by influencing the emotions the employees felt, or was it by other means? So they used a statistical technique called structural equation modeling which showed that *all* of the leaders' influence on their subordinates' performance was due to their influence on the subordinates' feelings of either frustration or optimism. They found that the effective leaders *reduced* the feelings of frustration their sales agents felt by a substantial amount. The good leaders also increased their sales agents' feelings of optimism, again by a sizeable amount. Employees who felt frustrated had lower performance; consequently, the leaders who had reduced their subordinates' feelings of frustration had higher performing sales agents.

A study of 229 entrepreneurs and small business owners (in the Vancouver, Canada, metropolitan area) also demonstrated that it makes good business sense to create positive moods and a positive emotional climate among employees (Ozcelik, Langton, & Aldrich, 2008). This study found that doing well and doing good are not mutually exclusive—the entrepreneurs who took good care of their employees by creating a positive emotional climate were more profitable over an 18 month time span as assessed by both company performance and growth. The following *Personal Reflections* feature also explains how leaders can benefit by helping employees enjoy their work.

PERSONAL REFLECTIONS: *WORK—DRUDGERY OR JOY?*

Throughout the centuries, philosophers, religious leaders, and other thinkers have differed in their opinions about work. Some viewed work as drudgery, an unpleasant task to be avoided if possible. Others, however, have viewed work more positively. To these thinkers, work can be a joy, a calling, a central part of our identity and life mission.

Fortunately, I was taught from an early age that work can be both fun and meaningful. When I was a young child, my older sisters

I had worked at an A&W like this one in Page, Arizona, only mine was located in a mall in Missouri. I still have positive feelings whenever I see an A&W.

Source: Wikipedia/Daniel Mayer (CC-BY-SA)

taught me that household chores could be fun. Whenever my parents were out of the house, Shirley and Sherry would tell us how wonderful it would be to surprise our parents with a clean house. Soon, I would be scurrying around the house with my brothers and sisters picking up toys and cleaning up the place. My sisters' positive attitudes made cleaning up the house seem like a game, and they piled on the praise as well. My parents would always act surprised and pleased when they returned, so I always thought my efforts were well rewarded.

Later, while in high school, I worked at an A&W, a fast food restaurant similar to McDonalds. Jimmy, the manager, gave me some of my first workplace lessons. Whenever the orders came in fast and furious, and it was hard to keep up, Jimmy would advise me and the other employees not to get *shook*. He knew the importance of regulating our emotions and staying calm. Jimmy also told me about the relaxation techniques he used at home. During the summers, Jimmy would take his teenage employees out camping with his own family, and he also had us over to his house for parties. Jimmy took a personal interest in his employees, and as a result, his A&W had unusually low turnover for a fast food restaurant. My professional jobs after college offered even more opportunities for me to identify with my career and to enjoy my work. However, my experiences at A&W have taught me that every job is important and can be fun. The fast-food industry has also been a major route to entrepreneurial success, and the most successful franchise owners usually know how to motivate their employees just like Jimmy did.

Objective factors, such as our pay, benefits, and working conditions, influence how much we like our jobs. However, research has found that other people's opinions also influence how much we like our jobs. If our coworkers seem to genuinely enjoy their jobs, we are likely to have a more positive attitude as well. On the other hand, if everyone is constantly griping about their work, it is much harder for us to enjoy our jobs. Coworkers' emotional reactions and facial expressions can have a powerful effect on how other workers, especially new workers, view the work. If we see the more experienced employees looking anxious, stressed out, or bored, we are more likely to judge the work as anxiety provoking or boring. If the other workers seem relaxed and in a good mood, however, we may think the work is easy and enjoyable. Leaders' attitudes can be especially contagious. If leaders imply by their coercive tone that our jobs are so unpleasant that we have to be forced to do the work, we are not likely to have a positive attitude toward our work. However, if our leaders are working right there beside us with a smile on their faces while they chat pleasantly with us, then we may well think that our jobs are reasonably fun and satisfying.

Often, all it takes is a playful, positive attitude to transform a dull task into a lively one. For example, after giving a test, I always collect the test booklets. Tests can be stressful, and collecting test booklets is a routine bureaucratic procedure. When collecting the tests I state, "Please pass in the tests—no keeping souvenir editions." The reference to souvenir editions usually gets a laugh and eases the tension, and at four extra words, it didn't take time away from class work. Likewise, managers can send out dull, bureaucratic sounding memos and e-mails, or they can liven up their communications with a casual tone. Adding a friendly sentence or two to an e-mail to a subordinate can change the entire emotional tone of the e-mail. Without the friendly sentence, the e-mail is a message from a distant and informal boss, with the friendly sentence, it can be a helpful piece of information from a supportive mentor. The casual, friendly tone is even more important when talking face-to-face.

Your Turn to Reflect: Were you taught that work could be fun and meaningful? Have you seen leaders imply by their attitudes that work can be fun and worthwhile? What can leaders do to make their interactions with subordinates and teammates more positive and appealing? Does your organization encourage dry formal e-mails and official communications or lively ones?

The following case is about an organization that sought to change how people are taught to think about work, especially with regard to emotions at work.

Case: *EMONET—A Worldwide Success*

At one time, popular organizational behavior textbooks had no mention of emotions in them, aside from brief references to how emotions can bias rational decision making or lead to interpersonal conflict. Now many organizational behavior textbooks have chapters on emotions, and millions of students and employees are being taught about the value of emotions in the workplace. EMONET—The Emotions in Organizations Network—has clearly had a large role in bringing this change about. When Goleman (1995) published his bestselling book, *Emotional Intelligence*, there was widespread public interest in the topic, but most academicians were skeptical and regarded emotional intelligence as just another fad. A small group of international scholars (from four different countries) came up with the idea for EMONET. Neal Ashkanasy had organized a Symposium on "Emotions in the Workplace: Not Just Skin Deep" at the 1996 Academy of Management conference. Blake Ashforth and Russell Cropanzano were part of the symposium and had contributed some ideas about forming EMONET. Later, some of the other participants in the symposium joined Neal for dinner; these participants were Sigal Barsade, Anat Rafaeli, and Michael Pratt. Together, they sketched out the basic concept behind EMONET, and early in 1997, EMONET was formed as an e-mail discussion group.

The e-mail discussion group was followed by the first conference on Emotions in the Workplace, held in San Diego in 1998 (in keeping with its international status, the location of the conference rotates among various nations). Normally, professors adopt a tone of professional reserve during conference sessions and are often more likely to express reservations, qualifications, and skepticism than enthusiasm—even for their own research. Yet at this conference, the optimistic sense that the members were starting a brand new area of research with great potential was overwhelming—at one point a faculty member was so enthusiastic that he jumped on a chair to address the audience (perhaps he had a little bit of Sir Richard's showmanship), and this spontaneous display of emotion was warmly received by the participants. The conference

(Continued)

(Continued)

organizers had picked an inspiring location for the conference dinner—a restaurant with a view over the San Diego Bay. The moon looked huge as it rose over the horizon and shone on the water and the conference members—truly a beautiful and stirring moment.

Neal Ashkanasy, Charmine Hartel, and Wilf Zerbe edited the books that came out of the EMONET sponsored conferences. These e-mail discussion groups, conferences, and books played a large role in gaining academic respectability for the field of emotions in the workplace. In order to gain credibility, scholars interested in emotions needed to organize in order to share their enthusiasm and ideas about the topic, as well as lobby for the value of emotions in the workplace. Affect scholars needed the opportunity to present their research and publish their findings; otherwise they would run the risk of having their work rejected by more cognitively oriented conferences and journals. And of course, scholars, especially the young, untenured assistant professors and graduate students at the conferences needed presentations and publications in order to get jobs and gain tenure.

All of the faculty members present at Neal's initial symposium who helped come up with the idea behind EMONET have gone on to become prominent, internationally known researchers. A good example would be Blake Ashforth, the 2009 Organizational Behavior Division Chair of the Academy of Management (this division has almost 6,000 faculty members from around the world, so being division chair is quite an honor). And EMONET itself has gone on to gain official recognition by the Academy of Management, which now hosts the EMONET e-mail discussion group. EMONET currently has about 1,300 members. In addition, a large proportion of those present at the first conference on Emotions in the Workplace have become known for their work on emotions. *Clearly, this shows that one way to become prominent in a field is to recognize when there is an opportunity to form a new group and then take the initiative to do so. Early members of these groups are likely to have a big advantage when it comes to gaining leadership positions in the organization. A few acquaintances or friends meeting over a dinner table can start an organization that has thousands of members a few years later.*

Applications: What organizations do you belong to? How were they founded? Did the originators go on to become successful leaders? Did they start out with a large budget, or did they start out with nothing more than a few ideas and a willingness to talk to people? Did they create opportunities for others to benefit by participating in the growing movement? What was done in the initial meetings to motivate people? Were they held in inspiring locations?

Some Other Organizations Related to Emotions

Geneva Emotion Group

The Consortium for Research on Emotional Intelligence in Organizations

International Society for Research on Emotions (ISRE)

Asia-Pacific Symposium on Emotions and Worklife

European Sociological Association—Sociology of Emotions Research Network

Sources: EMONET (2013, January 28). *About Us.* Retrieved from http://www.emotionsnet
.org/about/and personal experiences

Put It in Practice

1. Create a fun atmosphere to motivate yourself and your employees and to create a fun-filled experience for your customers.

2. Instead of attempting to suppress emotions at work, you should value and reward employees who provide emotional support to customers and coworkers.

3. Use neutralizing, buffering, prescribing, and normalizing tactics to regulate and control emotions at work.

4. Generate positive emotions to stimulate creativity, fuel the innovative drive, and power the passionate pursuit of excellence. Boost performance by helping teammates and followers transform feelings of frustration into feelings of optimism.

5. Lead by managing emotions at all five levels of the organization. Create positive affective events and use emotional contagion to uplift employees' moods above their normal emotional baseline.

6. Pay attention to your gut instincts—they may be right.

7. Improve job satisfaction by improving state positive affect at work.

8. Increase both individual and organizational performance by increasing job satisfaction.

9. Generate positive emotions to increase cognitive resources, intrinsic motivation, task performance, team performance, customer service performance, organizational citizenship, and creative performance.

10. Remember that leaders can have a powerful influence on the moods and morale of their team members and thereby influence their performance and productivity.

11. Transform dull work by adopting a playful and positive attitude—just a few lively words can make a big difference in your e-mails, memos, and personal talks.

12. You don't need permission to be a leader—take initiative to form groups to solve important problems. Motivate people to join by expressing positive emotions and by providing opportunities for advancement.

Exercises

1. Leaders As Mood Managers: Positive and Negative Emotional Contagion

Form groups and make a list of the emotions that leaders might display at work. For each emotion, list the expected outcome in terms of subordinates' emotional responses and behaviors. Can some leader emotional displays have both positive and negative outcomes? Share examples of some leader emotional displays you have witnessed at work, on sports teams, or other organizations.

Positive Leader Emotional Displays	Outcomes
a. _____	_____
b. _____	_____
c. _____	_____
d. _____	_____

Negative Leader Emotional Displays	Outcomes
a. _____	_____
b. _____	_____
c. _____	_____
d. _____	_____

2. Positive Affective Events at Work

Make a list of the things that supervisors and leaders can do to create positive affective events at work. Which of these are external to the job and the actual work tasks, such as a birthday party for employees during lunch time breaks? Which are actually related to the job, such as showing appreciation for someone's thoughtful comments during a committee meeting or helping an employee with a work task? Rate the items in your list in terms of effectiveness on a 1 to10 scale.

Visit the Student Study Site at **www.sagepub.com/humphreyel** for these additional tools:

- Learning Goals
- Leader's Book Case Articles
- Web Resources
- Student Self Assessments

References

Ashforth, B. E., & Humphrey, R. H. (1995). Emotion in the workplace: A reappraisal. *Human Relations, 48*(2), 97–125.

Ashkanasy, N. M. (2003a). Emotions in organizations: A multilevel perspective. In F. Dansereau & F. J. Yammarino (Eds.), *Research in multi-level issues: Multi-level issues in organizational behavior and strategy* (Vol. 2, pp. 9–54). Oxford, UK: Elsevier Science.

Ashkanasy, N. M. (2003b). Emotions at multiple levels: An integration. In F. Dansereau & F. J. Yammarino (Eds.), *Research in multi-level issues: Multi-level issues in organizational behavior and strategy* (Vol. 2, pp. 71–81). Oxford, UK: Elsevier/JAI Press.

Ashkanasy, N. M., & Humphrey, R. H. (2011). A multi-level view of leadership and emotions: Leading with emotional labor. In D. Collinson, K. Grint, B. Jackson, and M. Uhl-Bien (Eds.), *Sage handbook of leadership*. London, UK: Sage.

Ashkanasy, N. M., & Humphrey, R. H. (in press). Leadership and emotion: A multilevel perspective. In D. V. Day (Ed.), *The Oxford handbook of leadership and organizations.*

Ashkanasy, N. M., & Jordan, P. J. (2008). A multilevel view of leadership and emotion. In L. L. Neider & C. A. Schriesheim (Series Eds.) & R. H. Humphrey (Vol. Ed.), *Research in management: Vol. 7. Affect and emotion: New directions in management theory and research* (pp. 17–39). Charlotte, NC: Information Age.

Barger, P. B., & Grandey, A. (2006). Service with a smile and encounter satisfaction: Emotional contagion and appraisal mechanisms. *Academy of Management Journal, 49*(6), 1229–1238.

Barsade, S. G. (2002). The ripple effect: Emotional contagion and its influence on group behavior. *Administrative Science Quarterly, 47,* 644–675.

Boylan, A. L. (Ed.). (2011). *Thomas Kinkade: The artist in the mall.* Durham, NC: Duke University Press.

Branson, R. (2004). *Losing My Virginity: How I've survived, had fun, and made a fortune doing business my way.* New York, NY: Times Business.

Clark, L. A., Watson, D., & Leeka, J. (1989). Diurnal variation in the positive affects. *Motivation and Emotion, 13,* 205–234.

Damasio, A. R. (1994). *Descartes' error.* New York, NY: Grosset/Putnam.

De Rivera, J. (1992). Emotional climate: Social structure and emotional dynamics. *International Review of Studies of Emotion, 2,* 197–218.

Diener, E., Smith, H., & Fujita, F. (1995). The Personality Structure of Affect. *Journal of Personality and Social Psychology, 69*(1), 130–141.

Elfenbein, H. A., & Ambady, N. (2002). On the universality and cultural specificity of emotion recognition: A meta-analysis. *Psychological Bulletin, 128*, 203–235.

Erez, A., & Isen A. M. (2002). The influence of positive affect on the components of expectancy motivation. *Journal of Applied Psychology, 86*, 1055–1067.

Estrada, C., Isen, A. M., & Young, M. J. (1994). Positive affect influences creative problem solving and reported source of practice satisfaction in physicians. *Motivation and Emotion, 18*, 285–299.

Fisher, C. D. (2000). Mood and emotion while working: Missing pieces of job satisfaction? *Journal of Organizational Behavior, 21*, 185–202.

Fridja, N. H. (1993). Emotions are functional most of the time. In P. Ekman & R. J. Davidson (Eds.), *The nature of emotion: Fundamental questions* (pp. 112–122). Oxford and New York, NY: Oxford University Press.

Fried, Y., & Ferris, G. R. (1987). The validity of the job characteristics model: A review and meta-analysis. *Personnel Psychology, 40*, 287–322.

Friedman, H. S., & Riggio, R. E. (1981). Effect of individual differences in nonverbal expressiveness on transmission of emotion. *Journal of Nonverbal Behavior, 6*, 96–107.

Fritz, C., Lam, C. F., & Spreitzer, G. M. (2011). It's the little things that matter: An examination of knowledge workers' energy management. *Academy of Management Perspectives, 25*(4), 28–39.

Fulmer, I. S., Gerhart, B., & Scott, K. S. (2003). Are the 100 Best better? An empirical investigation of the relationship between being a "Great Place to Work" and firm performance. *Personnel Psychology, 56*, 965–993.

George, J. M., & Zhou, J. (2002). Understanding when bad moods foster creativity and good ones don't: The role of context and clarity of feelings. *Journal of Applied Psychology, 87*, 687–697.

Glomb, T. M., Steel, P. D. G., & Arvey, R. D. (2002). Office sneers, snipes, and stab wounds: Antecedents, consequences, and implications of workplace violence and aggression. In R. G. Lonr, R. J. Klimoski, & R. Kanfer (Eds.), *Emotions in the workplace: Understanding the structure and role of emotions in the workplace* (pp. 227–259). San Francisco, CA: Jossey-Bass.

Goleman, D. (1995). *Emotional intelligence: Why it can matter more than IQ.* New York, NY: Bantam Books.

Hannah, S. T., & Luthans, F. (2008). A cognitive affective processing explanation of positive leadership: Toward theoretical understanding of the role of psychological capital. In L. L. Neider & C. A. Schriesheim (Series Eds.) & R. H. Humphrey (Vol. Ed.), *Research in management: Vol. 7. Affect and emotion: New directions in management theory and research* (pp. 17–39). Charlotte, NC: Information Age.

Hardy, G. E., Woods, D., & Wall, T. D. (2003). The impact of psychological distress on absence from work. *Journal of Applied Psychology, 88*, 306–314.

Hochschild, A. R. (1979). Emotion work, feeling rules, and social structure. *American Journal of Sociology, 85*, 551–575.

Hochschild, A. R. (1983). How work rules influence perceptions: Structure-cognitive processes and organizational behavior. *American Sociological Review, 50*, 242–252.

Humphrey, R. H. (2002). The many faces of emotional leadership. *The Leadership Quarterly, 13*(5), 493–504.

Humphrey, R. H. (2006, August). *Leading with emotional labor.* Paper presented at The Academy of Management Conference, Atlanta, GA.

Humphrey, R. H., Pollack, J. M., & Hawver, T. (2008). Leading with emotional labor. *Journal of Managerial Psychology, 23*(2), 151–168.

Isen, A. M., Daubman, K. A., & Nowicki, G. P. (1987). Positive affect facilitates creative problem solving. *Journal of Personality and Social Psychology, 52,* 1122–1131.

Isen, A. M., Johnson, M. M. S., Mertz, E., & Robinson, G. F. (1985). The influence of positive affect on the unusualness of work associations. *Journal of Personality and Social Psychology, 48,* 1413–1426.

Johnson, S. K. (2009). Do you feel what I feel? Mood contagion and leadership outcomes. *The Leadership Quarterly, 20,* 814–827.

Jordan, P. J., Ashkanasy, N. M., & Hartel, C. E. J. (2002). Workgroup emotional intelligence: Scale development and relationship to team process effectiveness and goal focus. *Human Resource Management Review, 12*(2), 195–214.

Judge, T. A., & Kammeyer-Muellar, J. D. (2008). Affect, satisfaction, and performance. In N. M. Ashkanasy & C. L. Cooper (Eds.), *Research Companion to Emotion in Organizations* (pp. 136–151). Cheltenham, UK: Edward Elgar Publishing.

Judge, T. A., Scott, B., & Ilies, R. (2006). Hostility, job attitudes, and workplace deviance: Test of a multilevel model. *Academy of Management Journal, 91,* 126–138.

Judge, T. A., Thoresen, C. J., Bono, J. E., & Patton, G. K. (2001). The job satisfaction–job performance relationship: A qualitative and quantitative review. *Psychological Bulletin, 127,* 376–407.

Kelly, J. R., & Barsade, S. G. (2001). Mood and emotions in small groups and work teams. *Organizational Behavior and Human Decision Processes, 78,* 167–203.

Kraiger, K., Billings, R. S., & Isen, A. M. (1989). The influence of positive affective states on task perception and satisfaction. *Organizational Behavior and Human Decision Processes, 44,* 12–25.

Luthans, F., & Avolio, B. J. (2003). Authentic leadership development. In K. S. Cameron, J. E. Dutton, & R. E. Quinn (Eds.), *Positive organizational scholarship* (pp. 241–258). San Francisco, CA: Berrett-Koehler.

Martin, J., Knopoff, K., & Beckman, C. (1998). An alternative to bureaucratic impersonality and emotional labor: Bounded emotionality at the body shop. *Administrative Science Quarterly, 43,* 429–469.

McColl-Kennedy, J. R., & Anderson, R. D. (2002). Impact of leadership style and emotions on subordinate performance. *Leadership Quarterly, 13,* 545–559.

Morgan, G. (1986). *Images of organization.* Beverly Hills, CA: Sage.

Mumby, D. K., & Putnam, L. A. (1992). The politics of emotion: A feminist reading of bounded reality. *Academy of Management Review, 17,* 465–486.

Ozcelik, H., Langton, N., & Aldrich, H. (2008). Doing well and doing good: The relationship between leadership practices that facilitate a positive emotional climate and organizational performance. *Journal of Managerial Psychology, 23,* 186–203.

Pescosolido, A. T. (2002). Emergent leaders as managers of group emotion. *Leadership Quarterly, 13,* 589–599.

Phillips, D. T. (2008). *The founding fathers on leadership.* New York, NY: Business Plus.

Pirola-Merlo, A., Hartel, C., Mann, L., & Hirst, G. (2002). How leaders influence the impact of affective events on team climate and performance in R&D teams. *Leadership Quarterly, 13*(5), 561–581.

Plutchik, R. (1994). *The psychology and biology of emotion.* New York, NY: HarperCollins.

Pugh, S. D. (2001). Service with a smile: Emotional contagion in the service encounter. *Academy of Management Journal, 44,* 1018–1027.

Sy, T. S., Côté, S., & Saavedra, R. (2005). The contagious leader: Impact of the leader's mood on the mood of group members, group affective tone, and group processes. *Journal of Applied Psychology, 90,* 295–305.

Thoresen, C. J., Kaplan, S. A., Barsky, A. P., Warren, C. R., & de Chermont, K. (2003). The affective underpinnings of job perceptions and attitudes: A meta-analytic review and integration. *Psychological Bulletin, 129,* 914–945.

Tse, H. H. M., Dasborough, M. T., & Ashkanasy, N. M. (2008). A multi-level analysis of team climate and interpersonal exchange relationships at work. *The Leadership Quarterly, 19,* 195–211.

Van Maanen, J., & Kundra, G. (1989). "Real Feelings": Emotional expression and organizational culture. In L. L. Cummings & B. M. Staw (Eds.), *Research in organizational behavior* (Vol. 11, pp. 43–103). Greenwich, CT: JAI Press.

Vinnedge, M., & Nash, J. (2009). Virgin entrepereneur: Richard Branson started his first businesses as a youth. Decades later, he's still excited by the next new idea, the next challenge. *Success* [E-reader version]. Retrieved from http://www.thefreelibrary.com/Virgin+entrepreneur%3a+Richard+Branson+started+his+first+businesses+as...-a0202078557

Wagner, D. T., & Ilies, R. (2008). Affective influences on employee satisfaction and performance. In N. M. Ashkanasy & C. L. Cooper (Eds.), *Research companion to emotion in organizations* (pp. 152–169), Cheltenham, UK: Edward Elgar.

Watson, D., & Tellegen, A. (1985). Towards a consensual structure of mood. *Psychological Bulletin, 98,* 219–235.

Weber, M. (1968). *Economy and society: An outline of interpretive sociology* (Vols. 1-3, E. Fischoff et al., Trans.). In G. Roth & C. Wittich (Eds.). New York, NY: Bedminster Press.

Weiss, H., & Cropanzano, R. (1996). Affective events theory: A theoretical discussion of the structure, causes and consequences of affective experiences at work. In B. Staw & L. Cummings (Eds.), *Research in organizational behavior* (Vol. 18, pp. 1–74). Greenwich, CT: JAI Press.

Weiss, H. M., Nichols, J. P., & Daus, C. S. (1999). An examination of the joint effects of affective experiences and job reliefs on job satisfaction and variations in affective experiences over time. *Organizational Behavior and Human Decision Processes, 78*(1), 1–24.

9

Self-Leadership, Empowerment, Shared/Distributed Leadership, and Teams

Chapter Road Map

Virtual Leadership, Technology, and Distributed Teams
Collective Efficacy
Problems With Self-Managed Groups
Case: *Summit Fever on Mount Everest*
Put It in Practice
Exercise: (1) Mental Imagery and Cold Calling and (2) Empowerment Exercise

Case: *Do What You Have to Do*

How much self-motivation does it take to jump out of a helicopter... into a snow storm, above a raging sea with 25 foot waves, with a bleeding victim below whose arm was almost completely severed, in the dark? This was the situation that Patrick, a member of the U.S. Coast Guard, faced a few days after he completed his training to become an aviation survival technician. He was stationed off Kodiak, Alaska, when an emergency call came in from a fishing boat. In an attempt to land on the boat, Patrick descended on a mechanical hoist operated by a teammate, only to have a giant wave smack the boat, causing a steel girder to slap into Patrick and knock him

The Coast Guard uses realistic training to prepare their crew. This photo of a MH-60 Jayhawk helicopter shows its crew training to rescue someone stranded at sea.

Source: U.S. Coast Guard, Petty Officer 3rd Class Jonathan Klingenberg

wildly around. His flight mechanic was worried that Patrick might have been killed, so he quickly reeled him back in. Patrick was bruised but declared himself okay. The pilot wondered if the rough seas and Patrick's condition made it necessary to call off the rescue. It was up to Patrick to decide. Patrick knew that the fisherman with the nearly severed arm would die if they didn't get him to a hospital. He came up with a new approach. Rather than dropping straight down onto the boat, he had the helicopter swing him along the water toward the boat's railings. Patrick was inundated by waves several times, but he made it aboard the boat and rescued the injured man.

The above true story is from *Character in Action: The U.S. Coast Guard on Leadership*, by Donald Phillips and Admiral James Loy, USCG (retired) (2003). As the title of their book suggests, individual character plays a crucial role in the Coast Guard. It's "an organization where every person is a leader" (p. 6). This means that they have to recruit people with the personal qualities to be strong leaders. The seven characteristics they seek are (1) intelligence, (2) high energy, (3) self-confidence, (4) continual learning, (5) compassion, (6) courage with a bias toward action, and (7) character. These traits help them summon up the courage, confidence, and character necessary to risk their lives for others. These traits also help them lead their teammates as well. Caring, compassionate, and empathic individuals are a good fit with the Coast Guard's humanitarian mission, and this same caring attitude also creates followers and better relationships with teammates. Likewise, "Visible courage often inspires courage in others," and character is "the foundation of leadership" (p. 19).

In order to make everyone a leader, the Coast Guard has to empower people and give crew members the authority to act. This is a necessity in the Coast Guard where crew members may be hundreds of miles from headquarters in a situation that calls for immediate action and judgment. Thus, the Coast Guard has a standing order to leaders in the field: "Do what you have to do. Act first. Call me later" (Phillips & Loy, 2003, p. 83).

Phillips and Loy (2003) give two great examples of how crew members used their own judgment, even in one case violating standard protocol. In the first case, a Coast Guard helicopter flew for an hour to rescue fishermen from a vessel that was floundering and taking on water in 40-foot seas. However, the fishermen were reluctant to abandon their boat, and they waved the helicopter off. Rather than flying the hour back to base, the Coast Guard crew used their own judgment about whether the boat could withstand the storm, and they landed 10 minutes away on a remote island. Sure enough, the fishing boat again made an emergency call—a big wave had flooded their boat and they were going down. The boat sank immediately after the helicopter crew pulled the last man off the ship—if the Coast Guard helicopter had gone back to base, all the fishermen would have drowned.

In the second example, a 10-year-old was caught in the rip tide off of Atlantic City. The boy was drowning in the surf. The three person crew aboard the coast guard vehicle realized that their type of boat was not supposed to go into the surf (it could be dangerous to the crew). Yet they used their own judgment about

(Continued)

(Continued)

whether they could handle the surf, and they made the rescue safely. They discovered the boy's mother had been below him, holding him up. She was not breathing and barely had a pulse; the boy was also in shock and in need of immediate treatment. An ambulance was on the beach, whereas the Coast Guard dock was 10 minutes away. In violation of standard protocol, they ran the boat unto the beach. Although the mother still died, their quick action saved the life of the 10-year-old. Even though they violated standard protocol, the Coast Guard ruled they had acted properly.

Every year, the Coast Guard saves 3,000 lives. Truly, these heroes deserve our thanks.

Applications: Which of the seven characteristics that the Coast Guard recruits for are evident in the examples above? In most organizations, how useful would it be for employees to be able to act first and call their managers later? What are some other jobs where employees have to summon up their motivation in order to face daunting obstacles and challenges?

As the Coast Guard case illustrates, there are occupations where people have to summon up their courage and motivation in order to get the job done. These situations call for the best in self-leadership and self-control, so the tactics these leaders use can help the rest of us learn about how to handle unpleasant or intimidating tasks. Jobs do not have to be life threatening in order to require self-control and a certain amount of courage and confidence. Anyone who has had to make a sales call after several rejections knows how hard it can be to keep one's confidence up. In this chapter, we will explore the tactics that people use to motivate themselves to achieve goals and to take initiative and demonstrate leadership.

In addition, we will examine how leadership responsibilities can be shared among team members and how self-managed teams can demonstrate leadership. Shared leadership may be especially important among *extreme action teams*, such as medical teams in trauma centers (Klein, Ziegert, Knight, & Xiao, 2006) or in the Coast Guard. However, shared leadership may also be important in many other types of jobs as well. In self-managed work teams, members take responsibility for making many of the decisions that used to be made by managers in traditional hierarchical structures. Thus, in this chapter, we will explore the following questions:

- What are the major ways to perform self-leadership?
- How can organizations use shared leadership and empowered self-managed teams to distribute leadership responsibilities throughout the organization?
- Why are self-efficacy and collective efficacy important to self-leadership and teams?

What Is Character?

Many leaders talk about the need for character, but what exactly is character? According to Wright and Quick (2011), *character consists of moral discipline, moral attachment, and moral autonomy.* Leaders have moral discipline when they suppress "individual, personal needs for those of a greater societal good" (p. 976). It is not always easy to resist our selfish impulses and to consider the interests of others; it takes moral discipline to put others first. Leaders are more likely to consider others' interests when they have moral attachment, which is "a commitment to someone or something greater than" themselves (p. 976). Finally, leaders need to have moral autonomy, which requires individual responsibility, judgment, and the capacity to make ethical decisions. The following sections on self-leadership can help leaders develop the moral discipline essential to character.

What Is Self-Leadership?

Neck and Houghton (2006) reviewed 20 years' worth of research on self-leadership. They defined it this way: "*Self-leadership is a self-influence process through which people achieve the self-direction and self-motivation necessary to perform* (Manz, 1986; Manz & Neck, 2004)" [italics and boldface added]. The self-direction part of the definition means that self-leaders have to direct their attention and focus toward the goals they want—the ones they have consciously picked. This means they have to take initiative in choosing their goals. It also means they have to keep their focus on their goals and work on their goals instead of being distracted. The second part of the definition means that self-leaders take responsibility for motivating themselves. This is especially important when working on unpleasant or difficult tasks, or on tasks that have little immediate intrinsic value but great long-term benefits.

Much of the literature on self-leadership evolved out of the work on empowerment and self-managed work teams (Manz & Sims, 1994; Neck & Houghton, 2006). Thus, the material on self-leadership is a good match with the research on empowerment (Conger & Kanungo, 1988). We will cover these related approaches later in this chapter.

Although the research on self-leadership has focused on empowered teams, self-leadership concepts may be useful for managers and leaders in traditional settings as well. Managers and leaders almost by definition have to practice self-leadership. As the ones in charge, they have to determine the goals and the direction of effort both for themselves and their teammates and followers. Managers typically work on a wide variety of tasks. They are frequently interrupted with requests for action on minor issues while trying to work on their key priorities. The hectic and varied pace of managerial work means that leaders have many opportunities to lose their focus, become distracted, and in other ways, get bogged down. Lengthy projects also give leaders plenty of room for procrastination. The temptation to take a break and try to catch up later can be great. All these factors mean that leaders have to practice keen self-leadership to stay on track and on schedule. Moreover, in order to motivate others, leaders also have to be able to motivate themselves. Followers are not likely to be inspired by bored and apathetic leaders.

The Three Foes of Self-Management

Renn, Allen, and Huning (2009) demonstrated the negative effects that self-defeating behaviors can have on employees. They studied 298 counselors and teachers who worked in a nonprofit agency while providing a variety of counseling, adoption, and educational programs for children and families. They found three self-defeating behaviors that hindered some employees from using three types of effective self-management techniques (personal goal setting, self-monitoring of progress toward goals, and operating on or following through to achieve goals). First, they found that the *inability to delay gratification* hindered goal setting. It is often easier to choose short term, pleasant, and easily performed tasks than it is to set one's sights on more difficult, long term, and important tasks. Second, *procrastination* was even more devastating: It hindered goals, monitoring, and operating or following through. The third problem was *emotional self-absorption*, which is the endless obsession and rehashing over events and personal problems. It increased procrastination and reduced the use of effective monitoring of goal progress.

Neck and Houghton (2006) categorize self-leadership tactics into three categories: (1) behavior-focused strategies, (2) natural reward strategies, and (3) constructive thought pattern strategies. Many of the particular strategies advocated by self-leadership researchers are based on considerable research in the areas of psychology, counseling, and other social science areas.

In particular, self-leadership is based on the research on self-regulation theory, social cognitive theory, intrinsic motivation theory, and self-control theory.

Change Your Behavior

In order to improve at any endeavor, one must change one's behaviors. Changing one's behavior is especially important after encountering failure. As Boss and Sims (2008) observed, "To live is to experience failure" (p. 135). Everyone fails sometime or another. Some failures are due to random events, but many are learning opportunities. This is when you need to use behavioral focused self-leadership, which Boss and Sims define this way: *"Behaviour-focused self-leadership involves using action-oriented strategies to accomplish tasks that are difficult or are neither enjoyable nor motivating"* (p. 143) [boldface and italics added]. Sims and Manz (1996) and Boss and Sims (2008) described the steps involved in behavioral focused self-leadership, summarized below:

Self-observation: In order to change your behavior, you have to know what it is that you are doing. This calls for self-observation. How do you respond to criticism or failure? Do you interrupt others? How long do you work at your task before taking a break? Boss and Sims (2008) argue that self-observation calls for a high level of self-awareness, which is one of the four components of emotional intelligence. In-depth self-awareness calls for an understanding of how you behave, why you behave that way, and when or under what circumstances you behave that way.

Self-goal setting: This involves setting your own goals and deadlines instead of relying on others to set goals for you. Considerable research has documented that setting goals increases motivation (Locke & Latham, 2002). Boss and Sims (2008) regard this as the most important part of self-leadership. Moreover, they argue that organizations can support self-leadership by allowing participation in goal setting.

Self-rewards: Rewards are a powerful way to motivate people. Provide these rewards to yourself whenever you complete a difficult task or a goal. Some rewards can be intangible—give yourself a pat on the back for a job well done. For big projects, treat yourself to a night on the town, a vacation, or something else special. Positive rewards for task completion are generally much more effective than threats of negative rewards or punishments for failure. When you fail to complete a difficult task, you should focus on positive, self-correcting feedback.

Environmental cues: You can also shape your environment to facilitate task accomplish by increasing your organization, keeping your focus on the task, and eliminating distractions. For example, visibly posted lists, time schedules, computer generated reminders, and other tracking devices can help with your organization and keep you focused on your priorities. Motivational posters, encouraging slogans, and a pleasant, mood boosting environment also helps.

Natural Reward Strategies

Add pleasant activities: This strategy involves adding tasks that one enjoys doing to the work tasks to make the tasks more enjoyable. For example, at Pike's Place Fish Market in Seattle, the workers found that by throwing the fish around and adding fun, game-like activities to the process of selling fish, they enjoyed their jobs more. Leaders in particular have the chance to mix in social aspects with their committee work, networking, or other supervisory duties.

Focus on the pleasant aspects: Many jobs have tasks that are physically, mentally, or socially stimulating. Self-leaders focus on the intrinsically interesting parts of their jobs while diverting their attention away from the more routine, boring parts. Self-leaders shape their perceptions to appreciate the positive and downplay the negative aspects of their work.

Neck and Manz (2013, pp. 43–44) reasoned that jobs are naturally rewarding when people have feelings of competence, feelings of self-control, and feelings of purpose. Adding pleasant tasks and focusing on the intrinsic aspects of the job help self-leaders feel in control of their jobs and have a sense of self-determination. In addition, they make self-leaders feel more competent and have higher self-efficacy. Self-leaders can also develop a sense of purpose by practicing altruism. For example, they can focus on how their activities help out their clients, their coworkers, the new recruits they are mentoring, and so forth.

Constructive Thought Patterns

Identify thought patterns and beliefs: You should begin your journey toward self-leadership by analyzing your thought patterns. What is the message that you repeat to yourself every day? Is it a positive one? Keep track of how many times during a day you make negative self-evaluations, tell yourself the task is impossible, or in other ways repeat dysfunctional and unproductive thoughts and beliefs.

Replace negative self-talk with positive self-talk: Self-leaders take control of their thoughts by replacing negative, unproductive beliefs, recurring self-doubts, and other self-defeating messages with more productive ones. As Seligman (1991) argues in his book, *Learned Optimism*, people can learn to be more confident. If we think we can succeed, we are more likely to put effort into succeeding, explore different techniques to help us succeed, and in general, persevere in the face of obstacles. As Henry Ford stated, "If you think you can do a thing or think you can't do a thing, you're right" (Ford, retrieved 2012).

Use mental imagery and rehearsal: Image yourself succeeding at the task and being rewarded. Your mental imagery should have you perform all of the steps necessary for the task. If you are a company representative, you should imagine yourself greeting the clients, making your points, answering their questions, and staying confident.

> **Applications:** How difficult is it to motivate yourself to overcome procrastination and negative, self-defeating thoughts to work on your long-term priorities? What methods do you use to motivate yourself?

It can be hard to keep one's optimism and a positive attitude in any occupation. It is a rare job that doesn't have at least some frustrations, defeats, and setbacks. One of the toughest jobs is being a professional athlete. Half the competitors lose at any given match, and the competitors are contending against the best in the world, often before a large and hostile audience. The tactics that these world-class competitors use to keep their spirits up may help those of us in less challenging occupations.

Case: *Andre Agassi Opens Up*

In his *New York Times* number 1 bestselling autobiography, *Open*, Andre Agassi (2009) really opens up about the troubles he had keeping his morale up on his way to winning the U.S. Open's men's tennis championship, as well as the French Open, the Australian Open, the Olympics, Wimbledon, and the women of his dreams. Andre slams home the importance of keeping a positive attitude. During the times that he was motivated, he was ranked among the best in the world, and he held the number 1 ranking for 30 weeks in 1995. But when injuries and personal problems distracted him and he lost his focus, he tumbled out of the top 100, all the way into the minor league. What an embarrassing end to the career of someone

(Continued)

(Continued)

Steffi Graf and Andre Agassi warming up for an event at Wimbledon called "A Centre Court Celebration" on May 17, 2009.

who had been ranked number 1 in the world. But wait—there's more to the story. At an age when most tennis pros retire, Andre recovered his inner drive, along with his line drive. He gathered his friends around him and served, volleyed, and endured all the way back to the number 1 ranking in 1999 and again in 2003. So what are Andre's secrets to keeping up his morale?

Friends and family. Andre could always count on his older brother to listen and understand. Andre's best friend from high school also helped him see his problems in perspective and in new lights. His brother and his friend often traveled with him and gave him support when he needed it. Later, Andre gained a spiritual advisor when he met a Christian rock-song writer and pastor. Together, they had his back, clarified his thoughts, and soothed his troubled soul. On his path to number 1, Andre had his friends around him. But then he met the actress Brooke Shields and he was infatuated, distracted, and exasperated by the relationship (they were married in 1997). His friends also got married or in other ways had to attend to their own lives. Andre's relationship with his wife was troubled, he couldn't concentrate, and his game suffered as a result. When Andre separated from Brooke (in 1999) and won Steffi Graf's love, he began winning again. Steffi, who had 20 grand slam titles, understood the demands tennis made on Agassi.

Father figure and trainer. Gil Reyes became Andre's trainer and kept him focused on physical fitness. But more than that, he became a substitute father figure for Andre. Agassi also benefited from a new coach.

Self-talk: Andre discovered the value of positive self-talk. He learned to interpret his nervous butterflies and make them work for him.

Applications: How important is social support to your motivation? Does it help to have a friend to talk over your problems with? How do you calm yourself down when you are nervous?

Source: Agassi, A. (2009). *Open: An autobiography* [Kindle edition]. New York, NY: Knopf.

Self-Leadership and Performance

Driskell, Copper, and Moran (1994) performed a meta-analysis on 35 studies on mental imagery and performance. *They found overall positive support for the relationship between mental imagery and individual performance.* This positive relationship occurred for both physical and mental tasks, with even stronger effects for mental tasks. Thus, while mental imagery is commonly used for Olympic athletes and in sports, the benefits may be even greater for many types of office work, service encounters, and complex cognitive tasks.

A good example of the studies on self-leadership and performance was done by Neck and Manz (1996). They used a training intervention-based field study to teach thought based self-leadership in an organizational setting. The 48 employees who participated worked for an airline that was undergoing bankruptcy reorganization. Many employees had been laid off, and the remainder had seen their stock in the company disappear in value. Clearly, this was the sort of situation that would produce low morale that could hinder employees' job performance and morale and the chance that the airline could make a comeback. The employees who received the training in thought self-leadership were rated higher in job performance by their supervisors than were a matching group of employees (a control group) who received another type of training. In addition, the employees who received the thought self-leadership training had higher self-efficacy and job satisfaction than the control group.

Self-Leadership and Self-Efficacy

Improving self-efficacy may be one of the key ways in which self-leadership influences performance. For example, Prussia, Anderson, and Manz (1998) found that self-leadership influenced people's self-efficacy—their belief that they could do the tasks involved, and in turn, the improved self-efficacy beliefs influenced performance. In other words, their model, supported by their results, looks like this:

Self-leadership → Self-efficacy → Performance

The above model was also supported by research done by Konradt, Andreßen, and Ellwart (2009), researchers from universities in Germany and Switzerland. They studied 40 teams (total of 310 employees) of financial service providers, most of whom were directly involved in trading with customers, although some did back office work. Consistent with expectations, self-leadership strategies influenced self-efficacy, which in turn influenced performance.

Self-Leadership in a Paper Mill

Morin and Latham (2000) performed a field study in a Canadian paper mill to see if using mental imagery and self-leadership techniques could improve supervisors' self-efficacy and training outcomes. Forty-one supervisors and process engineers attended a one day training program on communications skills and then another one day refresher course. These covered 10 specific communication skills. Following the refresher course, the supervisors were randomly assigned to the following conditions: (1) control group; (2) goal-setting only group; (3) mental practice only; and (4) mental practice plus goal setting. In the goal-setting conditions, the supervisors were given instructions in goal setting and asked to publicly state their goals for applying the training they had received. In particular, they were asked to set a goal for how they would be rated on a 10-item behavioral ratings scale on communication skills. In the mental practice conditions, the supervisors were given a 30-minute exercise in which they were trained in how to engage in visualization techniques. For example, they were told to image very specific details, such as opening doors, smiling, shaking hands firmly but friendly, etc. Both the goal setting and mental practice conditions were followed up by three subsequent training sessions to reinforce their training in these areas. Six months after the initial training, the supervisors reported their self-efficacy with regard to applying the communication skills. The mental imagery training significantly improved their self-efficacy. The highest level of self-efficacy was in the condition where the supervisors received both mental imagery training and goal setting. Moreover, peers of the supervisors reported seeing a significant change in the communication skills of those supervisors who received mental imagery training, either with or without the goal-setting training. However, goal setting by itself did not have a significant effect. Overall, this study serves as a good example of how to use mental imagery techniques to teach supervisors and self-leaders specific leadership skills, such as communication skills.

PERSONAL REFLECTIONS: *THE MISERY ZONE*

When I was in my 20s, exercise was fun. Because I exercised every week, I never had to go through the agony of getting in shape. But then in my mid-30s, I discovered it wasn't always easy to find time to exercise. I was teaching classes at night and trying to publish during the day. Plus with two children and a commitment to being a modern dad, I found I was telling stories and changing diapers more than I was working out. When I did exercise, it was often in the *misery zone*—that first month of trying to get back in shape, marked by huffing and puffing and plenty of self-recriminations. If I kept at it, I would eventually go through the *okay* stage and back into the *performance* stage, where I could easily run five times the distance I ran in the misery stage. But one year I had exercised for a month or two, then stopped for a month while I focused on other priorities, then resumed running when I started feeling out of shape, then stopped again after a month, and so on. Result: 6 months in the misery zone and 6 months not exercising and regretting it, with a final fitness level right where I had started: in the misery zone. Compare this to the year when I had exercised continuously: 1 month in the misery zone: 1 month in the okay zone, and 10 months feeling great exercising in the performance zone and running five times farther than I had at the beginning of the year.

Many people do the same thing with their careers. Imagine Tom, a new hire. Month 1: Tom: "I'm eager to prove myself to the manager—I'm really going to work hard on this project." Manager: "Tom seems to have potential—he's still a rookie, but it looks like he's willing to learn." Month 2: Tom: "The boss seems impressed by me—maybe I can ease off a little—it wouldn't hurt to use the company computer to search for a new car—I deserve it." Tom spends much of the month using the computer for personal use. Manager: "Tom seems to have lost some motivation, but let's not judge too quickly. Let's see how he handles this next project." Month 3: Tom: "This is a big project—I'll show the boss he made the right choice giving it to me." Manager: "Tom seems to be picking up the pace—maybe he does have management potential." Month 4, the crucial presentation to the client: Tom: "Why did my buddies have to schedule their bachelor party in Vegas the weekend before my big presentation? Who knew a hangover could last so long?" Manager: "Tom just didn't seem very sharp during his presentation. I'm disappointed in him." The pattern continues for the rest of the year, with Tom alternating slacking off with efforts to perform. Result: Skill level: Tom's still a rookie; job satisfaction: His job satisfaction is low. Tom lacked confidence and felt like he was in the doghouse half the time. Manager's opinion: "I had thought Tom had potential, but I guess I was wrong. I just can't count on him and he doesn't seem to have improved his skills any. I'm going to give the promotion to Bob, who's shown steady improvement all year."

Your Turn to Reflect: How much more effective is steady, consistent effort than occasional bursts of trying to improve?

Self-Assessment: Rate your self-leadership skills by visiting the textbook website.

What Is Empowerment?

The earliest work on empowerment focused on efforts to give frontline workers greater autonomy in the workplace and to let them decide for themselves how to do the work. The initial efforts focused on empowering individual employees. During much of the last century, factory workers, clerical workers, and many other frontline workers were assigned by supervisors to perform individual tasks. Starting in the 1960s, the empowerment movement often called for employees to work in teams or to at least meet in groups on a regular basis. By meeting in teams, employees could further exercise leadership skills and have greater control over organizing how the work was done. *Thus, empowerment is a set of management practices that gives greater autonomy and control to workers.* For example, empowerment programs may give workers responsibilities formerly assigned to supervisors, such as scheduling production, scheduling workers for shifts, and coordinating work activities among employees. *Self-managed work teams are one type of empowerment practice in which group members take on many of the responsibilities formerly assigned to frontline supervisors.*

The use of teams became more popular in the late 1970s with the greater emphasis on quality control programs, and the team concept spread to many other areas. Although not all teams are empowered, the use of self-managed teams increased as well. By 1995, Lawler, Mohrman, and Ledford (1995) found that 68% of the Fortune 1000 companies used empowered teams for at least some work activities. Some experts believe that as much as 80% of medium (100 workers or more) to large organizations use some form of teams (Cohen & Bailey, 1997; Peterson, Mitchell, Thompson, & Burr, 2000; Solansky, 2008).

Teams became popular because they are often effective. Kirkman and Rosen (1999) argued that using self-managed teams can increase productivity, and that self-managed teams provide better customer service. They argued that empowered team members take a more proactive approach toward solving problems. When you are not in charge, you wait for your supervisors to spot problems and take corrective action. When you are empowered, you may feel it's up to you to solve the problems and make improvements. In addition, using empowered project teams increases employee satisfaction. Employees in these teams generally have better commitment to their team members as well as to the organization. Empowered teams may also be particularly useful for virtual teams operated at a distance from the leader (Kirkman, Rosen, Tesluk, & Gibson, 2004).

A second type of empowerment is psychological empowerment. *Employees feel psychological empowerment when they feel they have choices and the power to initiate action, when they feel competent, when they perceive they have an impact, and when they feel the job is meaningful* (Spreitzer, 1995;

Thomas & Velthouse, 1990). Briefly put, psychological empowerment involves *choice, competence, impact,* and *meaningfulness.* Psychological empowerment refers to employees' motivational levels: Psychologically empowered employees feel more motivated. People's level of psychological empowerment is influenced by their individual personality traits, such as generalized self-efficacy and locus of control. In order to initiate action, employees must have the confidence to believe they can be effective. In addition, psychological empowerment is influenced by the degree to which the organization practices empowerment, gives employees autonomy, and uses self-managed work groups. People are also more motivated by jobs that they feel are important and that have a meaningful impact on others (Hackman, 2002). Thus, people feel greater levels of psychological empowerment when they have the freedom to initiate action that they know will have tremendous benefits; in contrast, people are less motivated to work hard on trivial, relatively unimportant tasks. Organizations that provide extensive training and needed resources can also boost task-specific self-efficacy and feelings of competence, thus increasing psychological empowerment.

Training is particularly important to empowerment programs. Poorly implemented empowerment programs often fail because employees have not been trained in scheduling, budgeting, ordering inventories, leading teams, or in doing any of the other tasks that used to be done by supervisors (Quinn & Spreitzer, 1997).

Management empowerment programs are thought to work in part because they influence the intrinsic motivation levels of employees. Participation in decision making, for example, increases employees' intrinsic motivation (Conger & Kanungo, 1988; Deci & Ryan, 1985; Thomas & Velthouse, 1990). In a *meta-analysis*, Eby, Freeman, Rush, and Lance (1999) found that *supervisors' participative behaviors influenced employees' intrinsic motivation, which in turn influenced their organizational commitment.* Empowerment programs may also improve productivity by giving employees the opportunity to make process improvements. In general, management empowerment programs should strive to increase employees' sense of psychological empowerment. The following study demonstrates how senior managers' participative leadership increases middle managers' psychological empowerment and performance.

Empowerment in the Telecommunications Industry: A Chinese Example

Huang, Iun, Liu, and Gong (2010) surveyed 527 employees who worked for a Chinese telecommunications division of a Fortune 500 company. They argued that managerial level would determine how participative leadership benefits subordinates. Middle managers have to perform a wide variety of tasks and are held accountable for the performance of their units. Middle managers often face considerable uncertainly and a wide range of fluctuating factors that need to be constantly taken into account. Thus, according to these researchers, middle managers would especially appreciate greater autonomy from their supervisors. In contrast, they argued that when leaders use participatory leadership with frontline workers, they are demonstrating trust in the subordinates. Based on leader-member exchange theory, they argued that subordinates would return this trust by performing at higher levels.

The researchers tested their model with two samples. The first sample consisted of 314 middle managers and their 34 senior managers. The middle managers rated the degree to which their senior managers used participative management. Consistent with their hypotheses, they found that the *senior managers' use of participative leadership increased the middle managers' psychological empowerment, which in turn increased the middle managers' job performance and their organizational citizenship behaviors.* The second sample consisted of 213 frontline workers (call center agents; shop floor sales people). Consistent with their expectations, for *frontline workers, the subordinates' trust in their supervisors was more important than their psychological empowerment in explaining their job performance and organizational citizenship behaviors.*

Empowerment and Resistance

An empowering leadership style may be particularly useful because it reduces resistance from employees (Vecchio, Justin, & Pearce, 2010). It is only human nature to resist influence attempts. As Tepper, Duffy, and Shaw (2001) note, this resistance can take two forms. *The first is constructive or functional resistance, whereby the subordinates convey their concerns and suggestions to the leader and engage in problem solving and negotiation over what should be done. The second form of resistance is dysfunctional resistance, which consists of defiance, noncompliance, behind the scenes sabotage of the policies, and other efforts to undercut leaders' policies in nonconstructive ways.* People may resort to dysfunctional resistance when they feel they are being unduly bossed around by abusive managers.

Empowerment in Public School Systems

It can be tough to be an administrator and a leader in public school systems. For one thing, the subordinates are usually out of sight teaching their classes. This means they have opportunities to resist the administrators' directions and influence attempts. Vecchio, Justin, and Pearce (2010) reasoned that an empowering leadership style could improve employee performance and job satisfaction in school systems. For example, teachers, because of their expertise and frontline status working with students, may have valuable contributions to make about school policies. Principals who practice an empowering leadership style can benefit by listening to their teachers' concerns and recommendations and, together, arrive at better policies that improve performance. In addition, teachers may be more motivated to perform because they feel they have been consulted and empowered. Vecchio and his colleagues also hypothesized that an empowering leadership style would reduce dysfunctional resistance.

Vecchio, Justin, and Pearce (2010) surveyed 179 principal–teacher dyads from 179 public schools in California. The teachers were the lead teachers, similar to department heads, responsible for their subject matter areas. The areas were English, History, Mathematics, Physical Education, and Science. As expected, they found that *principals who practiced an empowering leadership style were able to improve the lead teachers' job satisfaction and their performance*. Moreover, the *empowering principals reduced dysfunctional resistance* among the teachers. This was important because dysfunctional resistance reduced both the performance and the job satisfaction of the teachers.

Empower Your Team to Sell

Traditionally, sales has been thought of as an individual activity, where a lone sales agent ventures forth and, unsupported, attempts to make a sale. However, now companies are realizing the benefits of team selling. Indeed, Cummings (2007) found that up to three quarters of companies now use some form of team selling. Team selling can increase cross selling, provide better customer service and support, and offer a more coordinated overall approach. In order for team selling to be effective, Ahearne and his colleagues argue that the team leaders need to empower the team (Ahearne, Mackenzie, Podsakoff, Mathieu, & Lam, 2010). In addition, they argue that they need to create positive team interpersonal climates and consensus among the team members. Positive interpersonal interactions among team members can help them keep their spirits up while making challenging and sometimes frustrating sales calls. On the other hand, bad team dynamics can exasperate the problems and further dampen morale. Empowered teams that have good interpersonal team climates and consensus would then develop team potency, which is similar to team efficacy. When team potency is high, the team members believe they can make their sales goals, and thus, they exert the required effort in terms of preparation and the number of sales calls.

Ahearne and his coauthors (2010) surveyed 1,070 pharmaceutical sales representatives who worked in 185 sales teams. The members had worked together in their teams on average for a little over 3 years, and part of their bonus was based on team sales. Interestingly, they found that the effect of leader empowerment behavior depended upon the degree of team interpersonal climate and consensus. *Leader empowerment only had positive effects on team potency when team interpersonal climate was strong*, otherwise it was nonsignificant. As expected, team potency influenced effort and objective sales performance. Their study shows the importance of considering team dynamics to empowerment programs. Leaders need to pay attention to creating positive interpersonal climates among the team members if they want to empower the team.

Shared Leadership and Distributed Leadership

Most models of leadership focus on a top-down approach, which assumes that leadership influence flows down from the top of a hierarchical organization. With regard to small groups, this top-down perspective assumes that there is one leader of a group who directs the others. This top-down approach is challenged, however, by shared leadership researchers. In 2003, Craig Pearce and Jay Conger edited an influential book called *Shared Leadership: Reframing the Hows and Whys of Leadership*. According to the shared influence perspective, lateral influences in organizations are particularly important. In other words, peers influence each other in a dynamic, interactive, back and forth fashion. This lateral influence takes place within groups in a single department and also among equal status department heads and managers throughout an organization. Moreover, this interactive influence extends both up and down the organizational hierarchy and middle-level managers and employees can exert a profound influence upon an organization's vision and direction. Pearce and Conger (2003b) formally *defined* **shared leadership** as

> A dynamic, interactive influence process among individuals in groups for which the objective is to lead one another to the achievement of group or organizational goals or both. This influence process often involves peer, or lateral, influence and at other times involves upward or downward hierarchical influence. (p. 1) [italics added]

Shared leadership is one type of distributed leadership; other types include coleaders and self-managed teams (Thorpe, Gold, & Lawler, 2011). *Distributed leadership consists of "a variety of configurations which emerge from the exercise of influence that produces interdependent and conjoint action"* (Thorpe et al., 2011, p. 241) [italics added]. In large organizations, knowledge and expertise is distributed throughout the organization, and even upper-level leaders may need to let themselves be influenced by lower-level managers and employees who have more knowledge about a particular problem. To be effective, people at every level need to engage in interdependent decision making and work together (i.e., take conjoint action).

Not all leaders recognize that they need to encourage the sharing of information among team members. In an experimental study, van Ginkel and van Knippenberg (2012) found that some leaders had mental models of leadership that emphasized that team members should spend time exchanging and sharing information, but that other leaders failed to realize the importance of this activity.

Using shared leadership can boost performance. For example, a study by Carson, Tesluk, and Marrone (2007) of 59 consulting teams found that teams that used a shared leadership approach were more productive.

As organizations grow larger, the need for various forms of distributed leadership becomes especially important. This is often a problem for entrepreneurs (Cope, Kempster, & Parry, 2011; Ensley, Hmieleski, & Pearce, 2006). In the beginning, their businesses are small and they may, out of necessity, have to make every decision. But as their organizations grow, they may find that many of their employees know more about a particular problem or task than they do. Successful entrepreneurs learn that they have to delegate leadership authority to people throughout the organization and engage in joint decision making.

Shared Leadership in the Knowledge Economy

Pearce and Manz (2005) argued that shared leadership is especially important in the knowledge economy. They reasoned that continuous innovation and creativity is improved in organizations that practice empowerment and shared leadership. Midlevel employees and professionals, as well as employees throughout the organization, have valuable knowledge and skills that could lead to improvements and innovations.

Friedrich, Vessey, Schuelke, Ruark, and Mumford (2009) also theorized that in modern organizations expertise is widely distributed among organizational members. As a result, leadership responsibilities must shift to those individuals with expertise relevant to the problems at hand. This results in leadership being distributed (e.g., Gronn, 2002) throughout the organization and across hierarchical levels, thus resulting in *collective leadership*.

Zárraga and Bonache (2005) also maintained that knowledge transfer and creation is enhanced in empowered, self-managed teams. Moreover, they reasoned that a *high care* team atmosphere best promotes innovation. High care team atmospheres exist when team members experience mutual trust, active empathy, leniency in judgment (about others' opinions), courage (to state one's own opinions), and access to help. They studied 363 members of self-managed teams from 12 companies in Spain. Consistent with their hypotheses, they found that the *high care variables were positively related to knowledge transfer and creation*. A high care atmosphere was even more important than the presence of a reward system linked with knowledge sharing in promoting innovation and knowledge transfer.

> **Applications:** Have you ever had a manager who didn't listen to you when you knew more about the task than the manager did? Do you feel freer to state your opinions and share your knowledge when managers demonstrate their concern for employees and their respect for employees' knowledge? What can leaders do to encourage employees to share their knowledge and opinions?

Virtual Leadership, Technology, and Distributed Teams

One of the biggest changes in the leadership of teams in the last 20 years has been due to technology. With the advent of the Internet and other electronic communication technologies, many employees now belong to teams whose members span the globe. Many leaders are also now responsible for supervising multiple teams located in various communities. As the following Leader's Bookcase reading indicates, shared leadership may be especially appropriate for leading teams in the Internet era.

> **The Leader's Bookcase:** Al-Ani, B., Horspool, A., & Bligh, M. C., (2011). Collaborating with 'virtual strangers': Towards developing a framework for leadership in distributed teams. *Leadership, 7,* 219–249.

Collective Efficacy

As mentioned earlier, self-leadership works in large part by boosting self-efficacy. When work is done in teams, it is also important to believe in the ability of the team as a whole to perform. Why work hard if the other team members are too lazy or incompetent to do their share of the task? Because so much work is now done in teams, researchers have begun studying collective efficacy (Brown, 2003; Chen & Bliese, 2002; Zaccaro, Blair, Peterson, & Zazanis, 1995; Zellars, Hochwarter, Perrewe, Miles, & Kiewitz, 2001). Shamir (1990) defines *collective efficacy* as *"the perceived probability that collective effort will result in collective accomplishments"* (p. 316) [boldface and italics added].

For individual tasks, meta-analysis has demonstrated that individual self-efficacy is a powerful determinant of performance (Stajkovic & Luthans, 1998). However, one study found that collective efficacy was more important than self-efficacy in determining how hard individuals worked on team projects (Kellett, Humphrey, & Sleeth, 2009). In other words, even if you believe that you can do the job, your perceptions of the team's collective efficacy might determine your own performance level. Consequently, team leaders need to boost team members' confidence in their teammates' abilities.

Problems With Self-Managed Groups

As Neck and Manz (1994) observed, empowered work groups can fall victim to the numerous problems that any group can have when making decisions. The following case is an example of how even groups with talented and experienced leaders and team members can make mistakes.

Summit Fever on Mount Everest

By Jeffrey M. Pollack, Jeni L. Burnette, and Donelson R. Forsyth, University of Richmond

> *"Dudes, what are you doing? Wake up! Guys, turn around, turn around."* (Viesturs, 1996, p. 1)

On May 10, 1996, two groups, one led by Rob Hall and one by Scott Fischer, set out for the summit of Mount Everest from their high camp at roughly 26,100 feet. Several expedition members did make the summit, but before the climbers could descend and reach the safety of their high camp, they were overtaken by a storm. After the storm passed, numerous climbers were missing

(Continued)

(Continued)

This photo shows the Everest southeast base camp with the Khumbu Icefall on the left. The remains of the helicopter that crashed in 2003 is a reminder of how dangerous Mount Everest can be.

Source: Wikipedia/Nuno Nogueira (CC-BY-SA)

and five climbers, including Rob Hall and Scott Fischer, perished. Mount Everest is one of the most dangerous climbs in the world, but a disaster of this magnitude, involving such talented guides, begs the question: Why?

In general, climbing experts agree that these two groups (Hall's expedition and Fischer's expedition) made a mistake—they all ignored their set turn-around time. Expeditions set this turn-around time to minimize the risks of lack of oxygen, darkness, and afternoon storms on the descent. For climbers on Mount Everest, a noon turn-around time is cautious, and a 2:00 p.m. time is risky. Edmund Hillary, who was one of the first climbers to reach the summit of Everest, heard about the disaster and felt that the tragedy was not an accident—it was caused by the slow ascent to the summit (quoted in Dowling, 1996). Ed Viesturs, an expert on high-altitude climbing, was there on May 10, 1996. He watched in disbelief as the teams climbed toward the top and exclaimed, "Guys, you left at midnight. It's two o'clock! It's going to be three or four before you get to the summit." As he watched the climbers continue upward he wondered, "Dudes, what are you doing? Wake up! Guys, turn around, turn around" (Viesturs, 1996, p. 1). Sadly, the two expeditions did not turn around—a terrible mistake that proved deadly.

Why did the groups push on past the turn-around time? Some claim that hypoxia (lack of oxygen), stormy weather, and too many inexperienced climbers on the mountain caused the tragedy. However, Rob Hall and Scott Fisher were very experienced lead guides and had successfully and safely climbed Mount Everest before. What, then, caused such a tragedy this time? We reviewed personal accounts, media descriptions, online interviews, and past empirical papers on risky decision making—in summary, we propose that a variant of the original groupthink model may have precipitated the disaster (Burnette, Forsyth, & Pollack, 2008; Dion, 2000). Specifically, in our groupthink type II model, we focus on task cohesion—the pursuit of a common goal. We suggest the two groups suffered from groupthink—but a form of groupthink where cohesion is rooted in the pursuit of a common goal, not necessarily strong emotional bonds.

Janis (1972, 1982) described groupthink as a faulty style of thinking that makes group members unable to evaluate decisions rationally. The key component of his model (Janis, 1972, 1982) was the presence of high interpersonal cohesion where members were overwhelmed by pressures to go along with the preferences of the group and failed to challenge bad reasoning or correct mistakes. However, according to Janis' model, the Everest climbers could not have experienced groupthink—all existing accounts of the groups stress their lack of interpersonal cohesion. We wondered about this paradox generated by Janis's (1972) classic theory—some groups display the symptoms and causes of groupthink, but they cannot be *victims* of groupthink as they are not interpersonally cohesive.

These two Everest expeditions were not cohesive in a social sense. However, they were cohesive in their shared pursuit of climbing the mountain. Everyone trained for months or years, endured ailments, painful coughing spurts, freezing temperatures, and months away from family and friends. Also, each person paid up to $65,000 for guiding fees and set aside personal issues during the climb (Emerson, 1966). Kayes (2004, 2006) coined the term *goalodicy* and suggested that members of these two groups focused too much on their collective goal and may have had what mountaineers often call *summit fever*.

In today's business environment, groups and project teams formed to address one specific issue are more common than ever. Two salient examples include the N.A.S.A. Challenger disaster and the 2000 (Y2K) information technology changeover—both examples illustrate the dire consequences that can result from a narrow focus on a common task (e.g., Moorhead, Ference, & Neck, 1991; Schiano & Weiss, 2006). A groupthink type II perspective may have important implications for reducing risky decisions in groups focusing on achieving a common goal—if your group is focused on one task, and you sense that mistakes are being made, turn around before it's too late! Don't fall prey to summit fever!

References for Summit Fever on Mount Everest

Burnette, J. L., Forsyth, D. R., & Pollack, J. M. (2008, November). *Groupthink type II: The role of task cohesion, closed leadership, and provocative contexts in collective decisions.* Paper presented at the annual meetings of the Southern Management Association (SMA), St. Pete Beach, FL.

(Continued)

(Continued)

Dion, K. L. (2000). Group cohesion: From "field of forces" to multidimensional construct. *Group Dynamics: Theory, Research, and Practice, 4*, 7–26.

Dowling, C. G. (1996, August). Death on the mountain. *Life, 32*–46.

Emerson, R. M. (1966). Mount Everest: A case study of communication feedback and sustained group goal-striving. *Sociometry, 29*, 213–227.

Janis, I. (1972). *Victims of groupthink*. Boston, MA: Houghton-Mifflin.

Janis, I. (1982). *Groupthink* (2nd ed.). Boston, MA: Houghton-Mifflin.

Kayes, D. C. (2004). The 1996 Mt. Everest climbing disaster: The breakdown of learning in teams. *Human Relations, 57*, 1236–1284.

Kayes, D. C. (2006). *Destructive goal pursuit: The Mount Everest disaster*. New York, NY: Palgrave-Macmillan Press.

Moorhead, G., Ference, R. J., & Neck, C. P. (1991). Group decision fiascoes continue: Space shuttle Challenger and a revised groupthink framework. *Human Relations, 44*, 539-550.

Schiano, W., & Weiss, J. W. (2006). Y2K all over again: How groupthink permeates IS and compromises security. *Business Horizons, 49*, 115–125.

Viesturs, E. (1996). Ed Viesturs on 1996: Turn around guys. *National Geographic Adventure*. Retrieved from http://www.nationalgeographic.com/adventure/everest/ed-viesturs-6.html

Applications: Have you witnessed people continuing on with a bad plan or course of action even after they started receiving bad signs? These don't have to be life or death stories—even an unsuccessful night out might count.

Put It in Practice

1. When immediate action is called for, empower your team members to make decisions and do what they have to do. Select team members who have character.

2. Practice self-leadership to focus on your goals and to stay motivated.

3. Use self-leadership tactics to overcome the inability to delay gratification, procrastination, and emotional self-absorption.

4. The three major self-leadership tactics involve changing your behavior, using natural rewards, and developing constructive thought patterns.

5. To hit a winner, surround yourself with a supportive team and use constructive self-talk.

6. Boost your self-efficacy and performance by using mental imagery.

7. Use empowered self-managed teams to motivate your workforce.

8. Remember that employees feel psychological empowerment when they feel they have choices and the power to initiate action, when they feel competent, when they perceive they have an impact, and when they feel the job is meaningful.

9. Remember that various studies have found that empowerment can increase performance, job satisfaction, and organizational citizenship behaviors while reducing dysfunctional resistance.

10. Recognize that shared leadership is especially important in the knowledge economy, but that in any organization, employees at any level may have useful knowledge and leadership skills.

11. Create a high care team atmosphere to encourage knowledge transfer and creation.

12. Create a sense of collective efficacy by getting team members to believe in each others' abilities.

13. Don't get summit fever—reevaluate your goals when you receive new information that suggests that your original goals are no longer achievable.

Exercises

1. **Mental Imagery and Cold Calling**

    A. *Round 1: Traditional Preparation:* In this exercise, imagine you have to make a sales pitch to a prospective client. Think of a particular item to pitch, like staplers, MP3 players, etc. Brainstorm about a couple of key selling points for the item. When the instructor says "go," find someone in the class you don't usually talk to and become partners. Take turns delivering your sales pitch and acting like the potential client. When playing the client, try to ask the type of questions you really would ask if you were suddenly confronted by a salesperson.

    B. *Round 2: Mental Imagery:* This time use mental imagery to help you prepare your sales pitch. Mentally rehearse each step of the sales process. Try to imagine performing each step in order, from introducing yourself, shaking hands, etc. Image the interaction in as much detail as possible, including physical sensations like speaking volume, body language, etc. Anticipate objections or tough questions, and imagine yourself calmly and professionally responding. Now when the instructor says "go," pick a different person to do the exercise with.

2. **Empowerment Exercise**

    Your teacher will give you instructions for this exercise.

Visit the Student Study Site at **www.sagepub.com/humphreyel** for these additional tools:

- Learning Goals
- Leader's Book Case Articles
- Web Resources
- Student Self Assessments

References

Agassi, A. (2009). *Open: An autobiography* [Kindle edition]. New York, NY: Knopf.

Ahearne, M., Mackenzie, S. B., Podsakoff, P. M., Mathieu, J. E., & Lam, S. K. (2010). The role of consensus in sales team performance. *Journal of Marketing Research, 47(6)*, 458–469.

Al-Ani, B., Horspool, A., & Bligh, M. C. (2011). Collaborating with 'virtual strangers': Towards developing a framework for leadership in distributed teams. *Leadership, 7,* 219–249.

Boss, A. D., & Sims, H. P. (2008). Everyone fails! Using emotion regulation and self-leadership for recovery. *Journal of Managerial Psychology, 23,* 135–150.

Brown, T. C. (2003). The effect of verbal self-guidance training on collective efficacy and team performance. *Personnel Psychology, 56,* 935–64.

Carson, J. B., Tesluk, P. E., & Marrone, J. A. (2007). Shared leadership in teams: An investigation of antecedent conditions and performance. *Academy of Management Journal, 50,* 1217–1234.

Chen, G., & Bliese, P. D. (2002). The role of different levels of leadership in predicting self- and collective efficacy: Evidence of discontinuity. *Journal of Applied Psychology, 8,* 549–56.

Cohen, S. G., & Bailey, D. E. (1997). What makes teams work: Group effectiveness research from the shop floor to the executive suite. *Journal of Management, 23,* 239–290.

Conger, J., & Kanungo, R. (1988). The empowerment process: Integrating theory and practice. *The Academy of Management Review, 13,* 639–652.

Cope, J., Kempster, S., & Parry, K. (2011). Exploring distributed leadership in the small business context. *International Journal of Management Reviews, 13,* 270–285.

Cummings, B. (2007). Group dynamics. *Sales & Marketing Management, 159,* 8.

Deci, E. L., & Ryan, R. M. (1985). *Intrinsic motivation and self-determination in human behavior.* New York, NY: Plenum.

Driskell, J. E., Copper, C., & Moran, A. (1994). Does mental practice enhance performance? *Journal of Applied Psychology, 79,* 481–492.

Eby, L. T., Freeman, D. M., Rush, M. C., & Lance, C. E. (1999). Motivational bases of affective organizational commitment: A partial test of an integrative theoretical model. *Journal of Occupational and Organizational Psychology, 72,* 463–483.

Ensley, M. D., Hmieleski, K. M., & Pearce, C. L. (2006). The importance of vertical and shared leadership within new venture top management teams: Implications for the performance of startups. *The Leadership Quarterly, 17*, 217–231.

Ford, H. Retrieved March 7, 2012 from http://www.brainyquote.com/quotes/authors/h/henry_ford_2.html#ixzz1oTtXUfBQ

Friedrich, T. L., Vessey, W. B., Schuelke, M. J., Ruark, G. A., & Mumford, M. D. (2009). A framework for understanding collective leadership: The selective utilization of leader and team expertise within networks. *The Leadership Quarterly, 20*, 933–958.

Gronn, P. (2002). Distributed leadership as a unit of analysis. *The Leadership Quarterly, 13*, 423–451.

Hackman, J. R. (2002). *Leading teams: Setting the stage for great performance.* Boston, MA: Harvard Business School Press.

Huang, X., Iun, J., Liu, A., & Gong, Y. (2010). Does participative leadership enhance work performance by inducing empowerment or trust? The differential effects on managerial and non-managerial subordinates. *Journal of Organizational Behavior, 31*, 122–143.

Kellett, J. B., Humphrey, R. H., & Sleeth, R. G. (2009). Career development, collective efficacy, and individual task performance. *Career Development International, 14*, 534–546.

Kirkman, B. L., & Rosen, B. (1999). Beyond self-management: Antecedents and consequences of team empowerment. *Academy of Management Journal, 42*, 58–74.

Kirkman, B. L., Rosen, B., Tesluk, P. E., & Gibson, C. B. (2004). The impact of team empowerment on virtual team performance: The moderating role of face-to-face interaction. *Academy of Management Journal, 47*, 175–192.

Klein, K. J., Ziegert, J. C., Knight, J. P., & Xiao, Y. (2006). Dynamic delegation: Shared, hierarchical, and deindividualized leadership in extreme action teams. *Administrative Science Quarterly, 51*, 590–621.

Konradt, U., Andreßen, P., & Ellwart, T. (2009). Self-leadership in organizational teams: A multilevel analysis of moderators and mediators. *European Journal of Work and Organizational Psychology, 2009, 18*, 322–346.

Lawler, E. E., Mohrman, S. A., & Ledford, G. (1995). *Creating high performance organizations: Practices and results of employee involvement and total quality management; practice and results in Fortune 1000 companies.* San Francisco, CA: Jossey-Bass.

Locke, E. A., & Latham, G. P. (2002). Building a practically useful theory of goal setting and task motivation: A 35-year odyssey. *American Psychologist, 57*, 705–717.

Manz, C. C. (1986). Self-leadership: Toward an expanded theory of self-influence processes in organizations. *Academy of Management Review, 11*, 585–600.

Manz, C. C., & Neck, C. P. (2004). *Mastering self-leadership: Empowering yourself for personal excellence* (3rd ed.). Upper Saddle River, NJ: Pearson Prentice-Hall.

Manz, C. C., & Sims, H. P. (1994). *Business without bosses: How self-managing work teams are building high performing companies.* New York, NY: Wiley.

Morin, L., & Latham, G. P. (2000). The effect of mental practice and goal setting as a transfer of training intervention on supervisors' self-efficacy and communication skills: An exploratory study. *Applied Psychology: An International Review, 49,* 566–578.

Neck, C. P., & Houghton, J. D. (2006). Two decades of self-leadership theory and research: Past developments, present trends, and future possibilities. *Journal of Managerial Psychology, 21,* 270–295.

Neck, C. P., & Manz, C. C. (1994). From groupthink to teamthink: Toward the creation of constructive thought patterns in self-managing work teams. *Human Relations, 47,* 939–952.

Neck, C. P., & Manz, C. C. (1996). Thought self-leadership: The impact of mental strategies training on employee behavior, cognition, and emotion. *Journal of Organizational Behavior, 17,* 445–467.

Neck, C. P., & Manz, C. C. (2013). *Mastering self-leadership: Empowering yourself for personal excellence* (6th ed.). Upper Saddle River, NJ: Pearson Prentice-Hall.

Pearce, C. L., & Conger, J. A. (Eds.). (2003a). *Shared leadership: Reframing the hows and whys of leadership.* Thousand Oaks, CA: Sage.

Pearce, C. L., & Conger, J. A. (2003b). All those years ago: The historical underpinnings of shared leadership. In C. L. Pearce & J. A. Conger (Eds.), *Shared leadership: Reframing the hows and whys of leadership* (pp. 1–18). Thousand Oaks, CA: Sage.

Pearce, C. L., & Manz, C. C. (2005). The new silver bullets of leadership: The importance of self- and shared leadership in knowledge work. *Organizational Dynamics, 34,* 130–140.

Peterson, E., Mitchell, T. R., Thompson, L., & Burr, R. (2000). Collective efficacy and aspects of shared mental models as predictors of performance over time in work groups. *Group Processes & Intergroup Relations, 3,* 296–316.

Phillips, D. T., & Loy, J. M. (2003). *Character in action: The U.S. Coast Guard on leadership.* Annapolis, MD: Naval Institute Press.

Prussia, G. E., Anderson, J. S., & Manz, C. C. (1998). Self-leadership and performance outcomes: The mediating influence of self-efficacy. *Journal of Organizational Behavior, 19,* 523–538.

Quinn, R. R., & Spreitzer, G. M. (1997). The road to empowerment: Seven questions every leader should consider. *Organizational Dynamics, 3,* 37–49.

Renn, R. W., Allen, D. G., & Huning, T. M. (2009). Empirical examination of the individual-level personality-based theory of self-management failure. *Journal of Organizational Behavior.* Retrieved from www.interscience.wiley.com .doi: 10.1002/job.667

Seligman, M. E. P. (1991). *Learned optimism.* New York, NY: Alfred Knopf.

Shamir, B. (1990). Calculations, values, and identities: The sources of collectivistic work motivation. *Human Relations, 43,* 313–332.

Sims, H. P., & Manz, C. C. (1996). *Company of heroes: Unleashing the power of self-leadership.* New York, NY: Wiley.

Solansky, S. T. (2008). Leadership style and team processes in self-managed teams. *Journal of Leadership & Organizational Studies, 14,* 332–341.

Spreitzer, G. M. (1995). Psychological empowerment in the workplace: Dimensions, measurement, and validation. *Academy of Management Journal, 38,* 1442–1465.

Stajkovic, A. D., & Luthans, F. (1998). Self-efficacy and work-related performance: A meta-analysis. *Psychological Bulletin, 124*(2), 240–261.

Tepper, B. J., Duffy, M. K., & Shaw, J. D. (2001). Personality moderators of the relationship between abusive supervision and subordinates' resistance. *Journal of Applied Psychology, 86,* 974–983.

Thomas, K. W., & Velthouse, B. A. (1990). Cognitive elements of empowerment: An "interpretive" model of intrinsic task motivation. *Academy of Management Review, 15,* 661–681.

Thorpe, R., Gold, J., & Lawler, J. (2011). Locating distributed leadership. *International Journal of Management Reviews, 13,* 239–250.

van Ginkel, W. P., & van Knippenberg, D. (2012). Group leadership and shared task representations in decision making groups. *The Leadership Quarterly, 23,* 94–106.

Vecchio, R. P., Justin, J. E., & Pearce, C. L. (2010). Empowering leadership: An examination of mediating mechanisms within a hierarchical structure. *The Leadership Quarterly, 21,* 530–542.

Wright, T. A., & Quick, J. C. (2011). The role of character in ethical leadership research. *The Leadership Quarterly, 22,* 975–978.

Zaccaro, S. J., Blair, V., Peterson, C., & Zazanis, M. (1995). Collective efficacy. In J. E. Maddux (Ed.), *Self-efficacy, adaptation, and adjustment: Theory, research, and application* (pp. 305–328). New York, NY: Plenum Press.

Zárraga, C., & Bonache, J. (2005). The impact of team atmosphere on knowledge outcomes in self-managed teams. *Organization Studies, 26,* 661–681.

Zellars, K. L., Hochwarter, W. A., Perrewe, P. L., Miles, A. K., & Kiewitz, C. (2001). Beyond self-efficacy: Interactive effects of role conflict and perceived collective efficacy. *Journal of Managerial Issues, 13,* 483–499.

10

Authentic Leadership Theory, Positive Organizational Scholarship, and Servant Leadership

❧

Chapter Road Map

Case: *Judy Vredenburgh, CEO of Girls Inc.: Know Thyself*
What Makes Someone an Authentic Leader or Servant Leader?
Develop Your Authentic Leadership Potential
What's Your Story?
Psychological Capital
You Can Learn to Be Confident, Optimistic, Hopeful, Resilient, and Happy
Case: *Resilience in the Desert*
Personal Reflections: *A Coffee Mug, a Newspaper, and Authentic Conversation*
Hopeful, Optimistic, and Resilient CEOs
Transparency
Pride—Deadly Sin or Positive Emotion?
Developmental Events in Famous or Infamous Leaders
Servant Leadership
Servant Leadership and Hope

Servant Leadership and Performance
Case: *Meg Whitman, former CEO of eBay: Transparency in Business*
Put It in Practice
Exercises: (1) What's Your Story? Develop Your Narrative Timeline and (2) Improve
Your Psychological Capital: confidence (self-efficacy), hope, optimism, and
resiliency

Case: *Judy Vredenburgh, CEO of Girls Inc.: Know Thyself*

In June of 2010, Judy Vredenburgh became President and CEO of Girls Inc. As CEO of Girls Inc., her mission is to empower girls to be smart, strong, and bold. Before joining Girls Inc., Judy was CEO of Big Brothers Big Sisters of America where she had won numerous awards for her outstanding leadership, including recognition by the United States Congress. It's not surprising she's been recognized: Under her leadership, the number of boys and girls helped by Big Brothers Big Sisters more than doubled, from 118,000 in 2000 to over a quarter of a million in 2008. The Big Brothers Big Sisters program has been effec-

This sign celebrates the 50th anniversary of the Santa Fe branch of Girls Inc. It also thanks some local businesses for supporting Girls Inc.—the right thing to do.

Source: Flickr/teofilo (CC-BY)

tive as well: The children mentored by the program have better relationships with their own families, are less likely to start using illegal drugs (47% less likely) or alcohol (27% less likely), and have half the rate of skipping school. During her tenure, the organization's revenue also increased from $171 million to $290 million.

Vredenburgh had earned an MBA degree from the State University of New York at Buffalo, and she had worked in retail for 20 years before switching to nonprofits. She moved to the nonprofit area because she wanted a chance to be more empathic. She advises leaders who move from profit to nonprofit organizations to use a more collaborative, shared leadership style. Nonprofit leaders have to work to build consensus among board members as well as direct reports. She recommends against using the old command and control approach. At the same time, everyone needs to be clear about goals, time lines, and who does what. There should be no ambiguity about expectations or responsibilities.

Bill George and Peter Sims (2007), in their book on authentic leadership called *True North*, cite Judy as an example of an authentic leader who knows herself. Judy states that "Having self-awareness early in life is very important. You need to understand ... the roles you are best in, your natural strengths, and your natural interests. Then put yourself in a place where you can shine" (p. 70).

Big Brothers Big Sisters is an organization which has people mentor the children they are helping. It is interesting that Judy recognizes the value of mentors in her own life. When joining a new organization, she recommends finding someone who can serve as a trusted advisor, someone who knows the organizational culture and values. When she joined Big Brothers Big Sisters, she established such a relationship with Joe Connolly. He served as her coach and sounding board. Not only did he understand the organization, but he also understood her. Judy also credits her husband for being part of her support team. He understood and supported her values and what she was trying to accomplish by working for a nonprofit agency. George and Sims (2007) argue that authentic leaders need at least one person they can count on unconditionally, someone they can be completely open and honest with, and someone who can see them when they are vulnerable. For Judy, that person was her husband.

Applications: What makes Judy an authentic leader? Is it easy to build consensus while also holding people accountable and setting firm deadlines?

Sources: Big Brothers Big Sisters president & CEO Judy Vredenburgh to receive 2008 Keynote Horizon Award. (2008, June 16). Retrieved from http://www.csrwire.com/press_releases/14556-Big-Brothers-Big-Sisters-President-CEO-Judy-Vredenburgh-To-Receive-2008-Keynote-Horizon-Award

George, B., & Sims, P. (2007). *True North: Discover your authentic leadership* [Kindle edition]. San Francisco, CA: Jossey-Bass.

Girls Inc. board of directors appoints Judy Vredenburgh as president and CEO. Retrieved November 18, 2010 from http://www.girlsinc.org/news/press-releases/vredenburgh-appointed-ceo.html

Transitioning into the ED role: Four keys to success. Retrieved November 18, 2010 from http://www.bridgestar.org/Library/TransitioningEDRole.aspx

Judy Vredenburgh has many of the characteristics of authentic leaders as defined in the following sections. She is aware of her values, and she has made acting on her values a key part of her career and her leadership style.

What Makes Someone an Authentic Leader or Servant Leader?

Authentic leadership research is part of the broader movement in positive psychology. Although psychologists and philosophers have examined the benefits of positive emotions and self-concepts for decades, researchers have only recently begun to examine positive organizational behavior (Cameron, Dutton, & Quinn, 2003; Nelson & Cooper, 2007) and authentic leadership. A popular book on authentic leadership by the former CEO of Medtronic, Bill George (2003), increased interest in the topic. Next, some influential articles on authentic leadership spurred academic interest (Avolio & Gardner, 2005; Avolio, Gardner, Walumbwa, Luthans, & May, 2004). Researchers have also developed scales, such as the Authentic Leadership Inventory (ALI), to measure authentic leadership (Neider & Schriesheim, 2011).

Avolio et al. (2004) described authentic leaders this way: "*We conceive of **authentic leaders** as persons who have achieved high levels of authenticity in that they know who they are, what they believe and value, and they act upon those values and beliefs while transparently interacting with others*" (p. 802) [italics and boldface added].

This chapter will also examine servant leadership, which like authentic leadership, is also concerned with values and ethical leadership. In 1977, Robert Greenleaf wrote an inspiring book entitled *Servant Leadership: A Journey into the Nature of Legitimate Power and Greatness*. In it, he argued that leaders should be servants to their followers. In particular, servant leaders need to work for the best interests of their followers, and they should focus on developing their followers' abilities and helping them live better lives. He stated,

> The best test and the most difficult to administer is: Do those served grow as persons? Do they, while being served, become healthier, wiser, freer, more autonomous . . . more likely themselves to become servants? (p. 21)

In this chapter, we will answer some of the following questions:

- How do leaders develop their values and leadership potential over the course of their lives? Is it their life events or their interpretation of their life story that matters most to their development?

- What is psychological capital? Can leaders learn to be more confident (self-efficacious), optimistic, hopeful, resilient, and happy?
- Can authentic leaders boost their followers' resilience?
- How is authentic leadership related to transformational leadership and performance?
- What are transparency, authentic pride, and psychological hardiness, and why are they important to leadership?
- How do developmental events shape leaders' personalities and leadership styles? Do these events influence whether leaders become ethical *socialized* leaders or more self-centered *personalized* leaders?
- What are the personality traits of servant leaders? How does servant leadership improve employee morale and job performance?

Develop Your Authentic Leadership Potential

Bruce Avolio is one of the foremost researchers on authentic leadership development. His book, *Leadership Development in Balance* (2005), has a two-word subtitle that succinctly captures the central message of the book: *MADE/Born*. *MADE* is in capital letters to emphasize the relative importance of developing our leadership potential compared to what we are born with. Avolio acknowledges that we are born with certain predispositions and abilities—that's why *Born* is the denominator of the *MADE/Born* equation. But he asks us to expand our conception of what we may become, to inflate our estimates of our full leadership potential. A narrow conception of self limits our potential to grow and to develop our abilities to the fullest.

Like scholars and philosophers before him, Avolio (2005) recommends self-reflection. In particular, we need to know how our life streams—all the events in our past—influenced our values, our competencies, and our sense of self. Avolio points out that two people may experience the same life event yet react quite differently to it based on their innate personality traits. Someone with a high energy level, for example, may react to a negative life event by learning from it and developing a capacity to handle challenge, whereas someone with a naturally low energy level may respond by becoming overwhelmed. By reflecting on our life stream, we can recognize the events that may have hindered us from developing our full potential as well as appreciate the people and events that contributed to our core values and beliefs.

In order to grow, we need to recognize that we have many possible selves in front of us. Avolio (2005) points out that many people have been taught to limit their range of possible selves. Avolio cites the example of abused children who have been encouraged to think of themselves as failures. In the same way, we can imagine subordinates who have been treated with a "Do as you're told" mentality—these subordinates are being taught not to see themselves as future leaders. To reach our full potential, we have to choose our own possible future selves and nurture our positive sense of self-worth.

What's Your Story?

What are the important events in your life, the events that have shaped your values, your beliefs, your career choices, your overall lifestyle, and sense of who you are? These life stories are not simply a collection of facts and events. It is the meaning that people attribute to events that creates a sense of self. For example, suppose two high school students are on a basketball team that made it to the state finals. Years later, one may recall every fumble and mistake made in the final game—yet another example of blowing big opportunities. In contrast, the second player may recall making it to the finals as an example of high achievement and leadership success. The event was the same, but their interpretation varied in important ways. Objective events do matter—if their team had never won a game, it would certainly have been harder to build a self-image as a basketball star, but around these objective events there is still considerable room for the players to develop their own meaning.

In their article called "What's Your Story?" Shamir and Eilam (2005) argued that authentic leaders attach meaning to the events in their life in a way that creates a life story. By understanding their life stories, authentic leaders understand their deepest values and convictions. They know their passions and what it is that they want to do with their lives. Shamir and Eilam reasoned that authentic leaders' self-concept includes being a leader. In other words, authentic leaders see behaving as a leader as an expression of their true selves. They are not acting as a leader because they have been appointed to a managerial role—a role that they find as unpleasant. Nor are they acting as a leader in order to gain rewards, status, or other perks. Instead, Shamir and Eilam argued that authentic leaders take on leadership responsibilities because they have a cause and a mission. Authentic leaders see performing the leadership role as consistent with their goals and convictions. Because they are acting out of their convictions, their behaviors are consistent with their underlying values and are thus *transparent* to observers.

Sparrowe (2005) theorizes that our self-narratives emerge in large part from our relationships with others. He argues, "To the extent that the narrative identity of a leader is derived from the provisional selves he or she has available from friends, colleagues, and acquaintances, understanding those other individuals and their own stories may prove important" (p. 435). His theories suggest that followers play an important role in shaping leaders' narratives and views about their leadership relationships.

Applications: Who has played an important role in your life in shaping your identity? Do most people take on leadership roles because they have a cause and a mission, or do they simply want the perks associated with being a leader?

Psychological Capital

The work world is filled with ups and downs. One month business is booming, the next it's in a slump. Production can be going smoothly when suddenly the machines malfunction, an employee gets hurt, or you run out of inventory because the parts weren't delivered as scheduled. Floods, fires, tornadoes, and other natural disasters can strike unexpectedly. Whether facing potential disaster or simple daily frustrations, it helps to have the confidence that you can succeed.

Luthans, Luthans, and Luthans (2004) theorized that people are more likely to succeed when they have *the four components of positive psychological capital: confidence (self-efficacy), hope, optimism, and resiliency.* They refer to human capital as what you know (your education, technical skills), social capital as who you know (your organizational contacts and relationships), and positive psychological capital as who you are. Traditional human resource departments have focused on human capital and social capital, but the three Luthanses reasoned that it is time to consider the benefits of these *who you are* psychological variables. Hannah and Luthans (2008) argued that psychological capital involves both cognitive elements, such as knowledge and beliefs, as well as affective responses. Optimism, for instance, is both a belief that you can succeed as well as a feeling. Many challenging situations require leaders to control their emotions while also planning what to do. For example, emergency technicians need to know how to control bleeding and handle life-threatening situations while also calming themselves down enough to perform their jobs.

Hope and optimism have well-known, commonsense meanings—indeed, the importance of hope and optimism is shown by how often people used these words. Resiliency may not be an everyday word; the American Heritage Dictionary (Resilient, 1985) defines "resilient" as "Recovering quickly, as from misfortunate or illness" (p. 586). However, anyone who has ever struggled to achieve a goal knows how important it is to recover from setbacks. Motivational speakers, coaches, song writers, and leaders all talk about how important it is to bounce back mentally from defeat and other losses. Authentic leadership scholars have developed some precise definitions of the four positive psychological capital variables as described below (Luthans, Avolio, Avey, & Norman, 2007).

Self-efficacy: Self-efficacy has been defined in earlier chapters and is an important predictor of performance. Trait self-efficacy refers to a more stable individual characteristic, whereas state self-efficacy refers to efficacy with regard to a particular task and to the individual's feeling of confidence and expectations for success at the time in question. Authentic leadership researchers are more concerned with state self-efficacy. Moreover, Luthans et al. (2007) argued that authentic leadership is concerned with **work domain self-efficacy** *(Bandura, 1998), which is the individual's belief that he or she has the abilities, skills, and resources to succeed across the entire range of activities at work* as opposed to expectations for success on a single specific task.

Hannah, Avolio, Luthans, and Harms (2008) reasoned that leadership efficacy is a specific type of efficacy. Many people may believe that they can be successful in performing their own work but lack confidence in their ability to influence others and lead groups. They state that "Leadership efficacy is a specific form of efficacy associated with the level of confidence in the knowledge, skills, and abilities associated with leading others" (p. 669). In order to have high leadership self-efficacy, you must believe that you can lead your individual followers and the group as a whole toward successful goal accomplishments. Hannah and Luthans (2008) argue that leaders gain experience over their lifetime that influences their psychological capital and efficacy and their knowledge about how to handle various leadership situations.

Hope: Luthans and his colleagues (Luthans et al., 2007) draw upon research by Snyder (2000) for their definition of hope, and they state that **"hope constitutes the <u>will</u> to succeed and the ability to identify, clarify, and pursue the <u>way</u> to success"** (p. 546) [boldface and italics added; underlining added where the original was already italicized]. They describe hope as a positive motivational state that energizes people to pursue goals. Moreover, they argue that hope includes contingency planning and an active search for ways to achieve a goal. Thus, we can think of hope as having two parts: the will and the way. Let's say you are pursuing a goal but encounter a problem. If you lack hope, you would remain passive and just give up. But if you are hopeful, you'll be energized to search for solutions to the problem. You might examine multiple ways to solve the problem, and you'll keep searching until you find the path to success.

Peterson and Luthans (2003) examined hope among fast food store managers. They found that the more hopeful managers had better financial performance and that their employees were also more satisfied and had lower turnover. Two studies of factory workers also found that hope was an important variable. Luthans, Avolio, Walumbwa, and Li (2005) found that Chinese factory workers high on hope were rated higher on performance appraisals and earned higher merit raises as a result. Likewise, Larson and Luthans (2006) found in a sample of American factory workers that hope was positively related with organizational commitment and job satisfaction.

Optimism: Luthans and his colleagues (2007) base their definition of optimism on work done by Seligman (1998). Luthans et al. (2007) state, "Seligman (1998) defines *optimists as those who make internal, stable, and global attributions regarding positive events (e.g., task accomplishment) and those who attribute external, unstable, and specific reasons for negative events (e.g., a missed deadline)*" (p. 547) [italics and boldface added]. By internal attributions, they mean that the person attributes the outcome to their own efforts rather than to external forces or luck. Thus, optimists attribute success to their own efforts and believe that they will continue to be successful. When something goes wrong, they attribute the failure to a specific environmental factor, perhaps an unlucky chance event, and they believe that in the long term the bad luck will end or that they can overcome the negative environmental factors and achieve success. Seligman has accumulated considerable evidence that indicates the importance of optimism to a wide variety of outcomes.

Resilience: Luthans (2002) defines **resilience** as the *"positive psychological capacity to rebound, to 'bounce back' from adversity, uncertainty, conflict, failure, or even positive change, progress and increased responsibility"* (p. 702) [italics and boldface added]. As the last part of this definition implies, even positive changes and many everyday work responsibilities call for resilience. Accidents, job loss, major work problems, and illnesses call for even greater levels of resilience. As Masten and Reed (2002) observe, humans have an impressive ability to bounce back from stressful life events. For example, most survivors of the 9/11 attack on the Pentagon did not need mental health counseling (Ritchie, Leavitt, & Hanish, 2006). Likewise, even the bombings of London during WWII, which killed 40,000, were not able to break the resilience or the determination of the Londoners (Jones, Woolven, Durodie, & Wessely, 2004).

Some work related to resilience has been done by Kobasa and her colleagues; they developed a hardiness scale which measures people's resistance to stressful events (Kobasa, Maddi, & Kahn, 1982). They found that scores on the hardiness scale predicted future health outcomes. In addition, executives who scored higher on hardiness suffered fewer illnesses and were more successful in their careers as well (Maddi & Kobasa, 1984).

Although negative events normally increase negative emotions, those who can maintain their positive emotions while facing these challenges have better resiliency (Tugade, Fredrickson, & Barrett, 2004). Indeed, overcoming obstacles seems to increase one's resilience (Luthans et al., 2007).

> **Applications:** Think of some of the obstacles you've faced in your own life. Did overcoming them help you become more confident and resilient?

You Can Learn to Be Confident, Optimistic, Hopeful, Resilient, and Happy

Luthans and his colleagues (Luthans et al., 2007) argue that psychological capital has state-like properties and thus can be developed. Gardner and Schermerhorn (2004) give useful advice about how to improve one's psychological capital. They reviewed the research on the four components of psychological capital and summarized the key advice from scholars in each area. In addition, another scholar gives advice on how to improve our overall happiness level.

Confidence and self-efficacy: Gardner and Schermerhorn (2004) recommend boosting confidence by giving people mastery opportunities. In other words, give people developmental task assignments that allow them to further develop their skills. They also recommend giving people the chance to practice ethical leadership. Leaders can also use role modeling and verbal persuasion to boost employees' confidence. Finally, leaders need to provide social support and find other ways to help employees handle physiological and emotional responses to failures and work challenges.

Hope: Gardner and Schermerhorn (2004) urge authentic leaders to use several tips from the clinical psychologist Snyder (cited earlier) to build hope. Leaders should match job assignments to the talents and abilities of their employees. There is nothing so demoralizing and hope destroying as being assigned a task you are not ready for. Leaders should also encourage employees to use *re-goaling* when they are trying to pursue unachievable goals. Participation in setting goals and subdividing goals into smaller units also helps with *waypower* and the ability of employees to see their way to success.

Optimism: Seligman (1998) entitled his book *Learned Optimism* because he believes that people can learn to become more optimistic. Gardner and Schermerhorn (2004) endorse Seligman's A-B-C-D-E steps for building optimism. They are

Adversity: List your adversities and obstacles.

Beliefs: Identify and understand your self-defeating thoughts and beliefs.

Consequences: Enumerate the results of the self-defeating thoughts (depression, inaction).

Dispute: Challenge the assumptions of self-defeating thoughts and replace them with realistic options for success.

Energization: Experience the energy that comes from having more enthusiastic thoughts.

Self-Assessment: *Optimism.* Go to the textbook website to rate yourself on optimism and to see tips for gaining a more optimistic outlook.

Resilience: Gardner and Schermerhorn (2004) advise authentic leaders to provide social and emotional support to employees facing adversity. They also state that authentic leaders "anticipate potential adversity or strains, make contingency plans to support and help employees cope with them, and are available and responsive when such persons reach out to them" (p. 278).

Imagine that you were taken thousands of miles from your home and placed in unfamiliar surroundings. Even worse, you're in a desert with blazing hot days and with few things to do for fun or recreation. Then imagine that you find yourself doing routine, boring work with no clear purpose to justify your time away from your family or the other sacrifices you are making. Chances are you'll find that stressful. The following case illustrates how a leader helped his team overcome their stress and boredom by giving them a common goal with clear, tangible benefits and worthwhile results.

Case: *Resilience in the Desert*

Bartone (2006) reviewed several empirical studies involving hundreds of cadets which demonstrated that leaders high on hardiness influenced their "subordinates to think and behave in more hardy and resilient ways" (p. S139). Bartone then provided a case study of a peace-time (1995) military leader who improved his subordinates' hardiness and resilience while they were on a 6 month tour of duty at a base in Saudi Arabia. During his visit to the base, Bartone conducted interviews and administered surveys which demonstrated that morale was poor in several of the companies in the battalion. The soldiers were stationed overseas far from home in a desert, and they found their work dull and predictable. However, one unit had high morale and cohesion. The company commander attributed his soldiers' high morale to the fact that they had a common goal and mission that produced tangible results. When the commander took charge of the company, he realized that there was a nearby military dump. The equipment in the dump was being buried by the sand—rusting out, going to waste, nothing but an eyesore. The commander took the following steps:

Create meaning out of an ambiguous situation: He found a mission that could give the company soldiers a purpose to their time in the field. They were able to salvage over one million dollars' worth of equipment by excavating and repairing the materials in the dump. In addition, they built a multipurpose athletic field on the spot of the former dump; this field provided much needed recreational opportunities for the base.

Participation and empowerment: He involved his subordinates in planning a way to excavate and restore the equipment. This created a shared sense of commitment.

A controllable task: The scope of the task was one that was under the control of the company and fit their collective abilities. Moreover, it could be accomplished within the 6 month time frame that the soldiers would be there.

Recognition: Before and after pictures of the excavation site were displayed in their work areas and meeting rooms, providing visible reminders of their accomplishments. The commander also arranged for the company to receive recognition from senior leaders and even from the national news media. This recognition increased the soldiers' pride in their accomplishments.

Applications: Relate the steps taken by the company commander to the suggestions made by Gardner and Schermerhorn (2004) about how to increase psychological capital. Which actions made the biggest differences?

Source: Bartone, P. T. (2006). Resilience under military operational stress: Can leaders influence hardiness? *Military Psychology, 18*(Suppl.), S131–S148.

Happiness: Sonja Lyubomirsky (2008) wrote a book called *The How of Happiness: A Scientific Approach to Getting the Life You Want.* In this book, she reviewed research which shows that *up to 40% of how happy we are is within our power to change.* Although genetics (50%) and life circumstances (10%) influence how happy we are, we can control to a considerable extent our own happiness. Sonja argued that the intent to be happy plays a key role in how happy we are. When we intend to be happy, we choose happiness activities such as showing gratitude and thinking positive thoughts, investing in social connections, living in the present, and committing to our goals. Why is happiness important to leadership? The research shows that happy people "are better leaders and negotiators and earn more money. They are more resilient in the face of hardship, have stronger immune systems, and are physically healthier. Happy people even live longer" (Lyubomirsky, 2008, p. 25).

PERSONAL REFLECTIONS: *A COFFEE MUG, A NEWSPAPER, AND AUTHENTIC CONVERSATION*

My stepdad, Bill Campbell, had the gift of authentic communication. He loved talking about politics. He would sit at the dining room table, coffee mug in one hand, the newspaper in the other, and go over the day's events. He used a traditional coffee mug, like you would see in the diners in old movies, with a thick rim to keep the coffee hot and with slightly curving sides so it was comfortable to hold. The mug was solid, functional, and dependable, just like my dad. He especially enjoyed a good debate with someone who disagreed with him. He had the knack of keeping these conversations fun and lighthearted. If the tension began to rise, he would come up with a quip worthy of Jay Leno, and everyone would have a good laugh. He could poke fun at his own side as well. The absurdities of both political parties were ample fodder for his wit. He never became angry with someone just because they belonged to another party or had a different opinion. I think it's because he saw people as human beings and individuals with unique life stories and backgrounds, not as political caricatures.

He would want to know what it was about their life and background that made them want to support a particular belief. And other people rarely became upset with him either during these discussions. Instead, they usually appreciated his honesty and good humor, and they became better friends as a result.

My dad is also my model of resiliency. He was a child during the Great Depression, and he served in the Korean War, so he learned to handle hardship at an early age. He handled problems with the same good humor he discussed politics with. If something at home broke down and needed repairing, he would roll up his sleeves and get to work. He was a courageous man. He kept his humor up even when he was dying with cancer in the hospital. His friends would come by the hospital room, looking sad and depressed because they knew my dad was dying. But my dad would tell them a joke and find some way to laugh about the situation. Nurses and other hospital staff are supposed to provide comfort to the sick, but with my dad, it sometimes seemed it was the other way around. Several times I saw him cheer up the nurses with his good humor.

It has been many years since my dad passed away. Sometimes I take out his coffee mug and think of him sitting at the table, with a wry grin on his face, talking about the day's events.

Your Turn to Reflect: What objects do you associate with your family members and friends? How have your role models taught you hope, resiliency, and authentic communication? How easy is it to have a friendly conversation with people who disagree with you? Does humor help prevent disagreements from becoming unfriendly? What is the best way to learn how to handle setbacks?

Hopeful, Optimistic, and Resilient CEOs

Peterson, Walumbwa, Byron, and Myrowitz (2009) wanted to know if CEOs who were more optimistic, hopeful, and resilient were more successful in starting new business ventures and in running already established businesses. They surveyed 49 CEOs who were running hi-tech business start-ups (less than 5 years old) as well as 56 CEOs who ran more established businesses (businesses older than 5 years with more than 100 employees and over $3 million in annual sales). They reasoned that CEOs who were high in these positive psychological characteristics would be more likely to use a transformational leadership style. In turn, the transformational leadership style should result in higher firm performance for the business start-ups and the more established firms. In other words, their model looks like this:

(Hope, Optimism, Resiliency) → Transformational Leadership →
Firm Performance

Peterson and her colleagues (2009) measured the CEOs' positive psychological traits by giving them survey items to assess themselves. Then, each CEO had on average three subordinates who rated them on their transformational leadership style. Finally, the researchers measured performance using company data from three time points: (1) when the surveys were done, (2) 1 year later, and (3) 2 years later. As expected, they found that the CEOs' levels of hope, resiliency, and optimism predicted their use of transformational leadership. Moreover, transformational leadership predicted firm performance 1 and 2 years later. Transformational leadership was slightly more important for the new business start-ups but was important for both new and established firms.

> **The Leader's Bookcase:** Go to the textbook website to download the article described above: Peterson, S. J., Walumbwa, F., Byron, K., & Myrowitz, J. (2009). CEO positive psychological traits, transformational leadership, and firm performance in high-technology start-up and established firms. *Journal of Management, 25,* 348–368.

Transparency

According to the authentic leadership philosophy, authentic leaders should be transparent, or open, about their values and beliefs. Vogelgesang and Lester (2009, p. 253) *define **transparency** in terms of the following sets of behaviors:*

- Sharing relevant information during interactions with followers;
- Being open to giving and receiving feedback;
- Being forthright about motives and reasons behind decisions.

Vogelgesang and Lester (2009) believe that transparent communication builds trust. We are more likely to trust people that we believe are being honest about their motives. They also argue that employees feel more engaged and are more creative when their leaders are open and honest about reasons for policies, mistakes they have made, or the various difficulties facing the organization. Open communication about problems encourages employees to take creative steps toward solving problems, and employees will be less likely to fear being punished for making mistakes while trying to come up with new approaches. If the boss admits trying a few approaches that didn't work, employees should feel empowered to experiment as well.

Transparent communication helps leaders and followers learn from mistakes. As a result, transparency should result in higher performance.

Norman, Avolio, and Luthans (2010) performed an interesting experiment that demonstrated the importance of transparency and positive emotions. They had 304 working adults (average age 47, with 26 years of work experience) read descriptions of a fictitious organization. The organization was described as undergoing difficult times and facing downsizing. The participants read a speech by the CEO, a newspaper article, and blog entries by employees. There were four different versions of these materials corresponding to these conditions: (1) high leader transparency, high leader positivity; (2) high leader transparency, low leader positivity; (3) low leader transparency, high leader positivity; and (4) low leader transparency, low leader positivity. The high transparency CEO held meetings and open forums to discuss the plans to handle the difficult times, whereas the low transparency CEO kept the planning process secret. In the high positive conditions, the CEO was described in terms to create the impression that he was optimistic, hopeful, and resilient, whereas in the low positive conditions, the CEO was described without these characteristics. *As expected, the researchers found that the participants rated the leaders as more effective and trustworthy when they were high on transparency and positivity.*

Pride—Deadly Sin or Positive Emotion?

What motivates people to behave ethically? Although pride is sometimes considered to be bad—it's listed as one of the seven deadly sins—perhaps it can have positive effects as well. Whether pride has positive or negative effects might depend on what type of pride we're talking about. Lewis (2000) argues that there are two different forms of pride: hubris and authentic pride. *Hubris is an excessive pride that is not based on accomplishments.* People with hubris resist feedback and fail to acknowledge or admit their mistakes. In contrast, **authentic pride** *is based on specific accomplishments that produce genuine feelings of self-worth* (Tracy & Robins, 2007). Indeed, Michie (2009) thinks that authentic pride motivates leaders to be altruistic. She argues that we feel pride when we attribute a positive outcome to our own efforts. Leaders may also be motivated to be altruistic by feelings of gratitude. She states that "**gratitude** *is felt when a positive outcome is attributed to the contributions of others*" (p. 395) [boldface and italics added]. Moreover, she argues that people experience authentic pride when they perform actions that are valued by other people. Because authentic pride produces intense pleasant feelings, it can motivate people to help others and to perform a variety of altruistic and prosocial behaviors.

Michie (2009) tested her theories with a sample of 71 managers who worked a variety of different industries, including retail, financial services, consulting, construction, health care, and manufacturing. The managers answered survey items that asked them how often they felt authentic pride and gratitude toward others at work. In addition, the managers were evaluated on altruism and social justice by roughly three direct reports each (for a total of 227 followers). Michie found that authentic pride was related to gratitude and to how the leaders were evaluated on altruism and social justice. *Thus, authentic pride based on accomplishments and feelings of self-worth can motivate leaders to be more altruistic.*

Prime Minister Winston S. Churchill, President Franklin D. Roosevelt, and Premier Josef Stalin meet at Yalta to plan winning the war. According to Ligon, Hunter, and Mumford (2008), Churchill and Roosevelt are socialized and charismatic leaders, whereas Stalin is a personalized and ideological leader.

Source: Department of Defense

Developmental Events in Famous or Infamous Leaders

Do crucial events in our early life shape our adult personalities? Are there some types of events that predispose us to have a certain leadership style or outlook on life? And are famous (or infamous) leaders more likely to have experienced certain unusual events that propelled them onto the path to fame, fortune, and influence? Ligon et al. (2008) explored these questions in their study of the lives of 120 of the most prominent leaders of the 20th century.

Ligon and her colleagues (2008) examined three pairs of related life events: originating events and turning points, anchoring events and analogous events, and redemption events and contamination events (Ligon et al., 2008 use the classification of events developed by Pillemer, 1998, 2001 and McAdams, 2001). *Originating events mark the start of a life path or career and result in goals and long term plans.* For example, as a child, Rupert Murdoch would visit the Herald newspaper with his dad, and this created his lifelong interest in publishing. *Turning points involve events that create major changes in direction*, and like originating events, they also result in the creation of new long term goals. *Anchoring events are those early life experiences that create a basis for a belief system* that guides leaders toward certain activities and away from others. The *analogous events are later life events that are similar to the anchoring events in some way*; leaders use the values and beliefs they formed during the anchoring events to guide their decision making when experiencing these later events. Finally, leaders can experience redemption and contamination events. *Redemption events occur when leaders experience negative events but later attribute some positive outcomes to the events*; these events teach leaders that they can turn around bad situations. In contrast, *contamination events are events that were initially positive but then resulted in failure or other negative outcomes*.

Ligon et al. (2008) classified leaders into two broad categories according to whether they were socialized leaders or personalized leaders (House & Howell, 1992; O'Connor, Mumford, Clifton, Gessner, & Connelly, 1995). *Socialized leaders focus on solving problems in a way that will benefit other people, such as the groups, organizations, or societies they belong to*. In contrast, *personalized leaders are motivated by their desire for personal dominance and by their own self-interests*. In addition, they classified leaders according to whether they were *charismatic* (inspirational, future oriented toward major change), *ideological* (tradition oriented, decisions made on values and beliefs), or *pragmatic* (problem-solving oriented, flexible, responds to environment) (these styles were defined in more detail in the chapter on intelligence). Because leaders with these styles could be either socialized or personalized leaders, there were six combinations of leaders. Ligon and her coauthors picked 20 leaders for each category, for a total of 120 leaders. They then examined the life narratives of the leaders as told in biographies.

The researchers found that socialized leaders (compared to personalized leaders) had considerably more early events that anchored their values and beliefs (Ligon et al., 2008). Moreover, socialized leaders had more redemption events that led them to be optimistic about their chances to overcome the later negative events they encountered in life. They also experienced more events in which they acted with kindness and compassion for others.

Ligon and her colleagues (2008) also found that ideological and pragmatic leaders differed in their early life experiences. Ideological leaders tended to have multiple anchoring events that caused them to rely on their values and beliefs to make decisions later on in their life. In contrast, pragmatic leaders had fewer early anchoring events and more originating events associated with problem solving and with gathering data and facts.

Compared to the other two types, charismatic leaders had more turning points events. This is consistent with their willingness as adult leaders to advocate major changes and a new vision.

Servant Leadership

For many years, the concept of servant leadership was popular as a philosophy of leadership. Servant leaders put their follower's interests above their own, and they are motivated by the opportunity to serve others. However, scholars have also put considerable effort into developing the principles of servant leadership into a testable set of leadership theories. Some scholars have developed scales that focused on three key dimensions of servant leadership: vision, empowerment, and service (Dennis & Winston, 2003; Page & Wong, 2000). Washington, Sutton, and Field (2006) used these scales in their study of servant leadership. They had 288 followers rate their 126 leaders on servant leadership. Sample items (p. 707): Vision: "My immediate supervisor actively seeks ways to utilize people's differences as a contribution to the group"; Empowerment: "My immediate supervisor is willing to share his or her power and authority with others"; and Service: "My immediate supervisor does not seek recognition or rewards in serving others." The researchers were curious: What type of person would become a servant leader? What personality traits would cause a leader to want to serve others? They found as expected that four personality traits together explained a considerable portion of the variance in servant leadership. *Servant leaders were higher in empathy, integrity, competence, and agreeableness.*

Servant Leadership and Hope

Barbuto and Wheeler (2006) also developed servant leadership scales based on earlier descriptions of servant leaders (Greenleaf, 1977; Spears, 1995). They developed five dimensions—*altruistic calling, emotional healing, wisdom, persuasive mapping,* and *organizational stewardship.* Searle and Barbuto (2011) further related these dimensions to positive psychological variables such as hope. Altruistic calling refers to the servant leaders' conscious decision to serve others and willingness to sacrifice their own self-interests in order to aid their followers. Servant leaders promote emotional healing by helping followers recover from traumatic events. Servant leaders display wisdom when they understand the environment and the causes and consequences of various behaviors. Searle and Barbuto argued that altruistic calling promotes hope in followers, and that emotional healing helps with the *will* component of hope, whereas wisdom helps followers figure out the *way*. Persuasive mapping refers to the ability to use sound reasoning to develop mental models of the issues facing the followers. Like wisdom, it helps followers find the path and the way to success. Because servant leaders present their mental maps in an inspiring way, Searle and Barbuto argue that persuasive mapping also helps with willpower. Although servant leaders are highly concerned with individual followers, they also care about the overall community and society. Organizational stewardship thus refers to servant leaders' desire to help the organizations they lead benefit their communities and all stakeholders involved. In terms of overall effectiveness, Searle and Barbuto (2011) argued that servant leadership should increase hope, which in turn should increase organizational performance.

Servant Leadership and Performance

With all the talk about ethics and community service, skeptics might be inclined to think that servant leaders would lack the focus on productivity necessary to have high performance. Fortunately, research consistently shows that servant leadership actually improves performance while maintaining high employee job satisfaction and organizational commitment.

A study by van Dierendonck and Nuijten (2011) developed a scale that had eight dimensions of servant leadership: standing back (i.e., backing off and letting employees take credit for their contributions), forgiveness, courage, empowerment, accountability, authenticity, humility, and stewardship. They developed and tested these scales using eight different samples (mostly employees) from the UK and the Netherlands with a combined sample size of 1,571 people. They found that *the servant leadership measures were related to employee engagement, job satisfaction, and organizational commitment.* Moreover, five out of the eight dimensions were related to self-assessed performance: empowerment, accountability, standing back, forgiveness, and stewardship.

Another study examined how servant leadership is related to high performance organizations (de Waal & Sivro, 2012). The researchers classified organizations as high performance organizations if they had both financial and nonfinancial performance that was superior to their industry competitors for a period of at least 5 years. Nonfinancial performance included factors such as customer and employee loyalty that ultimately influence performance in the long run. Based on their prior research, the authors concluded that high performance organizations have five important characteristics that contribute to their outstanding performance. The first is *management quality*, which refers to the degree to which management develops trusting relationships with employees at every level and treats people fairly and with respect. High performance organizations also focus on *workforce quality*; in other words, they recruit employees who are flexible, resilient, creative, and highly skilled. The organizations also provide training to employees to keep their skills current. High performance organizations also have a *long-term orientation*, are high on *openness and action orientation* (i.e., they are open to suggestions from employees and they take risks in order to quickly take action), and they focus on *continuous improvement and renewal*. The researchers used the same eight dimensions of servant leadership described in the previous study by van Dierendonck and Nuijten (2011). The researchers surveyed 116 employees and leaders in a medical center in the Netherlands. They found that five of the eight servant leader dimensions were significantly related to all five of the high performance characteristics. These were humility, empowerment, standing back, stewardship, and forgiveness. The other servant dimensions were also related to at least some of the dimensions. *Thus, servant leadership was related to high performance characteristics.*

Another group of researchers developed a measure of servant leadership that had seven dimensions (Liden, Wayne, Zhao, & Henderson, 2008): behaving ethically, putting subordinates first, helping subordinates grow and succeed, emotional healing, empowering, conceptual skills, and creating value for the community. Hu and Liden (2011) used this scale to study how servant leadership influences team effectiveness. They studied 71 teams that had a total of 304 employees who worked in five banks located in China. The team members rated their leaders on servant leadership, and two upper-level managers rated each team on performance and on organizational citizenship behavior. *The researchers found that servant leadership was strongly correlated with team performance and team-level organizational citizenship behavior.* In addition, servant leadership helped increase the relationship between goal clarity and team potency. With high servant leadership, high goal clarity increased team potency. In contrast, when servant leadership was low, high goal clarity reduced team potency. The authors reasoned that this is because servant leaders empower their followers and also look out for their followers' welfare, which builds commitment to the goal.

As these servant leadership studies show, once again the evidence indicates that doing good and doing well are not mutually exclusive. The following case is about Meg Whitman, who also found that you can do well by doing good. She was made CEO of Hewlett-Packard in September 2011. Before that, she was CEO of eBay (from 1998 to 2007), and she is credited with developing eBay from a small company with 30 employees into a corporation with 15,000 employees and $8 billion in revenue. She attributes her success to her values and authentic leadership style. She has many of the characteristics of socialized leaders. She has donated $30 million to her alma mater, Princeton University. In 2006, Meg and her husband set up a charitable foundation with their eBay stock worth $9.4 million. The foundation has grown in value, and Meg and her husband have used the foundation to donate $10 million dollars to Teach for America and another $2.5 million to 10 charter high schools.

Case: *Meg Whitman, former CEO of eBay: Transparency in Business*

Under Meg Whitman's leadership, eBay has changed the way the world buys and sells secondhand goods. Before eBay, individual owners of antiques, family heirlooms, used equipment, collectors' curios, etc., would take their items for sale to antique dealers, pawn shops, etc., and hope to get a fair deal. They depended on the dealers to assess their item and tell them what a fair price would be. Unless you were an expert, you would have little idea how much that silver teapot you inherited from your grandmother might be worth. Even the dealers might be uncertain—how much would someone pay for a picture of Elvis made with dried beans? As Meg Whitman pointed out in her book (with Joan Hamilton, 2010), *The Power of Many: Values for Success in Business and Life*, eBay added

Meg Whitman, former CEO of eBay and current CEO of Hewlett-Packard

Source: Flickr/Max Morse (CC-BY)

transparency to the buying and selling process. Potential buyers, including professional dealers as well as hobbyists and other nonprofessionals, would have to compete with each other to buy the products. Thus, sellers could be assured that their items would be sold at fair market price regardless of their own knowledge. At the same time, sellers had to be transparent and ethical as well: eBay set up chat rooms where hobbyists could comment on sellers who inaccurately described their products.

Pierre Omidyar founded eBay and came up with the basic idea to sell used goods over the Internet. Pierre knew he needed someone with administrative experience to grow eBay from a small start-up with 30 employees to a major corporation. Meg Whitman had experience as a consultant and as a business executive at major corporations like Disney and Hasbro. Meg left her secure, high-paying executive job to join eBay in part because she liked Pierre's sense of ethics. Meg stated that it's a myth that leaders have to be unethical to win and "that great success demands that we give up, or at least fudge, our relationship to what most of us recognize as decent, commonsense values. Honesty. Family. Community. Integrity. Generosity. Courage. Empathy" (Whitman & Hamilton, 2010, p. 5). Meg believed that if they had treated eBay community members (i.e., users) as a resource to be exploited, eBay would never have grown and prospered.

Interestingly, Pierre and Meg assumed that "most people are basically good" (Whitman & Hamilton, 2010, p. 28). In other words, they believed that most eBay community members would describe their secondhand products in a fairly accurate and transparent manner and in general would treat each other ethically. Notice that Pierre and Meg didn't say that all people are always good. They realized that fraud and theft over the Internet occurs, so they created eBay's Trust & Safety division to monitor the transactions to prevent the selling of counterfeit goods, devious bidding tactics, or other inappropriate behavior. But Meg argued that eBay works because most of their customers are basically honest. She recommended that business leaders be realistic but not cynical.

Applications: How important is transparency to your interactions with your leaders? Is transparency good for business? Have you had any experience buying things over eBay? Are most of the products described accurately? Can leaders trust most of their employees and customers to be basically good?

Sources: Noguchi, S. (2011, October 26). Whitman gives $10 million to Teach For America. Retrieved from http://www.mercurynews.com/education/ci_19196351

Whitman, M., & Hamilton, J. (2010). *The power of many: Values for success in business and in life* [Kindle edition]. New York, NY: Crown Publishers.

Put It in Practice

1. Be a mentor and a mentee: Find someone to mentor you while also mentoring others. Don't be too proud to ask for help: Even top leaders need mentors and advisors.

2. Choose your own possible future self—become the person you want to be.

3. Understand your life story and choose to interpret your life events in a way that will inspire you to achieve leadership success.

4. Develop your psychological capital: You can learn to be more confident (self-efficacious), optimistic, hopeful, resilient, and happy.

5. Improve your followers' resilience by giving them a meaningful task, empowering them, giving them a controllable task they can successfully complete, and by recognizing their accomplishments.

6. Practice authentic communication by accepting differences of opinion and by using humor to diffuse tension and establish positive relationships.

7. Use hope, optimism, and resiliency to aid your transformational leadership style and boost performance.

8. Create trusting relationships with your employees by being transparent; share information with others, be honest and open in your feedback and accept feedback from others, and be forthright about your motives.

9. Don't be as Greek tragedy: Avoid hubris. Develop your authentic pride based on your actual accomplishments and your positive contributions to others' welfare.

10. Understand how developmental events influence your life and leadership approach (charismatic, ideological, and pragmatic). You can choose to be a socialized leader concerned with the welfare of others instead of a personalized leader.

11. Be a servant leader: You can boost employee commitment and job performance by serving those you lead.

12. You don't have to give up your ethical values to be successful: Being an ethical, transparent leader may actually help you achieve great success. Be realistic but not cynical: Most people are basically good!

Exercises

1. **What's Your Story? Develop Your Narrative Timeline**

    A. Develop a list of some of the major events in your life—those events that have shaped your personality, values, and life goals. Do these events form a narrative timeline so that you can see how early events shaped later outcomes?

    B. How many of these events were capable of being interpreted in different ways? For example, could you have interpreted a sports loss as a sign that this was not the right sport for you or as a sign that you needed to practice more?

C. How many of the events could be classified:

    a. Originating events   _____

    b. Turning points   _____

    c. Anchoring events   _____

    d. Analogous events   _____

    e. Redemption events   _____

    f. Contamination events   _____

D. Which of these events have helped develop your leadership potential?

E. Share one of these events either in a small group discussion or in class discussion (as directed by your instructor).

2. **Improve Your Psychological Capital: confidence (self-efficacy), hope, optimism, and resiliency**

Form groups and share examples of events that called upon you to have confidence, hope, optimism, and resiliency. Describe to your classmates what you did during the event to bolster your psychological capital and leadership skills. Which tactics worked best? Prepare one or two examples to share with the class.

Visit the Student Study Site at **www.sagepub.com/humphreyel** for these additional tools:

- Learning Goals
- Leader's Book Case Articles
- Web Resources
- Student Self Assessments

References

Avolio, B. J. (2005). *Leadership development in balance: MADE/Born.* Mahwah, NJ: Lawrence Earlbaum.

Avolio, B. J., & Gardner, W. L. (2005). Authentic leadership development: Getting to the root of positive forms of leadership. *The Leadership Quarterly, 16*, 315–338.

Avolio, B. J., Gardner, W. L., Walumbwa, F. O., Luthans, F., & May, D. R. (2004). Unlocking the mask: A look at the process by which authentic leaders impact follower attitudes and behaviors. *The Leadership Quarterly, 15*, 801–823.

Bandura, A. (1998). Personal and collective efficacy in human adaptation and change. In J. G. Adair, D. Belanger, & K. L. Dion, (Eds.), *Advances in psychological science: Vol. 1. Personal, social and cultural aspects* (pp. 51–71). Hove, UK: Psychology Press.

Barbuto, J. E., & Wheeler, D. W. (2006). Scale development and construct clarification of servant leadership. *Group & Organization Management, 31*, 300–326.

Bartone, P. T. (2006). Resilience under military operational stress: Can leaders influence hardiness? *Military Psychology, 18*(Suppl.), S131–S148.

Cameron, K. S., Dutton, J. E., & Quinn, R. E. (2003). *Positive organizational scholarship.* San Francisco, CA: Barrett-Koelher.

Dennis, R., & Winston, B. E. (2003). A factor analysis of Page and Wong's servant leadership instrument. *Leadership & Organization Development Journal, 24*, 455–459.

de Waal, A., & Sivro, M. (2012). The relation between servant leadership, organizational performance, and the high-performance organization framework. *Journal of Leadership & Organizational Studies, 19*, 173–190.

Gardner, W. L., & Schermerhorn, J. R., (2004). Unleashing individual potential: Performance gains through positive organizational behavior and authentic leadership. *Organizational Dynamics, 33*, 270–281.

George, B. (2003). *Authentic leadership: Rediscovering the secrets of creating lasting value.* San Francisco, CA: Jossey-Bass.

Greenleaf, R. K. (1977). *Servant leadership: A journey into the nature of legitimate power and greatness.* Mahwah, NJ: Paulist Press.

Hannah, S. T., Avolio, B. J., Luthans, F., & Harms, P. D. (2008). Leadership efficacy: Review and future directions. *The Leadership Quarterly, 19*, 669–692.

Hannah, S. T., & Luthans, F. (2008). A cognitive affective processing explanation of positive leadership: Toward theoretical understanding of the role of psychological capital. In R. H. Humphrey (Ed.), *Research in management: Vol. 7. Affect and emotion: New directions in management theory and research.* Charlotte, NC: Information Age Publishing.

House, R. J., & Howell, J. M. (1992). Personality and charismatic leadership. *The Leadership Quarterly, 3*, 81–108.

Hu, J., & Liden, R. C. (2011). Antecedents of team potency and team effectiveness: An examination of goal and process clarity and servant leadership. *Journal of Applied Psychology, 96*, 851–862.

Jones, E., Woolven, R., Durodie, W., & Wessely, S. (2004). Public panic and morale: A reassessment of civilian reactions during the Blitz and World War 2. *Journal of Social History, 17*, 463–479.

Kobasa, S. C., Maddi, S. R., & Kahn, S. (1982). Hardiness and health: A prospective study. *Journal of Personality and Social Psychology, 42*, 168–177.

Larson, M., & Luthans, F. (2006). Potential added value of psychological capital in predicting work attitudes. *Journal of Leadership and Organizational Studies, 13*, 44–61.

Lewis, M. (2000). Self-conscious emotions: Embarrassment, pride, shame, and guilt. In M. Lewis & J. M. Haviland-Jones (Eds.), *Handbook of emotions* (pp. 623–636). New York, NY: Guilford.

Liden, R. C., Wayne, S. J., Zhao, H., & Henderson, D. (2008). Servant leadership: Development of a multidimensional measure and multilevel assessment. *Leadership Quarterly, 19,* 161–177.

Ligon, G. S., Hunter, S. T., & Mumford, M. D. (2008). Development of outstanding leadership: A life narrative approach. *The Leadership Quarterly, 19,* 312–334.

Luthans, F. (2002). The need for and meaning of positive organizational behavior. *Journal of Organizational Behavior, 23,* 695–706.

Luthans, F., Avolio, B. J., Avey, J. B., & Norman, S. M. (2007). Positive psychological capital: Measurement and relationship with performance and satisfaction. *Personnel Psychology, 60,* 541–572.

Luthans, F., Avolio, B. J., Walumbwa, F., & Li, W. (2005). The psychological capital of Chinese workers: Exploring the relationship with performance. *Management and Organization Review, 1,* 247–269.

Luthans, F., Luthans, K. W., & Luthans, B. C. (2004). Positive psychological capital: Beyond human and social capital. *Business Horizons, 47,* 45–50.

Lyubomirsky, S. (2008). *The how of happiness: A scientific approach to getting the life you want.* New York, NY: The Penguin Press.

Maddi, S. R., & Kobasa, S. C. (1984). *The hardy executive.* Homewood, IL: Dow Jones-Irwin.

Masten, A. S., & Reed, M. G. J. (2002). Resilience in development. In C.R. Snyder & S. J. Lopez, (Eds.), *Handbook of positive psychology* (pp. 74–88). Oxford, UK: Oxford University Press.

McAdams, D. P. (2001). The psychology of life stories. *Review of General Psychology, 5,* 100–123.

Michie, S. (2009). How positive emotions influence the prosocial behaviors of organizational leaders. *Journal of Leadership & Organizational Studies, 15,* 393–403.

Neider, L. L., & Schriesheim, C. A. (2011). The Authentic Leadership Inventory (ALI): Development and empirical tests. *The Leadership Quarterly, 22,* 1146–1164.

Nelson, D., & Cooper, C. L. (Eds.). (2007). *Positive organizational behavior: Accentuating the positive at work.* Thousand Oaks, CA: Sage.

Noguchi, S. (2011, October 26). Whitman gives $10 million to Teach For America. Retrieved from http://www.mercurynews.com/education/ci_19196351

Norman, S. M., Avolio, B. J., & Luthans, F. (2010). The impact of positivity and transparency on trust in leaders and their perceived effectiveness. *The Leadership Quarterly, 21,* 350–364.

O'Connor, J. A., Mumford, M. D., Clifton, T. C., Gessner, T. E., & Connelly, M. S. (1995). Charismatic leadership and destructiveness: A historiometric study. *The Leadership Quarterly, 6,* 529–555.

Page, D., & Wong, T. P. (2000). A conceptual framework for measuring servant leadership. In S. Adjibolosoo (Ed.), *The human factor in shaping the course of history and development.* Lanham, MD: University Press of America.

Peterson S., & Luthans, F. (2003). The positive impact of development of hopeful leaders. *Leadership and Organization Development Journal, 24,* 26–31.

Peterson, S. J., Walumbwa, F., Byron, K., & Myrowitz, J. (2009). CEO positive psychological traits, transformational leadership, and firm performance in high-technology start-up and established firms. *Journal of Management, 25,* 348–368.

Pillemer, D. B. (1998). *Momentous events, vivid memories.* Cambridge, MA: Harvard University Press.

Pillemer, D. B. (2001). Momentous events and the life story. *Review of General Psychology, 5*(2), 123–134.

Resilient. (1985). *American Heritage Dictionary* (p. 586). New York, NY: Dell.

Ritchie, E. C., Leavitt, F., & Hanish, S. (2006). The mental health response to the 9/11 attack on the Pentagon. In Y. Neria, R. Gross, R. Marshall, & E. Susser (Eds.), *9/11: Mental health in the wake of a terrorist attack.* New York, NY: Cambridge University Press.

Searle, T. P., & Barbuto, J. E. (2011). Servant leadership, hope, and organizational virtuousness: A framework exploring positive micro and macro behaviors and performance impact. *Journal of Leadership & Organizational Studies, 18,* 107–117.

Seligman, M. E. P. (1998). *Learned optimism.* New York, NY: Pocket Books.

Shamir, B., & Eilam, G. (2005). "What's your story?" A life-stories approach to authentic leadership development. *The Leadership Quarterly, 16,* 395–417.

Snyder, C. R. (2000). *Handbook of hope.* San Diego, CA: Academic Press.

Sparrowe, R. T. (2005). Authentic leadership and the narrative self. *The Leadership Quarterly, 16,* 419–439.

Spears, L. C. (1995). Servant-leadership and the Greenleaf legacy. In L. C. Spears (Ed.), *Reflections on leadership* (pp. 1–14). New York, NY: Wiley.

Tracy, J. L., & Robins, R. W. (2007). The psychological structure of pride: A tale of two facets. *Journal of Personality and Social Psychology, 92,* 506–525.

Tugade, M. M., Fredrickson, B. L., & Barrett, L. F. (2004). Psychological resilience and positive emotional granularity. *Journal of Personality, 72,* 1161–1190.

van Dierendonck, D., & Nuijten, I. (2011). The servant leadership survey: Development and validation of a multidimensional measure. *Journal of Business and Psychology, 26,* 249–267.

Vogelgesang, G. R., & Lester, P. B., (2009). Transparency: How leaders can get results by laying it on the line. *Organizational Dynamics, 38,* 252–260.

Washington, R. R., Sutton, C. D., & Field, H. S. (2006). Individual differences in servant leadership: The roles of values and personality. *Leadership & Organization Development Journal, 27,* 700–716.

Whitman, M., & Hamilton, J. (2010). *The power of many: Values for success in business and in life* [Kindle edition]. New York, NY: Crown Publishers.

11

Identity Processes: Individual, Relational, Social, Organizational, and Cultural

Cross-Cultural Differences in Leadership
Case: *Carnegie Creates His Ideal Self*
Put It in Practice
Exercises: (1) Relational Identity Exercise and (2) Collective and Social Identity

Case: *Martha Stewart—People Want Leaders They Can Identify With*

Like most leaders, Martha is a controversial person. Unlike in fairy tales, real leaders are actual people with all the mix of good and bad traits that being human entails. And like some other human beings, she's had some trouble obeying the law (her insider trading is nothing to take lightly). But whatever her faults, it is clear that through her work with discount retailers and her advice about do-it-yourself projects, she has added a touch of affordable elegance to millions of working-class and middle-class homes.

Martha Stewart became America's first female self-made billionaire entrepreneur because she recognized that people want and need leaders, role models, and people they can identify with. Most cookbooks are filled with recipes and have only one or two pages about the author. In contrast, Martha Stewart's first book, *Entertaining*, devotes only about half the book to recipes. The rest of the book portrays Martha and her family living the good life entertaining at her Turkey Hill residence and gardens. The book also includes numerous photos of her and her family as well as suggestions about how the readers can follow Martha's lead into a more elegant lifestyle. The result? A publishing phenomenon—the bestselling cookbook in over 2 decades. Her next three books were also bestsellers and resulted in her gaining her lucrative endorsement deal with Kmart.

Martha used this same formula with her TV shows and her magazine, *Martha Stewart Living*. When *Martha Stewart Living* first hit the newsstands,

Martha Stewart looks elegant at the 2009 Metropolitan Opera in New York City.

other publishers criticized it because it featured Martha instead of focusing 100% on recipes, gardens, furniture, and architecture. They thought she was simply being egotistical, and they launched their own competing magazines that focused on the product instead of on an actual person. What happened? Martha's magazine continued to grow in sales while her competitors floundered. Unlike her competitors, Martha realized that her fans wanted to see someone they could admire and identify with enjoying the lifestyles featured in her magazines and television shows.

Martha realized the value of creating positive moods and emotions. Many TV shows portray various negative emotions in their efforts to be dramatic. Stewart realized that there was a need for a more positive, relaxing show. Her shows featured pleasant music and had an overall happy tone—many of her fans watched her shows every day because of the enjoyable moods they evoked. Martha also knew the value of displaying positive emotions during her numerous television appearances and public presentations—at one time, the only other woman in the world with more media attention was the Queen of England (this was even before Martha's stock scandal and brief jail term). She had an incredibly hectic schedule and as CEO she had to solve numerous frustrating problems, but when the cameras came on, she could put her frustrations aside and portray the positive, uplifting emotions her fans needed.

Martha Stewart illustrates the wide variety of roles a leader must play—roles that sometimes seem contradictory. As a former stockbroker, she knew how to use the stock market to raise money so she could buy her magazine and TV shows from their corporate owners and to become her own boss: a shrewd corporate move that you might not expect from someone known for homemaking skills. As CEO of Martha Stewart Living Omnimedia, she provided leadership for the employees who worked on her magazines, television shows, DVDs, Internet, and retail businesses. Martha's a perfectionist, and she drove her employees just as hard as she drove herself. Her angry outbursts at employees might seem inconsistent with the pleasant, charming identity she presented on TV. Nonetheless, both sides of her, the demanding boss and the gracious host, may reflect her true, multifaceted personality.

Martha Stewart was convicted of lying to federal investigators about a stock tip involving less than $50,000 worth of stock, and she spent 5 months in prison as a result. The short stint in prison did not seriously affect the ability of her magazine to offer decorating tips, recipes, etc., but it did influence the degree to which her fans identified with her. Who wants to identify with a

(Continued)

(Continued)

jailbird? As a result, she lost millions of fans and hundreds of millions of dollars in the stock value of her company. However, Martha has continued working on her magazines and TV shows, and almost two million people now follow her on Twitter. It's clear that many people still identify with her.

Applications: Do you think most people want to have a leader? Someone they can look up to, admire, and identify with? Do companies that have highly visible leaders, such as Martha Stewart or Steve Jobs, attract more loyal customers than companies without high profile leaders? How often do people have identities, such as the demanding boss and the gracious host, that seem inconsistent to observers? Martha accepted her punishment (instead of waging lengthy legal appeals) and did her time in jail; should her fans accept her back?

Sources: Byron, C. (2002). *Martha, INC.: The incredible story of Martha Stewart Living Omnimedia.* New York, NY: Wiley.

Carr, A. Martha Stewart's Twitter tips. *FASTCOMPANY.* Retrieved June 16, 2010 from http://www.fastcompany.com/1660328/facebook-and-twitter-tips-from-martha-stewart?partner=homepage_newsletter

Martha Stewart is a good example of how important leaders are to organizations and to people. Without the intense identification that many of her fans felt for her, her business enterprises would never have succeeded, and many observers wonder what will happen to her magazines and other businesses once she is gone. Martha the gracious host behaved quite differently than Martha the demanding boss. Thus, Martha also illustrates how we have different identities according to the roles we are playing. Do you act the same way at work as you do when you are hanging out with your friends on the weekend? Chances are you act quite differently. At work, you may dress more formally or even wear special clothing, such as a nurse's outfit, a doctor's white overcoat, a mechanic's outfit, or a company shirt or blouse. You might speak more formally at work while using slang or casual language with your friends. You probably act differently with different groups of friends as well. Perhaps with your sports team one side of your personality comes out while with another group a different aspect emerges. We may be serious, formal, and practical with one group of people while with another we are humorous and carefree. In other words, most of us adopt at least a slightly different persona depending on who we are with, what we are doing, and where we are at. In other words, all of us have multiple identities that we draw upon as needed.

We also have several layers of identity. At the most basic level is our individual identity. However, we also have social identities that reflect our one-on-one relationships, our group identities, our organizational identities, and our cultural and national identities. Although social psychologists and sociologists have studied identities for over a century, leadership scholars have only begun to pay significant attention to identity theory in the last quarter century. These scholars have begun to examine how leaders can build followers' identification with their roles and with their organizations. In this chapter, we will explore the following questions:

What are the components and levels of identity?

How can leaders influence their followers' identification with their job and thus their job performance and organizational commitment?

How do organizational members adopt leadership and other professional identities?

What are the main dimensions that distinguish cross-cultural differences in leadership?

The Components of Identity

Ashforth, Harrison, and Corley (2008) argued that we can think of *identity in narrow terms, comprising our self-definition, our values, and our feelings about our self*. Or they stated we can think about *identity in somewhat broader terms that include our goals, beliefs, skills and abilities, and typical behaviors*. Their model is presented in Figure 11.1, and you can also learn more about their model by downloading their article from the Leaders' Bookcase section in the textbook website. As Figure 11.1 indicates, our identity concerns our deepest beliefs about who we are, what we stand for, and what we can do. Our core identity includes not only our beliefs about ourselves, but also our feelings about ourselves, our values, and other people that we identify with. At the broadest level, our identity consists of our everyday behaviors—we are what we do.

The Leaders' Bookcase: Ashforth, B. E., Harrison, S. H., & Corley, K. E. (2008). Identification in organizations: An examination of four fundamental questions. *Journal of Management, 34,* 325–374.

Figure 11.1   Identification: A Fuzzy Set

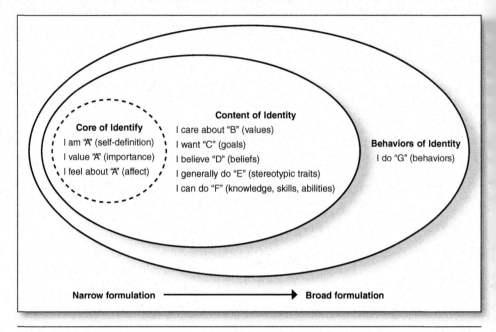

Source: Ashforth, B. E., Harrison, S. H., & Corley, K. E. (2008). Identification in organizations: An examination of four fundamental questions. *Journal of Management, 34,* 325–374.

Levels of Identity

We have many different levels of identity, including our individual identity, our interpersonal identity, and our collective identity (Brewer & Gardner, 1996). In addition, we can analyze identity at organizational and cultural levels. The different levels of identity are defined as follows:

Individual and independent identity: Our **individual identity** *is based on our perceptions of our individual traits, characteristics, and behaviors, especially those that distinguish us from other people.* At this level, self-esteem is based on a comparison with other people (Hogg & Abrams, 1990). People may label themselves with favorable terms that highlight some skill or ability that they possess while giving unflattering labels to those low on that skill (Ashforth & Humphrey, 1995, 1997). When an individual identity is activated, people usually operate to maximize their own self-interests rather than considering group or collective interests.

Interpersonal and relational identity: Our **interpersonal and relational identity** *is based on our interdependent role relationship with another individual, such as our relationship with a spouse, coworker, or supervisor or subordinate* (Brewer & Gardner, 1996; Sluss & Ashforth, 2007). At this level, people derive their self-esteem from fulfilling their obligations and duties to their partner; when people feel a sense of interpersonal identity, they take their partner's interests into account.

Collective identity and social identity: **Social identity** *has been defined as "that* <u>part</u> *of an individual's self-concept which derives from his knowledge of his membership of a social group (or groups) together with the value and emotional significance attached to that membership"* (Tajfel, 1978, p. 63) [boldface and italics added, underlining added to show original italics]. When people identify with a group, they care about the welfare of the group and part of their self-esteem is based on their group membership. People want to belong to high status groups, and as a result, people are more likely to identify with high status groups. As Tajfel and Turner (1986) argued, our social identities have an evaluative component: We compare the groups that we belong to with other groups. This can create *labeling contests when members of different groups attempt to label their own group with high status descriptions while assigning less prestigious labels to rival groups* (Ashforth & Humphrey, 1997).

As the above definitions indicate, *when our individual identity is activated, we care about our own welfare; when our relational identify is activated, we care about our partner as well; and when our collective identity is aroused, we care about the group.* People may also care about their organizations and their national or ethnic culture.

Organizational identity: Albert and Whetten (1985) defined **organizational identity** *in terms of properties of the organization that are distinctive, enduring, and central to the way the organization operates.* For example, Starbucks and McDonalds have distinct organizational identities. This is why buying coffee at Starbucks is quite a different experience than buying coffee at McDonalds. Their distinct identities and culture also explain why working at Starbucks is a considerably different experience than working at McDonalds. Both organizations are highly successful, yet in their own way.

Cultural or national identity: In addition, *there are cultural values and characteristics that distinguish cultures and nations from one another and create distinctive **national or cultural identities**.* Cultures differ in their beliefs about how leaders should behave. Leaders who manage people in different cultures need to understand these differences if they want to be successful.

Collective Identity and Altruistic Leadership

Sosik, Jung, and Dinger (2009) wanted to know how managers' levels of identity influenced their altruistic behaviors and job performance. They had 218 leaders provide measures of their identity. These leaders were frontline managers (20%), middle managers (65%), senior managers (12%), and executives (3%). They were on average 31 years old and had 8 years of company tenure. They then had 935 subordinates rate the managers on their altruistic behaviors at work. The managers' job performance was evaluated by their own superiors. The researchers found that the managers' altruistic behaviors were a good predictor of their job performance. Managers who were most concerned with their individual identity were less likely to perform altruistic behaviors. Relational identity was not related to altruistic behaviors. The managers who were high on collective or social identity were more likely to perform altruistic behaviors. Their model (slightly simplified) found the following:

Leaders' Collective Identity →
Altruistic Behaviors → Leader Performance

Their study is consistent with prior research which found that empathic, caring, ethical leadership helps people emerge as leaders and perform more effectively.

Identity, Roles, and Cognitive Categories

Roles and identity: Much of our identity and sense of self is based on the roles we play in life. Thus, Stets and Burke (2000) *defined core identity in terms of roles and state that* **core identity** *is "the categorization of the self as an occupant of a role, and the incorporation, into the self, of the meanings and expectations associated with that role and its performance"* (p. 225) [italics and boldface added].

Cognitive categories: We usually think of ourselves in terms of our occupational roles such as student, teacher, accountant, or supervisor as well as in other roles such as parent, athlete, and team member. Researchers argue that we have knowledge structures about these roles that tell us how to behave as a parent or child, how to perform as a student, and what to do as a subordinate, manager, or leader. In essence, these knowledge structures form the core of our self and our identity (Kihlstrom, Beer, & Klein, 2003; Lord, Brown, & Freiberg, 1999). These knowledge structures form cognitive categories. Each category is called to mind as needed. Our total knowledge structure about how to behave in every situation and role is too large to be held in working memory at any one time. The situation we are in cues which cognitive category we call to mind and access at any given moment.

Multiple selves: Because we have multiple categories, we have multiple selves that can be quite distinct (Markus & Nurius, 1986; Markus & Wurf, 1987; Thoits, 1983). We draw upon these identities as needed—the serious, ambitious, hardworking identity while we are at work; the carefree and fun loving identity while at a party; the loving, caring, and supportive identity while with our children. Even within the workplace we have multiple selves that correspond to our multiple roles at work (Ashforth & Johnson, 2001). Navigating between these multiple identities can be tricky (Ashforth, 2001).

For example, when we are at a party or nightclub, we may activate a cognitive category—a sense of self—that tells us that we talk loud, laugh a lot, perhaps even act a little wild and irresponsible. In the office, however, we may have quite a different sense of who we are. We may frown at those who bend the rules, come in late, speak loudly, etc. *Because our working memory does not allow us to hold both sets of cognitive categories in mind at once, we are often not aware of how different the two sets of identities can be.* Middle managers, for example, are both leaders and followers: They enact leader roles when supervising those below them but play subordinate roles when interacting with their own superiors. When a subordinate identity is activated, someone's self-conception about how employees should act may be quite different from that same person's perception as to how employees should behave when their own leader identity is triggered. When acting as a manager and leader, a person may express scorn and firm disapproval of subordinate behaviors such as being slightly tardy to meetings, while as a subordinate, the same person may call up a cognitive category and sense of self that treats such behaviors more leniently.

Although some part of our self varies with each role, there are some parts of our self-identity that are active in almost every setting and are part of all or almost all of our multiple selves. Some people's self-identities may, for example, include being punctual in almost every setting. Sometimes the roles that we perform cause us to act in ways inconsistent with how we behave in the majority of our other roles. This inconsistency may cause us to feel that the role we are playing is inconsistent with our true self. People in these situations may feel they are being forced to behave in an inauthentic way. For example, suppose someone is normally easygoing, friendly, and unassertive. When placed in a supervisor role where he or she has to frequently reprimand tardy or poor performing subordinates, the supervisor may feel that the leadership role is inconsistent with his or her true self.

Ashforth and Humphrey (1993) stated,

> Proponents of social identity theory suggest that individuals who strongly identify with their organizational roles (or, relatedly, their occupations, departments, or organizations)—that is, individuals who regard their roles as a central, salient, and valued component of who they are—are apt to feel most authentic when they are conforming to role expectations. (p. 98)

Thus, the more a leader identifies with the leadership role, the more authentic the leader will feel when acting as a leader. Burke (1991), for example, argued that the psychological effects of performing a behavior depends upon how relevant that behavior is to your identity. Someone who strongly identifies with being a leader may feel joy when successfully performing a leadership task, but someone who does not identify with the leadership role may not care whether the task was done successfully or not. Failure to perform a task that is relevant to your identity can be stressful, while successfully performing an identity relevant task can enhance your psychological well-being (Thoits, 1991). For example, an engineer with a strong leadership self-identity might be elated to be appointed to chair a committee, whereas an engineer whose self-identity centers on his or her mathematical skills might regard the appointment as an unpleasant chore.

Although identities have a strong cognitive component, emotional processes are important as well. Indeed, as we will see in the chapter on charismatic leadership, charismatic leaders use emotional appeals to establish a common identity with their followers. We are more likely to identify with a leader when we feel an emotional attachment to the leader. In addition, Humphrey (2012) argued emotions are important to every level of identification and that leaders need to take a role in creating emotional climates that promote identification. At the individual identity level, people are more likely to identify with their role when they feel the emotions that are appropriate to that role. For example, caregivers are more likely to identify with their occupations when they genuinely experience compassion when helping others. Leaders can promote identification by role modeling and displaying the appropriate emotions and by creating affective events that promote the desired emotions. Leaders may also need to reduce or remove events that create emotions like frustration that hinder identification. At the interpersonal and relational level of identification, leaders can promote identification with individual followers by creating resonance and interactive, two-way empathic bonds. We are more likely to identify with others when we feel they are on the same emotional wavelength that we are on and when they are experiencing the same emotions that we are feeling. Likewise, leaders can promote collective and social identification by creating common emotional bonds among team members.

> **Self-Assessment:** Visit the textbook website to compare the relative importance of your different identities.

Leader Identity, Follower Identity, and Effectiveness

Barbara van Knippenberg, Daan van Knippenberg, David De Cremer, and Michael A. Hogg (2005) outlined some of the ways in which identity processes can influence leadership effectiveness (see also their earlier review, van Knippenberg, van Knippenberg, De Cremer, & Hogg, 2004). First, they argued that leaders can have an important influence on their followers' identity and sense of self (e.g., Lord et al., 1999). As Figure 11.1 indicates, our identities include our beliefs about our capabilities as well as our beliefs about what it is that we desire and value. Leaders can increase their subordinates' performance by helping them identify with their role. This would increase their followers' motivation—performing the job correctly would be a way to validate their new identity as a teacher, engineer, accountant, truck driver, etc. Leaders also help shape their followers' sense of individual or collective efficacy. Our beliefs about what we are capable of doing are an important part of our identity. This approach states the following:

Leaders → Followers' Identity (efficacy, values, goals) →
Followers' Performance

Second, van Knippenberg et al. (2005) argued that follower identity also determines how the followers react to the leader (Hogg & van Knippenberg, 2003). When followers identify more strongly with the group or collective identity, they respond better to leaders who are also seen as prototypical of the group (i.e., the leaders are seen to have personal characteristics that best represent the group as a whole). Moreover, followers who strongly identify with the collective want their leaders to be group oriented and to treat the members of the group as a group rather than as a collection of individuals.

Building Follower Identification

Prior research has described a number of ways in which leaders and organizations can shape followers' identity. Michael Pratt (2000) described the ways in which Amway used identification tactics to build intense loyalty among its distributors. For example, Amway encouraged their employees to socialize together, thus building a sense of collective identity, and to identify themselves as Amway people in all aspects of their lives. Many other organizations such as universities and colleges, military organizations, and religious groups also attempt to extend their followers' identification with the organization to a large part of their lives. Universities, for example, encourage students to socialize with other college students by hosting a wide range of activities unrelated to studying and learning. Thus, universities offer music events, free movies, athletic events, and a wide range of clubs and other activities on campus to encourage students to make the college experience an all-encompassing part of their identity. The extent to which these tactics are successful is demonstrated by the large number of alumni who return to college campuses for sporting and other events decades after they've graduated. Organizations such as Google use similar tactics by creating campus-like company headquarters and by offering a wide range of events that encourage employees to eat together (company dining rooms, local hangouts) and spend time together.

Organizations also frequently use clothing and distinctive fashion apparel to create a common identity and to help people take on their occupational and organizational identity (Dutton, Dukerich, & Harquail, 1994; Pratt & Rafaeli, 1997). Moreover, organizations use a wide variety of symbols (logos, distinctive architecture, furniture, equipment, flags, mascots, color schemes, and job titles) and specialized language and jargon to create a unique organizational identity (Pratt & Rafaeli, 2001).

> **Applications:** What does your organization do to promote identification with the organization?

Employees also have to take initiative in forming their own identity. As the following research found, this is not always a simple process.

Constructing Your Identity

Many professions require a deep level of commitment and personal identification from those who want to join their profession. Students who identify with their future occupation—who see the occupation as consistent with their personal identity—are also more likely to endure the hardships and lengthy training it takes to obtain professional status. This process is especially important in the medical field, which requires would-be doctors to endure lengthy residences and internships as well as medical school. Unfortunately, sometimes reality conflicts with our naïve expectations about what a profession is really like.

This McDonalds is the third one built and the oldest one still in use; it was built in 1953 in Downey, California, and shows some of the early features of the McDonalds' architecture—notice the two arches used as decorative supports and the arch for the sign. McDonalds' arches are a key part of its brand identity and have helped make it one of the most recognized brands in the world.

Source: Wikipedia/Bryan Hong (CC-BY-SA)

Pratt and his two colleagues (Pratt, Rockmann, & Kaufmann, 2006) conducted a 6-year-long study to find out how medical residents and interns adjusted their identities to match the reality of their occupations. They found that medical residents and interns often encounter "***work-identity integrity violations: an experienced mismatch between what physicians did and who they were***" (p. 235) [italics and boldface added]. The following quote illustrates how a first year intern had to perform many tasks that were not part of the intern's initial expectations and identity:

> An intern [first-year medical resident] is something like a *secretary* and a *social worker* and a *physical therapist* and an *errand boy.* You just take care of business as an intern. . . . That means you know—that means writing down hundreds of pages a day of text into different places—patients' charts and forms. It is just an unbelievable pile of paperwork that somebody has to do. . . . The interns get left to do all that sort of crap. (Pratt et al., 2006, p. 243)

Pratt and his colleagues discovered that the interns and residents had to do what they called *identity customization* to fit their identity to their actual job. In other words, the residents couldn't change their work to match their naïve expectations about what doctors actually did, so they had to change their identity to match the reality. For example, they found that over time some residents began talking about being doctors in a more encompassing way that included caring for patients in wide variety of ways as a positive outcome—as being their ally, advocate, friend, guide, etc. These residents engaged in *identity enrichment* to broaden their understanding of what their professional identity encompassed. Other residents used a variety of other tactics to help them handle the work-identity violations.

Applications: Think of your first professional job or your first experiences as a manager trainee, assistant manager, or other initial leadership experience. How did this match your initial expectations or sense of identity? When thinking about your initial experiences, how would you have filled in the blanks in this sentence: "A _____ is something like a _____ and a _____ and a _____ and an _____." How would you have filled this sentence out after a few years of experience? Did you come to identify more with the role?

Claim Your Leadership Identity

There is often a struggle for leadership positions, whether the positions are formal or informal. Among peer work groups and committees, an informal leader often emerges. Even when someone is a manager and has formal leadership authority, there can still be a struggle for leadership. Subordinates do not always recognize or respect a manager's expertise and leadership abilities. Managers themselves may also doubt their own leadership abilities. If they do not see others responding appropriately to their leadership, they may not think of themselves as leaders. DeRue and Ashford (2010) discuss this issue in their article, "Who Will Lead and Who Will Follow? A Social Process of Leadership Identity Construction in Organizations." According to their model, *people who want to be leaders have to **claim the leadership role**, in other words, they have to present themselves to others as a leader.* However, you can't be a leader without followers. In order for your claim to be successful, others have to accept your leadership claim and adopt the role of follower. In other words, *they have to **grant you leadership status** by responding to you as a leader and by reinforcing your leadership claims with* *their own follower behaviors.* This is a reciprocal process, and people need some reinforcement of their role as a valued subordinate if they are going to reciprocate your claim as a leader. When people find others responding to them as a leader, then people begin to internalize the role of leader and make it part of their identity.

DeRue and Ashford (2010) argue that problems are likely to occur when would-be leaders and followers have different cognitive categories or expectations about the roles of followers and leaders. For example, they describe how a manager might have a cognitive category that tells him or her that leaders act in a hierarchical, top-down manner when interacting with subordinates. If the subordinates also believe this is how leaders should behave, then there would be no problem. But if the subordinates' mental model of how leaders should behave is based on concepts of shared leadership, then problems would ensue, and the subordinates would resist reinforcing the manager's self-image as a leader.

PERSONAL REFLECTIONS: *MY FAMILY, FRIENDS, COWORKERS, AND STUDENTS: THE HEART OF MY IDENTITY*

Social identity theory states that our relationships with others form a crucial part of our own personal identity. We carry in our hearts, our minds, and our identity a piece of our family members, friends, coworkers, leaders, and mentors. My two children are certainly a core part of my identity. Here's a sample of how my identity as a scholar, teacher, and leader has been formed by my relationships with other people.

Self-esteem and My Mother. My mom could have taught Carl Rogers a thing or two about the benefits of unconditional positive regard. She showered me with praise and love and an unwavering belief in my potential. Like many American mothers, she always told me that I could grow up to be president. Psychologists tell us that our self-esteem is very heavily influenced by our early childhood experiences. In my mid-30s, I encountered some difficult times and some challenges to my self-esteem. Although by that time I had won many academic awards and honors—objective evidence for self-efficacy—I found my thoughts flying back for support to those early childhood days with my mom—the true source of my self-esteem.

My Coauthors and My Identity as a Scholar. I identify with being a scholar and active researcher—an identity validated by my publications with my coauthors. These coauthors also shaped my research identity by helping me choose what topics to investigate; because of them, I see myself as an emotions researcher, an identity researcher, and a leadership scholar.

My Students and My Identity as a Teacher. I also strongly identify with being an effective teacher. I've tried to claim the status of being a good teacher by putting a lot of effort into my teaching; fortunately, my students have reciprocated by granting me the status of an effective teacher with their words of praise. Although a few words of praise may seem like a simple thing, they are the food that sustains my identity as an effective teacher. I especially enjoy running into former students who greet me with smiles and comments about how class was awesome. These authentic displays mean a lot to me. When I think of myself as a teacher, I often recall very specific interactions with students. These students have become part of my self-concept, part of my identity, part of who I am. Each semester, my sense of identity is reaffirmed by my positive interactions with students, by their lively responses to my questions, by their spirited discussions, and by their willingness to open up and share their own stories and life events. These students have my profound thanks and gratitude for helping make me who I am.

Your Turn to Reflect: Who has helped make you who you are? Can you enrich your own identity by developing closer, more supportive relationships with others? Are there times when you have needed to distance yourself from others in order to build your individual identity?

Are You Dedicated?

Ng and Feldman (2008) wanted to know what makes someone dedicated, what makes someone willing to put in the long hours necessary for career success? They thought that the degree to which people identified with their jobs would be an important predictor of the number of hours that people worked. People who identified with their jobs and occupations, who saw their work as a central and salient part of their identity, should be more willing to devote extra hours to their careers. **Work centrality *was defined as the "Self-reported extent to which work is central to one's life"*** (Ng & Feldman, 2008, p. 865) [italics and boldface added]. Ng and Feldman tested their theory by conducting a meta-analysis of 222 independent samples (all but eight were of working adults). The people in the studies averaged 42.4 hours of work per week, 48 percent were female and most were Caucasian (96%), and the average age was 39. Most (93%) of the studies were done in the United States. They were largely nonmanagement employees (92%). The number of studies and the sample size varied for each of the different variables they examined; for work centrality they examined 38 studies that had a combined sample of 17,846 employees. *As predicted, they found that work centrality was positively related to the number of hours worked.* In other words, the more people saw work as central to their lives, the more hours they worked. *The number of hours that people worked was related to career success, salary, promotions, and career satisfaction.* So if you want to be promoted to leadership positions, you need to be willing to put in the extra hours. On the negative side, however, the number of hours worked was related to work-to-family conflict and was somewhat related to job stress. The number of hours worked had no effect on physical health problems, however.

Team Identification, Affect, and Performance

An interesting study demonstrated the powerful effect that team identification has on performance and work related attitudes (Tanghe, Wisse, & van der Flier, 2010). Jacqueline Tanghe and her coauthors studied 171 employees who worked in 71 teams from a variety of service industries, including shops, restaurants, and bars. The employees had over 9 years of work experience, and a little over half (57%) of the employees were female. The employees filled out confidential surveys in which they were asked how much they identified with their team and also about their current level of affect at work. For outcome measures, they also described the team's performance and the amount of organizational citizenship behaviors they performed. The researchers found that the teams with a high level of identification performed more organizational citizenship behaviors. Moreover, they also found that *when employees had high levels of identification with the team, performance was higher as well.* Interestingly, they also found that when people identified with their teammates, they had higher levels of affective convergence. In other words, team members who identify with each other are more likely to have high emotional contagion and to experience the same emotions. This is important because the level of team affect also influenced performance and organizational citizenship behaviors among high identifying teams. The authors concluded that leaders need to pay attention to team affect and identification. *The highest performing teams had both high team identification and high positive affect, so leaders should encourage identification while creating positive affective climates at work.*

How *Not* to Build Identification With the Leader

Many managers want their employees to identify with them and look up to them as role models. Unfortunately, some managers and leaders also find themselves doing things that undermine their efforts to build identification and positive team affect. One such activity is surveillance. It is natural for managers to want to know if their employees are working and doing their job right, but spying on them and overmonitoring them reduces trust and the chance that employees will identify with the manager. O'Donnell, Jetten, and Ryan (2010) used an experimental design to vary the extent to which a fictitious workplace used surveillance (cameras, timed breaks, and phone calls, etc.). They also varied the extent to which the workplace team was described as having high or low team identification. For each condition, the participants who read about the company were asked whether they would regard the leader as part of the team or not. *As expected, surveillance undermined the perceptions that the leaders were part of the team.*

Conformity Pressures, Overidentification, and Other Problems

Have you ever joined a sports team, music band, club, or other organization because you loved the activity the group did? Perhaps you loved playing soccer or performing rock music. People often show their identification with these activities in a wide variety of ways. Soccer team members often wear sweats and soccer-related clothing even when they are not playing soccer, and rock band members often dress in distinctive fashions as well. This can result in conformity pressures—perhaps you love soccer, but you would rather dress more professionally when away from the field. Or maybe you love rock music, but you really don't want another tattoo. The same peer pressures can happen at work—perhaps you love accounting, but you would rather dress like a rock star than an accountant. Leaders in particular may come under intense pressure from their organization and even from their followers to conform to their organization's stereotypical leader identity (Sinclair, 2011). This can make it difficult for leaders to be their authentic selves.

Problems may also occur when people overidentify with their leaders or organizations. Followers who overidentify with their leaders or their organization may fail to question ethically dubious directions from their leaders. Or they may fail to question bad planning and poor decision making. As will be discussed in later chapters, history is full of charismatic and narcissistic leaders who have convinced their followers to carry out unethical and unwise policies.

Applications: Have you ever felt pressures to conform to informal dress codes, i.e., dress the way your teammates, band mates, or coworkers dress? What other types of behaviors are subjected to conformity pressures at work and in social groups? Does conforming have some positive aspects? Which is worse, conforming or not fitting in?

Case: *DEC's Organizational Identity*

Walsh and Glynn (2008) provided a powerful example of how organizational identity is important to people. They also demonstrated that organizational identity is a true organizational phenomenon that exists independently of any single individual. They studied how the organizational identity of the Digital Equipment Corporation (DEC) persisted long after it was no longer a recognizable legal entity. DEC was bought by Compaq and later merged with Hewlett-Packard, thus officially dying as an organization. Yet as Walsh and Glynn observed, it still existed as an organizational identity a decade after its legal death. As they argued, "DEC is still very much alive, persisting in the collective memory and activities of former DEC members through alumni associations, online message boards, newsletters and publications ... that preserve valued aspects of DEC's identity" (p. 262). The fact that former employees persisted in maintaining their DEC identity years later shows how important an organizational identity can be to people.

Applications: Do you participate in any company related associations such as sports teams, social clubs, or Internet sites? Should organizational leaders sponsor these types of activities as a way of increasing organizational identification?

Cross-Cultural Differences in Leadership

Many people identify with the cultures that they grow up in. When people learn their culture, they develop cognitive categories or knowledge structures that tell them how leaders in their culture should behave. Javidan, Dorfman, Sully de Luque, and House (2006) reasoned that *members of a culture share these cognitive structures and beliefs about the traits and behaviors of outstanding leaders and thus have a **culturally endorsed implicit leadership theory.*** As previously discussed, our identities are composed to a large extent of knowledge structures like these that tell us how we should behave in various roles. Thus, our identities are partially based on these culturally endorsed implicit leadership theories. As part of the 62 country GLOBE study (Global Leadership and Organizational Behavior Effectiveness; House et al., 2004), Javidan and his colleagues studied people's perceptions of outstanding leaders. They grouped leadership behaviors and traits into six main leadership dimensions, as shown below and in Table 11.1.

> *Charismatic/Value-Based:* Javidan et al. (2006) define this as, "A broadly defined leadership dimension that reflects the ability to inspire, to motivate, and to expect high performance outcomes from others on the basis of firmly held core beliefs" (p. 73). The Anglo cultures score highest on this dimension (see Table 11.1).

> *Team-Oriented:* Cultures are high on team orientation when leaders emphasize "effective team building and implementation of a common purpose or goal among team members" (Javidan et al., 2006, p. 73).

> *Participative:* Leaders in participative cultures involve others in decision making and in the implementation of plans.

> *Humane-Oriented:* Outstanding leaders in humane-oriented cultures are supportive, considerate, compassionate, and generous.

> *Autonomous:* Javidan and his colleagues (2006) state that this new dimension "refers to independent and individualistic leadership" (p. 73).

> *Self-Protective:* This new dimension "focuses on ensuring the safety and security of the individual. It is self-centered and face saving in its approach" (Javidan et al., 2006, p. 73).

Although Javidan and his colleagues found that there were cross-cultural differences, there were also similarities. In particular, all cultures gave relatively high marks to the importance of charismatic and value based leadership and relatively low marks to self-protective leadership. Thus, the high, medium, and low scores in Table 11.1 refer to the comparisons among the countries and not to whether they rated the particular behavior high or not. Thus, while the Anglo cultures had the highest scores on charismatic leadership, all the other countries had scores above 5 as well. Likewise, even though Southern Asia and the Middle East had the highest scores on self-protective behaviors, their scores were still below 4. The researchers noted that there were culturally contingent differences of opinion about the value of autonomous leader behaviors, because some cultures endorsed autonomous leader behaviors while others looked down upon such behaviors.

Applications: How does your culture rate on the various leadership dimensions? Which cultures are closest to your own? Which ones are most different?

Table 11.1   Cultural Differences on Leadership Dimensions

Societal Cluster	Culturally Endorsed Implicit Leadership Dimensions					
	Charismatic/ Value-Based	Team-Oriented	Participative	Humane-Oriented	Autonomous	Self-Protective
Eastern Europe	M 5.74	M 5.88	L 5.08	M 4.76	H 4.20	H 3.67
Latin America	H 5.99	H 5.96	M 5.42	M 4.85	L 3.51	M 3.62
Latin Europe	M 5.78	M 5.73	M 5.37	L 4.45	L 3.66	M 3.19
Confucian Asia	M 5.63	M 5.61	L 4.99	M 5.04	M 4.04	H 3.72
Nordic Europe	H 5.93	M 5.77	H 5.75	L 4.42	M 3.94	L 2.72
Anglo	H 6.05	M 5.74	H 5.73	H 5.08	M 3.82	L 3.08
Sub-Sahara Africa	M 5.79	M 5.70	M 5.31	H 5.16	L 3.63	M 3.55
Southern Asia	H 5.97	M 5.86	L 5.06	M 5.38	M 3.99	H 3.83
Germanic Europe	H 5.93	M 5.62	H 5.86	M 4.71	H 4.16	L 3.03
Middle East	L 5.35	L 5.47	L 4.97	M 4.80	M 3.68	H 3.79

High scores (relative to other cultures) are denoted by "H," medium scores by "M," and low scores by "L." After each letter, the actual cluster absolute score is given.

Source: Adapted from Tables 2 and 3 of Javidan, M., Dorfman, P. W., Sully de Luque, M., & House, R. J. (2006). In the eye of the beholder: Cross cultural lessons in leadership from project GLOBE. *The Academy of Management Perspectives, 20,* 67–90.

What sort of person does it take to rise from poverty to become the second richest person in world history? Perhaps it takes someone tough—a man of steel—ruthless and willing to stomp on anyone who gets in his way? Perhaps it takes a cold hearted pragmatist who doesn't care about anyone but himself? Or maybe, just possibly, could it take a starry eyed dreamer? Someone motivated by a vision of making the world a better place, a more prosperous, more educated, more peaceful place? Someone who argued early in life that industrialists should earn wealth in the first half of life so they could *give it all away* to philanthropic causes during the second half of their life—and proceeded to do exactly that? *Forbes,* in 2008, declared that Andrew Carnegie was the second richest person in world history with an estimated worth (of $298 billion in 2007 dollars) that dwarfs Bill Gates' wealth. As we see below, Carnegie is another example of how high IQ plus high EQ equals phenomenal success along with empathy for the poor and downtrodden. Carnegie (1920) thought that his autobiography should be edited by "a man with a heart as well as a head" ("Preface," location 27)—a good description of Carnegie himself. The case also illustrates how Carnegie achieved success by striving to improve himself and to become his ideal self.

Case: *Carnegie Creates His Ideal Self*

In the *Autobiography of Andrew Carnegie* (1920), Carnegie describes growing up with his family while living in one or two room houses or apartments in Scotland and later in America. His father was a weaver whose earnings were hurt by the introduction of steam powered looms, while his mother had to labor long into the night binding shoes. Yet despite living in what most of us would consider poverty, Carnegie describes his childhood in almost idyllic terms. Rather than being embittered by his parents' poverty, he was inspired by their dedication and hard work. He describes his mother as sweet, saintly, and loving, while his father was the image of Scottish manliness and reserve. When the family moved to America, Carnegie had to drop out of school (at age 13) and start work full time. After working briefly in a factory, Carnegie started working as a messenger for the telegraph office running messages across town, often working until 11:00 p.m. From there, he worked his way into becoming a telegraph operator, then joined the railroads as a telegraph operator and clerk, then supervisor, and finally into several joint partnerships producing railroad sleeping cars, iron and steel mills, a steel bridge building company, and oil wells. Much of his success was due to his constant desire to improve himself and his ability to create positive relationships with others. In his own words, here are Carnegie's secrets to success:

Andrew Carnegie (on the right) and James Bryce, 1st Viscount Bryce (on the left)

Source: Andrew Carnegie

Have role models: In addition to his parents, Carnegie drew great inspiration from Scottish history, literature, and poetry. He especially admired William Wallace, the Scottish commoner, rebel, and freedom fighter. Carnegie states, "It is a tower of strength for a boy to have a hero" (1920, "Parents and Childhood," location 347).

Cultivate positive thoughts and attitudes: "A sunny disposition is worth more than fortune. Young people should know that it can be cultivated; that the mind like the body can be moved from the shade into the sunshine.... Laugh away trouble if possible" (1920, "Parents and Childhood," location 123).

Know others: "My material success in life has hung—a success not to be attributed to what I have known or done myself, but to the faculty of knowing and choosing others who did know better than myself. Precious knowledge this for any man to possess. I did not understand steam machinery, but I tried to understand that much more complicated piece of mechanism—man" (1920, "Dunfermline and America," location 419).

Reading and self-improvement: Carnegie describes how he felt when a local gentleman opened up his personal library of 400 books to working children to borrow:

> There came, however, like a blessing from above, a means by which the treasures of literature were unfolded to me.... the windows were opened in the walls of my dungeon through which the light of knowledge streamed in. Every day's toil and even the long hours of night service were lightened by the book which I carried about with me. (Carnegie, 1920, "Colonel Anderson and Books," location 705)

Years later, Carnegie helped create the free public library system in America and in other countries by building 3,000 public libraries.

Choose uplifting friends and activities: Carnegie and his teenage friends formed a debating club and also starting attending the local literary society. These activities taught him public speaking skills:

> The self-possession I afterwards came to have before an audience may very safely be attributed to the experience of the 'Webster Society'. My two rules for speaking then (and now) were: Make yourself perfectly at home before an audience, and simply talk to them, not at them. Do not try to be somebody else; be your own self (Carnegie, 1920, "The Telegraph Office," location 929).

Form positive relational identities with superiors: Carnegie admired and identified with his superiors, and this positive attitude helped him gain important business partnerships throughout his life. He described his supervisor at the railroad this way:

> Mr. Scott was one of the most delightful superiors that anybody could have and I soon became warmly attached to him. He was my great man and all the hero worship that is inherent in youth I showered upon him" (Carnegie, 1920, "Railroad Service," location 1041).

(Continued)

(Continued)

Mr. Scott reciprocated the warm feelings by giving Carnegie rapid promotions and investment opportunities.

Demonstrate your talents: Time and time again Carnegie demonstrated his talents by performing tasks far beyond his normal job duties. He stated,

> The battle of life is already half won by the young man who is brought personally in contact with high officials; and the great aim of every boy should be to do something beyond the sphere of his duties—something which attracts the attention of those over him. (Carnegie, 1920, "Railroad Service," location 1085)

While a messenger, he learned (on his own time) how to be a telegraph operator; while an operator, he amazed others by being among the first to learn how to record teletype messages by sound alone; as a simple clerk to Mr. Scott, he learned how to perform many of Scott's duties—and amazed Scott by performing them when Scott was absent.

Applications: Carnegie grew up in modest circumstances. How difficult do you think it was for him to develop a vision of a possible self as an educated, refined, and sophisticated man destined to become a millionaire and the world's greatest philanthropist? Many subordinates resent their bosses instead of identifying with them. What role do you think Carnegie's hero worship of his superiors played in their willingness to mentor him? Do you identify with your manager and with the other leaders of your organization?

Source: Carnegie, A. (1920). Autobiography of Andrew Carnegie [E-reader version]. Ithaca, NY: Cornell University Library.

Put It in Practice

1. People want leaders they can identify with. Build your customer base by creating an image that customers can identify with.

2. Develop all the components of your identity from a narrow focus on yourself and your values to a broader definition that includes your skills and behaviors.

3. Build self-esteem by activating the right level of identity: individual identity, interpersonal and relational identity, and collective and social identity.

4. Boost your leader performance by activating your collective identity and by acting altruistic to your subordinates.

5. Recognize that you have multiple identities. To maximize your sense of authenticity, pick roles that are relatively consistent with each other. The more you identify with your leadership role, the more authentic you will feel when performing your leader duties.

6. Increase your followers' performance by helping them identify with their role. When they identify with their role, they will want to validate their role identity by performing their jobs correctly. Increase group identity by treating followers as members of a group.

7. Build follower identification with the organization by encouraging followers to socialize together and by tying in a large number of extracurricular activities to their organizational membership. Use distinctive clothing, logos, colors, symbols, lingo, and even architecture to build your organizational identity.

8. Construct your own identity and overcome work-identity integrity violations by engaging in identity customization and identity enrichment.

9. Claim your leadership identity by valuing and rewarding subordinates who grant your claim to leadership. Make sure you and your subordinates have a common mental model of leader-follower interactions.

10. Develop your own identity by building deeper and more meaningful relationships with others: Our relationships with others form the heart of our identity. Save a part of your heart for your individual identity.

11. Increase your career success, salary, promotions, and career satisfaction by making work a central part of your identity and by putting in the extra hours.

12. For high performing teams, create high team identification and positive affective climates.

13. Trust your employees: Surveillance and overmonitoring reduces the odds that your followers will identify with you.

14. Beware conformity: Build organizational identity while still respecting people's right to have their own individual identities. Encourage people to express their doubts about the wisdom of organizational policies.

15. Organizational identity is important to people and people may still identify with an organization after they leave or after it ceases to exist. Build that type of strong identification by sponsoring organization-related clubs, associations, sports teams, networks, etc.

16. When leading people from different cultures, recognize that cultures differ in their beliefs about how leaders should behave. In particular, pay attention to these dimensions: Charismatic/Value-Based, Team-Oriented, Participative, Humane-Oriented, Autonomous, and Self-Protective.

17. Create your own ideal self by having role models, cultivating positive thoughts and attitudes, knowing others, reading and striving for self-improvement, choosing uplifting friends and activities, forming positive relational identities with superiors, and by demonstrating your talents.

Exercises

1. Relational Identity Exercise

Pick three or four of your managers, coworkers, teammates, etc., to think about for this exercise. For each person, list five things that you think are part of their identity, such as being a parent, sports fan, accountant, person with a sense of humor, etc. Now make your own list. What things do you have in common? What could you do to establish a better relational identity and sense of common identity with each person? For example, if the other person frequently mentions his or her role and identity as a parent, could you bring up stories about your own family, ask questions about his or her family, and so forth? Do you have better leader-member relationships with the people that you have more things in common?

2. Collective and Social Identity

Make a list of the organizations or groups that you belong to. Rate how much you identify with each group on a 1 to 10 scale. Form groups and compare your list with your teammates. Why do you identify more with some groups and organizations than with others? What can leaders do to increase collective and social identification?

Visit the Student Study Site at **www.sagepub.com/humphreyel** for these additional tools:

- Learning Goals
- Leader's Book Case Articles
- Web Resources
- Student Self Assessments

References

Albert, S., & Whetten, D. A. (1985). Organizational identity. *Research in Organizational Behavior, 7,* 263–295.

Ashforth, B. E. (2001). *Role transitions in organizational life: An identity-based perspective.* Mahwah, NJ: Erlbaum.

Ashforth, B. E., Harrison, S. H., & Corley, K. E. (2008). Identification in organizations: An examination of four fundamental questions. *Journal of Management, 34,* 325–374.

Ashforth, B. E., & Humphrey, R. H. (1993). Emotional labor in service roles: The influence of identity. *Academy of Management Review, 18*, 88–115.

Ashforth, B. E., & Humphrey, R. H. (1995). Labeling processes in the organization: Constructing the individual. In L. L. Cummings & B. M. Staw (Eds.), *Research in Organizational Behavior* (Vol. 17, pp. 413–461). Greenwich, CT: JAI Press.

Ashforth, B. E., & Humphrey, R. H. (1997). The ubiquity and potency of labels in organizations. *Organization Science, 8*, 43–58.

Ashforth, B. E., & Johnson, S. A. (2001). Which hat to wear? The relative salience of multiple identities in organizational contexts. In M. A. Hogg & D. J. Terry (Eds.), *Social Identity Processes in Organizational Contexts* (pp. 31–48). Philadelphia, PA: Psychology Press.

Brewer, M. B., & Gardner, W. (1996). Who is this "we"? Levels of collective identity and self-representations. *Journal of Personality and Social Psychology, 71*, 83–93.

Burke, P. J. (1991). Identity processes and social stress. *American Sociological Review, 56*, 836–849.

Carnegie, A. (1920). *Autobiography of Andrew Carnegie* [E-reader version]. Ithaca, NY: Cornell University Library.

DeRue, D. S., & Ashford, S. J. (2010). Who will lead and who will follow? A social process of leadership identity construction in organizations. *Academy of Management Review, 35*, 627–647.

Dutton, J. E., Dukerich, J. M., & Harquail, C. V. (1994). Organizational images and member identification. *Administrative Science Quarterly, 39*, 239–263.

Hogg, M. A., & Abrams, D. (1990). Social motivation, self-esteem and social identity. In D. Abrams & M. A. Hogg (Eds.), *Social identity theory: Constructive and critical advances* (pp. 28–47). New York, NY: Springer-Verlag.

Hogg, M. A., & van Knippenberg, D. (2003). Social identity and leadership processes in groups. In M. P. Zanna (Ed.), *Advances in Experimental Social Psychology* (Vol. 35, pp. 1–52). San Diego, CA: Academic Press.

House, R. J., Hanges, P. J., Javidan, M., Dorfman, P. W., Gupta, V., & GLOBE Associates. (2004). *Leadership, culture and organizations: The GLOBE study of 62 societies.* Thousand Oaks, CA: Sage.

Humphrey, R. H. (2012). How leading with emotional labour creates common identities. In M. White (Ed.), *Leadership as emotional labour: Management and the managed heart* (pp. 80-105). London, UK: Routledge.

Javidan, M., Dorfman, P. W., Sully de Luque, M., & House, R. J. (2006). In the eye of the beholder: Cross cultural lessons in leadership from project GLOBE. *The Academy of Management Perspectives, 20*, 67–90.

Kihlstrom, J. F., Beer, J. S., & Klein, S. B. (2003). Self and identity as memory. In M. R. Leary & J. P. Tangney (Eds.), *Handbook of self and identity* (pp. 68–90). New York, NY: The Guilford Press.

Lord, R. G., Brown, D. J., & Freiberg, S. J. (1999). Understanding the dynamics of leadership: The role of follower self-concepts in the leader/follower relationship. *Organizational Behavior and Human Decision Processes, 78*, 1–37.

Markus, H., & Nurius, P. (1986). Possible selves. *American Psychologist, 41*, 954–969.

Markus, H., & Wurf, E. (1987). The dynamic self-concept: A social psychological perspective. *American Review of Psychology, 38*, 299–337.

Ng, T. W. H., & Feldman, D. C. (2008). Long work hours: A social identity perspective on meta-analysis data. *Journal of Organizational Behavior, 29,* 853–880.

O'Donnell, A. T., Jetten, J., & Ryan, M. K. (2010). Watching over your own: How surveillance moderates the impact of shared identity on perceptions of leaders and follower behavior. *European Journal of Social Psychology, 40,* 1046–1061.

Pratt, M. G. (2000). The good, the bad, and the ambivalent: Managing identification among Amway distributors. *Administrative Science Quarterly, 45,* 456–493.

Pratt, M. G., & Rafaeli, A. (1997). Organizational dress as a symbol of multilayered social identities. *Academy of Management Journal, 40,* 862–898.

Pratt, M. G., & Rafaeli, A. (2001). Symbols as a language of organizational relationships. *Research in Organizational Behavior, 23,* 93–132.

Pratt, M. G., Rockmann, K. W., & Kaufmann, J. B. (2006). Constructing professional identity: The role of work and identity learning cycles in the customization of identity among medical residents. *Academy of Management Journal, 49,* 235–262.

Sinclair, A. (2011). Being leaders: Identities and identity work in leadership. In A. Bryman, D. Collinson, K. Grint, B. Jackson, & M. Uhl-Bien (Eds.), *Sage handbook of leadership* (pp. 508–517). London, UK: Sage.

Sluss, D. M., & Ashforth, B. E. (2007). Relational identity and identification: Defining ourselves through work relationships. *Academy of Management Review, 32,* 9–32.

Sosik, J. J., Jung, D., & Dinger, S. L. (2009). Values in authentic action: Examining the roots and rewards of altruistic leadership. *Group & Organization Management, 34,* 395–431.

Stets, J. E., & Burke, P. J. (2000). Identity theory and social identity theory. *Social Psychology Quarterly, 63,* 224–237.

Tajfel, H. (1978). Social categorization, social identity and social comparison. In H. Tajfel (Ed.), *Differentiation between social groups: Studies in the social psychology of intergroup relations* (pp. 61–76). London, UK: Academic Press.

Tajfel, H., & Turner, J. C. (1986). The social identity theory of intergroup behavior. In S. Worchel & W. G. Austin (Eds.), *Psychology of intergroup relations* (2nd ed.) (pp. 7–24). Chicago, IL: Nelson-Hall.

Tanghe, J., Wisse, B., & van der Flier, H. (2010). The formation of group affect and team effectiveness: The moderating role of identification. *British Journal of Management, 21,* 340–358.

Thoits, P. A. (1983). Multiple identities and psychological well-being: A reformulation and test of the social isolation hypothesis. *American Sociological Review, 48,* 174–187.

Thoits, P. A. (1991). On merging identity theory and stress research. *Social Psychology Quarterly, 54,* 101–112.

van Knippenberg, B., van Knippenberg, D., De Cremer, D., & Hogg, M. A. (2005). Research in leadership, self, and identity: A sample of the present and a glimpse of the future. *The Leadership Quarterly, 16,* 495–499.

van Knippenberg, D., van Knippenberg, B., De Cremer, D., & Hogg, M. A. (2004). Leadership, self, and identity: A review and research agenda. *The Leadership Quarterly, 15,* 825–856.

Walsh, I. J., & Glynn, M. A. (2008). The way we were: Legacy organizational identity and the role of leadership. *Corporate Reputation Review, 11,* 262–276.

12

Authority, Power, and Persuasion

Chapter Road Map

Case: *Jordan Belfort: A Cautionary Tale for Rich and Poor Alike*

Jordan Belfort (2007) wrote his book, *The Wolf of Wall Street*, to be "a cautionary tale to the rich and poor alike" (p. 11). Jordan's well qualified to give such a tale: He went from rags to riches to prison—all within a few years. Along the way, he almost died a few times. In addition to endangering his own life, he risked the lives of his family members and friends as well as the lives of subordinates and innocent strangers. What caused this reckless behavior? Jordan succumbed to three of the biggest disrupters of leadership success: greed, abuse of power and wealth, and drug addiction.

Belfort founded Stratton Oakmont, a stock brokerage firm that grew to have a thousand employees. Unlike most stock market firms, he didn't require his employees to have an understanding of finance or of the intricacies of the stock market. Instead, he taught his employees, some of whom were

This is the headquarters of the U.S. Securities and Exchange Commission, located in Washington, DC. Its glass walls suggest openness, transparency, and the shining of light on illegal activities.

Source: Wikipedia/AgnosticPreachersKid (CC-BY-SA)

not even high school graduates, how to sell stock over the phone by using aggressive sales tactics. He used direct appeals to people's most basic instincts: greed, fear, the desire for status and domination. Jordan motivated his employees the same way, telling them that they could solve all of their problems, even those with their girlfriends or boyfriends or other family members, by becoming rich. Jordan also mocked, ridiculed, and fired those employees who wouldn't buy into his cult-like ideology and become dedicated *Strattonites*.

Most investors, when they receive these overly aggressive phone calls from unknown stockbrokers, are smart enough to hang up. But with a thousand employees cold-calling all day long, Jordan and his Strattonites were bound to turn up some naive investors. Belfort reeled in the investors by using a well-known and illegal tactic called *pump and dump*. His legion of employees would encourage their clients to bid up the stock price of a company well above its real market value. The victims, who saw the price of the stock rising, would think they were receiving good advice. When the price was high enough, Belfort would sell his own stock (held illegally under assumed names or by fellow conspirators). It doesn't take a genius to use these tactics—just a willingness to risk going to prison. His investors lost about $200 million.

To his credit, Belfort makes clear in his book that his ill-gotten gains did him little good. His expensive houses, yachts, and other excessive items brought him more headaches than joy. And his model wife, who loved spending his money, would belittle him and make him feel inferior. Even worse, his drug addiction meant that he spent much of his time in a drug-induced stupor or in a paranoid state. It's hard to enjoy your wealth when you are lying on the floor drooling in a drug-induced semi-catatonic state. While on drugs, he wrecked cars (breaking an innocent woman's arm) and ordered his yacht out in a storm (where it sank, endangering his life, his families' and friends' lives, and the crew and rescuers' lives). The law finally caught up with him, too. He had to testify against his friends, sending them to prison, and he spent 22 months in prison and was ordered to repay $100 million. His wife filed for divorce as soon as he was arrested.

Jordan has been off drugs for a long time, and he now gives motivational talks. He has two internationally best-selling books, and a movie starring Leonardo DiCaprio as Jordan is in the works. It's a shame that drugs and greed wrecked Belfort's early life—a sure testament to the corrupting power these have over even highly talented people like Jordan.

Applications: Is 22 months in prison a long enough sentence for someone like Belfort? How many leaders and potential leaders that you know have had their careers wrecked by illegal drug use? Belfort used high pay and coercive tactics to motivate his 1,000 employees to use unethical sales tactics. Have you witnessed leaders using similar techniques to encourage questionable behavior?

Sources: Belfort, J. (2007). *The wolf of Wall Street* [Kindle edition]. New York, NY: Bantam. Belfort, Jordon. Retrieved February 4, 2013 from http://en.wikipedia.org/wiki/Jordan_Belfort

Jordan Belfort is undoubtedly a very persuasive person, and he was able to get a large number of people to follow him. He is a good example of what can go wrong when leaders use power and persuasion tactics for the wrong purposes. However, all leaders, even the most ethical ones, have to use at least some persuasion tactics to reach consensus among group members and to motivate their followers to perform their duties. Organizations need to give leaders enough power to get the job done but not so much that they can abuse others. Thus, in this chapter, we will address the following questions:

What are the major sources of leaders' power?

What are the most commonly used and most effective influence and persuasion methods?

How does political skill influence leadership effectiveness?

Do people differ in their motivation to use power, and does this vary by culture?

What are the harmful effects of abusive leadership, and how do employees react to unfair treatment?

What Is Power?

Power is usually defined in terms of the ability of one person (the agent) to influence another person (the target); moreover, power also consists of the ability to resist influence attempts from others. In organizations, power often consists of control over people; over rewards, promotions, and benefits; over decisions; and over resources.

Control Over People: Leaders with authority to direct those under them can have considerable power over their subordinates. In some cases, their authority gives them the ability to direct their subordinates' behavior in very detailed and controlling ways.

Control Over Rewards, Benefits, and Promotions: Obviously, control over these types of rewards gives leaders considerable power and authority. Even among peer work group members, power struggles can often take place as group members negotiate with each other for the right to perform career enhancing developmental work tasks that eventually lead to promotions to leadership positions (de Pater et al., 2009).

Control Over Decisions: Many of the day-to-day power struggles in organizations are over the ability to make decisions. Some decisions are made by those higher in authority, but others are made by groups of peers. Boards of directors, executive committees, regular committees, project teams, and empowered work groups all have to make numerous decisions. These decisions have important implications that influence the behaviors and work assignments of employees, organizational policies, and a wide range of other issues.

Control Over Resources: In order to get the job done, leaders need various work-related resources. Other types of resources, such as comfortable office furniture and funds for training and development, are also needed in order to maintain a motivated and committed work force. Control over these resources is an important source of power.

Power: Too Little, Too Much, and Just Right

When we think of the word *power*, the word *abuse* often comes to mind as well. In other words, to many of us, power has a negative connotation. As Lord Acton stated, "Power tends to corrupt, and absolute power corrupts absolutely" (Acton, 2013). However, managers need the power and authority necessary to get the job done. As Churchill stated, "What you have no right to do is to ask me to bear responsibilities without the power of effective action" (Hayward, 1997, p. 42). Managers and other leaders need the authority to make decisions, to appropriate resources, and to direct others if they are to achieve the tasks given to them to do.

Midlevel managers and leaders in particular often lack the power of effective action. Red tape, micromanaging executives, and uncooperative peers often limit the ability of these leaders to get the job done in a timely fashion. On the other hand, upper-level executives have to be sure that managers and employees are following organizational policies and implementing the overall organizational strategy. Abuse of power can take place at any level, and often, organizational policies protect frontline employees from unfair treatment by their immediate supervisors. Thus, one of the most difficult tasks in any organization is to ensure that managers and leaders up and down the hierarchy have the right amount of power. Leaders need enough power to get the job done, but they should not have so much power that they can ignore organizational policies and strategies and abuse their subordinates.

Empowerment programs have been useful in part because they have given more authority to the people who have the most information about the tasks at hand and because they limit the chances to abuse power. In other words, these programs have helped give organizational members the right amount of power.

We can also think about power in terms of the personality traits and individual characteristics of the leaders. There are many leaders who have considerable power but are never tempted to abuse it. There are also leaders who, even though they have the authority and sources of power necessary for their job, are too timid to use their authority. In essence, they let others, including their subordinates and fellow managers, push them around.

Finally, there are leaders who, even though they lack much formal authority, still manage to have considerable influence over decisions.

Does Power Corrupt?

A fascinating study suggests that the adage that *power corrupts* may not generally be true. Instead, it could be that it's the *lack of power* that causes people to be aggressive, insensitive, and uncaring toward others. People in high power, high control situations tend to experience positive emotions and lower frustration levels, and positive moods promote prosocial behaviors. In contrast, people in low power, low control situations tend to experience negative emotions and high frustration, which tends to promote aggression and hostility. Mast, Jonas, and Hall (2009) wanted to test if having high power made people less interpersonally sensitive to others. They noted that prior research had documented that high status people (i.e., better educated, higher incomes) scored higher on a measure of interpersonal sensitivity (nonverbal decoding accuracy); moreover, those who scored higher on trait measures of power were also higher on nonverbal decoding accuracy (see the meta-analysis by Hall, Halberstadt, & O'Brien, 1997). However, Mast and her two colleagues (2009) acknowledged that interpersonal sensitivity could help people become more successful, so it's hard to tell from these correlational studies what impact having power has on people. So they conducted four experimental studies in which they manipulated people's feelings of power. For example, in one study, subjects were either assigned to be the high-powered leader or the low-powered assistant. In another study, they primed feelings of power by asking people to recall a time in which they experienced feelings of either high power or low power. After manipulations of power, the subjects were given various tests to measure their interpersonal sensitivity at that particular moment. For example, in two of the studies, the subjects watched videotapes of people interacting, and they had to guess what feelings and thoughts the actors experienced at various points in the film. In all four studies, when the participants were primed to experience feelings of power, they scored higher in interpersonal sensitivity.

The studies by Mast and her colleagues (2009) did not directly test whether people in high power positions actually treat others better. However, the fact that being in high power positions increases interpersonal sensitivity and accuracy suggests that it may also increase empathic concern. After all, the ability to perceive others' emotions is a key component of empathy. And in democratic societies such as Switzerland and the United States (the two countries where Mast and her colleagues did their studies), it is clear that high status people, those with higher education and income, are also the ones who contribute the most to charity, are most involved in community groups, and are most likely to do volunteer work.

The Bases of Power

Suppose you were a manager and you wanted to influence others to achieve some goal. What types of power would you have available to you? French and Raven (1962) developed the most commonly used classification of the types of power available to leaders. According to French and Raven, the five major sources of power are reward power, coercive power, legitimate power, expert power, and referent power.

Reward Power: Leaders have **reward power** *when they control pay raises, bonuses and benefits, special perks such as opportunities for travel or extra training, or other resources valued by the target of their influence attempts.* Rewards can have a powerful impact on people's behavior. In order to be effective, the rewards have to be fair and in proportion to effort required by the subordinates to carry out the requests.

Coercive Power: Leaders have **coercive power** *when they can punish others who do not comply with the leaders' requests, for example, by docking workers' pay, assigning unpleasant tasks, issuing verbal or written reprimands, or even firing employees.* The frequent use of coercive power tends to create resistance from employees and followers.

Legitimate Power: When managers occupy positions of formal authority over others in organizations they have **legitimate power**. In order to use legitimate power, leaders have to make sure that their requests fall within the scope of the authority granted to them by the organization and that the requests serve organizational goals and are consistent with the values of the organization. For example, leaders should not use their authority to have subordinates do non-work-related personal tasks for the leader.

Expert Power: When leaders have special knowledge and expertise relevant to the tasks at hand they have **expert power**. People comply with leaders' requests when they believe that the leaders' expertise allows them to know what should be done to successfully achieve the goal. Leaders gain expert power through their education and training and through job experience. Expert power is enhanced when the followers believe that the leader knows more than they do about how to perform the task or achieve the goal. Expert power is related but somewhat distinct from *information power, which involves control over specific pieces of information that others may need or want.* People who control the distribution of key information to others may have considerable power as a result.

Referent Power: Leaders who are perceived to be attractive, charismatic, friendly and likable, trustworthy, or have other desirable traits admired by the followers have referent power. When subordinates identify with the leader and use the leader as a role model, they are more willing to comply with the leader's requests—they may even imitate the leader's behaviors in a wide range of ways.

Three of the sources of power derive from the leader's position in the organizational hierarchy: reward power, coercive power, and legitimate power. Information power can also be a result of a person's particular position in the organization. The other two sources of power, expert power and referent power, derive from the personal characteristics of the leader and thus do not depend on the leader's position in the formal chain of command. Thus, a subordinate who is an expert in a particular area may even hold expert power over his or her superiors. Likewise, informal leaders often emerge because of their referent power and personal characteristics.

The different sources of power influence people in different ways and tend to have different outcomes. *Expert power and referent power operate by changing people's attitudes.* If an expert tells you that following a particular procedure or course of action gets the best results, then you will follow the expert's advice based on your belief in the accuracy of the expert's advice. Likewise, when followers use a leader as a role model, they follow the leader's example because they believe in what the leader is doing. In both of these cases, followers may not feel that the leader is *exerting power* on them. Instead, they may feel that the leader is helping them out by giving them good advice or by role modeling the path to success. *Thus, expert power and referent power tend to produce commitment among followers.*

Reward power, legitimate power, and coercive power operate directly on people's behaviors. In other words, they do not depend on changing people's attitudes. People may not believe that the policy advocated by the leader is the best, but they will comply if the rewards are large enough or if they feel that the leader has the legitimate authority to direct their behavior. Although some researchers argue that reward and legitimate power produce compliance (conformity, but not necessarily enthusiasm and agreement) instead of commitment (enthusiastic agreement and dedication), people who are fairly rewarded may develop positive expectations toward their leaders, and people may be highly motivated to achieve large financial rewards.

A number of studies have found that legitimate power produces behavioral compliance but not attitudinal change and commitment (Yukl, 2010). However, it seems reasonable to believe that legitimate power would also have some impact on attitudes if the leader emphasizes the values of the organization rather than the leader's position power. Legitimate power is ultimately based on the belief that the leader's requests are consistent with the values of the organization and society and serve a useful purpose. Leaders can enhance their legitimate power by explaining how their requests serve the interests of the employees or organizational members, their customers, or society at large. Although legitimate power is often conceived of as a downward flow of requests from the top to the bottom, even subordinates can make legitimate requests of their superiors for resources or for necessary managerial action.

Coercive power tends to create resistance—attempts by the followers to avoid the directives and orders of the leader. In general, punishments and coercive behaviors should not be the main way to motivate followers toward goals. Instead, coercive behavior should only be used to punish employees for major violations of company policies or similar offenses.

A meta-analysis found that leaders' use of referent power, expert power, and reward power were positively related to high employee performance (Carson, Carson, & Roe, 1993). Moreover, these may be the three most useful power bases for creating positive, affective responses. A good example of this research is a study done by Carson, Carson, and Pence (2002). They surveyed 128 members of the Medical Library Association. They asked the members about the degree to which they perceived organizational support and also about their managers' use of the five power bases. As expected, referent power, reward power, and expert power were all positively related to perceived organizational support. In addition, legitimate power was also positively related, although not as strongly as the other three. Coercion was not related to perceptions of organizational support.

> **Applications:** Which type of power do you think would be most useful for influencing subordinates? How do you feel when managers use their position power to influence you? How about when they use their personal powers?

The Bases of Power and Empowerment

Which types of power bases would be most useful for leaders to use if they also wanted to practice empowerment? Randolph and Kemery (2011) answered this question in their study of a cross section of managers and their subordinates. They surveyed 195 pairs of employees and their supervisors from the mid-Atlantic region of the United States. The managers on average were 41 years old and had been in their current position for approximately 9 years. The subordinates had a mean age of 29 and had worked for slightly under 5 years at their current job. The managers were surveyed about their empowerment practices, whereas the subordinates were given surveys that measured the extent to which they felt psychologically empowered. In addition, the subordinates answered questions about their managers' use of the five power bases.

As expected, Randolph and Kemery (2011) found that subordinates reported feeling more psychological empowerment when the managers reported using more empowerment practices. They also found that the *subordinates experienced greater psychological empowerment when the managers used reward power and referent power*. In addition, *the empowering managers refrained from using their expert power*: Expert power was negatively related to psychological empowerment. This makes sense because empowerment involves letting subordinates make their own decisions and use their own expertise and judgment. Coercive power and legitimate power were unrelated to feelings of psychological empowerment.

> **The Leaders' Bookcase:** To learn more about this study, download it from the textbook website: Randolph, W. A., & Kemery, E. R. (2011). Managerial use of power bases in a model of managerial empowerment practices and employee psychological empowerment. *Journal of Leadership & Organizational Studies, 18,* 95–106.

Facilitation Power and Ecological Power: Although the five types of power classified by French and Raven (1962) are the best known, researchers have extended the French and Raven taxonomy to include leaders' influence on the environment. According to this perspective, leaders can change the environment that employees operate in, which in turn changes the employees' behaviors. For example, Humphrey, O'Malley, Johnston, and Bachman (1988) theorized that facilitation power was an additional base of power:

> . . . **facilitation power** as the ability to influence behavior either by providing social cooperation or by altering environmental circumstances. Facilitation may take the form of making desirable behaviors easier to perform, shifting the focus of attention or activity, or providing resources logically necessary for the completion of the behaviors. (p. 330)

Facilitation power does not require changing organizational members' attitudes or using additional rewards or coercion. People often resist efforts to change their attitudes or other efforts to control them. Because facilitation power does not require changing attitudes or using coercion, it does not provoke resistance among organizational members. Facilitation power can also be used to decrease undesirable behaviors by shifting people's focus of attention and activity toward more desirable behaviors.

Humphrey and his colleagues (Humphrey, O'Malley, Johnston, & Bachman, 1988) tested the effects of facilitation power in a study of over 27,000 high school students from across the United States. They classified different groups and organizations (peers, schools, religious organizations) according to their ability to use facilitation power and the five original bases of power to influence students' drug use. They found support for French and Raven's (1962) model of how the bases of power influence either attitudes or behaviors. Moreover, they found that including measures of facilitation power increased the explained variance by over one third; in other words, *facilitation power was one of the most important predictors*. Their results demonstrated the importance of facilitation power and suggest that it should be added to the original bases of power.

Yukl (2010) used the term *ecological power to refer to the way leaders indirectly influence people by controlling the physical environment, technology, or organization of the work*. For example, leaders can change the work environment by means of job enrichment. If the job enrichment is successful in making the work more intrinsically interesting, then the leaders may have influenced the employees' productivity levels without having to use the other bases of power. Yukl also pointed out that technology, such as the speed of an assembly line, can control an employee's behavior. However, more research needs to be done on ecological and facilitative power to fully understand the relative importance of these variables to the other power bases.

Persuasion

Suppose you were trying to influence one of your coworkers to do something. You are not the coworker's boss so you have no formal authority over the coworker. How would you go about it? Or suppose you were trying to persuade your boss to do something for you. You certainly couldn't use most of the power bases on your boss. So there's a good chance you'll try one of the influence methods recommended by Kipnis, Schmidt, and Wilkinson (1980). They studied how organizational members used a variety of tactics to influence each other, such as using rational arguments, ingratiation, exchanging favors, acting assertively, building coalitions, and appealing to higher authorities. Other scholars verified that these tactics can even be used to *influence one's superiors* (Hochwarter, Harrison, Ferris, Perrewe & Ralston, 2000; Schriesheim & Hinkin, 1990; Wayne, Liden, Graef & Ferris, 1997). Rational arguments are generally the most useful for influencing one's superiors. In contrast, the more aggressive strategies can backfire when trying to influence one's superiors.

Rational, Consultative, Inspirational, and Collaborative Leaders

Yukl and his colleagues developed one of the more recent scales to measure types of influence tactics, an extended version of the Influence Behavior Questionnaire (IBQ) (Yukl, Seifert, & Chavez, 2008). Although the scales measure 11 different types of proactive influence tactics, Yukl and his colleagues argued that there are four core tactics: rational persuasion, consultation, inspirational appeals, and collaboration. These are described below:

> **Rational Persuasion:** *The use of logic and facts to explain why the request is reasonable and beneficial.*

> **Consultation:** *Involving others in making suggestions for improvements to the plan in order to win their support for the proposed activity.*

> **Inspirational Appeals:** *The use of emotionally arousing appeals to values and ideals that support the request.*

> **Collaboration:** *Offers of assistance in terms of either help in performing the requested task or providing resources used to carry out the request.*

Yukl and his colleagues validated the extended IBQ by administering it to four different samples of working adults and their superiors (Yukl et al., 2008). *They found that these four core tactics were effective in gaining commitment* (i.e., a willingness to carry out the requested actions) both when they were used on peers and on subordinates (this was tested in three of the samples). In addition, they wanted to know how using these tactics influenced the quality of the leader-member exchange relationships. In two of the studies, the subordinates rated both their leaders' use of the influence tactics and their evaluation of the quality of the leader-member exchange relationship. They found that the four core influence tactics were positively related to the quality of the leader-member exchange relationship. *Their findings suggest that more effective leaders use these influence tactics and that using them improves the quality of relationships with others.* After all, who wouldn't want to work with a leader who's rational and logical, who's collaborative and helps out with the work tasks, who consults others about decisions that concern them, and who's inspiring and has good values? In addition to these four core tactics, the researchers also found that ingratiation (using praise and flattery) was also useful for influencing peers and that ingratiation positively influenced the quality of the leader-member relationships.

In contrast to the more positive, collaborative forms of influence, *using pressure tactics and coalition building were ineffective and in most cases negatively related to commitment and the quality of the leader-member exchange* (Yukl et al., 2008). Exchange tactics were also ineffective, although not negatively so.

Persuasion: The Power of Beliefs and Peer Pressure

One of the most influential models of attitudes and behaviors was developed by Fishbein and Ajzen (1975); this model gives great weight to the importance of beliefs (i.e., information and facts that people believe) and values in determining one's attitudes. The model states that people's behaviors are determined to a large extent by their attitudes and beliefs. However, the model also recognizes that sometimes we do things that go against our attitudinal desires because of the influence of peer pressure or other subjective social norms. The following case demonstrates how a business leader is fighting illegal drug use by providing information about the dangers of crystal meth and by influencing beliefs about peer opposition to drug use.

Case: *Dangerous and Unpopular*

Tom Siebel knows how to persuade people. He's even written a book called *Virtual Selling*. He was one of the best salespeople at Oracle, where he rose up the ranks to become a top executive. He then became the CEO of Gain Technology before he founded his own company, Siebel Systems. Tom knew how to use the bases of power: His employees were rewarded with generous stock options that made many of them rich; on the negative side, he fired the bottom 5% of performers. After selling Siebel Systems to Oracle for $5.9 billion, Tom became chairman of a holding and investment company, and he now

(Continued)

(Continued)

This antimeth mural in Drummon, Montana, was created by the local community as part of the Montana Meth Project.

devotes much of his time to philanthropy. In 2009 and 2010, he was listed as one of the top five philanthropists in the world by Barron's. Since 2000, the Thomas and Stacey Siebel Foundation has distributed over $229 million to charities (as of April 2012). One of his major philanthropies is the Meth Project, where Tom's trying to use his powers of persuasion to convince people not to use crystal meth.

Tom became aware of the crystal meth problem in Montana through a friend of his who was a sheriff. He learned that by 2005 half of all the incarcerations in Montana were meth related. Siebel then talked to teenage meth users and heard firsthand horrifying stories about what meth did to them. Most antidrug ads try to avoid sounding oversensationalistic and thus avoid going into the gory details. Seibel took the opposite approach: He hired famous movie directors to produce television and radio ads that showed young girls prostituting themselves for $50, meth users getting into fights with their family members and friends, and users losing complete control over their lives. Rock songs often portray drug use as glamorous; to combat this, Seibel portrayed crystal meth users as dirty and sickly looking, with unattractive vacant stares. One of the more effective ads focused on *meth mouth* and showed how meth use leads to rotting, unattractive teeth (visit http://www.methproject.org to see the ads). His ads revealed how meth use was both dangerous and socially unpopular. As a result, Montana's per capita meth use rate dropped from 5th worst to 39th, and overall meth use among teens has dropped by half. Other states are now adopting the Meth Project techniques.

Applications: How much do peers influence our behavior? Is providing facts a good way to influence others, or do people ignore facts whenever they want to? What type of ad do you think would be more effective: an emotionally neutral ad or a more sensationalistic one?

Sources: Meth Project. Retrieved April 14, 2012 from http://www.methproject.org/about/

Siebel Foundation. Retrieved April 14, 2012 from http://www.siebelfoundation.org/

Siebel, Thomas. Retrieved April 14, 2012 from http://en.wikipedia.org/w/index.php?titl
e=Special:Book&bookcmd=download&collection_id=e745865d4cc617ab&writer=rl
&return_to=Thomas+Siebel

Verini, J. (2009, May). What meth made this billionaire do. *FASTCOMPANY*, 84-89.

Tom Siebel is not the only leader who uses power for ethical purposes. As the following case indicates, the leader of PepsiCo also knows the power that comes from having a purpose.

Case: *PepsiCo Chair and CEO Indra K. Nooyi: Power Through Purpose*

As head of PepsiCo, Indra Nooyi has been ranked as the most powerful woman in business 5 years in a row by *Fortune* magazine. You might think that with a title like that she would lead by being dominating, aggressive, and powerful. Instead, Indra leads through trust and the power of purpose. That's why Stephen Covey, Greg Link, and Rebecca Merrill (2012) feature her in their book, *Smart Trust: Creating Prosperity, Energy, and Joy in a Low-Trust World.* Indeed, Indra even wrote the foreword to their book. In the foreword, Nooyi described how after becoming CEO of PepsiCo, her team

Indra K. Nooyi, Chairman and Chief Executive Officer, PepsiCo, taken during a press conference for the 2008 Annual Meeting of the World Economic Forum held in Davos, Switzerland

felt they needed to make clear how they would manage the company. They came up with the phrase, "Performance with Purpose," to describe PepsiCo's mission. They

(Continued)

(Continued)

also developed three planks to guide PepsiCo's future: human sustainability (healthier food and beverages), environmental sustainability (protecting natural resources), and talent sustainability (help employees succeed and create employment opportunities). Indra deplores the crisis of trust that has emerged as a result of financial scandals and the world economic crisis. She stated (Covey et al., 2012, "Foreword," location 270) that companies need "to ensure that we embrace not just the commercial idea of value, but the ethical ideal of values, too. Again, in a word, *trust*." Companies need to develop trusting relationships with their employees as well as with their customers. Indra makes this clear when she declared,

> We also have to take great care with the emotional bond that employees feel for our companies, because unless we have that emotional bond, companies cannot reach their potential. At the heart of that emotional bond is trust. (Covey et al., 2012, "Foreword," location 282)

Indra is a good example of how leaders can be powerful, ethical, and successful. Under her leadership, PepsiCo has outperformed by a 2 to 1 margin in the S&P 500 while at the same time making the 100 Best Corporate Citizens List (Covey et al., 2012). As the following section indicates, being politically skillful may also help leaders accomplish worthwhile goals.

Source: Covey, S. M. R., Link, G., & Merrill, R. R. (2012). *Smart trust: Creating prosperity, energy, and joy in a low-trust world* [Kindle edition]. New York, NY: Free Press.

Political Skill

Have you ever known someone who seemed politically skillful at work? Someone who knew how to navigate the office landscape without getting stuck in the quagmires of career-killing assignments or lost and isolated far away from the centers of influence? Someone socially astute, who knew what to say during politically sensitive discussions? Although we often think of office politics in negative terms, leaders have to be able to handle office politics if they want to be effective and help their followers and teammates. Indeed, Ahearn, Ferris, Hochwarter, Douglas, and Ammeter (2004) found that *politically skillful leaders helped their work teams be more effective and even increased the team members' feelings of empowerment.* Likewise, Treadway and his colleagues (Treadway et al., 2004) found that leaders high on political skill created a greater sense of organizational support for their subordinates, which in turn enhanced the subordinates' feelings of trust, reduced their cynicism, and increased their job satisfaction. As a result, *subordinates whose leaders were more politically skillful had higher organizational commitment.*

Ferris, Perrewé, and Douglas (2002) argued that political skill is a key component of social competence at work. Ferris et al. (2005) developed the *Political Skill Inventory (PSI)* to measure this type of social ability. They validated their scale using seven different samples and four different studies. They concluded that *political skill involves the following four dimensions: (1) social astuteness, (2) interpersonal influence, (3) networking ability, and (4) apparent sincerity.* Although research on political skill is still fairly new, a review of the literature suggests that it has considerable promise (Yammarino & Mumford, 2011).

> **Self-Assessment:** Visit the textbook website to see how you rate on political skill.

It's Who You Know: Networking and Leadership Success

As Brass (2001) argued, who you know has a large influence on your ability as a leader to influence others and get things done. In other words, your social capital (your friendship ties and informal network) has a lot to do with your leadership success. A leader with influential ties throughout the organization may even be in a better position to influence his or her subordinates. A study found that subordinates perceived well-connected leaders to have higher status and a better reputation throughout the organization (Venkataramani, Green, & Schleicher, 2010). Because of their better reputation, the influential and well-connected leaders were able to establish better leader-member relationships with their own subordinates.

> **Applications:** How important is networking and political skill to a leader's success? What makes someone a center of a network? Are leaders high on political skill more trustworthy? Who would you rather work for: a leader low or high on political skill and networking ability?

Power Motivation Across Cultures

*McClelland argued that individuals and societies differ in their **power motivation**, or desire to control and influence others* (McClelland, 1985; McClelland & Boyatzis, 1982). Power motivation is an individual difference variable in that within societies there are considerable differences between people in their desire for power. However, McClelland and his colleagues also believed that people acquire some of their power motivation from their culture and that there are differences between cultures in the percentages of people with high power motivation. For some people, the power motivation is a major motivator that causes them to seek administrative positions or other sources of power and influence over others. McClelland maintained that people also differ in terms of whether they want to use power for socially beneficial purposes or for selfish reasons.

A study conducted in 24 countries demonstrated that there are important differences among cultures in power motivation (van Emmerik, Gardner, Wendt, & Fischer, 2010). Here is a brief list on how some of the countries rate on power motivation:

Philippines	1.42
South Korea	1.25
Japan	1.19
United States	1.02
Italy	.98
Canada	.87
Spain	.82

As this demonstrates, some societies, like the Philippines, are high in power motivation; some, like the United States, are moderate; and some, like Spain, are apparently low on power motivation. When working with people from other cultures, make sure to consider their power motivation levels.

As the following *Personal Reflections* feature demonstrates, some people give orders due to their personal power motivation, whereas others give orders because they are trying to achieve organizational goals.

PERSONAL REFLECTIONS:
THE TWO "NEEDS" TO GIVE ORDERS

Some people seem to get a real thrill out of giving orders to other people. Giving orders to other people makes them feel powerful, important, and in control. These leaders give orders because of their own psychological needs. Other leaders give orders because they need to instruct someone in how to do the job, because they need to coordinate the activities of multiple workers, or even because they want to bolster a subordinate's confidence that he or she can accomplish the goal. These leaders give orders because of the second type of need—the need to get the job done. I've seen both types of leaders in action. I've noticed that the first type of leader often gives orders in a way that emphasizes their own power and right to control their subordinates. "I'm the boss" is the not-too-subtle message that accompanies every order. In contrast, the best leaders I've seen make requests in a way that respects the autonomy and dignity of those they lead. When leading a group, they may specify the three key tasks that need to be done and then ask for volunteers. They get to thank the team members for their help every time they volunteer. Leaders high on the psychological need for power often emphasize their own expertise and frequently explain to subordinates how to do tasks they already understand. In contrast, the second type of leader gives requests in a way that supports the self-esteem and confidence of their subordinates: "Jane, you're our statistical analysis wizard, could you take charge of getting that graph prepared?"

Directing others is one of the hardest tasks for a new manager to learn. Years ago, as an assistant professor, I was a little hesitant about directing the activities of my research assistants. I wasn't much older than they were, sometimes even younger, and I tried to act more like a friend than a boss. Most of the assistants showed great initiative in doing their tasks, but one was obviously not putting in the hours that he was supposed to on my projects. Since I was trying to act friendly, I always accepted his excuses about how much pressure he was under to finish his dissertation or work on his other projects. For years afterward, I berated myself over this as an example of how I wasn't assertive enough. But then something interesting happened: My former assistant was now a faculty member at another university and in a position to do me an important favor. It turns out he appreciated my consideration of his situation when he was a student and he wanted to return the favor. Perhaps being considerate of my assistant was the right way to go after all.

Your Turn to Reflect: Have you witnessed leaders giving orders just to show they are the boss? How can you give directions to subordinates and make sure they do their work without sounding like an abusive boss?

Petty Tyrants and Abusive Bosses

Have you ever known a manager who's always criticizing his or her subordinates? Someone who's always eager to point out to others any mistakes subordinates might have made? Someone who seems to delight in ridiculing employees? Someone who never trusts subordinates to take responsibility? Someone who gives orders for the sake of giving orders? If so, then you probably know what Ashforth (1994) is talking about in his article on petty tyrants. *Petty tyrants are self-aggrandizers who treat their subordinates in an arbitrary, belittling, inconsiderate, and overcontrolling manner*. Petty tyrants are generally low-level supervisors who are more concerned with their own power than they are with the welfare of their subordinates. As Ashforth observes, petty tyrants generally have negative effects both on performance and on their subordinates' welfare. Their subordinates generally feel stress and frustration, and in addition, they feel helpless to take initiative to solve work-related problems. Moreover, subordinates respond to petty tyrants with reactance and sometimes engage in indirect, covert opposition to the dictates and commands of the petty tyrants.

Considerable research has documented the harmful effects that abusive supervision can have on employees (Tepper, 2000). A meta-analysis has summarized 66 studies (39 that measured supervisor aggression) that examined the effects of supervisor aggression, coworker aggression, and outsider aggression on the work-related attitudes and health of employees (Hershcovis & Barling, 2010). *When comparing coworker to supervisor aggression, the supervisor aggression had the strongest negative effects on employees' job satisfaction, affective commitment, and job performance, and supervisor aggression also caused the biggest increase in intent to turnover.* Coworker aggression, in turn, had bigger negative effects on job satisfaction and affective commitment than did outsider aggression. *Aggression also had negative effects on the employees' physical health, with coworker and supervisor aggression being equally harmful.*

There are steps that employees can take to help them cope with the negative effects of supervisor abuse. For example, Harvey, Stoner, Hochwarter, & Kacmar (2007) found that employees who used ingratiation to build their support network among their peers and who were also high on positive affect were better able to cope with abusive supervision.

The following case written by a guest author shows how subordinates react to unfair treatment and abuse, and it also demonstrates that sometimes justice prevails in the long run.

Case: *Abusive Leadership and Retaliation*

By Rebecca Michalak

The consequences of a lack of or poor leadership can be very negative. Top-down mistreatment of employees is one type of poor leadership behavior, which can have dire effects on an organization. In line with this, recent research has begun to explore how different leadership styles, including laissez-faire and abusive leadership, may result in employees engaging in negative behavior, including acts of retaliation. For example, an interview study conducted in Australia found that approximately one quarter of employees that experience bad behavior from individuals in leadership positions at work engage in some form of retaliation. A further 30% spend significant amounts of time considering what they might do to seek revenge but do not actually carry out their plans.

Retaliation can take several forms and may be directed at the perpetrator or displaced—i.e., directed at another person in the organization or the organization itself. In cases such as top-down mistreatment (where power plays a critical role), retaliation is most often displaced at the organization, rather than the leader themselves. Retaliation also varies in its severity. An employee may simply withdraw work effort, resulting in lower productivity. However, others will go to rather extreme lengths to seek revenge for their poor leadership experiences, as the following case demonstrates.

While negotiating a new enterprise employment agreement, the executive of a services-based organization used a large group of its frontline employees as a *bargaining tool* with the unions. Whenever the negotiation was not going the way of the leadership team, this employee group found entitlements such as their previously guaranteed training programs (completion of which was contractually linked to their salary increases) under threat of renunciation. This manipulative, mistreatment tactic went on for months, wreaking havoc on employee rosters and annual leave plans. Employees (and their immediate managers) were unsure whether these employees were to remain available for an already scheduled four week intensive training program or not. Concurrently, long awaited and sizeable pay rises (in the order of $8,500) for the employees who were due to complete the program were indefinitely delayed.

Even after the employment agreement was finalized and training programs were formally reinstated, the apparent disgust among affected employees over the actions of the senior leadership team remained high. Eventually, in an attempt to soothe employees, the executive held an open feedback session where employees were encouraged to vent their frustrations in a *strictly off the record* forum so that *we can learn to do it better next time*. One affected employee had been elected a spokesperson for the group and told the leadership team that due to all the to-ing and fro-ing in regard to training entitlements, they felt they had been used as pawns for the executives to get what they wanted out of the negotiation process.

Little did this employee know that despite the leadership team's assurances otherwise, she had just placed a target on her own back. The CEO in particular

(Continued)

(Continued)

seemed unimpressed by the feedback, even though it was truthful, fair, and delivered tactfully. However, at that stage, he was unable to do much about it. The elected spokesperson in question was, after all, a multiple award winning employee and the very popular face of public relations for the organization.

It was many months later that the opportunity arose for the CEO to get his own back. A miscommunication between venues resulted in some items being picked up by this employee and her coworker that were not actually intended for their organization. The owner of the items reported it and the CEO seized his chance. The employee received a phone call on her day off, demanding she attend the office immediately. Upon doing so, she was seated on her own on one side of a board table, faced off by the entire executive team, who bluntly told her she was being summarily dismissed for stealing. When she attempted to tell her side of the story and clarify what had actually occurred, she was forcefully silenced. Knowing what this would do to her reputation and trying to buy some time, she demanded she be allowed to resign instead of being terminated. However, rather than allowing her to go home and return the following day with her own resignation, they left her in the room and sometime later returned, placing an already typed letter in front of her. Handed a pen, she was told that if she did not resign from her position by 4:30 p.m., she would be sacked. This all occurred in the absence of any investigation into what had actually occurred (which would have cleared the employee of the accusations), with the employee denied her rightful request to access to a union representative or legal counsel. With the executive staring her down, isolated from anyone to assist her, and not knowing what else to do, she signed the papers at 4:28 p.m. As the employee said in her interview, it had become crystal clear to her that "They (the leadership team) were only going to try and hunt me down anyway."

The story does not end there however. Nothing short of furious with the way she had been treated by the leadership of the organization, this employee retaliated. She went on to start her own business—in direct competition with her former employer. As a long term employee, she was well aware of the issues that some of their clients were having with lucrative mining contracts, and she designed the bulk of her business around addressing these. In the space of a few months, she had successfully poached several of these cash cow clients, and as her business expanded, she continued to chip away at their market share. Before long, she had made a significant dent in one of their most profitable service areas, and she showed no signs of slowing down.

Seeking revenge helped her deal with the feelings of frustration and anger she had toward the organization as a result of its poor leadership behavior.

"I'd be lying if I said it wasn't part of my own form of retaliation because I've already bought the CEO a very nice card. Very nice, it's not horrible, but I'll send him that and say thanks very much for the step up to get to the position where I was, and without what you've done to me, I would never be where I am today. Oh, and here's my company folder, and this is why you've just lost 10 contracts."

Not all employees will go to this extent in retaliating. For example, others may simply engage in widespread word of mouth criticism of the organization, which can severely damage its reputation. As another interviewee who experienced ongoing bullying by the leader of her work team said, "You know, I told everyone—I'm sure I told the clerk at the grocery store that I was miserable about my boss.... I told a lot of people, and of course again, they didn't have the benefit of hearing the other side of the story—they only had my side." This form of retaliation may seem minor in comparison but can have severe effects on the organization's reputation both as an employer and as a supplier of goods or services.

These cases show that poor leadership has the potential to harm the organization in many ways, for example via damage to reputation, reduced productivity, and the loss of clients. These outcomes can result in anything from minor to significant decreases in profitability, indicating that without doubt, poor leadership is bad for business.

Rebecca Michalak is a former Director of HR in professional services and Principal Consultant for Advantage People Management Australia Pty Ltd. Her doctoral research at the University of Queensland explores the victim's perspective on interpersonal deviance, including perpetrated perpetrators and the use of retaliation as an emotion-focused coping strategy.

Applications: How would you respond to unfair treatment by your leader or your organization? Have you witnessed any examples of retaliation?

Put It in Practice

1. Avoid prison: Don't be too greedy, don't abuse your power and make subordinates do unethical things, and don't become a drug addict.

2. Use the right amount of power: Give leaders and employees the right amount of power, not too much or too little. Leaders need the authority to take effective action.

3. Power doesn't always corrupt: Lack of power causes feelings of frustration, which can lead to aggression. High power, high status people often have better interpersonal sensitivity.

4. Bases of power: Use referent power, expert power, and reward power to create high employee performance; legitimate power usually creates compliance but not high levels of commitment. Coercion produces resistance.

5. Psychological empowerment: Use reward power and referent power to enhance your followers' psychological empowerment; let them be the experts.

6. Be facilitative: Use facilitation power and ecological power to change the environment in a way that naturally guides behavior toward goal performance. Provide resources and change the environment to make desirable behaviors easier to perform.

7. Be persuasive: Use rational persuasion, consultation, inspirational appeals, and collaboration to gain compliance and improve leader-member relationships. Ingratiation may also help, but pressure tactics usually backfire.

8. Attitudes and peer pressure: Influence attitudes and beliefs by providing facts, and don't forget to show that peers also support the desired behaviors.

9. Use power with a purpose: That way you can achieve financial goals and societal goals.

10. Be politically skillful: Politically skillful leaders can help their teams be more effective and increase followers' feelings of empowerment and commitment. Political skill involves (1) social astuteness, (2) interpersonal influence, (3) networking ability, and (4) apparent sincerity.

11. Network your way to success and better leader-member relationships.

12. Power motivation: Recognize cultural differences in power motivation; also, use your own power motivation to achieve socially worthwhile goals, not just to boss others around.

13. Don't be a tyrant: Negative comments to subordinates may be more harmful than you think, and subordinates sometimes find ways to retaliate.

Exercises

1. Bases of Power Skits

Form teams and develop short skits that illustrate how leaders use the expanded six bases of power to influence a subordinate (rewards, coercion, expert, legitimate, referent, and facilitation/ecological power). For each basis of power, have one person play the leader and at least one person play the subordinate. Try to demonstrate how the respondents would react to the leader's use of power. You may want to show the subordinates reacting to the leader's influence attempt when the leader is not around to monitor them.

2. Persuasion

Form groups and discuss examples of times others have tried to influence you to do something. How successful was the effort? How would you classify the attempts according to the various persuasion strategies discussed in this chapter? Which methods seem most effective?

Visit the Student Study Site at **www.sagepub.com/humphreyel** for these additional tools:

- Learning Goals
- Leader's Book Case Articles
- Web Resources
- Student Self Assessments

References

Acton J. Retrieved February 4, 2013 from http://en.wikipedia.org/wiki/Lord_Acton

Ahearn, K. K., Ferris, G. R., Hochwarter, W. A., Douglas, C., & Ammeter, A. P. (2004). Leader political skill and team performance. *Journal of Management, 30,* 309–327.

Ashforth, B. E. (1994). Petty tyranny in organizations. *Human Relations, 47,* 755–778.

Belfort, J. (2007). *The wolf of Wall Street* [Kindle edition]. New York, NY: Bantam.

Belfort, Jordon. Retrieved February 4, 2013 from http://en.wikipedia.org/wiki/Jordan_Belfort

Brass, D. J. (2001). Social capital and organizational leadership. In S. J. Zaccaro & R. J. Klimoski (Eds.), *The nature of organizational leadership: Understanding the performance imperatives confronting today's leaders* (pp. 132–152). San Francisco, CA: Jossey-Bass.

Carson, P. P., Carson, K. D., & Pence, P. L. (2002). Supervisory power and its influence on staff members and their customers. *HOSPITAL TOPICS: Research and Perspectives on Healthcare, 80*(3), 11–15.

Carson, P. P., Carson, K. D., & Roe, C. W. (1993). Social power bases—a meta-analytic examination of interrelationships and outcomes. *Journal of Applied Social Psychology, 23,* 1150–1169.

Covey, S. M. R., Link, G., & Merrill, R. R. (2012). *Smart trust: Creating prosperity, energy, and joy in a low-trust world* [Kindle edition]. New York, NY: Free Press.

de Pater, I. E., Van Vianen, A. E. M., Humphrey, R. H., Sleeth, R. G., Hartman, N. S., & Fischer, A. H. (2009). Task choice and the division of challenging tasks between men and women. *Group and Organization Management, 34,* 563–589.

Ferris, G. R., Perrewé, P. L., & Douglas, C. (2002). Social effectiveness in organizations: Construct validity and directions for future research. *Journal of Leadership and Organizational Studies, 9,* 49–63.

Ferris, G. R., Treadway, D. C., Kolodinsky, R. W., Hochwarter, W. A., Kacmar, C. J., Douglas, C., & Frink, D. D. (2005). Development and validation of the political skill inventory. *Journal of Management, 31,* 126–152.

Fishbein, M., & Ajzen, I. (1975). *Belief, attitude, intention and behavior.* Reading, MA: Addison-Wesley.

French, J. R. P., & Raven, B. (1962). The bases of social power. In D. Cartwright (Ed.), *Group dynamics: Research and theory* (pp. 607–623). Evanston, IL: Row, Peterson.

Hall, J. A., Halberstadt, A. G., & O'Brien, D. E. (1997). "Subordination" and nonverbal sensitivity: A study and synthesis of findings based on trait measures. *Sex Roles, 37,* 295–317.

Harvey, P., Stoner, J., Hochwarter, W., & Kacmar, C. (2007). Coping with abusive supervision: The neutralizing effects of ingratiation and positive affect on negative employee outcomes. *The Leadership Quarterly, 18,* 264–280.

Hayward, S. F. (1997). *Churchill on leadership: Executive success in the face of adversity.* Rocklin, CA: Prima.

Hershcovis, M. S., & Barling, J. (2010). Towards a multi-foci approach to workplace aggression: A meta-analytic review of outcomes from different perpetrators. *Journal of Organizational Behavior, 31,* 24–44.

Hochwarter, W. A., Harrison, A. W., Ferris, G. R., Perrewe, P. L., & Ralston, D. A. (2000). A re-examination of Schriesheim and Hinkin's (1990) measure of upward influence. *Educational and Psychological Measurement, 60,* 751–771.

Humphrey, R. H., O'Malley, P. M., Johnston, L. D., & Bachman, J. G. (1988). Bases of power, facilitation effects, and attitudes and behavior. *Social Psychology Quarterly, 51,* 329–345.

Kipnis, D., Schmidt, S. M., & Wilkinson, I. (1980). Intra-organizational influence tactics: Explorations in getting one's way. *Journal of Applied Psychology, 65,* 440–452.

Mast, M. S., Jonas, K., & Hall, J. A. (2009). Give a person power and he or she will show interpersonal sensitivity: The phenomenon and its why and when. *Journal of Personality and Social Psychology, 97,* 835–850.

McClelland, D. C. (1985). *Human motivation.* Cambridge, UK: Cambridge University Press.

McClelland, D. C., & Boyatzis, R. E. (1982). Leadership motive pattern and long-term success in management. *Journal of Applied Psychology, 67,* 737–743.

Meth Project. Retrieved April 14, 2012 from http://www.methproject.org/about/

Randolph, W. A., & Kemery, E. R. (2011). Managerial use of power bases in a model of managerial empowerment practices and employee psychological empowerment. *Journal of Leadership & Organizational Studies, 18,* 95–106.

Schriesheim, C. A., & Hinkin, T. R. (1990). Influence tactics used by subordinates: A theoretical and empirical analysis and refinement of the Kipnis, Schmidt, and Wilkinson subscales. *Journal of Applied Psychology, 75,* 246–257.

Siebel Foundation. Retrieved April 14, 2012 from http://www.siebelfoundation.org/

Siebel, Thomas. Retrieved April 14, 2012 from http://en.wikipedia.org/w/index.php?t itle=Special:Book&bookcmd=download&collection_id=e745865d4cc617ab& writer=rl&return_to=Thomas+Siebel.

Tepper, B. (2000). Consequences of abusive supervision. *Academy of Management Journal, 43*, 178–190.

Treadway, D. C., Hochwarter, W. A., Ferris, G. R., Kacmar, C. J., Douglas, C., Ammeter, A. P., & Buckley, M. R. (2004). Leader political skill and employee reactions. *Leadership Quarterly, 15*, 493–513.

van Emmerik, H., Gardner, W. L., Wendt, H., & Fischer, D. (2010). Associations of culture and personality with McClelland's motives: A cross-cultural study of managers in 24 countries. *Group & Organization Management, 35*, 329–367.

Venkataramani, V., Green, S. G., & Schleicher, D. J. (2010). Well-connected leaders: The impact of leaders' social network ties on LMX and members' work attitudes. *Journal of Applied Psychology, 95*, 1071–1084.

Verini, J. (2009, May). What meth made this billionaire do. *FASTCOMPANY,* 84–89.

Wayne, S. J., Liden, R., Graef, I., & Ferris, G. (1997). The role of upward influence tactics in human resource decisions. *Personnel Psychology, 50,* 979–1006.

Yammarino, F. J., & Mumford, M. D. (2011). Leadership and organizational politics: A multi-level review and framework for pragmatic deals. In G. R. Ferris & D. C. Treadway (Eds.), *Politics in organizations: Theory and research considerations (SIOP frontier series).* New York, NY: Taylor & Francis/Routledge.

Yukl, G. (2010). *Leadership in organizations.* (7th ed.). Upper Saddle Brook, NJ: Prentice Hall.

Yukl, G., Seifert, C., & Chavez, C. (2008). Validation of the extended Influence Behavior Questionnaire. *The Leadership Quarterly, 19,* 609–621.

13

Charisma, Rhetoric, and Impression Management

Chapter Road Map

Case: *Steve Jobs: Master of Impression Management*

The late Steve Jobs, cofounder of Apple and former CEO of Pixar, was undoubtedly one of the most charismatic business leaders of the last century. His speeches to Apple employees and to technology conferences were enthusiastically shared on Internet sites and have been watched by millions. He was also a master of *impression management— the art of creating favorable impressions on others* (Rosenfeld, Giacalone, & Riordan, 1995). Although Steve Wozniak may have been the computer genius responsible for design-

Steve Jobs and Bills Gates at the 2007 'D5: All Things Digital' conference held in Carlsbad, California

Source: Wikipedia/Joi Ito (CC-BY)

ing Apple's first personal computer, it was Steve Jobs who had the business sense and personal charisma necessary to attract investors and market Apple. Jobs knew how to create the impression that he was an eccentric genius. When courting investors, he wore sandals instead of dress shoes and had unkempt, long hair. Perhaps he was trying to create the impression that he was like Einstein, who was also known for his unruly hair and for wearing shoes without socks. Whatever his motives, Jobs was often successful: Within minutes of meeting him, many seasoned business leaders formed the impression that Jobs had a great intellect.

Jobs also knew how to create visionary appeals. Jobs inspired investors with talks about how personal computers would change the world. Early investors felt they had an almost moral obligation to invest in Apple and thus bring about the personal computer revolution. Jobs applied his charisma and impression management techniques to vendors as well. One software supplier accepted a small fee (instead of more profitable royalty payments) because Jobs convinced him that he would be "providing a service to humanity" (Rosenfeld et al., 1995, p. 2); the supplier stated, "He made me feel like I should pay him for letting him use my software" (quote taken from Butcher, 1989, p. 219 and reported in Rosenfeld et al., 1995, p. 2).

Later, Jobs used visionary appeals and impression management tactics to sell computers to high schools and universities. He emphasized how he was trying to save the failing American education system by bringing schools into the technological age. Thus, he made it seem like he was doing school systems a favor by selling them computers. More recently, Jobs' personal charisma and marketing genius helped make Apple's portable music players the chic choice over cheaper MP3 players.

Steve's charisma and legacy are still working on investors today. Apple's market capitalization surpassed Microsoft's market value on May 26, 2010. There's good reason to think that Apple's market value was inflated due to the public frenzy that Jobs created over the iPad and other Apple products. Microsoft's revenue at the time was substantially higher than Apple's ($58.4 billion vs. $42.9 billion, respectively); moreover, Microsoft had more cash on hand than Apple ($35.7 billion vs. $23 billion, respectively). Microsoft also had a much wider range of products, including a near monopoly in computer operating software. Apple's stock prices continued to rise (even after Steve's death), and by April 2012, Apple was the most valuable publicly traded company on the New York stock exchange, with a market capitalization of $570 billion. This made it worth as much as Microsoft, Google, Hewlett-Packard, Dell, and Yahoo *combined.* Analysts disagree over whether Apple is overpriced, but whatever the verdict, Apple's success and market value is a vivid testament to Steve Job's legacy and the power of charisma and impression management.

Although it's easy to be skeptical of grand visionary appeals, Jobs made most of his visions come true. As we all know, the introduction of personal computers did change the world as Jobs had promised. High schools and universities now make extensive use of computers in the classroom. And Jobs revolutionized two other industries as well: movies and music. Billions of people have enjoyed Pixar movies, and iPods have transformed the music industry and changed the way music is both sold and played. All in all, Jobs used his charisma and impression management skills to make the world a better place.

Applications: How important is a leader's charisma to an organization's success? What do you think made Steve Jobs so successful? Will Apple continue to be successful without Jobs?

Web Exercise: Watch some of Jobs' speeches over YouTube.com or other Internet sites.

Sources: Butcher, L. (1989). *Accidental millionaire: The rise and fall of Steve Jobs.* New York, NY: Paragon House.

Nosowitz, D. (2010, May 26). Microsoft's and Apple's product lines compared: This is why Apple wins. *FastCompany.com.* Retrieved from http://www.fastcompany.com/1652843/microsoft-vs-apple-product-line-market-cap-wall-street-valuation-steve-jobs

Rosenfeld, P., Giacalone, R. A., & Riordan, C. A. (1995). *Impression management in organizations.* London, UK and New York, NY: Routledge.

Russolillo, S., & Cheng, J. (2012, April 25). Apple's stock-market sway. *Wall Street Journal.* Retrieved from http://online.wsj.com/article/SB10001424052702303990604577366332861232436.html

Steve Jobs exhibited many of the characteristics of charismatic leaders. He was able to create a sense of awe among his followers, which as the following section demonstrates, is a key feature of charismatic leaders. He also developed several visions of a better future for both his employees and his customers, and charismatic leaders excel at creating new visions. His first rise to success occurred during a period of great entrepreneurial possibilities, and later, he helped Apple emerge from a financial crisis. As we will see in this chapter, charismatic leaders are more likely to emerge during times of crisis or great opportunity. Jobs was also a great speaker and presenter, and charismatic leaders are usually exceptional communicators. Steve was also able to regulate his own emotions to create the emotional displays that would influence others to have a positive impression of his abilities. Steve was not above yelling at others and manipulating others, and quite a few observers have accused him of using his charisma for selfish purposes. Again, as the chapter will demonstrate, the misuse of charisma and other forms of influence is always a possibility. In this chapter, we will explore the following questions:

- What makes someone a charismatic leader? Is charisma a learned behavior or an inborn trait?
- Why is the development of a new vision important to charismatic leadership? What role does the environment (crisis vs. great opportunity) play in the emergence of charismatic leadership?
- Do charismatic leaders have to take risks in order to inspire others?
- What rhetorical techniques create an impression of charisma?
- How do leaders use emotional labor methods to control emotional contagion among their followers?
- What are the most common impression management techniques?
- What differentiates *dark-side* leaders from other influential leaders?

Charisma: Divine Gift or Learnable Behavior?

Early researchers defined charisma as a type of *divine gift* that separated history's greatest leaders from more ordinary leaders (Weber, 1947). In other words, these charismatic leaders were thought to have special characteristics and abilities, and only prominent leaders of social or religious movements, nations, or large organizations were described as charismatic (Shamir, 1995). Frontline leaders, supervisors, middle managers, or other types of routine, everyday leaders were not classified as charismatic. According to the divine gift perspective, charismatic leaders inspired feelings of awe among their followers and a reverential belief that the charismatic leaders were special and far above the common leader.

Of course, we are not likely to have this reverential awe for people that we can observe closely. As the Duke of Conde observed, "No man is a hero to his valet" (Pepys, 1854, p. 172). Great leaders are people too who make mistakes and are sometimes uninformed or ignorant about a topic and can be insecure, indecisive, vain, petty, or vindictive just like anyone else. Thus, it is easier to believe charismatic leaders have a divine gift when we observe them from afar and cannot see up close their human flaws. Although early scholars focused on the feelings of awe inspired by charismatic great leaders, latter scholars recognized that frontline leaders may also have a certain type of charisma even though it may differ in important ways from the charisma demonstrated by more distant leaders (Shamir, 1995). Leaders throughout the organization are also able to inspire those who know them well even if they can't create feelings of reverential awe.

Scholars also begin to think of charisma in terms of behaviors instead of in terms of special traits possessed only by a few (Conger & Kanungo, 1987). In particular, researchers began to focus on rhetorical skills that could be used to inspire others, to create a sense of common values and identity, and to motivate followers to achieve difficult goals and overcome obstacles (Shamir, Arthur, & House, 1994; Shamir, House, & Arthur, 1993). If charisma consists of specific behaviors, then it could, at least to some extent, be learned. For example, politicians and other would-be charismatic speakers were taught that they should use "we" statements instead of "I" statements in order to create a sense of a common collective identity (e.g., "Together, we can solve this problem" instead of "I can solve this problem").

The Need for Vision

Many scholars posit that charismatic leaders are those who create a new plan and vision to better meet their followers' needs. Conger, Kanungo, and Menon (2000) state, "Charismatic leadership is distinguished from other forms by the followers' perceptions of the manager's formulation of a shared and idealized future vision as well as his or her effective articulation of this vision in an inspirational manner" (p. 749). Charismatic leaders make their followers feel empowered by giving them a clear sense of purpose associated with high moral principles, a worthy cause, and a confidence boosting plan of action.

"Me" vs. "We"

The use of "we" statements and other devices to create a sense of a common collective identity may be particularly important to developing relationships with followers. Indeed, some scholars emphasize how charisma creates a special type of relationship between leaders and followers; the strength of this relationship also varies because the forms of charisma can vary from strong to weak (Bratton, Grint, & Nelson, 2005). In particular, *charismatic leaders may create a sense of a common social identity* (Conger et al., 2000; Shamir et al., 1994; Shamir et al., 1993). Followers are more likely to believe they are in a charismatic relationship with a leader when they identify with the leader and believe that the leader shares their values and goals. Thus, charismatic leaders exert part of their influence by getting followers to internalize the goals and values of the social movement, group, or organization they are leading.

A study by Sosik (2005) demonstrated that leaders who are concerned with values and the good of the collective team members are more likely to be perceived as charismatic leaders. Although charismatic leaders are known for advocating change, they also seek to build on their common values with followers, which are usually traditional values for most people. Thus, charismatic leaders link the past to the future and show how their common values support the changes they are advocating. Sosik's study is consistent with the earlier quantitative summary of the literature which found that charismatic leadership does contribute to follower job performance and commitment (Fuller, Patterson, Hester, & Stringer, 1996).

To the Rescue: Crisis and Charisma

A considerable body of research suggests that leaders are more likely to be perceived as extraordinary, charismatic leaders when they help their followers handle a crisis or cope with a major change (Conger et al., 2000; Pillai, 1996). During times of change or crisis, most people may be confused, uncertain, anxious, and clueless about what to do. Someone who can take charge and solve a seemingly unsolvable problem is thus more likely to be seen as extraordinary. Routine, everyday meetings may also give leaders little opportunity to make value-laden, extraordinary statements. Soaring rhetoric may seem inappropriate in a meeting devoted to reordering staples and office supplies. This is one reason why after the 9/11 attacks that the use of charismatic language increased dramatically among American leaders—the situation now called for such a response (Bligh, Kohles, & Meindl, 2004).

An experimental study demonstrated that stressful situations and crisis situations can increase the perceptions that a leader is charismatic (Halverson, Murphy, & Riggio, 2004). The researchers had 55 groups (three people each) work on project planning tasks. In each group, one person was randomly assigned to be the leader. Half the groups had the bad luck to be in the stressful condition. Moreover, all of the groups experienced a crisis midway through the project. As expected, the leaders in the stressful condition rose to the occasion and were rated as more charismatic. Moreover, the introduction of the crisis boosted the ratings of the leaders in the nonstressful situation to be equivalent to that of the leaders who were already experiencing stress.

Although many charismatic leaders may support change, social groups that are resisting proposed changes may also perceive themselves to be in a crisis. Their way of life, their culture, their careers, or their standard of living may be threatened by the projected transformations. These groups may want a charismatic leader who can mount the defense against the undesirable changes (Levay, 2010). A study of leaders in a Scandinavian university hospital found that leaders who opposed dreaded changes were considered to be charismatic by their supporters (Levay, 2010).

Charismatic Opportunities

Many successful leaders who are widely regarded as charismatic are known more for their successes than for handling crisis. Entrepreneurs with personal charm who have astonishing success stories are often regarded as extraordinary and charismatic individuals. Thus, instead of a crisis environment, an environment of great entrepreneurial possibilities may allow leaders to develop grand visions with the promise of a considerably better future (Conger, 2011). During the hi-tech boom, thriving entrepreneurs were treated with rock-star like status and with the sort of reverential awe that most politicians can only dream of.

> **The Leader's Bookcase:** To learn more about charisma, see: Conger, J. A. (2011). Charismatic leadership. In A. Bryman, D. Collinson, K. Grint, B. Jackson, & M. Uhl-Bien (Eds.), *Sage Handbook of Leadership* (pp. 86-102). London, UK: Sage.

Caught in the Middle

In typical organizations, creating charismatic relationships can be challenging for midlevel leaders because they must balance both upward and downward demands. Cowsill and Grint (2008) illustrated the dilemmas faced by middle managers in a mythologically inspired article called "Leadership, Task and Relationship: Orpheus, Prometheus and Janus." They argued that midlevel leaders must be like Janus, the two-faced Roman god of doorways and bridges. One face must look downward toward their subordinates while the other face looks upward to their own superiors. Subordinates desire their midlevel leaders to display supportive and friendly faces, but the upper-level executives expect the managers to display more stern task-oriented faces. It is hard to create a sense of "we" while expressing a stern visage.

Yet supportive midlevel leaders have to be careful to avoid the fate of Prometheus (Cowsill & Grint, 2008). Prometheus defied the gods and supported mankind by giving humanity the gift of fire; as a result, Prometheus was chained to a rock and had his liver eaten every day by vultures until he was freed by Hercules. To be considered charismatic, leaders must, like Prometheus, display a self-sacrificing concern and risk their own interests on behalf of their followers (Conger & Kanungo, 1987; Conger et al. 2000). In other words, they must prove they are more concerned with the "we" than with the "me." *When subordinates see leaders take personal risks on behalf of the group and organization, they are more willing to attribute benevolent motives to leaders and accord them heroic, charismatic status.* This is one reason why Winston Churchill is considered to be charismatic: He defied his own party's leadership and was expelled from governmental office as a result of his continuing insistence that the United Kingdom needed to be wary of the Nazis. Likewise, Teddy Roosevelt risked his own life by fighting corruption and by leading his troops up San Juan Hill. George Washington, who believed in listening more than speaking, is still considered charismatic because he led his soldiers from the front lines and often was the last to retreat.

Nonetheless, midlevel leaders still need to make sure the work is done. Thus, they must balance their downward displays of supportive, relationship-oriented behaviors with their subordinates with their need to carry out task duties consistent with their upward facing obligations to their own superiors. Therefore, charismatic leaders need to be both supportive and task-oriented. Charismatic leaders achieve this goal in part by role modeling the correct behavior by performing exemplary acts that prove their dedication and ability. The following case is about a political leader who role modeled the correct behavior by taking a personal risk for freedom.

Case: *Aung San Suu Kyi and a Personal Risk for Freedom*

Aung San Suu Kyi is a charismatic leader of the prodemocracy movement in Burma (aka Myanmar). It took some bravery for her to head up a dissident party. She knew from her own family experiences what standing up for freedom might cost: Her father, a leading political figure in the 1940s, had been killed by a rival political hit squad in 1947. Moreover, in 1988, the military rulers had shot and killed thousands of students and protesters. Despite the risk, she led the National League for Democracy to an election victory in 1990. Unfortunately, the dictators refused to yield power to the duly elected Aung San Suu Kyi, and they placed her under house arrest.

The repressive violence continued, and in 2007, hundreds of Buddhist monks and students were shot and beaten during the Saffron Revolution protest marches. Aung San Suu Kyi was freed from a 7 year stint under house arrest in November 2010; altogether, she's spent 15 years under house arrest because of her campaigns for freedom. Because of her courage and bravery, she was awarded the Nobel Peace Prize.

Nobel laureate Aung San Suu Kyi prepares to speak with her constituents during the 2012 by-election campaign (Kawhmu township, Myanmar; March 22, 2012).

Source: Wikipedia/Htoo Tay Zar (CC-BY-SA)

The military rulers imposed a strict censorship on artwork and public broadcasts. Inspired by Aung San Suu Kyi, many youth defied the censors by watching satellite TV broadcasts from the free world and by listening to Voice of America radio. These brave protestors achieved a major victory when Aung San Suu Kyi and 42 other members of her party were elected to the country's parliament in April 2012.

Sources: Hammer, J. (2011, March). Myanmar's free thinkers. Smithsonian, 28–36.

Voice of America News. (2012, April 30). Burma opposition ends boycott as UN chief addresses parliament. Retrieved from http://www.voanews.com/english/news/Burma-Opposition-Ends-Boycott-149459405.html

Express Your Charisma

The importance of effective communication skills to charisma is shown by a study that asked 422 students to define charisma (Levine, Muenchen, & Brooks, 2010). When the researchers coded the words the students used to define charisma, they found that the words grouped into five factors or clusters, all of which included some aspect of communication. The first factor related to having an outgoing personality, and included words such as "strong, charming, confident, and being a good speaker." Charismatic leaders also have to be good listeners: The second factor included the "ability to listen," "empathize with and understand others," be "genuine" and "knows when to talk and when to listen." The third and fourth factors directly focused on specific speaking skills, such as "the ability to speak well," having a "large vocabulary" and the ability "to maintain effective eye contact," and to have "a genuine speaking style." The fifth factor included being powerful and "loud." Although the factors included many words not related to communication, the considerable number of speaking skill-related words shows the importance of outstanding communication skills to charisma.

It is interesting that Winston Churchill, widely regarded as one of the most charismatic leaders in history, began his career by studying rhetoric. As a young man, he studied the greatest political speeches in English history, as well as poetry and literature. He had a phenomenal memory and could recite long poems decades after reading them (a divine gift?). As a 24-year-old, he wrote a short piece called "The Scaffolding of Rhetoric," in which he explains the principles that guided his future history-making speeches (Hayward, 1997). Later in his life, Churchill became the highest paid journalist in the world, and after WWII, he won a Nobel Prize in Literature for his historical writings. The following case goes over Churchill's advice on how to communicate and write speeches.

Case: *Winston Churchill on Rhetoric*

As Churchill stated in 1897, "Of all the talents bestowed upon men, none is so precious as the gifts of oratory... Abandoned by his party, betrayed by his friends, stripped of his offices, whoever can command this power is still formidable" (Hayward, 1997, p. 97). This statement proved to be prophetic in that in the early to mid-1930s Churchill was abandoned by his party and he did not hold office, yet his speeches and writings still made him one of the leading political figures of the decade.

The best possible word: Churchill stated, "There is no more important element in the technique of rhetoric than the continual employment of the best possible word" (Hayward, 1997, p. 99). Churchill preferred short, easily understandable words. He avoided jargon and he especially disliked using bureaucratic sounding expressions. He criticized bureaucratic proposals for using terms such as "communal feeding centers" and "accommodation units." Churchill thought that highfalutin words and phrases were often used to hide a speaker's real meaning or to disguise sloppy and confused thinking.

The power of rhythm: Churchill believed that "the great influence of sound on the human brain is well known" and that "the sentences of the orator when he appeals to his art become long, rolling and sonorous. The peculiar balance of the phrases produces a cadence which resembles blank verse rather than prose" (Hayward, 1997, p. 101). Churchill's speeches had a poetic rhythm to them and his handwritten notes often showed they were written in poetic style with line breaks to emphasize the rhythm. This rhythm was helped by his use of short words.

While on a speaking tour in the United States in 1900, Winston Churchill addresses a joint session of the United States Congress. This would have been about a year after he wrote the "Scaffolding of Rhetoric," and he would only have been about 25 years old—fairly young for addressing Congress.

Build your argument: Churchill also paid attention to logic and organization. Churchill used accumulation of argument, in which "a series of facts is brought forward all pointing in a common direction." As a result, "the end appears in view before it is reached" (Hayward, 1997, p. 102). The accumulating facts guide the listeners toward Churchill's conclusions.

Use analogies: Churchill wrote that an analogy "appeals to the everyday knowledge of the hear-

Source: Library of Congress

er and invites him to solve the problems that have baffled his powers of reason by the standard of the nursery and the heart" (Hayward, 1997, p. 102). Throughout his career, Churchill used vivid analogies to explain complex issues in a few readily understandable sentences.

Web Exercise: Use YouTube.com or other Internet sites to find some of Churchill's most famous speeches. Which of his four principles can you detect in his speeches? How much more powerful do you think his speeches would have been if you had been a British citizen during WWII?

Research generally confirms Churchill's advice to use analogies and vivid, visual imagery when making speeches. For example, a study examined the inaugural addresses of 36 United States presidents (Mio, Riggio, Levin, & Reese, 2005). Roughly half the presidents were rated as high on charisma (17) and half low (19). When the inaugural speeches were coded for their use of metaphors, it was found that the charismatic presidents used almost twice as many metaphors as did the noncharismatic presidents. Moreover, in a second study, the researchers had judges rate sections of the inaugural speeches on how inspirational they were. The findings again demonstrated the importance of metaphors to creating inspiring, charismatic speeches.

Another study used an experimental design to confirm the importance of speech imagery to perceptions of charisma (Naidoo & Lord, 2008). The study used two experimental conditions, one in which subjects listened to a speech with a high rate of imagery and the other with a low rate of imagery. For the high imagery condition, the researchers took the speech from U.S. President Franklin Delano Roosevelt's (FDR) 1933 inaugural address. FDR has been ranked as one of the United States's most charismatic presidents and his inaugural address is a great example of a high imagery speech. For the low imagery condition, they replaced high imagery words in the FDR speech with low imagery words that had the same meaning. For example, they replaced "dark hour" with "troubled moment"; and the phrase, "the withered leaves of industrial enterprise lie on every side" with "the effects of industrial folly lie on every side." For both speeches, references to specific historical events that would give away the identity of the speaker were removed. As expected, the participants rated the high imagery speech as higher in charisma. This effect worked in part by boosting the state positive affect (the moods the participants were experiencing while listening to the speech). The high imagery condition put the listeners in a better mood, which resulted in them rating the speech as more charismatic. This study confirms the importance of choosing the right word because the two speeches were identical except for the substitution of certain key words with identical meaning words that had less vivid imagery.

Charisma may be important to a president's ability to perform effectively. In order to carry out their agenda, presidents and other leaders have to be able to persuade others to support their plans. Thus, more charismatic presidents may be able to persuade congressmen to pass their legislative agenda and the overall public to support their programs. This may be one reason why studies have found that speech imagery and charismatic language are positively related to ratings of presidential greatness (Emrich, Brower, Feldman, & Garland, 2001).

A study of prominent television directors found that they used words related to optimism, praise, action, and movement more frequently than most people do (Murphy & Ensher, 2008). Their positive and vivid action-oriented communication style helped these leaders develop and communicate their vision to their crew and cast members. Waples and

Connelly (2008) also found that leaders who expressed active emotions had superior vision-related performance. Another study of leaders in a governmental agency in the Netherlands found that charismatic leaders had a supportive and assured communication style (de Vries, Bakker-Pieper, & Oostenveld, 2010).

Self-Assessment: Visit the textbook website to assess your skills at charismatic communication.

PERSONAL REFLECTIONS: *THE WORDS*

First, you need the words. Are you a master of the words? Can you make them stand on end, spin, and dance? Can you make them a chisel sharp enough to etch your meaning onto others' minds? Can you send them sliding down the neural pathways of their brains, free of obstruction, faster than any nagging doubt? Can you sculpt a slogan out of a shapeless mass of abstract ideas, give it form and a shape that others can see, that a child can understand? Can your words conjure the wind, make your listeners feel its caress? Can your words summon the touch of a mother's hand, make your listeners feel her warm embrace? Can you speak the tongue of scholars, the language of laborers? Can you make them hear your words with equal approval? Can your words soar above the crowd, yet be one with the people?

Second, you need the cause. Without the cause, your words may be a thing of beauty, but lack the weight to move people's hearts, to set their limbs in action, their hands to a purpose. You must search for the cause, delve deep into your followers' hearts, and discover what they most desire. Their desires give weight to your words; the stronger and more fervent their passions, the more powerful your words become. Let your words be the torrent of their deepest needs, and you can carve a stream through the bedrock of history.

Third, you need the path, the channel, to direct the mighty stream of humanity's needs. Your words must be the blueprints for the channels, the canals, the dams that shape and alter the flow of humanity. Plan foolishly, and the stream becomes a flood, a disaster, a waste. Plan wisely, and the stream powers turbines, lights up homes, waters fields and feeds the hungry. Do this, and the people will proclaim your greatness: *Charisma*.

Your Turn to Reflect: How important is vivid language to leadership and charisma? Are the leaders you admire good speakers? Which is easy to remember: the literary description of charisma or the academic version?

Coaches With Charisma

A leader's personal charisma may influence what type of leadership style he or she should use. Researchers assigned 400 undergraduate students to 80 five-person teams that worked on a dynamic simulation task (DeRue, Barnes, & Morgeson, 2010). In each team, one person was randomly assigned to be the leader. The teams were also motivated by the possibility of earning up to $50 in bonus money for good performance. Two experimental conditions were used: In one, the leader was told to use a coaching style that focused on developing and supporting the growth of the team members' abilities. In the second condition, the leaders were assigned to use a directive leadership style in which they actively set the team goals, provided specific directions, and monitored the teams' performance. The researchers found that leaders who were rated as charismatic (as measured by both self-ratings and follower ratings) were more effective at using a coaching, supportive style. In contrast, leaders without charismatic personal appeal were more effective when they used a directive leadership style. This study shows the importance of individual personal charisma to the charismatic leadership style.

Charisma and Emotional Contagion

Charismatic leaders may be especially emotionally contagious. In an impressive series of four studies, Bono and her colleague, Ilies (2006), demonstrated that charismatic leaders generally exhibit more positive emotions than do less charismatic leaders. Leaders who displayed positive emotions were rated as more effective. Moreover, Bono and Ilies provided evidence that one of the main ways that charismatic leaders influence others is by influencing their moods through emotional contagion—the spreading of the positive emotions from the leaders to the followers. When the followers' moods were boosted by their leaders' positive emotional displays, the followers rated the leaders as more effective. In a follow-up study, Bono, Jackson Foldes, Vinson, and Muros (2007) found that transformational leaders also influenced their followers to experience more positive moods (components of transformational leadership are related to charisma).

Leading With Emotional Labor

Have you ever led a team that was going through some difficult times, perhaps a crisis? Your employees, teammates, or players are feeling discouraged—what do you do? Chances are you'll try to buck up their spirits by displaying confidence. The trouble is you might be feeling a little down too. You might catch some of the negative moods from your teammates and subordinates; it's hard to feel confident when everyone around you is feeling pessimistic and depressed (Dasborough, Ashkanasy, Tee, & Tse, 2009). As Humphrey, Pollack, and Hawver (2008) stated, "Leaders may have to display confidence . . . even when they are experiencing the doubts and worries of their group members" (p. 157).

During difficult times, leaders may have to use emotional labor and regulation tactics to manage their own emotions. These tactics can help leaders display the right emotions to motivate their followers and team members. Hochschild (1983) was the first to study emotional labor; she focused on service workers like airline attendants and waiters and waitresses. She argued that *employees perform **emotional labor** when they are required to display emotions, such as smiling at customers, as part of their job*. In many restaurants and shops, employees are encouraged to provide service with a smile. She defined two methods that employees can use to put on the right emotional displays for their job. Employees use **surface acting** *when they change their outward displays of emotions without really trying to feel the emotions they are displaying*. In contrast, *when employees use **deep acting**, they first try to summon up the emotions and feelings they want to display and then let their generated feelings animate their outward displays of emotions.*

Ashforth and Humphrey (1993) argued that there is a third way to perform emotional labor: ***Genuine emotional labor** takes place when employees' spontaneous, natural, and genuine emotions also meet the emotional display rules of the organization*. When employees identify with their jobs and enjoy their work, they may not have to fake their emotional displays or try to feel emotions they are not naturally feeling. Research has confirmed that genuine emotional labor is a valid form of emotional labor that often results in better outcomes for both the employees and customers (Dahling & Perez, 2010; Diefendorff, Croyle, & Gosserand, 2005; Diefendorff & Gosserand, 2003; Glomb & Tews, 2004).

Although most research focused on service workers, Mann (1997) studied how employees (including managers) used emotional labor to communicate up and down the hierarchy. It is probably not a surprise to you to find that employees do not always express their true emotions to other employees (i.e., they sometimes use surface acting). Employees may also have to summon up (through deep acting) displays of enthusiasm and confidence when telling the boss that they will get the project done on time, make the big sale, improve production, reduce defects, etc. Later, Brotheridge and Grandey (2002) found that managers performed emotional labor as frequently as many service workers do; their research suggested that leaders also use emotional labor. Humphrey (2005, 2006, 2008) was the first researcher to develop a model of how leaders use emotional labor, and he coined the phrase "leading with emotional labor." Humphrey (2008) [italics and bold-faced added] stated

> *Leading with emotional labor refers to the whole process in which leader emotional displays influence subordinates' moods and thus their performance, and includes the leader's use of surface acting, deep acting, and genuine emotional expression, as well as their effects on the subordinates' moods and performance.* (p. 5)

By leading with emotional labor, managers can take control of their own feelings and emotional displays. Once they have their own emotional displays under control, leaders can use emotional contagion to help their followers feel the right emotions for the current situation.

Emotional labor tactics may help leaders express charismatic emotions, especially during difficult times and crisis situations. For example, emotional labor can help leaders in the public service sector express optimistic feelings; by displaying confidence, leaders can help governmental workers believe that they too can handle the difficult tasks facing them (Kiel & Watson, 2009; Newman, Guy, & Mastracci, 2009). A study of college leaders found that leaders may use deep acting to express emotions that they do not typically express (Iszatt-White, 2009; 2012). For example, a normally agreeable and easy-going leader might have to use deep acting to show irritation toward a poor performer who seems to be slacking off.

Leaders are also responsible for managing emotional labor processes at all levels, ranging from within-person daily variations in moods up to the setting of organization-wide display rules (Ashkanasy & Humphrey, 2011a, 2011b, in press; charismatic processes also vary by level; e.g., Waldman & Yammarino, 1999). For example, Sir Richard Branson and Tony Hsieh both created emotional display rules that encouraged greater freedom in emotional self-expression and the use of genuine natural emotions when dealing with customers. Leaders also have to exercise greater judgment in their use of emotional labor than do most other workers who perform emotional labor (Humphrey et al., 2008). Many service workers have to use a fairly narrow range of emotional expressions in a highly repetitive manner that requires little judgment about what emotions to portray. Restaurant workers, for example, know they should smile and act friendly to customers. In contrast, when an employee comes in late for work due to a personal problem, a leader may have to decide if he or she should express sympathy and support or stern disapproval. Leaders may have to display a wide range of emotions such as friendliness, sympathy, enthusiasm, optimism, and even anger or irritation. Moreover, leaders may have to switch rapidly from one type of emotional display to another—the employee needing sympathy may walk in right after the leader had to display irritation at a poor performing subordinate.

It takes skill to lead with emotional labor, and the effects of a leader's emotional labor depends on how it is perceived by the subordinates (Jones, Kane, Russo, & Walmsley, 2008). Few people may be skilled in using all three types of emotional labor; Jordan, Soutar, and Kiffin-Petersen (2008) found that only 4% of the service workers in their sample were high on all three types of emotional labor, and only 28% were high on both deep acting and genuine emotional expression.

There is a payoff for using emotional labor, because leaders who use emotional labor are rated higher on transformational leadership (Epitropaki, 2006). In general, leaders who effectively use emotional labor, especially deep acting and genuine emotional labor, should be perceived as more charismatic. One study of small business owners found that entrepreneurial leaders who used natural and genuine emotional labor to express positive emotions like enthusiasm and liking had employees with higher job satisfaction; these leaders also had higher overall firm performance (Batchelor, Humphrey, & Burch, 2012). When leaders use surface acting, however, they may actually lower their followers' job satisfaction (Fisk & Friesen, 2012).

Performing emotional labor can be stressful. Even putting on a smile may feel stressful at the end of a long work day. In particular, surface acting may create feelings of stress (Bono & Vey, 2005; Brotheridge & Grandey, 2002; Bryant & Cox, 2006; Van Dijk & Kirk-Brown, 2006). One study of how leaders use emotional labor found that the leaders' stress levels depended on their level of emotive awareness (Jones, Visio, Wilberding, & King, 2008).

Dissonance occurs when employees portray emotions that are discrepant with how they really feel, and thus, surface acting (and possibly deep acting) can cause feelings of inauthenticity among leaders (Gardner, Fischer, & Hunt, 2009; Hunt, Gardner, & Fischer, 2008). For example, midlevel leaders ordered to *get tough* with subordinates may use surface acting to express anger toward their subordinates, but they might feel a sense of inauthenticity as a result. The leaders may not feel that their expressed emotions represent the real them. Moreover, even when leaders use surface acting to portray positive emotions, subordinates may see through the surface acting and perceive the leaders to be inauthentic and untrustworthy. Even expressing genuine emotions can produce a bad impression on employees if the emotions are not consistent with social norms or the organization's display rules: Sometimes it is best not to express that rude urge (Hunt et al., 2008).

When leaders identify with their job and leadership role, however, performing emotional labor may have beneficial effects. Deep acting may even help leaders feel better themselves. A good example would be Eisenhower during WWII. Few leaders have ever had such awesome responsibilities as he did—the fate of the free world depended on his winning the war, and millions of lives were at stake. Eisenhower resolved to always display a cheerful, optimistic attitude. He believed that portraying optimism "tends to minimize potentialities within the individual himself to become demoralized" and that it also

> has a most extraordinary effect upon all with who[m] he comes into contact. With this clear realization, I determined that my mannerisms and speech in public would always reflect the cheerful certainty of victory—that any pessimism and discouragement I might feel would be reserved for my pillow. (Ambrose, 1990, p. 82)

Eisenhower also set the emotional display rules for his officers. He refused to consider the possibility of defeat or let his officers display defeatist, pessimistic attitudes either (Axelrod, 2006).

Applications: Have you ever worked at a job where you were told what emotions you should express to others? How difficult is it to display the right emotions? How does expressing an emotion you are not really feeling make you feel? Should leaders display confidence during crisis situations even if they are feeling anxious? Do you pay attention to your leaders' emotions?

The Dark Side of Charisma

As Kets de Vries and Balazs (2011) argued in "The Shadow Side of Leadership," leaders like any other people may suffer from narcissism, irrationality, and dark unconscious motivations. Many powerful leaders exhibit signs of **narcissism**, *defined as "a personality trait encompassing grandiosity, arrogance, self-absorption, entitlement, fragile self-esteem, and hostility"* (Rosenthal & Pittinsky, 2006, p. 617) [italics and boldface added]. Narcissistic leaders are often motivated by a need to be admired and by a desire for power, while at the same time lacking empathic concern for others.

Although most charismatic leaders are probably beneficial, there always exists the possibility that charismatic leaders may use their ability to influence others for selfish or destructive purposes (House & Howell, 1992). There may be particular personality traits, such as narcissism and a personal power motive (as opposed to socialized power motive), as well as environmental factors that distinguish destructive charismatic leaders from more beneficial ones (O'Connor, Mumford, Clifton, Gessner, & Connelly, 1995). Nonetheless, research suggests that charismatic leaders may be less prone to violent, destructive leadership than ideological leaders (Mumford et al., 2007). Mumford and his colleagues (Mumford et al., 2007, p. 227) found that *selective information processing—"a tendency to reject or discount objective information" with a "reality-distorting" view of the world, was characteristic of violent leaders*. Moreover, violent leaders scored high on ideological extremism. Thus, it might be traits like narcissism, ideological extremism, and reality-distorting selective information processing rather than charisma per se that creates destructive behavior on the part of leaders.

Impression Management and Charisma

Erving Goffman (1959) pioneered the field of impression management in his classic book, *The Presentation of Self in Everyday Life*. According to Goffman, impression management is an essential part of everyday life; it is part of the process of communicating to others who we are. Far from being a method of conning others, impression management can have many socially beneficial purposes. For example, impression management is often used to help others save face. When a subordinate or coworker makes an embarrassing mistake, a leader or team member can use impression management techniques to smooth over the embarrassing moment. Considerable research has confirmed these beneficial results (Rosenfeld et al., 1995). For instance, a study of 246 working adults found that subordinates responded more positively to constructive negative feedback when the supervisors included face-saving statements as well as the negative feedback; moreover, subordinates had more positive impressions of the supervisors (Kingsley Westerman & Westerman, 2010).

Although there are many types of impression management tactics, scales developed by Bolino and Turnley (1999) measure five common impression management tactics that people use to advance their own careers or to obtain aid:

Self-promotion: This involves talking to others about your relevant experiences, education, talents, value to the organization, and accomplishments.

Ingratiation: This consists of complementing and praising others, taking an interest in colleagues' personal life, or doing favors to demonstrate your friendliness and likeability.

Exemplification: This requires demonstrating your dedication by arriving early to work, staying late, or always looking busy even if it's slow.

Intimidation: This is engaging in intimidation or other forceful and aggressive behavior when it helps you do your job or when it helps you prevent others from interfering with your work.

Supplication: This is gaining aid and assistance from others by pretending to be ignorant or uninformed or needy in some way to avoid doing unpleasant chores.

Research using three different samples has confirmed the overall validity of the Bolino and Turnley scale (Kacmar, Harris, & Nagy, 2007). Another recent study, by Nguyen, Seers, & Hartman (2008), examined two of the dimensions, self-promotion and ingratiation, and found that they were related to organizational citizenship behaviors, team member satisfaction, and the degree of liking team members felt for each other. The beneficial effects were strongest when the motives behind the behaviors were seen as sincere. Supervisor's perceptions of the motives behind subordinates' behavior are also particularly important and may determine whether the supervisors regard the behavior as a form of impression management or as sincere organizational citizenship behavior (Halbesleben, Bowler, Bolino, & Turnley, 2010).

In addition to the above tactics, other tactics exist as well. For example, the Impression Management by Association Scale (IMAS) (Andrews & Kacmar, 2001) measures the extent to which people try to associate themselves with influential, successful others and distance themselves from unproductive others.

Some people have a negative view of impression management and assume that leaders high on impression management praise their superiors while backstabbing their competition and coercing their subordinates. However, some evidence suggests quite the opposite—that leaders high on impression management might be *less likely* to use punishment or coercion as a motivating tool. After all, these leaders generally want to be admired, liked, and respected by others, including their subordinates. Gray and Densten (2007) surveyed a national cross sample of 2,376 Australian business executives. They found that impression management was associated with greater amounts of transformational leadership behavior. In particular, leaders high on impression management were likely to report higher levels of providing individual support. This shouldn't be surprising—ingratiation is one of the key forms of impression management. Moreover, the use of impression management was negatively correlated with contingent punishment. After all, it's hard to get employees to admire you while you are punishing them.

The following case demonstrates how one of the most charismatic leaders in history used charm, ingratiation, and self-promotion to become Emperor.

Case: *Napoleon: The Most Persuasive Man in History?*

How persuasive was Napoleon? His parents fought against the French, and he was born in the Corsican Mountains while his mother was hiding from the French invaders, yet he convinced the French conquerors of Corsica to make him their leader. When the revolutionaries beheaded the French king and queen, they put up a sign on the palace declaring that France would never again be ruled by a king. The revolutionaries also guillotined thousands of other nobles in the name of equality. Yet Napoleon convinced these same revolutionaries to make him an Emperor with more absolute power than the kings of France ever had. Two American presidents had their reputations tarnished by the deaths of 58,000 U.S. soldiers in the Vietnam War (out of a population of 200 million). Up to *1.7 million* French soldiers were causalities in the Napoleonic wars (out of a population of 28 million), yet Napoleon remained beloved by his soldiers and countrymen. What made Napoleon so charismatic?

Napoleon in Alexandria, July 3, 1798

Source: Guillaume-François Colson. The Yorck Project

"I have only one counsel for you—be master" (Napoleon, retrieved 2013).

Master Writing: Napoleon scored his first major victory with the pen, not the sword. The young Napoleon developed his writing skills by entering literary contests and by writing a romantic novella. Napoleon first gained national attention by writing his Address to the National Assembly, in which he pledged Corsican support for the French Revolution. The National Assembly was so impressed by the address that they granted Corsicans the "full rights and liberties of French citizens" (Markham, 1966, p. 21). (Not all of the Corsicans were impressed: Napoleon and his family had to flee Corsica.) Later, Napoleon gained the attention and support of the French revolutionary leaders by writing a pamphlet.

(Continued)

(Continued)

During his military campaigns, Napoleon would send back to Paris dramatic bulletins that glorified his victories. These bulletins made him the best known general even though other French generals were also winning battles. He used poetic images, for example, he called one fight the "Battle of the Pyramids" even though it took place in a melon patch 30 miles from the pyramids.

Master Your Voice: Napoleon knew the powerful effect that emotionally expressive voices can have on others. The diplomat Caulaincourt said of Napoleon, "He had, when he wanted, something seductive, persuasive, in his voice and manner.... no man ever had more charm." Here's how a battle-hardened general described Napoleon: "When he wanted to seduce, his manner was one of ineffable charm, a kind of magnetic power. The person he wishes to attract seems to lose control of himself" (both quotes are from Aronson, 1990, p. 151).

Don't Hold Back: Napoleon knew the value of an all-out impassioned plea. While still a relatively poor, unknown junior officer, Napoleon won the affections of the most sought after woman in France, Josephine (who was also well connected politically), by writing her a letter worthy of Shakespeare:

> I awaken full of you. Between your portrait and the memory of our intoxicating night, my senses have no respite. Sweet and incomparable Josephine, what is this strange effect you have upon my heart? What if you were to be angry? What if I were to see you sad or troubled? Then my soul would be shattered by distress. Then your lover would find no peace, no rest. But I find none, either, when I succumb to the profound emotion that overwhelms me, when I draw from your lips, from your heart, a flame that consumes me.... I send you a thousand kisses—but send me none in return, for they set my blood on fire. (Aronson, 1990, p. 57)

Napoleon used the same sort of all-out appeals to inspire his troops. During his resignation speech to his troops, he let tears fall down his cheeks. The soldiers were touched by his unrestrained emotional displays and later supported his reinstatement as Emperor.

Master Art and Ceremony: Napoleon's coronation was a masterpiece of pomp, circumstance, and symbolism. A famous painter who had supported the republican cause by signing death warrants for many nobles now glorified Napoleon's coronation as Emperor in an awe-inspiring painting. By inviting the Pope to participate in his coronation, Napoleon publicly expressed his desire to make peace with the church. Yet Napoleon grabbed the crown from the Pope and placed it on his own head, thus symbolically demonstrating his supremacy over the Church.

Rule With Praise: Napoleon created The Legion of Honor to motivate soldiers with praise and public recognition (contrary to the earlier revolutionary prohibition on nonegalitarian honors). Napoleon stated, "A soldier will fight long and hard for a bit of colored ribbon" (Napoleon, retrieved 2013).

Master the Grand Gesture: In one battle (at Tilsit, in 1807), Napoleon and his army killed thousands of Russian soldiers. Yet a few days later, Napoleon had a Russian soldier kissing his hand in gratitude. How? He gave the soldier a medal for bravery. Napoleon also charmed Czar Alexander I, who became a big admirer of Napoleon. He convinced the Czar to join in an embargo against the English that the Czar's own nobles strongly opposed.

On his return from exile in 1815, Napoleon encountered on the road the troops who had been sent to arrest him. Napoleon boldly faced the troops alone and cried, "Kill your Emperor if you wish" (Markham, 1966, p. 141). The troops broke ranks and crowded around him, cheerfully welcoming him back. These soldiers must have known that welcoming Napoleon back would mean war.

Master Your Craft: Napoleon knew that his public support ultimately depended upon his military victories. As a student, he studied and mastered the mathematics behind artillery. He also read books on the latest military tactics and theoretical articles about how the new types of artillery might transform warfare. Napoleon is one of history's greatest military geniuses.

Applications: Napoleon abhorred the Reign of Terror and he was merciful to his political opponents, many of whom he invited to join his government. Is Napoleon a dark-side leader or a heroic reflection of his times and culture? What do you think made him so charismatic? How can his tactics be used in more ordinary circumstances and in typical organizations?

Sources: Aronson, T. (1990). *Napoleon & Josephine: A love story.* New York, NY: St. Martin's Press.
Markham, F. (1966). *Napoleon.* New York, NY: Penguin.

Put It in Practice

1. Master impression management: Create favorable impressions by relating your product to broader societal goals.

2. Be awe-inspiring: You can learn to be charismatic by using "we" statements and performing other charismatic behaviors.

3. Create a common social identity: Create a common identity with and among your followers by emphasizing common values and a shared vision of an idealized better future.

4. Crisis and opportunity: Take advantage of both great opportunities and crisis situations to become a charismatic leader.

5. Be heroic: Demonstrate your commitment by taking personal risks for your followers.

6. Express your charisma: Speak well and listen to others.

7. Rhetoric: Use the best possible word (short is better) and the power of rhythm. Build your arguments and use analogies.

8. Use metaphors, imagery, and vivid language: Direct your way to success with optimistic, action-oriented words.

9. Coach with charisma: If you are personally charismatic, focus on coaching and developing your subordinates; otherwise, be directive, set goals, and monitor progress.

10. Control emotional contagion: Use your own emotional displays to create positive moods among your followers and to boost perceptions of your charisma.

11. Use deep acting and genuine emotional labor to motivate both yourself and the troops. Avoid surface acting and inauthenticity.

12. Don't go to the Dark Side: Avoid narcissism and selective information processing.

13. Master impression management: Use impression management to help others save face and to create positive impressions of your skills and abilities. Use self-promotion and ingratiation to improve team members' satisfaction and liking for each other.

14. Become an emperor (or at least a leader): Master writing, master your voice, don't hold back, master art and ceremony, rule with praise, master the grand gesture, and master your craft.

Exercises

1. Web Exercise: Charismatic Images

Look up some of the famous paintings of Napoleon, such as the painting by J. L. David of Napoleon crossing the Alps on a magnificent horse (he actually crossed on a more sure-footed mule). How inspirational are they? You can also find quotes from Napoleon on brainyquote.com. Is a picture worth a thousand words, as Napoleon stated? What do the quotes say about Napoleon and his leadership style?

2. Vivid Words

Look up this article and read the two different versions of the speech by FDR at the end of the article: Naidoo, L. J., & Lord, R. G. (2008). Speech imagery and perceptions of charisma: The mediating role of positive affect. *The Leadership Quarterly, 19,* 283–296. Then take a typical article from a newspaper or a magazine. Try to replace some of the words in the article with the sort of vivid word images used in the actual FDR speech.

Visit the Student Study Site at **www.sagepub.com/humphreyel** for these additional tools:

- Learning Goals
- Leader's Book Case Articles
- Web Resources
- Student Self Assessments

References

Ambrose, S. E. (1990). *Eisenhower: Soldier and president.* New York, NY: Simon & Schuster.

Andrews, M. C., & Kacmar, K. M. (2001). Impression management by association: Construction and validation of a scale. *Journal of Vocational Behavior, 58,* 142–161.

Aronson, T. (1990). *Napoleon & Josephine: A love story.* New York, NY: St. Martin's Press.

Ashforth, B. E., & Humphrey, R. H. (1993). Emotional labor in service roles: The influence of identity. *Academy of Management Review, 18,* 88–115.

Ashkanasy, N. M., & Humphrey, R. H. (2011a). A multi-level view of leadership and emotions: Leading with emotional labor. In A. Bryman, D. Collinson, K. Grint, B. Jackson, & M. Uhl-Bien (Eds.), *Sage handbook of leadership* (pp. 365–379). London, UK: Sage.

Ashkanasy, N. M., & Humphrey, R. H. (2011b). Current emotion work in organizational behavior. *Emotion Review, 3,* 1–11.

Ashkanasy, N. M., & Humphrey, R. H. (in press). Leadership and emotion: A multi-level perspective. In D. V. Day (Ed.), *Oxford handbook of leadership and organizations.*

Axelrod, A. (2006). *Eisenhower on leadership: Ike's enduring lessons in total victory management.* San Francisco, CA: Jossey-Bass.

Batchelor, J. H., Humphrey, R. H., & Burch, G. F. (2012, April). *How entrepreneurs use emotional labor to improve employee attitudes and firm performance.* Presentation at the Society for Industrial and Organizational Psychology, San Diego, CA.

Bligh, M. C., Kohles, J. C., & Meindl, J. R. (2004). Charisma under crisis: Presidential leadership, rhetoric, and media responses before and after the September 11th terrorist attacks. *The Leadership Quarterly, 15,* 211–239.

Bolino, M. C., & Turnley, W. H. (1999). Measuring impression management in organizations: A sale development based on the Jones and Pittman taxonomy.
Organizational Research Methods, 2, 187–206.

Bono, J. E., & Ilies, R. (2006). Charisma, positive emotions, and mood contagion. *The
Leadership Quarterly, 17,* 317–334.

Bono, J. E., Jackson Foldes, H., Vinson, G., & Muros, J. P. (2007). Workplace emotions: The role of supervision and leadership. *Journal of Applied Psychology, 92,*
1357–1367.

Bono, J. E., & Vey, M. A. (2005). Toward understanding emotional management at
work: A quantitative review of emotional labor research. In C. E. J. Härtel,
W. J. Zerbe, & N. M. Ashkanasy (Eds.), *Emotions in organizational behavior*
(pp. 213–233). Mahwah, NJ: Lawrence Erlbaum.

Bratton, J., Grint, K., & Nelson, D. (2005). *Organizational leadership,* Mason, OH:
Thomson/South-Western.

Brotheridge, C. M., & Grandey, A. A. (2002). Emotional labor and burnout: Comparing
two perspectives of "People Work." *Journal of Vocational Behavior, 60,* 17–39.

Bryant, M., & Cox, J. W. (2006). The expression of suppression: Loss and emotional
labour in narratives of organizational change. *Journal of Management &
Organization, 12,* 116–130.

Butcher, L. (1989). *Accidental millionaire: The rise and fall of Steve Jobs.* New York,
NY: Paragon House.

Conger, J. A. (2011). Charismatic leadership. In A. Bryman, D. Collinson, K. Grint,
B. Jackson, and M. Uhl-Bien (Eds.), *Sage handbook of leadership* (pp. 86–102).
London, UK: Sage.

Conger, J. A., & Kanungo, R. N. (1987). Toward a behavioral theory of charismatic leadership in organizational settings. *Academy of Management Review, 12,* 637–647.

Conger, J. A., Kanungo, R. N., & Menon, S. T. (2000). Charismatic leadership and
follower effects. *Journal of Organizational Behavior, 21,* 747–767.

Cowsill, R., & Grint, K. (2008). Leadership, task and relationship: Orpheus,
Prometheus and Janus. *Human Resource Management Journal, 18,* 188–195.

Dahling, J. J., & Perez, L. A. (2010). Older worker, different actor? Linking age and
emotional labor strategies. *Personality and Individual Differences, 48,* 574–578.

Dasborough, M. T., Ashkanasy, N. M., Tee, E. E. J., & Tse, H. H. M. (2009). What
goes around comes around: How meso-level negative emotional contagion can
ultimately determine organizational attitudes toward leaders. *The Leadership
Quarterly, 20,* 571–585.

DeRue, D. S., Barnes, C. M., & Morgeson, F. P. (2010). Understanding the motivational contingencies of team leadership. *Small Group Research, 41,* 621–651.

de Vries, R. E., Bakker-Pieper, A., & Oostenveld, W. (2010). Leadership = communication?
The relations of leaders' communication styles with leadership styles, knowledge
sharing and leadership outcomes. *Journal of Business Psychology, 25,* 367–380.

Diefendorff, J. M., Croyle, M. H., & Gosserand, R. H. (2005). The dimensionality and
antecedents of emotional labor strategies. *Journal of Vocational Behavior, 66,*
339–357.

Diefendorff, J. M., & Gosserand, R. H. (2003). Understanding the emotional labor process: A control theory perspective. *Journal of Organizational Behavior, 24,* 945–959.

Emrich, C. G., Brower, H. H., Feldman, J. M., & Garland, H. (2001). Images in words: Presidential rhetoric, charisma, and greatness. *Administrative Science Quarterly, 46,* 527–557.

Epitropaki, O. (2006, August). '*Leading the show*': *The impact of leader's emotional labor on subordinates' transformation leadership perceptions and collective emotional labor.* Paper presented at *The Academy of Management,* at Atlanta, GA.

Fisk, G. M., & Friesen, J. P. (2012). Perceptions of leader emotion regulation and LMX as predictors of follower's job satisfaction and organizational citizenship behaviors. *The Leadership Quarterly, 23,* 1–12.

Fuller, J. B., Patterson, C. E. P., Hester, K., & Stringer, D. Y. (1996). A quantitative review of research on charismatic leadership. *Psychological Reports, 78,* 271–287.

Gardner, W. L., Fischer, D., & Hunt, J. G. (2009). Emotional labor and leadership: A threat to authenticity? *The Leadership Quarterly, 20,* 466–482.

Glomb, T. M., & Tews. M. J. (2004). Emotional labor: A conceptualization and scale development. *Journal of Vocational Behavior, 64,* 1–23.

Goffman, E. (1959). *The presentation of self in everyday life.* New York, NY: Doubleday.

Gray, J. H., & Densten, I. L. (2007). How leaders woo followers in the romance of leadership. *Applied Psychology: An International Review, 56,* 558–581.

Halbesleben, J. R. B., Bowler, W. M., Bolino, M. C., & Turnley, W. H. (2010). Organizational concern, prosocial values, or impression management? How supervisors attribute motives to organizational citizenship behavior. *Journal of Applied Social Psychology, 40*(6), 1450–1489.

Halverson, S. K., Murphy, S. E., & Riggio, R. E. (2004). Charismatic leadership in crisis situations: A laboratory investigation of stress and crisis. *Small Group Research, 35,* 495–514.

Hammer, J. (2011, March). Myanmar's free thinkers. *Smithsonian,* 28–36.

Hayward, S. F. (1997). *Churchill on leadership: Executive success in the face of adversity.* Rocklin, CA: Prima.

Hochschild, A. R. (1983). *The managed heart: Commercialization of human feeling.* Berkeley, CA: University of California Press.

House, R. J., & Howell, J. M. (1992). Personality and charismatic leadership. *The Leadership Quarterly, 3,* 81–108.

Humphrey, R. H. (2005, November). Empathy, emotional expressiveness, and leadership. *Proceedings of the Southern Management Association.* Charleston, SC.

Humphrey, R. H. (2006, August). Leading with emotional labor. *The Academy of Management Conference.* Atlanta, GA.

Humphrey, R. H. (2008). The right way to lead with emotional labor. In R. H. Humphrey (Ed.), *Affect and emotion: New directions in management theory and research* (pp. 1–17). Charlotte, NC: Information Age Publishing.

Humphrey, R. H., Pollack, J. M., & Hawver, T. (2008). Leading with emotional labour. *Journal of Managerial Psychology, 23,* 151–168.

Hunt, J. G., Gardner, W. L., & Fischer, D. (2008). Leader emotional displays from near and far: The implications of close versus distant leadership. In R. H. Humphrey (ed.), *Affect and emotion: New directions in management theory and research* (pp. 43–65). Charlotte, NC: Information Age Publishing.

Iszatt-White, M. (2009). Leadership as emotional labour: The effortful accomplishment of valuing practices. *Leadership, 5,* 447–467.

Iszatt-White, M. (2012). Leadership as emotional labor: So what's new? In M. Iszatt-White (Ed.), *Leadership as emotional labor.* New York, NY: Routledge.

Jones, R. G., Kane, T., Russo, J., & Walmsley, P. (2008, July). *What you see is what you feel: Leader emotional labor is in the eye of the beholder.* A symposium presentation at the meeting of The Sixth International Conference on Emotions and Organizational Life (EMONET VI), Fontainbleau, France.

Jones, R. G., Visio, M., Wilberding, K., & King, H. (2008, July). *Leader emotive awareness, emotional labor, burnout and work-family conflict.* A symposium presentation at the meeting of The Sixth International Conference on Emotions and Organizational Life (EMONET VI), Fontainbleau, France.

Jordan, C., Soutar, G., & Kiffin-Petersen, S. (2008, July). *Are there different 'types' of emotional laborers?* A symposium presentation at the meeting of The Sixth International Conference on Emotions and Organizational Life (EMONET VI), Fontainbleau, France.

Kacmar, K. M., Harris, K. J., & Nagy, B. G. (2007). Further validation of the Bolino and Turnley impression management scale. *Journal of Behavioral and Applied Management,* 16–32.

Kets de Vries, M., & Balazs, K. (2011). The shadow side of leadership. In A. Bryman, D. Collinson, K. Grint, B. Jackson, & M. Uhl-Bien (Eds.), *Sage handbook of leadership* (pp. 380–392). London, UK: Sage.

Kiel, L. D., & Watson, D. J. (2009). Affective leadership and emotional labor: A view from the local level. *Public Administration Review, 1,* 21–24.

Kingsley Westerman, C. Y., & Westerman, D. (2010). Supervisor impression management: Message content and channel effects on impressions. *Communication Studies, 61,* 585–601.

Levay, C. (2010). Charismatic leadership in resistance to change. *The Leadership Quarterly, 21,* 127–143.

Levine, K. J., Muenchen, R. A., & Brooks, A. M. (2010). Measuring transformational and charismatic leadership: Why isn't charisma measured? *Communication Monographs, 77,* 576–591.

Mann, S. (1997). Emotional labour in organizations. *Leadership & Organization Development Journal, 18,* 4–12.

Markham, F. (1966). *Napoleon.* New York, NY: Penguin.

Mio, J. S., Riggio, R. E., Levin, S., & Reese, R. (2005). Presidential leadership and charisma: The effects of metaphor. *The Leadership Quarterly, 16,* 287–294.

Mumford, M. D., Espejo, J., Hunter, S. T., Bedell-Avers, K. E., Eubanks, D. L., Connelly, S. (2007). The sources of leader violence: A comparison of ideological and non-ideological leaders. *The Leadership Quarterly, 18,* 217–235.

Murphy, S. E., & Ensher, E. A. (2008). A qualitative analysis of charismatic leadership in creative teams: The case of television directors. *The Leadership Quarterly, 19*, 335–352.

Naidoo, L. J., & Lord, R. G. (2008). Speech imagery and perceptions of charisma: The mediating role of positive affect. *The Leadership Quarterly, 19*, 283–296.

Napoleon. (n.d.). BrainyQuote.com. Retrieved February 4, 2013 from http://www .brainyquote.com/quotes/quotes/n/napoleonbo150173.html

Newman, M. A., Guy, M. E., & Mastracci, S. H. (2009). Beyond cognition: Affective leadership and emotional labor. *Public Administration Review, 1*, 6–20.

Nguyen, N. T., Seers, A., & Hartman, N. S. (2008). Putting a good face on impression management: Team citizenship and team satisfaction. *Journal of Behavioral and Applied Management*, 148–167.

Nosowitz, D. (2010, May 26). Microsoft's and Apple's product lines compared: This is why Apple wins. Retrieved from http://www.fastcompany.com/1652843/ microsoft-vs-apple-product-line-market-cap-wall-street-valuation-steve-jobs

O'Connor, J. A., Mumford, M. D., Clifton, T. C., Gessner, T. E., & Connelly, M. S. (1995). Charismatic leaders and destructiveness: A historiometric study. *The Leadership Quarterly, 6*, 529–555.

Pepys, S. (1854). *Diary and correspondence of Samuel Pepys, F.R.S.: Secretary to the Admiralty in the reigns of Charles II and James II* (Vol. 1). London, UK: Hurst & Blackett.

Pillai, R. (1996). Crisis and the emergence of charismatic leadership in groups: An experimental investigation. *Journal of Applied Social Psychology, 26*, 543–562.

Rosenfeld, P., Giacalone, R. A., Riordan, C. A. (1995). *Impression management in organizations*. London, UK and New York, NY: Routledge.

Rosenthal, S. A., & Pittinsky, T. L. (2006). Narcissistic leadership. *The Leadership Quarterly, 17*, 617–633.

Shamir, B. (1995). Social distance and charisma: Theoretical notes and an exploratory study. *The Leadership Quarterly, 6*, 19–47.

Shamir, B., Arthur, M. B., & House, R. J. (1994). The rhetoric of charismatic leadership: Theoretical extension and a case study. *Leadership Quarterly, 5*, 25–42.

Shamir, B., House, R. J., & Arthur, M. B. (1993). The motivational effects of charismatic leadership: A self-concept based theory. *Organization Science, 4*, 577–594.

Sosik, J. J. (2005). The role of personal values in the charismatic leadership of corporate managers: A model and preliminary field study. *The Leadership Quarterly, 16*, 221–244.

Van Dijk, P. A., & Kirk-Brown, A. (2006). Emotional labor and negative job outcomes: An evaluation of the mediating role of emotional dissonance. *Journal of Management & Organization, 12*, 101–115.

Waldman, D. A., & Yammarino, F. J. (1999). CEO charisma leadership: Levels-of-management and levels-of-analysis effects. *Academy of Management Review, 24*, 266–285.

Waples, E. P., & Connelly, S. (2008). Leader emotions and vision implementation: Effects of activation potential and valence. In R. H. Humphrey (Ed.), *Affect and emotion: New directions in management theory and research* (pp. 66–96). Charlotte, NC: Information Age Publishing.

Weber, M. (1947). *The theory of social and economic organization* (A.M. Henderson & T. Parsons, Trans.; T. Parsons, Ed.). New York, NY: The Free Press. (Original work published 1924).

14

Transactional Leadership and Goal Setting

Chapter Road Map

Case: *Emilio Estefan and The Rhythm of Success*

In his 2010 book, *The Rhythm of Success*, Emilio Estefan drums home the importance of planning and setting goals. Hundreds of millions of people know Emilio because of his 19 Grammy Awards and because of his marriage to Gloria Estefan. With his band, the Miami Sound Machine, he made Latin music popular in the United States during the 1980s. Emilio later used his expertise as a producer to help other Latino musicians. Over the years, he and his production/songwriting crew have worked with such notables as Shakira, Jennifer Lopez, Ricky Martin, and Marc Antony. But Estefan is more than a musician and music publisher/producer; he's also an entrepreneur who invests in real estate and who operates restaurants and hotels.

The Cardozo Hotel is one of the many businesses owned by Emilio and Gloria Estefan. The patio looks like the perfect place to read *The Rhythm of Success* or listen to Latin music.

Source: Wikipedia/Elmschrat (CC-BY-SA)

Although many rock stars are known for their wild excesses and burnout after a few years, Emilio has a business-like attitude toward life that has kept his career strumming along for over 30 years. Instead of sleeping late, he gets up at 5:00 a.m. every day—holidays included. And his biography has chapter titles that wouldn't be out of place in the biographies of the most-task-oriented straightlaced business leaders. Emilio has a chapter called "Develop a Plan," which is followed by chapters called "Keep Planning" and "Work Hard." Other chapters are called "Get an Education and Keep Developing Your Skills and Talents" and "Manage Yourself."

Emilio made his first life-changing plan when he was only a teenager. He had an idyllic childhood growing up in pre-Castro Cuba. He lived in a large house that had plenty of room for his parents, his brother, an uncle, and two grandparents. His grandfather ran a greengrocery and also bought and sold real estate; Emilio and his extended family lived comfortably even though they weren't rich. His grandfather's brothers also ran small businesses and lived nearby, and once a week, the whole extended family would gather for dinner and conversation. That all changed when Castro took power. The family businesses were confiscated and put under the control of bureaucrats who didn't know how to run them. His cousin was arrested, and one of his aunts was thrown in prison for 20 years for trying to obtain a visa for his cousin. And one day, scary and rude soldiers waving machine guns showed up at Emilio's house looking for U.S. dollars. There was an old safe in his parents' bedroom wall that hadn't been used for years, and the soldiers threatened his father and demanded that he open it. His father couldn't remember the combination, so the soldiers blew up the safe with dynamite. Nothing but old papers and a bit of forgotten jewelry was inside. His parents remained worried—they might be on the communist regime's bad side, and who knew what might happen? That's when Emilio made his first life-changing plan: He became determined to leave Cuba behind and find a way to reunite his family in America.

Emilio and his father were able to get a passport to Spain (where his mother had relatives), but his older brother was approaching draft age and the Cuban government wouldn't let him go. His mother wouldn't leave without his older brother or her parents. Heartbroken, Emilio boarded the plane for Spain, worried he would never see his mother again. After a year and a half, the 15-year-old Emilio left Spain for America, and he worked hard to find the money and the method to bring his parents to America. Eventually, he succeeded, but it took all his planning and resourcefulness to bring his family together again.

Emilio attributes his success in life to his careful planning. He advises others to "plan for all the goals in your life: your studies, your finances, your vacations, and especially your family" (Estefan, 2010, p. 74). He recommends making "plan, plan, plan your mantra" (p. 77). He advocates short term, medium term, and long term plans and revising plans as necessary. He also believes in detailed daily schedules: "Time is one of your most important resources and you have to use it wisely, so you need to plan your day—or schedule, in other words. Even down to small things." (p. 75). When he travels, his suitcase is organized by each day, and he's always ready to leave in 2 minutes' time if necessary. He's never late to an appointment. His wallet is organized for maximum efficiency; his iPod loaded with all his important files, his office neat and his desk spotless. Emilio lives an active life, and he states, "The only way I can live my life so fully is by planning" (p. 75).

Emilio carefully planned all the details of his Miami South Beach restaurant, which he and Gloria named *Larios on the Beach*. Although by this time Emilio could afford to hire employees to do all of the work renovating the restaurant, Emilio worked *hombro a hombro* (shoulder to shoulder) with the workers carrying

(Continued)

(Continued)

buckets and pounding nails. As Emilio put it, although he could afford to hire workers, "I couldn't hire someone else to set the example as the boss... Nothing replaces hard work, and few things are more effective at motivating people than a hardworking boss" (Estefan, 2010, p. 81).

Applications: What are some of your short term, medium term, and long term plans? Without a daily plan, how easy is it to waste large chunks of the day? Why do detailed schedules improve efficiency so much? Is overall productivity a matter of doing many small things in the most efficient way?

Source: Estefan, E. (2010). *The rhythm of success.* New York, NY: Penguin.

Taking Care of Business

There are many routine managerial tasks that may not seem glamorous but that are still essential. Returning client phone calls, filling out everyday reports, completing performance appraisals, ordering supplies, and managing unexpected work problems—however minor they may seem—are all ultimately important to keeping a business running smoothly. Emilio Estefan attributed much of his success to his ability to handle these details by careful planning and goal setting. As Mintzberg (1973) observed in his classic study of what managers do every day, managers and other leaders make thousands of small decisions and perform thousands of minor tasks every year. Mintzberg found that these details are interspersed with the top priorities. While working on their top priorities, managers are often interrupted to answer annoying questions from subordinates or from their own superiors. Each seemingly trivial detail may not be very important by itself, but cumulatively they form an important part of what leaders do, and performing them can make the difference between success and failure. By way of analogy, stopping to get gas on your way to work may not seem like a very important, crucial task, but if you failed to get gas when needed, you'll soon realize how important it is. As Michelangelo once said, "Trifles make perfection," yet "perfection is no trifle" (Michelangelo, retrieved 2013).

Transactional leaders tend to be good at handling the routine administration of business. In addition, the goal setting programs described in this chapter help leaders plan, set goals, and ensure that work tasks are completed correctly and on time. This chapter reviews the evidence that transactional leadership and goal setting are important to overall leadership effectiveness. This chapter will help us answer the following questions:

- Do transactional leadership behaviors improve follower job performance and job satisfaction? Are contingent rewards more useful than the other forms of transactional leadership?
- Why are specific and difficult goals effective in boosting performance, and why does goal commitment matter? What are stretch goals?
- How does goal orientation affect performance, and which orientation (learn, prove, or avoid) is most effective?
- How can top leaders use goals, financial incentives, and consideration for employees' welfare to unite the interests and motivations of their midlevel leaders and employees with the goals and interests of the organization?

Applications: How important are routine managerial and administrative tasks to a leader's success? How much of a leader's time is usually taken up with budgeting, scheduling, planning, processing routine paperwork, returning calls, etc.? Are there some leaders who seem great at motivating others but just can't seem to get the routine stuff done?

Transactional Leadership: The Basis of Transformational Leadership

Although charismatic, transformational leaders seem to get all the good press, transactional leadership may be almost as important to the successful leadership of organizations. James MacGregor Burns (1978) first described transactional and transformational leaders as two separate types of leaders, yet later scholars argued that transformational leaders also perform transactional leadership behaviors. Early research and theory suggested that transactional leadership, although important, was not nearly as effective as transformational leadership. However, there is growing recognition that at least one form of transactional leadership—the use of contingent rewards—plays an important part in overall leadership success. As Avolio (2011) stated, he and his colleagues "have argued that transactional leadership was the basis for developing transformational leadership" (p. 24). Indeed, research has demonstrated that there is a high correlation between transactional and transformational leadership (Judge & Piccolo, 2004). Thus, good leaders perform both types of leadership behaviors.

Bass and Riggio (2006/2007) described transactional and transformational leaders this way:

Transactional business leaders offer financial rewards for productivity or deny rewards for lack of productivity. Transformational leaders, on the other hand, are those who stimulate and inspire followers to both achieve extraordinary outcomes and, in the process, develop their own leadership capacity. Transformational leaders help followers grow and develop into leaders by responding to individual followers' needs by empowering them. (p. 3)

This brief description of transactional leadership emphasizes the importance of contingent rewards, which is the most important dimension of transactional leadership. As previously defined in Chapter 1, *leaders use contingent rewards when they set up clear expectations for performance, specify what should be done, and reward employees based on their meeting goals and expectations.* Because of the importance of goal setting to transactional leadership, this chapter will cover goal setting in considerable detail. The motivational approaches based on contingent rewards are quite different from those used to inspire followers via transformational leadership. Thus, contingent rewards will be covered in this chapter while the next chapter will go over the specific tactics that transformational leaders use to motivate their followers.

Chapter 1 also defined the other two types of transactional leaders: *management by exception—active and management by exception—passive. As their names suggest, the former type is characterized by leaders who take a more active role in spotting and correcting problems before they become major issues, whereas the more passive leaders wait until problems become more noticeable.* The final leadership style described by transformational leadership researchers is called *laissez-faire, which as previously defined in Chapter 1 is basically a manager who fails to exert leadership and avoids making decisions and carrying out other leadership responsibilities.* Research has confirmed that this last style is highly ineffective (Judge & Piccolo, 2004).

A study by O'Shea, Foti, Hauenstein, and Bycio (2009) examined the effectiveness of 726 leaders who performed different combinations of transformational, contingent reward, and passive management by exception leader behaviors. They argued that the optimal combination would be for the leaders to be high on both transformational leadership and the use of contingent rewards but low on passive management by exception. Consistent with their hypothesis, they found that leaders with the optimal combination had subordinates who were more satisfied with their leader and rated their leader as more effective; moreover, these subordinates reported that their own motivation was higher as well.

The most recent meta-analysis by Wang, Oh, Courtright, and Colbert (2011) found that transformational leadership and contingent rewards had consistently positive effects on followers' individual performance and on team performance. In contrast, *management by exception had largely negative effects on follower performance.* As Avolio (2011) states, "The management-by-exception form of corrective transaction tends to be more ineffective, particularly when used in excess" (p. 64). However, Avolio argues that there may be occasions, particularly during emergencies, when leaders may have to use this style and take corrective action. Avolio (2011) described the active form of management by exception this way: "When active, the leader arranges to actively monitor deviations from standards, mistakes, and errors in the follower's assignments and to take corrective action as necessary. Such leadership involves a constant vigilance for possible mistakes" (p. 64). However, this style should not be a leader's predominant style, so this chapter will focus instead on the benefits of goal setting and contingent rewards.

> **Applications:** Have you ever had a leader who was constantly trying to catch you in a mistake? How did this make you feel? Are leaders more effective when they focus on what to do right instead of on what has been done wrong?

Transactional Leadership and Follower Performance

Wang and his colleagues' meta-analysis examined how transactional leaders influenced three types of follower performance (Wang et al., 2011). First, they found that leaders' use of contingent rewards positively influenced their followers' individual task performance. Second, they found leaders' use of contingent rewards positively influenced their followers' team level of performance. Third, they found that the use of contingent rewards also positively influenced overall organizational performance. Thus, to sum up, *using contingent rewards improves individual performance, team performance, and organizational performance.*

> **The Leader's Bookcase:** To learn more, download this article: Wang, G., Oh, I., Courtright, S. H., & Colbert, A. E. (2011). Transformational leadership and performance across criteria and levels: A meta-analytic review of 25 years of research. *Group & Organization Management, 36,* 223–270.

Transactional Leadership and Satisfaction

Judge and Piccolo (2004) used a meta-analysis to examine whether transactional leadership improved follower job attitudes. They found that the leader's use of contingent rewards increased followers' job satisfaction.

In addition, using contingent rewards increased followers' satisfaction with the leader—apparently followers like leaders who reward them for good performance. Finally, leaders who used contingent rewards improved followers' motivation levels—rewards really do work. *Thus, leaders who use contingent rewards improve followers' job satisfaction, followers' satisfaction with their leaders, and followers' motivation levels.* As a result, *using contingent rewards improved the leader's own job performance and effectiveness.* Their results are consistent with the results of another meta-analysis which also found that leader rewarding behaviors generally improve follower attitudes (Podsakoff, Bommer, Podsakoff, & MacKenzie, 2006).

> **Applications:** Do rewards for performance generally improve your attitudes? What does your organization do to reward performance? Does your organization do enough to reward performance, not enough, or too much?

Goal Setting: A Thousand Studies Strong

One of the major duties of leaders is to set goals both for themselves and for those they lead. Indeed, setting goals is one of the most effective ways that leaders have to motivate followers and to direct their attention to the most important work tasks and priorities. The evidence behind goal setting is strong. As Latham and Locke (2009) point out, *over 1,000 studies have found support for the basic principles of goal setting* (Mitchell & Daniels, 2003). What are these basic principles? As the following sections will reveal, leaders should set specific goals, maximize production by setting difficult yet attainable goals, and ensure that their followers are committed to achieving the goals.

Be Specific

Most employees hate it when their managers give them vague, unspecific goals. When the boss gives a vague goal, such as "I want you to do your best," the employees are likely to feel uncertain about what it will take to satisfy the boss. The slackers are likely to feel that they don't have to produce too much. After all, the manager didn't tell them exactly how much to produce, so they can always claim they thought they had produced enough. This can produce arguments with the boss later on, so both parties may feel unhappy as a result. The more conscientious employees are not likely to be happy either—they are likely to worry about what the performance target should be. Decades of psychological research has convincingly demonstrated that worry interferes with performance. Conscientious employees tend to prefer clear and specific targets.

When leaders give specific performance standards and production goals, followers have less uncertainty and anxiety. If the followers are a little short of reaching the goal, then they know they should work a little harder to achieve the goal. Once they achieve the goal, they can relax and be reasonably certain they have satisfied managerial expectations. *Over 500 hundred studies have verified that setting specific goals produce the best results* (Seijts, Latham, Tasa, & Latham, 2004).

Set Difficult Yet Attainable Goals

The advice to set difficult goals is well supported by the research on goal setting, which has found that *difficult goals yield higher output than easy to moderate goals*. This is only logical: Easy and moderate goals are by definition ones that you can achieve without putting forth your best effort. Difficult goals encourage people to produce at the highest levels they can reasonably perform at. However, followers need to believe that the goal is achievable, so leaders need to make sure that they do not set unrealistic goals for their employees and that their employees or followers believe that the goals are attainable. *Studies have shown that performance decreases when goals are set too high.*

Leaders need to know the highest level of goal performance they can reasonably expect from each follower. Leaders with considerable experience doing the work may have a solid understanding of the work processes and a good understanding of how long it takes to complete the work. When leaders lack this experience, they may need to consult with employees about what is possible or check performance records. Leaders also need to understand the performance capabilities of individual team members—new employees especially may not be capable of performing as much as more experienced employees. Even among experienced employees, there are likely to be differences in abilities that should be taken into account when setting goals.

Goal Commitment

Followers are not likely to commit themselves to achieving goals if they believe the goals are unrealistic. *A meta-analysis with a sample size of 7,952 has found that goal commitment is important to performance at all levels of task difficulty, but that it is especially important when goal difficulty is high* (Klein, Wesson, Hollenbeck, & Alge, 1999). Even at low levels of difficulty, employees who are not committed to achieving the goals produce less than employees with high goal commitment. Commitment to the goal becomes even more important when goal difficulty is high. The high goal difficulty increases the temptation to give up—only the more committed will persevere and maintain their full effort when goal difficulty is high. In addition, the meta-analysis found that *employees are more likely to have high goal commitment when they expect to be rewarded for achieving the goal (no surprise here) and when they find the goal attractive for various reasons.*

Who Sets High Goals for Themselves?

Why do some people set high goals, while others set easy or moderate goals? One answer is personality. A meta-analysis summarized the studies that had examined how the Big Five personality traits are related to whether people set high goals or not (Judge & Ilies, 2002). *This meta-analysis found that people high on Conscientiousness, Openness to Experience, and Extraversion were more likely to set higher goals for themselves, whereas people high on Neuroticism and Agreeableness were more likely to set lower goals.* These results make sense. Conscientiousness by definition refers to the willingness to work hard at completing tasks, so naturally conscientious people are willing to set high goals. As we learned in a meta-analysis in a prior chapter (Judge, Bono, Ilies, & Gerhardt, 2002), people high on Openness to Experience are more likely to emerge as leaders and to be effective leaders, so it makes sense that they would recognize the need to set high goals for themselves. Extraverts are also more likely to emerge as leaders and to strive for success, so again it makes sense that Extraverts would set high goals. The prior study on leadership emergence also had results consistent with this study's finding on Agreeableness. People high on Agreeableness were *less* likely to emerge as leaders, so it's not surprising that agreeable, easy-going people are less likely to set high goals for themselves. They are not bucking for promotion or leadership positions, so why should they try to stand out by setting high goals for themselves? Finally, people high on Neuroticism are likely to focus on their own personal problems and concerns instead of on organizational goals, and they are more likely to find difficult goals to be stressful. Consequently, people high on Neuroticism set lower goals for themselves. The flip side of this dimension is Emotional Stability, and these results mean that emotionally stable individuals are more likely to set high goals.

It is important to realize that the associations between personality and goal setting are not nearly perfect. There are many agreeable people who set high goals and many extraverts who prefer to socialize rather than work on difficult goals. Thus, while personality traits suggest who might be a high goal setter, leaders should judge employees on their actual performance. The following is a summary of the Big Five personality traits:

High Goal Setters

Conscientiousness

Openness to Experience

Extraverts

Low Goal Setters

Neuroticism

Agreeableness

Leaders as Goal-Focused Coaches

Because some teammates and followers tend to set their goals too low, leaders need to be able to coach followers into setting more productive goals. With help, many people can be taught to seek more challenging goals. Effective coaching requires skill and sensitivity to people's feelings and personalities. A study conducted in Australia examined the characteristics of professional management coaches and compared them to nonprofessional coaches (Grant & Cavanagh, 2007). The study found that the most effective coaches were higher in emotional intelligence. In order to be effective goal-focused coaches, leaders need to have five key skills (Grant & Cavanagh, 2007). First, leaders need to have *goal-setting skills* themselves so they can teach these skills to the *coachees*. The leaders need to be able to teach the coachees how to set realistic short-term and long-term goals as well as how to set goals that develop their skills and abilities over time. Equally important, the coachees need to learn how to set goals that are aligned with their personal values and that are personally satisfying to them. Second, coaches need to develop a *strong working alliance* with those they coach. The coaches need to demonstrate empathy and understanding, and make the coachees feel free to express their own ideas.

Third, leaders need to take a *solution-focused* approach that encourages coachees to develop their own insights and solutions. Coachees should focus on future plans and goals and not on the past. Fourth, the leaders need to be skilled in *managing process and accountability*. The leaders need to make sure that the coachees complete the agreed upon steps. Coachees also need to be held responsible for monitoring their own progress, and leaders need to be prompt in alerting the coachees to any shortfall in performance. Fifth and finally, the process should result in the coachees obtaining *outcomes that are valued and meaningful*. The accomplishment of important goals is what makes the coaching experience worthwhile to the coachees and to the organization. In sum, *effective* **goal-focused coaching** *requires effective goal-setting skills, the development of a strong working alliance, a solution-focused approach, managing process and accountability, and obtaining outcomes that are valued and meaningful.*

> **Applications:** Has your manager or leader ever asked you about your goals or talked with you about your goals in any meaningful way? Does your organization provide any training in how to achieve goals? How important is it to be able to talk over your goals with a friend, a colleague, or a mentor?

The research on goal-focused coaching has found that goals are far more motivating when they are consistent with our values, our identity, and our personality. The following case shows how important knowing her own desires and true goals was to helping Barbara Corcoran achieve both success and happiness.

Case: *Barbara Corcoran Learns Her Heart's True Desires*

In her hilarious and lighthearted book, *Shark Tales: How I Turned $1,000 Into a Billion Dollar Business*, Barbara Corcoran demonstrates the importance of knowing what you really want out of life (Corcoran & Littlefield, 2011). As her title suggests, Barbara founded her real estate company, The Corcoran Group, with only $1,000 and some big dreams. Shortly after founding the company, Barbara took out a piece of paper and wrote down some big goals for herself and the company. In 1978, she had only 14 sales agents working for her, who earned a total of $250,000 in commissions. She set a goal of doubling the number of agents and the commissions every year. So she put down 28 salespeople for 1979, 56 for 1980, and so on, all the way up to 1,792 salespeople in 1985 with total commissions of $32,000,000. Barbara was amazed when she saw the fantastic sums projected for 1985, and of course many people, when they see such amazing sums, would dismiss the calculations as a fantasy. But as Barbara put it, she went to work the next day hustling hard for her $32 million.

Real estate agents are paid largely by commission, which is about as close as you can get to a pure form of contingent reward for performance. However, Barbara didn't rely solely on the commissions to motivate her workers. She threw theme parties and held numerous social events to build a committed workforce. Good sales agents could always move to another firm, but not every firm had Barbara's positive attitude and fun-filled atmosphere. In the early years of the firm, when money was tight, Barbara and her relatives did the cooking for the outings and parties, and she found clever ways to entertain people with skating parties and other lively activities. As the firm became larger and more profitable, she even hired professional entertainers for the company's midweek picnics, which included elephant shows, daring rides on hot air balloons, horses, or Harley Davidsons, etc. Barbara stated, "I built my company on pure fun, and believe that fun is the most underutilized motivational tool in business today. All of my best ideas came when I was playing outside the office with the people I worked with" (Corcoran & Littlefield, 2011, p. 283). What did she get in return for the fun atmosphere? She had the "most profitable real estate company per person in the United States" (p. 284). By the time she sold her agency in 2001, she had 1,000 agents working for her, and she had the largest real estate agency in New York—clearly her motivational strategies attracted a large number of productive employees.

Barbara Corcoran had sold her firm for $66 million. She thought that would make her happy, but instead, it made her sad. Although she pretended to be happy with her new wealth and freedom, she was "secretly miserable" (Corcoran & Littlefield, 2011, p. 232). She had lost her purpose in life. Barbara stated, "I felt my entire identity gone—wiped out" (p. 232). In addition to losing her personal identity, she lost much of her social identity as well when the new owners blocked her former employees from sending her emails. Without a purpose and an identity, she felt like a nobody.

Barbara set to work making some new goals for herself. She took out her trusty yellow legal pad and drew a line down the center of the page. On one side of the page, she listed everything she hated, on the other side, everything she loved. When doing exercises like this, it's important to be honest with oneself. Barbara was honest enough to realize that she loved the power of her old position. She also liked being creative and helping other people. She especially loved being the center of attention. These honest self-evaluations and goals helped her realize that she wanted a new career in the mass media. This set her on the path to her current job

(Continued)

(Continued)

as a cohost of ABC's show *Shark Tank*. On *Shark Tank*, she can listen to creative would-be entrepreneurs pitch their ideas for new companies, and she has the opportunity to help them out by investing her own money in their businesses. And as a TV host, she gets plenty of attention as well: a true happy ending to her tale.

Applications: Are you motivated by ambitious goals, such as doubling the number of sales agents every year, or intimidated? Barbara's rivals in the real estate industry probably paid the same commissions on sales to their agents that she did to hers. Given that all the agencies paid the same rate, why was Barbara able to grow her firm so rapidly? What else did she do to motivate and attract the best agents?

Source: Corcoran, B., & Littlefield, B. (Ed.). (2011). *Shark Tales: How I turned $1,000 into a billion dollar business.* New York, NY: Penguin.

Barbara set herself some stretch goals. As the following section demonstrates, many organizations also set stretch goals for their employees.

The Ampera (the European version of the Chevy Volt) is a good example of a product developed by motivating stretch goals. It is a plug-in electric hybrid vehicle. The Volt won the 2011 North American Car of the Year Award, while the Ampera version won the 2012 European Car of the Year award.

Source: Wikipedia/Noebu (CC-BY)

Stretch Goals: Make No Small Plans

As Daniel Burnham stated, "Make no small plans: They have no magic to stir men's blood, and probably themselves will not be realized. Make big plans; Aim high in hope, and work" (White, 1986, p. 183). Today, many leaders use *stretch goals* as a way to get their employees to make big plans. According to Sim Sitkin and his colleagues, a *stretch goal is defined as "an organizational goal with an objective probability of attainment that may be unknown but is seemingly impossible given current capabilities (i.e., current practices, skills, knowledge)"* (Sitkin, See, Miller, Lawless, & Carton, 2011, p. 547). Wow: "Seemingly impossible"—that sure sounds difficult! However, the last part of the definition provides some hope: The stretch goals are only impossible using current practices, skills, and knowledge. This suggests that the stretch goals may be achievable by getting rid of outdated practices or by researching and developing new procedures. Thus, stretch goals give employees freedom to be innovative. As Rousseau (1997) stated, stretch goals enable "creativity and assumption-breaking thinking" (p. 528). As Burnham poetically stated, stretch goals may stir our blood and encourage us to dream big (White, 1986).

Sim and his colleagues gave three examples of the successful use of stretch goals (Sitkin et al., 2011). First, John F. Kennedy stirred the world's imagination when he declared the goal to send mankind to the moon. At the time, no existing rockets were capable of taking people to the moon, but as we know, NASA scientists were eventually able to stretch our capabilities all the way to the moon and back. Second, Southwest Airlines used stretch goals when it set a goal to have 10 minute turnaround times (the time between when a plane unloads one group of passengers and departs with the next group). By reducing turnaround times, it was able to make more flights with fewer planes—a huge savings. Third, the automobile industry set ambitious plans to dramatically increase fuel economy over what was possible using their then-current technology. Their stretch goals resulted in the development of hybrid technology that is now being used in thousands of cars on the road today.

When properly managed, stretch goals may encourage flexible thinking as well as positive affect and enthusiasm. Employees may be inspired by thoughts of making it to the moon or of achieving goals, like greater fuel economy, that would be of great benefit to mankind. However, when improperly used, stretch goals may create feelings of fear and anxiety over the ability to achieve the goal and as a result, may actually reduce creativity and the ability to process new information (Sitkin et al., 2011).

Far better it is to dare mighty things, to win glorious triumphs, even though checkered by failure, than to take rank with those poor spirits who neither enjoy nor suffer much, because they live in the gray twilight that knows neither victory nor defeat. —*Theodore Roosevelt*. (Theodore Roosevelt Association, 2013)

As Roosevelt's quote suggests, stretch goals are not always achievable— sometimes dreamers suffer the agony of defeat. Sim and his colleagues (Sitkin et al., 2011) argued that organizations should pursue stretch goals when they have the slack resources that allow them to afford experimentation and the occasional failed venture. Paradoxically, however, organizations with slack resources are usually those who are making a tidy profit using their existing procedures and thus may see no reason to change those procedures; consequently, they may be less likely to invest in grand plans and unproven, risky ventures. In contrast, organizations with few slack resources may unwisely gamble on risky stretch goals they might not be able to afford.

Goal Orientation: Learn, Prove, or Avoid

Researchers have discovered that people tend to have one of three types of goal orientation (Button, Mathieu, & Zajac, 1996; Dweck & Leggett, 1988; VandeWalle, 1997). *People with a learning goal orientation are eager to learn new tasks and are willing to try challenging tasks that take some time to master.* People with this orientation understand that when they learn new tasks they will make mistakes; they view these mistakes as learning opportunities, and they are not embarrassed by the mistakes. They recognize that while learning a new task they will not be as accomplished at performing the task as a more experienced person would be. When playing a sport or game, people with a learning orientation often seek to play better players as a way to learn from their opponents and improve their own skills.

In contrast, people with a *performance goal orientation focus more on the end result and on achieving the goal than on learning and development.* There are two main types of performance goal orientations: prove and avoid. *People with a prove goal orientation seek to demonstrate their competence to others by achieving goals and by doing tasks that they are good at performing.* Employees with a prove goal orientation may work hard at tasks they already know how to do. However, they may be reluctant to try new tasks or projects. In their efforts to impress others with their productivity, they may also try to start producing before they have fully learned the best and most efficient ways to proceed. When playing sports or games, people with this orientation may prefer to play people they can beat. *People with an avoid goal orientation want to avoid any tasks that might cause others to question their competence*; because they worry about making mistakes in front of others, they are not eager to attempt activities they have not already mastered. Consistent with this perspective, a study found that people with an avoid goal orientation were less likely to pick challenging tasks during an assessment center exercise and instead picked simple tasks to perform (De Pater et al., 2009). This has important implications for career success because the study also found that performing the complex tasks increased perceptions of competency for career advancement.

Although most employees are predisposed to a particular goal orientation, managers and other *leaders can influence employees' state goal orientations by the instructions they give them* (Button et al., 1996; Dragoni, 2005). (As explained in prior chapters, *state* refers to the attitude being experienced at the time in contrast to a more stable and long lasting personality trait or disposition.) For example, a leader could tell new employees that their main goal is to learn all they can about how to do the work. When working with more experienced employees, leaders can create a climate that supports the learning goal orientation by emphasizing continuous learning, skill development, experimentation, and learning from failures (Dragoni, 2005).

When leaders have positive leader-member relationships with their followers, the followers are also more willing to adopt a learning orientation and to be open to feedback. The beneficial effects of positive leader-member relationships on learning was demonstrated in a study of 1,112 employees and their 233 leaders from seven organizations in the Netherlands (Bezuijen, van Dam, van den Berg, & Thierry, 2010). These employees and leaders worked in a variety of industries (healthcare, police, penitentiary, social services, security services, high tech, and vocational training). According to both the employees' self-reports and the leaders' ratings, the *employees were more likely to engage in learning activities when they had positive leader-member relationships.*

Leaders may want to encourage employees to adopt a learning goal orientation because a *learning goal orientation often results in higher performance than either of the two performance goal orientations*; this is especially true when the employees perform complex work and need to search for information. For example, one study found that a specific learning goal produced better results than specific performance goals (Seijts et al., 2004). The following Personal Reflections feature shows the importance of setting learning goals for oneself.

PERSONAL REFLECTIONS: *THE COURAGE TO FAIL A THOUSAND TIMES*

Once when I was watching the Winter Olympics, the announcer described how long it takes the skaters to learn the jumps they were doing. Before they could perform the jump correctly even once, they would have to attempt the jump 1,000 times. A thousand times! That's an awful lot. And to perfect the jump enough to perform it in competition, they would have to attempt the jump thousands more times. Imagine: The first 1,000 times you try something, *failure*. It takes courage and confidence to fail that many times and not give up. This is why many athletes believe that the right mental attitude is the most important characteristic it takes to win.

The Olympic athletes' experiences are not unique. It takes about a thousand repetitions to program a reflexive response—the type of rapid almost instantaneous movement that many athletes use. Many factory workers also need thousands of repetitions to perform their work as fast and as accurately as more experienced workers. In some cases, it may take new workers up to three months to achieve *mastery*, or the performance level of most experienced workers. During the first few weeks, the new employees' performance levels may fall far below that of the more experienced workers.

It can be tough to keep up your confidence in your abilities when so many people around you are outperforming you by a wide margin. Many new employees quit before they have a chance to achieve the mastery level because they lack confidence in their ability to learn the job. For many professional jobs, the learning curve is much longer; often years of experience are required to become an expert—the temptation to quit can be great when it takes years to become as good as your office mates. Who wants to feel inferior to the guy or gal in the next desk?

I had some personal experiences with the learning curve when I succumbed to the *Guitar Hero* craze. I decided to buy the complete band set. I didn't know how to play any musical instruments, and I didn't play video games, so I had no relevant experience. But hey, it was a game for teenagers, how difficult could it be? And besides, I told myself I was really buying it for my teenage son as a way to teach him about great rock music. My son helped me set up the game. He demonstrated how it worked by easily playing a song on one of the more difficult levels. He had no musical training, but after years of video game playing, his reflexes were good. On *Guitar Hero* you control the game with a plastic guitar with buttons on the guitar neck and a strum bar; you watch a video screen that shows notes coming down the guitar strings, and when the notes hit the strum bar, you have to hold down the right buttons on the neck of the guitar while hitting the strum bar. I decided to try a song on the level for beginners. The notes seemed to be coming down the strings at a slow, easy pace, nothing like the rapid pace on the song my son had played. Surely it should be easy, but I found it hard to make my clumsy, inexperienced fingers hit the notes and strum bar at the right time. The virtual audience started booing. Oh no! My son gave me helpful advice, "Hit the notes more rhythmically, Dad." I was booed off the stage, right in front of my son—how embarrassing! Fortunately my son didn't gloat—perhaps I was never enough competition to warrant gloating.

It was tempting to give up on the game. Perhaps I should stick to things that I could already do well. But fortunately I could practice alone out of sight of an embarrassing audience. Eventually I became better. I watched my accuracy rate creep up, and I moved on to playing songs on levels that seemed impossible to me when I first started. Like the research on learning suggested, it took about three months for me to develop the automatic reflexes necessary to play the game well. A few months later, I even performed at a faculty office party—a rock star at last!

Your Turn to Reflect: Do you prefer to do activities that you can already do well, or do you enjoy learning new things? Have you seen people avoid trying new things that they might actually enjoy because they were afraid to try something new? How does it feel when you are first learning a job—can learning a new job be anxiety provoking? What can leaders do to ease this anxiety and help make new employees confident they can eventually succeed?

Self-Assessment: Visit the textbook website to evaluate your goal orientation.

Leaders need to provide emotional support and training to help their followers learn new skills. In addition, as the next case indicates, leaders also have to give financial incentives to others to achieve the goals.

Case: *Truett Cathy, Founder of Chick-fil-A, Splits the Profits*

Imagine you are 30 years old. You are a hard worker, a responsible person, and you would like to start your own business or at least make some good money. The trouble is, you only have a few thousand dollars in savings, and even a fast food restaurant costs millions of dollars to build or buy. But suppose someone offered to make you a partner in a 2 million dollar plus restaurant, where you could take almost half the profits for managing it? To many people, this would be a dream come true. If someone sent you a letter in the mail offering you this deal, you would probably suspect it's a scam—it sounds too good to be true. Yet this is the deal that Truett Cathy and Chick-fil-A makes with his *Operators*, or restaurant managers. In his 2002 book, *Eat Mor Chikin: Inspire More People*, Truett explains how he inspires his employees to provide

(Continued)

(Continued)

The playful cows greatly boosted Chick-fil-A sales. Notice also how the "C" in Chick-fil-A resembles a chicken. Truett Cathy loves giving out toy Chick-fil-A cows to children

Source: Wikipedia/Mav (CC-BY-SA)

the outstanding service that Chick-fil-A is known for. Chick-fil-A builds the restaurant (and still owns it); the Operator pays a 15% of gross sales franchise fee to Chick-fil-A; and after that, the Operator and Chick-fil-A split the net profits 50-50 (Cathy, 2002, p. 99). This policy results in pretty high earnings for the Operators: In 2002, the majority made more than $100,000, many earned over $200,000, and some even earned over $300,000.

People ask Truett how he can afford to be so generous with his Operators. Truett states (Cathy, 2002, p. 99), "We love it when an Operator earns a lot of money because that means we are also earning a lot of money from the restaurant." He wants the Operators to share this attitude by thinking, "The more successful I make Chick-fil-A, the more successful I make myself." When Operators share in the profits they make from every sale, they are motivated to treat customers right as well. As one Operator, Alex Rodriguez, stated, "The customer right in front of you is funding your paycheck" (p. 101).

Truett also knows that money is only part of what it takes to motivate employees. For many years he tried to personally know every Operator as well as their family (with over 1,500 Operators, he can no longer do that). He shows consideration for his Operators and Chick-fil-A employees by closing restaurants on Sundays so employees can spend time with their families. Chick-fil-A also was one of the first fast food restaurant chains to give college scholarships to their employees ($1.6 million during 2011). Truett believes that part of his mission is to help develop young people—he and his wife personally have been foster parents to over 150 children, and he has funded the WinShape Foundation, which supports foster homes, counseling programs, and a summer camp (13,000 campers in 2011 alone). This caring attitude is part of how Chick-fil-A Operators treat their employees. As Rodriguez stated (Cathy, 2002, p. 101), "I take a personal interest in the people who work in our restaurant, dropping personal notes in with their paychecks, buying cake on their birthdays, attending softball games and track meets. My goal for them first is to be successful in life, and then to be a good Chick-fil-A team member."

Although many businesses had slow sales during 2010, the Chick-fil-A restaurant chain reported an astonishing 11.4% sales increase over its 2009 sales figures. Its figures for 2011 were just as impressive: a 13.08% increase over the 2010 overall sales performance, and total revenue now exceeds $4 billion. Indeed, Chick-fil-A has had a 44 year streak of positive sales growth.

Truett grew up during hard economic times. Before he was born, his once prosperous father lost his farm and real estate investments when the real estate market collapsed (their house also burned down in a fire), his older brother had died from an infection, and his demoralized father had to go to work as a sales agent. By the time Truett was born, his family was poor. To make ends meet, his mother had to run a boarding house, and she did the cooking, cleaning, and laundry for the boarders as well as for her own family. As an 8-year-old, Truett started selling Coca-Cola door to door. At that age, his speech impediment was so bad he couldn't pronounce his own name, and he had to show strangers a handwritten card with his name on it. Later he sold magazine subscriptions and delivered newspapers. While delivering newspapers, he learned to treat every customer as important; he tried not to lose a single customer. On the weekends, he helped out his mother. Truett learned his cooking skills from her. During WWII, he served in the army (stateside), and after the war, he opened his first restaurant, The Dwarf Grill, in 1946.

Truett founded the first Chick-fil-A in the early 1960s. Two factors were important to the early growth of his company. One was his invention of the boneless chicken sandwich. Today, with chicken sandwiches in almost all fast food restaurants, it's hard to imagine that boneless chicken sandwiches ever needed inventing. Second, he was the first to operate fast food restaurants inside malls. Because he rented the space inside the malls, he was able to expand rapidly without taking out large loans to buy land and build freestanding restaurants. By the time the nation-wide construction of new malls slowed down (which limited his expansion into new malls), Truett had enough revenue and resources to grow by building freestanding restaurants.

Applications: How is a typical restaurant manager compensated? How does this compare to the Chick-fil-A method? Do you think the Chick-fil-A method of splitting the profits with Operators is an effective way to provide contingent rewards? Why or why not? How important is the personal, caring attitude to Chick-fil-A's success?

Sources: Cathy, S. T. (2002). *Eat mor chikin: Inspire more people.* Decatur, GA: Looking Glass Books.

Chick-fil-A. (2012, February 6). Chick-fil-A achieves record annual sales of $4 billion. Retrieved from http://www.chick-fil-a.com/Pressroom/Press-Releases#?release=sales-release

A simplistic reading of goal theory suggests that all you have to do is set goals like improving productivity and profits by 10%, and like magic the goals are achieved! However, every business that has gone bankrupt has undoubtedly had goals to improve profits and sales. Goals work best when they are united with passion and a purpose, and when they focus on meeting the needs of both employees and customers. The following case about Howard Schultz and Starbucks shows how goals need to be meaningful in order to be truly motivating.

Case: *Howard Schultz, Chairman and CEO of Starbucks, Brews a Strong Cup of Goals*

Howard tells us about the origins of Starbucks in his first book (Schultz & Yang, 1997) entitled *Pour Your Heart Into It: How Starbucks Built a Company One Cup at a Time*. His second book (Schultz & Gordon, 2011) is called *Onward: How Starbucks Fought for Its Life Without Losing Its Soul*.

Goals and Dreams Can Come True: Howard is another true rags to riches life story: His family was part of the working poor, and he grew up in a public housing project in New York. Howard became the first person in his family to graduate from college, and he also attended Xerox's famous corporate sales training program. He eventually became the vice-president and general manager of Hammarplast's national sales force before finding his passion selling coffee.

Passionate Goals: Hammarplast sold kitchen products (like coffee makers). Howard travelled to Seattle to find out why a small company—Starbucks—was selling so many coffee makers. Starbucks specialized in selling coffee beans from around the world and sold drip coffee makers so their customers could brew their own coffee at home. The Starbucks owners offered him a cup of freshly brewed dark roasted coffee, and Howard was smitten with the love of fine coffee. He was so passionate about his love of coffee that he was willing to take a steep pay cut (with a small cup of equity in Starbucks) to begin working at Starbucks.

Learning Goals: Howard didn't just jump into opening his own coffee shops after his first sip of Starbuck's coffee. He first set himself some learning goals. When describing how he became successful, Howard stated that he "learned from anyone I could" (Schultz & Yang, 1997, p. 19). He advises people to "lay your foundations well, absorb information like a sponge" (p.19). Howard laid his foundation well and learned about coffee and the retail business by working for Starbucks for several years before opening his own coffee shops. He also *visited almost 500 coffee bars* in Italy and took detailed notes on how they were operated.

Make No Small Plans: Before he was even hired at Starbucks, Howard had the ambitious goal of expanding Starbucks to all the major cities in America. He wanted to share his love of coffee with everyone! As he told the Starbucks owners during his job interview, "If Starbucks opened stores across the United States and Canada, you could share your knowledge and passion with so many more people. You could enrich so many lives" (Schultz & Yang, 1997, p. 41). The Starbucks owners, however, were content to sell roasted coffee beans from their four small stores in Seattle—they were intimidated by Howard's big plans and almost didn't hire him as a result.

After working at Starbucks for a year, Howard (in 1983) travelled to Italy where he was smitten with an even bigger vision. Everywhere he went in Milan he saw coffee bars. The coffee bars were a place to socialize while drinking fine coffees and espressos made fresh to order. The social aspects of drinking coffee struck Howard like a double shot of espresso—he was even shaking with the intensity of his vision. At that time, Starbucks only sold coffee beans; why not sell coffee by the cup? Howard had a vision of recreating the Italian coffee bar culture in America. He wanted to make Starbucks coffee bars a place where people went to socialize and drink coffee on a daily basis. He envisioned Starbucks as an *experience* and not just a bag of beans. His plan involved changing the daily routines and habits of millions of people—truly an ambitious goal!

After much prodding and stirring, Howard managed to convince the Starbucks owners to open up a small espresso bar to test the market. The bar was an immediate hit, and within weeks, people were lined up outside the store waiting for their turn to buy espresso and lattes. Despite the immediate hit, Howard couldn't convince the owners to focus on creating a chain of coffee bars. Instead, they used their limited resources to buy another small chain of coffee bean stores. Howard believed in his dream enough to leave Starbucks and start his own espresso bars, and after making his espresso bars a success, he went back and bought the original Starbucks stores and took the Starbucks name as well.

(Continued)

(Continued)

Ethical Goals: Right from the start, Howard had the goal of making Starbucks an ethical company with a deep commitment to its employees and to the world. When Howard was growing up, his father was injured on the job, and because he couldn't work while in a cast, his father also lost his job. This made a deep impression on Howard, and when he became CEO of Starbucks, he offered comprehensive health-care even to part-time employees and he also gave them stock options—both rare benefits for part-timers (the stock options were playfully called *bean stock*). Instead of regarding these benefits as expenses, Howard regarded them as a key part of his competitive strategy. The benefits saved Starbucks money by dramatically reducing turnover costs, and in addition, the more experienced and motivated employees provided better customer service and thus increased sales.

Don't Sell Your Soul for Growth, Growth, Growth: After making Starbucks a nation-wide success, Howard turned over the CEO job to others, and eventually an outsider was hired as CEO. At the time, Starbucks was still focusing on rapid growth. Over the years, Starbucks's emphasis on its employees and on the authentic *coffee experience* had slowly been watered down, and in 2007, it experienced its first quarter without an increase in sales, and its stock price tumbled an astonishing 42%. The problems had begun earlier. Starting in 2006, employees had been quietly approaching Howard with their concerns. As Howard put it (Schultz & Gordon, 2011), "People wanted something other than Grow! Grow! Grow!" (p. 22). Howard took up the CEO job again, and by 2010, Starbucks had its best quarter ever. If you truly want amazing growth, you have to focus first on your customers and on your employees—make them your goals, and the sales goals will follow naturally.

> **Applications:** How important is it to have a passion for the product you are selling? Do you think Howard's intrinsic love of coffee motivated him as much as his extrinsic rewards did? Do you think his background helped him identify more with his frontline employees? Can an overemphasis on growth actually hurt growth?

Source: Schultz, H., & Gordon, J. (2011). *Onward: How Starbucks fought for its life without losing its soul.* New York, NY: Rodale.

Put It in Practice

1. Pound out the rhythm of success: Plan, plan, plan.

2. Taking care of business: Use transactional leadership and goal setting to help you manage all the details and work tasks that come your way.

3. Use transactional leadership: Use contingent rewards to set up clear expectations for performance, specify what should be done, and reward employees based on their meeting goals and expectations.

4. Rewards work: Use contingent rewards to boost follower's job performance, their job satisfaction, their satisfaction with your leadership, and your own leader performance.

5. Set specific, difficult, attainable, and acceptable goals.

6. Build goal commitment: Reward goal accomplishment and make goals intrinsically attractive to followers—this is especially important when goal difficulty is high.

7. Select high goal setters: those high on extraversion, openness, and conscientiousness.

8. Be a coach: Effective goal-focused coaching requires effective goal-setting skills, the development of a strong working alliance, a solution-focused approach, managing process and accountability, and obtaining outcomes that are valued and meaningful.

9. Know your true desires: You will be more motivated and successful when your goals reflect your true desires.

10. Stretch your followers' creativity: Use stretch goals to stimulate creativity, stir your followers' blood and inspire them, and get them to make big plans.

11. Set learning goals: Boost your followers' performance and help them overcome proving and avoiding orientations by instructing them to learn all they can about the work tasks.

12. Have the courage to fail 1,000 times: It's the only way to learn new skills.

13. Split the profits: The more they make, the more you make. Be friendly and considerate too.

14. Brew strong goals by following your passions, learning all you can about your product, by dreaming big, and by focusing your goals on meeting your employees' and customers' needs.

Exercises

1. Your True Heart's Desires

On a sheet of paper, draw a line down the middle. On one side, list all the things you want to avoid in your career and your life. On the other side, list the things that you love and want to have in your career and life. What sort of goals can you set for yourself to help you achieve the things you love and avoid the things you hate? (Instructor: Let the class know at the beginning of the exercise if students will be asked to share their lists in small groups or with the class as a whole. Usually a few students will volunteer to share their lists even if the majority get to keep their list confidential.)

2. **Shoot to Win**

Form teams of about five people. Each team should pick an athlete to represent them in the contest. The team should make three paper wads suitable for throwing. Then the team should advise their athlete about whether to try for 5 pointers, 10 pointers, or 15 pointers. The instructor will use a trash can for the basket and place markers on the floor to indicate where the 5 point, 10 point, and 15 point lines are. The athletes will line up and throw their three balls one at a time. The team with the highest point total wins. After the contest is over, the instructor will explain how this relates to goal setting.

Visit the Student Study Site at **www.sagepub.com/humphreyel** for these additional tools:

- Learning Goals
- Leader's Book Case Articles
- Web Resources
- Student Self Assessments

References

Avolio, B. J. (2011). *Full range leadership development* (2nd ed.). Thousand Oaks, CA: Sage.

Bass, B. M., & Riggio, R. E. (2006/2007). *Transformational leadership* (2nd ed.) [E-library edition]. Mahwah, NJ: Lawrence Erlbaum.

Bezuijen, X. M., van Dam, K., van den Berg, P. T. & Thierry, H. (2010). How leaders stimulate employee learning: A leader–member exchange approach. *Journal of Occupational and Organizational Psychology, 83,* 673–693.

Burns. J. M. (1978). *Leadership.* New York, NY: Harper & Row.

Button, S. B., Mathieu, J. E., & Zajac, D. M. (1996). Goal orientation in organizational research: A conceptual and empirical foundation. *Organizational Behavior and Human Decision Processes, 67,* 26–48.

Cathy, S. T. (2002). *Eat mor chikin: Inspire more people.* Decatur, GA: Looking Glass Books.

Chick-fil-A. (2012, February 6). Chick-fil-A achieves record annual sales of $4 billion. Retrieved from http://www.chick-fil-a.com/Pressroom/Press-Releases#?release=sales-release

Corcoran, B., & Littlefield, B. (Ed.). (2011). *Shark Tales: How I turned $1,000 into a billion dollar business.* New York, NY: Penguin.

De Pater, I. E., Van Vianen, A. E. M., Humphrey, R. H., Sleeth, R. G., Hartman, N. S., & Fischer, A. H. (2009). Task choice and the division of challenging tasks between men and women. *Group and Organization Management, 34,* 563–589.

Dragoni, L. (2005). Understanding the emergence of state goal orientation in organizational work groups: The role of leadership and multilevel climate perceptions. *Journal of Applied Psychology, 90,* 1084–1095.

Dweck, C. S., & Leggett, E. L. (1988). A social-cognitive approach to motivation and personality. *Psychological Review, 95,* 256–273.

Estefan, E. (2010). *The rhythm of success.* New York, NY: Penguin.

Grant, A. M., & Cavanagh, M. J. (2007). The goal-focused coaching skills questionnaire: Preliminary findings. *Social Behavior and Personality, 35,* 751–760.

Judge, T. A., Bono, J. E., Ilies, R., & Gerhardt, M. W. (2002). Personality and leadership: A qualitative and quantitative review. *Journal of Applied Psychology, 87,* 765–780.

Judge, T. A., & Ilies, R. (2002). Relationship of personality to performance motivation: A meta-analytic review. *Journal of Applied Psychology, 87,* 797–807.

Judge, T. A., & Piccolo, R. F. (2004). Transformational and transactional leadership: A meta-analytic test of their relative validity. *Journal of Applied Psychology, 89,* 755–768.

Klein, H. J., Wesson, M. J., Hollenbeck, J. R., & Alge, B. J. (1999). Goal commitment and the goal-setting process: Conceptual clarification and empirical synthesis. *Journal of Applied Psychology, 84,* 885–896.

Latham, G. P., & Locke, E. A. (2009). Science and ethics: What should count as evidence against the use of goal setting? *Academy of Management Perspectives, 23*(3), 88–91.

Michelangelo. (n.d.). BrainyQuote.com. Retrieved February 4, 2013 from http://www.brainyquote.com/quotes/quotes/m/michelange127407.html

Mintzberg, H. (1973). *The nature of managerial work.* New York, NY: Harper & Row.

Mitchell, T. R., & Daniels, D. (2003). Motivation. In W. C. Borman, D. R. Ilgen, & R. J. Klimoski (Eds.), *Comprehensive handbook of psychology: Industrial organizational psychology* (Vol. 12, pp. 225–254). New York, NY: Wiley & Sons.

O'Shea, P. G., Foti, R. J., Hauenstein, N. M. A., & Bycio, P. (2009). Are the best leaders both transformational and transactional? A pattern-oriented analysis. *Leadership, 5,* 237–259.

Podsakoff, P. M., Bommer, W. H., Podsakoff, N. P., & MacKenzie, S. B. (2006). Relationships between leader reward and punishment behavior and subordinate attitudes, perceptions, and behaviors: A meta-analytic review of existing and new research. *Organizational Behavior and Human Decision Processes, 99,* 113–142.

Rousseau, D. M. (1997). Organizational behavior in the new organizational era. *Annual Review of Psychology, 48,* 515–546.

Schultz, H., & Gordon, J. (2011). *Onward: How Starbucks fought for its life without losing its soul.* New York, NY: Rodale.

Schultz, H., & Yang, D. J. (1997). *Pour your heart into it: How Starbucks built a company one cup at a time*. New York, NY: Hyperion.

Seijts, G. H., Latham, G. P., Tasa, K., & Latham, B. W. (2004). Goal setting and goal orientation: An integration of two different yet related literatures. *Academy of Management Journal, 47*, 227–239.

Sitkin, S. B., See, K. E., Miller, C. C., Lawless, M. W., & Carton, A. M. (2011). The paradox of stretch goals: Organizations in pursuit of the seemingly impossible. *Academy of Management Review, 36*, 544–566.

Theodore Roosevelt Association. (2013). Theodore Roosevelt. Retrieved February 4, 2013 from http://www.theodoreroosevelt.org/life/quotes.htm

VandeWalle, D. (1997). Development and validation of a work domain goal orientation instrument. *Journal of Educational and Psychological Measurement, 57*, 995–1015.

Wang, G., Oh, I., Courtright, S. H., & Colbert, A. E. (2011). Transformational leadership and performance across criteria and levels: A meta-analytic review of 25 years of research. *Group & Organization Management, 36*, 223–270.

White, R. B. (1986). *The great business quotations*. New York, NY: Dell.

15

Transformational Leadership, Change, and Sensemaking Perspectives

❧❦

Chapter Road Map

❧❦

Case: *Ford CEO Alan Mulally Drives Home "One Ford"*

Alan Mulally has been hailed as one of the greatest CEOs of all time. Bryce G. Hoffman's (2012) book about Alan is entitled *American Icon: Alan Mulally and the Fight to Save Ford Motor Company*. Bill Vlasic (2011) also praises Alan in his book, *Once Upon a Car: The Fall and Resurrection of America's Big Three Automakers—GM, Ford, and Chrysler*. Bill Ford and Ford board members hired Alan Mulally in 2006 to be Ford's CEO. They picked him because they wanted "somebody with vision" but also "an operating guy who can drive it home" (Hoffman, "The Man on the White Horse," location 1375). In other words, they wanted someone high on both transformational and transactional leadership. The 60-year-old Mulally had proven experience: He had transformed the organizational culture at Boeing while overseeing the development of highly profitable new airplanes, and he also helped Boeing survive a financial crisis after the 9/11 attacks caused multiple cancellations in orders for Boeing planes. Ford Motors was facing its own financial crisis. Bill Ford, the great-grandson of Henry Ford, would lie awake at nights worrying about the company's future. But when he was with Alan, he would relax: Alan's obvious competence along with his trademark grin and enthusiastic, optimistic demeanor inspired confidence. Alan was known for giving people hugs, and at Boeing he signed his name with a cartoon of a smiling jet under his signature. At the same time, Alan knew how to hold people accountable by setting goals and by monitoring their progress. Alan also had rules for working together to stop executive backstabbing and to get people to work together as a team for the good of the company.

Alan Mulally, CEO of Ford

In part, Ford was a victim of its own success. In the 1980s, Ford's revolutionary Taurus became the bestselling car in America, and by 1987, Ford was making more profit than all the *European and Japanese car manufacturers combined*. In 1990, Ford introduced the Ford Explorer, which quickly became the world's bestselling SUV. In 1998, Ford's $22 billion profit set a record in the automobile industry. Good sales continued for a few more years, but eventually the market became saturated—almost everyone who wanted a new Ford had one.

Moreover, the high quality and longevity of Ford vehicles also meant that their customers didn't need to replace their vehicles anytime soon. Rising gas prices were also shifting consumer demand away from Ford's profitable SUVs and trucks. In October 2006, a month after Mulally became Ford's CEO, Ford posted its worst quarterly loss in 14 years—a staggering $5.8 billion.

Mulally developed a plan and vision which he called "One Ford." Alan developed his vision by listening to employees, reading all he could about the auto industry, and by trying to make sense of Ford's production process and overall organization. Alan would astonish lower-level employees by popping into their offices, joining them for lunch in the employee cafeteria, and chatting with them as they walked down the halls. Alan would ask them for their insights into Ford and for suggestions for improvement. One engineer took Alan up on his open door policy and walked in with a bunch of engineering schematics. He showed Alan how Ford had over a dozen different hood structures. Soon, Alan was covering a table in his office with different models of door handles, switches, and other car parts. Alan wondered why there were so many different versions all designed to do the same thing? Mulally also tried to make sense of Ford's worldwide production strategy. Alan noticed that the many Ford regional divisions (Europe, Asia, Latin America, and North America) produced their own models of vehicles instead of using common, worldwide platforms. Even within a division many parts were not standardized across vehicle types. Thus, Ford had to spend money designing and producing a wide variety of latches, door handles, dashboards, and thousands of other components. The One Ford plan called for uniting the independent Ford divisions into a truly unified company that used standardized parts for a much smaller number of brands and models. This reorganization would reduce engineering and production costs and allow for greater economies of scale.

Mulally implemented his vision with hands-on leadership. He eliminated layers of bureaucracy that had isolated Bill Ford from his top executives. Alan required all of his top executives to meet each week with him in a Thursday morning business plan review. The executives had to present their status reports in color-coded Powerpoint slides. Green for on schedule, yellow for somewhat short, and red for in trouble. Alan emphasized that the purpose was to help them uncover problems that needed to be fixed, but the executives all thought that the first one to reveal a red color code would be fired. The charts all kept turning up green. Finally an executive, Mark Fields, had the courage to post a red dot indicating a delay in the launch of the Ford Edge—a key new vehicle. The room grew quiet. Mark thought he might be fired—then Alan stood

(Continued)

(Continued)

up and started clapping! "Mark, that is great visibility," Mullaly applauded. "Now is there any help you need from any member of the team?" (Vlasic, 2011, p. 283). Other executives quickly jumped in with offers of help. This marked a turning point in the team: The executives knew they could trust Alan and they began fixing their problems instead of hiding them.

The 2008 economic crisis made the market for vehicles even worse. Fortunately, the reorganization worked, and Ford began making a profit again. By 2010, it posted a first quarter profit of $2.1 billion. Its market share also climbed 2.5% in a single quarter, a record increase. Ford has also maintained its quality. The 2012 JD Power dependability ratings are based on surveys of owners of 2009 model year vehicles. This survey found that three of Ford's products ranked number 1 (or tied for first) for dependability in their category: Ford Fusion, Ford Explorer, and the Lincoln MKZ. In addition, the Ford Taurus, the Lincoln MKX, and the Ford Ranger also won awards for being in the top three in their categories. Clearly, Mulally's transformational and transactional leadership is working.

Applications: Think of the organizations that you belong to. Have the top leaders ever asked you for advice and input about the organization's vision? Alan is known for his big grin and friendly hugs—can good guys be just as effective as *tough* bosses in holding people accountable? Why do you think Alan was so successful?

Source: J.D. Power and Associates 2012 U.S. Vehicle Dependability Study[SM] (VDS) (2011, December 30). Retrieved from http://autos.jdpower.com/content/study-auto/V8Ois5x/2012-vehicle-dependability-study-results.htm?page=2

As the Ford case demonstrates, transformational leaders often use transactional leadership and goal-setting techniques. By combining inspiration with goal setting, transformational leaders can achieve superior results when it comes to motivating followers. The word *transformation* also conjures up images of change. As this chapter demonstrates, transformational leadership is especially important when organizations need to make major changes in order to survive. Change is threatening to many people, and transformational leaders need to help their followers cope with their fears and insecurities and help them feel positive emotions about the changes. Organizations have to change in order to adapt to changes in the external environment. Transformational leaders need to make sense of changes in the external environment and understand how these changes impact their organization. Thus, this chapter will also discuss sensemaking processes related to changing environments and organizational change. This chapter will in particular address three important questions:

- How does transformational leadership add to the goal-setting process and improve individual, team, and organizational performance and follower satisfaction?
- How does transformational leadership help followers cope with change and improve the odds of having a successful change?
- What steps can leaders take to manage the unexpected and handle the complex changes in the environment that frequently occur?

Transformational Leadership and Goal Setting

As discussed in Chapter 14, transformational leaders use transactional leadership to set goals for their followers. However, transformational leaders add to the goal-setting process by inspiring followers as well as by offering them financial rewards for performance. As a result, transformational leadership *augments*, or increases, leaders' overall effectiveness. Avolio (2011, p. 51) described several ways in which transformational leadership augments the goal-setting process. First, transformational leaders help followers see their short-term goals in terms of the bigger picture and the relevance of their goals to other employees, their organization, and their customers. Second, transformational leaders use challenging goals as a way to further develop their followers' skills and abilities. Third, transformational leaders challenge basic assumptions about how the work is usually done, and as a result, they increase creativity and efficiency. Fourth, transformational leaders emphasize moral responsibilities and values and encourage followers to achieve their goals without compromising ethical standards. As the following paragraphs indicate, transformational leaders may also help followers agree on common goals.

When everyone on a team agrees about the importance of various goals, they have high **goal importance congruence,** *or goal importance agreement.* When team members disagree about priorities and about which goals are most important, they are not likely to work well together. Because transformational leaders are effective communicators, they can communicate their vision for the organization in a way that helps team members understand their top priorities. Transformational leaders develop organizational goals by working together with their followers; as a result, they build consensus about the team goals and priorities.

A study by Colbert and her colleagues demonstrated how vital goal importance congruence is to top management teams and organizational performance (Colbert, Kristof-Brown, Bradley, & Barrick, 2008). They surveyed CEOs from 94 credit unions, along with 517 members of their top management teams. They found that CEOs who had a transformational leadership style were more likely to have top management teams with high goal importance congruence. In turn, this high goal importance congruence created higher organizational performance. In brief, their results looked like this:

Transformational Leadership → Goal Importance Congruence →
Organizational Performance

Applications: Have you ever worked on teams where people couldn't agree about what goals to pursue? How much conflict did the lack of agreement create? Did the lack of agreement interfere with the group's success? What can leaders do to promote agreement about goals and priorities?

The Four "I's" of Transformational Leadership

There are four main methods, called the four "I's," which transformational leaders use to encourage followers to achieve goals (Avolio, 2011; Bass & Riggio, 2006/2007). As previously defined in Chapter 1, *transformational leaders use idealized influence, inspirational motivation, intellectual stimulation, and individualized consideration to transform followers' beliefs and to create a new, more motivating vision.* A questionnaire, called the Multifactor Leadership Questionnaire, or MLQ, has four subscales to measure these aspects of transformational leadership (Avolio & Bass, 2004). The first two dimensions, idealized influence and inspirational motivation, are sometimes called the charismatic components of transformational leadership, and they are sometimes used as a measure of charisma. Here is how the four components are described:

Idealized Influence: Transformational leaders demonstrate idealized influence when they act as role models for their followers. Here is how Bass and Riggio (2006/2007) explained idealized influence:

> Transformational leaders behave in ways that allow them to serve as role models for their followers. The leaders are admired, respected, and trusted. Followers identify with the leaders and want to emulate them; leaders are endowed by their followers as having extraordinary capabilities, persistence, and determination. (p. 6)

A study by Epitropaki and Martin (2005) demonstrates that transformational leaders can get followers to identify with their overall organization. They surveyed 502 service employees who worked in four banks in Greece. They found that service employees who had transformational leaders were more likely to identify with the banks that employed them. Transactional leadership also increased employee organizational identification, but not as much as transformational leadership did. As a result, transformational leadership did augment, or increase, organizational identification over the amount of identification due to transactional leadership.

Inspirational Motivation: Transformational leaders use inspirational motivation when they inspire others by providing meaning and challenge to their work. As Avolio (2011) stated,

> Transformational leaders behave in ways that motivate and inspire those around them by providing meaning and challenge to their followers' work. Team spirit is enhanced. Such leaders display enthusiasm and optimism. They get followers involved in thinking about various attractive future states or scenarios. . . . They can inspire others by what they say, by what they do. (p. 61)

A study done by Piccolo and Colquitt (2006) demonstrated that transformational leaders can help their followers see their jobs as more meaningful and worthwhile. Employees are not likely to do their best when they do not believe that their jobs are important, worthwhile, or in other ways meaningful. Piccolo and Colquitt measured employees' jobs in terms of five core job characteristics (Hackman & Oldham, 1976): the variety of work tasks performed, the task identity or completion of a whole piece of work, the autonomy or amount of freedom employees had on the job, the significance or impact the job had on others, and the amount of clear feedback employees had about their performance. This study found that employees with transformational leaders were more likely to rate their jobs higher on the five job characteristics—in other words, employees with transformational leaders were more likely to believe they had more meaningful, significant, and important jobs. As a result, these employees were more intrinsically motivated, had higher levels of goal commitment, and had better task performance and organizational citizenship behavior.

Applications: Have you ever done work that you thought was boring, trivial, and meaningless? How did that make you feel? Have you witnessed managers contributing to this sense of meaninglessness by implying that the work their subordinates did was less important than their own work? What can leaders do to make every employee feel that their work is meaningful and important?

As the following case indicates, the company you work for can make a big difference in whether you find your work meaningful or not, even for the same type of work.

Case: *Phone Monkey or Agent With a Mission?*

Phone Monkey: The Secret Diary of a Frustrated Call Centre Worker (Anonymous, 2012) screams out the aggravation that the anonymous British author felt while selling insurance over the phone. He wrote the book to try to find some meaning and purpose in his work experiences. Apparently, he wasn't very successful in seeing his job as meaningful. The fact that he calls himself and his fellow call center workers Phone Monkeys shows how alienated he felt from his work. The contingent rewards were good: When he was hired, he was impressed with his opportunity to make big bucks on bonuses. The free coffee and tea was great also. But he and his colony of Phone Monkeys rarely felt any dedication to their jobs, their employer, their customers, or each other. Although the Phone Monkeys were supposed to help retain disgruntled customers by offering discounts and persuasive explanations of policies, none of them put much effort into trying to retain customers. They could make more bonus money by quickly hanging up and moving on to the next call. As the experienced call center worker told the author during his training (Anonymous, 2012, "Day One," location 73), "We're all only here for the money, it's not a labor of love, and the next call could have a bonus attached to it." The Phone Monkeys referred to irate customers—about 10% of the people they talked to—as "The Crazies" (2012, "Day Nine," location 714); admittedly, every business has some rude customers, but at 10% it seems like the company must not be doing enough to keep their customers happy. The company also had an incentive system that pitted the interests of the call center employees against the interests of the customers: The bigger the discounts the employees gave customers, the lower their own bonuses would be. The Monkeys also lacked team spirit: They were constantly gossiping about each other and making fun of their coworkers' personal lives.

It's tempting to assume that call center work is simply a bad job—that the work itself is alienating and lacking in intrinsic meaning. But is this true? The call center agents at United Services Automobile Association (USAA) also sell insurance, yet USAA is ranked as the 20th best company to work for (Moskowitz, 2012). J.D. Power and Associates also recognized USAA in 2011 for being a Customer Service Champion. The satisfied and dedicated workers at USAA helped it grow from a net worth of $13.1 billion in 2006 to $18.7 billion in 2010. Why are the employees so dedicated? It could be that they believe in the mission and values of their organization. USAA was founded in 1922 by 25 Army officers who had trouble getting private insurance, so they created their own insurance company for military families. Today, USAA's members number 8 million strong, and the membership still consists of military families and the adult children of members. Many of the employees are either former military members or spouses of current service members. The employees identify with their customers and with USAA; after all, they are providing a service to other military families.

Applications: Monkey see, monkey do: The Phone Monkey learned some of his bad attitudes toward customers from his trainers, who also showed up late for training sessions. Do you think that if his managers and trainers had role modeled better customer service that the author might have turned into a dedicated employee instead of a Phone Monkey? What can leaders do to help employees have a positive attitude toward customers? Why do you think the employees at USAA have such a different attitude toward their jobs than the Phone Monkeys do?

Sources: Anonymous (2012). *Phone monkey: The secret diary of a frustrated call centre worker* [E-reader version]. Great Britain, UK: Underglow Books.
Moskowitz, M., & Levering. (2012, February). The 100 best companies to work for. *Fortune,* 117–127.
USAA. Retrieved April 9, 2012 from https://www.usaa.com/inet/pages/why_choose_usaa_main?wa_ref=pub_global_usaaandu

Some interesting research by Sosik and Dinger (2007) suggests that transformational leaders and transactional leaders use different approaches to influence and motivate their followers. They surveyed 183 corporate leaders from six different industries as well as 809 of their subordinates. The followers rated their leaders on inspirational motivation, idealized influence, transactional contingent reward, and laissez-faire leadership. The leaders, who were enrolled in a management development class, wrote a vision statement for a university alumni association. The vision statement was supposed to encourage alumni to become more committed to the alumni organization as well as more active in its meetings. In addition, the leaders were told to write a vision statement that they thought would get the alumni to identify with them as a leader. The researchers found that leaders who were rated as transformational leaders by their subordinates wrote vision statements that were optimistic and confident. Moreover, their vision statements stressed values, the importance of participation, and intrinsic benefits. In contrast, the vision statements written by the transactional leaders emphasized goals, time frames, and extrinsic benefits.

> **Applications:** Which type of vision statement, transformational or transactional, would most motivate you to join and participate in an alumni association? Why?

Intellectual Stimulation: Transformational leaders increase their followers' innovation and creativity by getting them to question assumptions and see problems from new perspectives and approaches (Avolio, 2011; Bass & Riggio, 2006/2007). Transformational leaders help reframe problems in a way that encourages creativity and new insights. Instead of using a top-down approach, transformational leaders encourage their followers and teammates to be creative and fully engaged in the problem solving process. Transformational leaders are willing to reexamine their organization's way of doing things, and they listen to opinions that differ from their own.

Individualized Consideration: Transformational leaders act as coaches and mentors to their followers by recognizing that individuals differ in their abilities as well as in their needs for growth and achievement (Avolio, 2011; Bass & Riggio, 2006/2007). Transformational leaders recognize that they need to use different approaches with different people. Some followers may need encouragement and emotional support to boost their sagging confidence levels, whereas overconfident and aggressive followers may need a firmer approach. Some followers may benefit from high levels of autonomy, whereas others may feel lost if given too little direction. Transformational leaders know their followers and their individual strengths and weaknesses and thus adjust their leadership style according to each person's individual needs. Transformation leaders are willing to delegate tasks to subordinates, but they follow up their subordinates' progress and offer help and constructive feedback when necessary. Subordinates generally do not resent the constructive advice offered by transformational leaders because they realize that the transformational leader is trying to help them grow, learn, and advance in their skills, abilities, and careers.

A study of U.S. West Point cadets found that both intellectual stimulation and individualized consideration are important to leading change (Matthew, 2009). Although intellectual stimulation can help people come up with new approaches, leading change also involves leading groups of people and managing the socio-emotional dynamics of the change process. Many people find change threatening or at least uncomfortable, and change leaders need to be able to manage people's emotions in order to get people to go along with the proposed changes. This study found that intellectual stimulation was the most important predictor of the cadet's ability to lead change, and that individualized consideration was the second best predictor. Both of these measures were more important than cognitive intelligence (as measured by the SAT; however, there was considerable range restriction on the SAT measures as all the cadets had high scores). Intellectual stimulation and individualized consideration were also more important than another commonly used measure of creativity.

The Transformational Leadership Inventory

In addition to the MLQ, there are other ways to measure transformational leadership. One of the other more popular scales is the Transformational Leadership Inventory, or TLI (Podsakoff, MacKenzie, Moorman, & Fetter, 1990). Instead of the four "I's," this has six subscales: Articulates Vision, Provides Appropriate Role Model, Fosters the Acceptance of Goals, Sets High Performance Expectations, Provides Individual Support, and Provides Intellectual Stimulation.

A study of 1,158 managers in Australia used the TLI to see if transformational leaders are more effective at creating a climate for innovation (Sarros, Cooper, & Santora, 2008). The managers were from a variety of private sector companies; 31% listed themselves as top-level managers, 21% as executives, and 48% as upper-middle managers. The study found that articulating vision was the most important dimension of the Transformational Leadership Inventory for predicting a climate of innovation. The study also examined whether transformational leadership affected a second type of organizational culture, which consisted of having a competitive and performance-oriented culture. They found that three of the Transformational Leadership Inventory subscales (articulates vision, individual support, and performance expectations) predicted to a competitive and performance-oriented culture. In turn, the competitive and performance-oriented culture predicted to the climate for innovation. In simplified terms, their results look like this:

Transformational Leadership → Competitive/Performance Culture → Climate of Innovation

Self-Assessment: Evaluate your own levels of transformational leadership by visiting the textbook webpage.

Creating a climate for innovation is one way in which transformational leaders improve productivity and performance. As the following meta-analysis demonstrates, transformational leadership is effective in boosting performance at a variety of levels in the organization.

Transformational Leadership and Follower Performance

The meta-analysis from Chapter 14 on transactional leadership by Wang, Oh, Courtright, & Colbert (2011) also examined transformational leadership and performance. *This study found that transformational leadership is positively related to individual performance, organizational citizenship behavior, team performance, and organizational performance.* It also found that transformational leadership enhanced the creative performance of individual followers.

The researchers also wanted to know if transformational leadership augmented or increased the ability to explain performance over the beneficial effects of contingent rewards (Wang et al., 2011). Although transformational leadership is positively related to individual performance, it did *not* augment the ability to explain individual performance over the amount due to contingent rewards. Consequently, to improve employees' individual performance, leaders should concentrate on rewarding employees for good performance. The researchers used a statistical technique that examines the relative importance of variables. They found that 28% of the leaders' influence on their followers' individual performance was due to transformational leadership, whereas 72% was due to contingent rewards.

As transformational leadership theory advocates, transformational leadership did augment the ability to explain organizational citizenship behavior over and above the effects of contingent reward (Wang et al., 2011). The relative importance analysis found that 71% of the leaders' influence on followers' organizational citizenship behavior was due to transformational leadership, and the remaining 29% was due to contingent rewards. With regard to team performance, the meta-analysis found that transformational leadership did augment performance over and above the effects due to contingent reward (Wang et al., 2011). The relative importance analysis found that 72% of the leaders' influence on team performance was attributable to transformational leadership, and the remaining 28% was attributable to contingent rewards.

What conclusions can we draw from the above study? First, leaders should seek to influence followers' individual performance by using contingent rewards like pay raises, bonuses, and individual praise and recognition. It doesn't hurt to give these rewards while also emphasizing values, so support your use of contingent rewards with inspirational appeals and personal consideration. Second, to get people to help out the organization by doing voluntary good deeds, leaders should emphasize values and use inspirational appeals, backed up with an occasional reward for good citizenship. Third, to get people to work together as a team, leaders need to proclaim the values of working together for the common good. Transformational leaders also need to role model cooperation and unselfish support for coworkers and teammates, and personally demonstrate their care and concern for each follower. Finally, it helps to back up inspirational appeals to work together with some concrete rewards for demonstrating team spirit.

Transformational Leadership and Follower Satisfaction

Judge and Piccolo's (2004) meta-analysis of transformational leadership examined 93 studies with a combined sample of 17,105. They found that transformational leadership had a strong positive relationship with followers' job satisfaction. Thus, followers were more likely to like their jobs when they had leaders who used a transformational leadership style. Moreover, transformational leadership was strongly related to how satisfied the followers were with their leader. Clearly, employees are more satisfied when their leaders use transformational leadership. The followers also had higher levels of motivation when their leaders used transformational leadership. *Thus, transformational leadership improves followers' job satisfaction, their satisfaction with the leader, and their motivation levels.*

Judge and Piccolo (2004) also used a multiple-regression analysis to see if transformational leadership improved satisfaction levels over and above the improvement due to the use of transactional leadership and contingent rewards. They found that transformational leadership had a considerably larger effect on follower satisfaction with the leader than did transactional leadership (although contingent reward was still positively related to satisfaction with the leader). In addition, transformational leadership also augmented the ability to increase follower motivation over the effects of contingent rewards (contingent rewards was still important). *Thus, to improve followers' satisfaction with the leader and followers' motivation levels, leaders should use both transformational leadership and contingent rewards.*

Transformational Leadership Around the World

Leong and Fischer (2011) used meta-analysis to examine the levels of transformational leadership in 18 countries. Their results are shown in Table 15.1. Many of the countries are only represented by single studies or small

Table 15.1   Countries Included in the Analysis, Number of Participants, Samples, and Average Transformational Leadership Means

Country	Size	Samples	Transformational Leadership Leadership Mean
Australia	83	1	0.62
Canada	655	3	0.66
China	213	1	0.48
France	617	1	0.65
Germany	608	2	0.61
Greece	502	1	0.77
India	210	1	0.55
Israel	3,187	7	0.74
Italy	456	1	0.54
Kenya	158	1	0.55
Korea, South	507	2	0.61
Netherlands	870	2	0.61
New Zealand	2,764	3	0.66
Singapore	1,450	4	0.55
Spain	590	4	0.69
Taiwan	139	2	0.49
United Kingdom	751	2	0.61
United States	6,313	16	0.67

Source: Used with permission from: Leong, L. Y. C., & Fischer, R. (2011). Is transformational leadership universal? A meta-analytical investigation of multifactor leadership questionnaire means across cultures. *Journal of Leadership & Organizational Studies, 18*(2), 164–174.

sample sizes, so caution should be used when interpreting the results for these countries. The researchers also correlated the countries' scores with other variables such as the country's Gross Domestic Product (GDP) per capita. GDP correlated well with transformational leadership (0.30), which suggests that transformational leadership may help countries become more prosperous. Transformational leadership was also negatively related with countries' power distance scores. Thus, nations with lower power distance were more likely to have leaders who used a transformational leadership style. Power distance was also negatively correlated with GDP, which suggests that low power distance also contributes to economic prosperity.

Transformational leadership may help nations prosper by increasing employees' productivity. The following feature study was done in Germany, which has one of the world's most productive workforces.

Transformational Leadership Climate, Affective Climate, and Trust

Menges, Walter, Vogel, and Bruch (2011) theorized that transformational leaders exert much of their influence on organizations by creating the appropriate organizational climate. Thus, transformational leaders teach other managers and employees how to be transformational leaders. As a result, organizations with a high transformational leadership climate have transformational leaders throughout the organization and at every level of the organization. Transformational leaders also work to create a positive affective climate throughout the organization. When organizations have a positive affective climate, members share positive feelings with each other through a process of emotional contagion. These positive feelings in turn boost motivation and performance. They also argued that trust is important as well and that a trusting climate contributes to performance and enhances the benefits of having a transformational leadership climate.

Menges and his colleagues (Menges et al., 2011) tested their theories by surveying 158 small to medium size enterprises in Germany. A total of 18,094 employees participated in their study, including top management (3%), middle management (9%), and first-line supervisors (10%); the remaining sample consisted of nonmanagers. As expected, they found that a *transformational leadership climate is positively related to having a positive affective climate.* Employees were more likely to report that the employees in their organization experienced feelings of being cheerful, content, elated, and satisfied when their organization had a transformational leadership climate. The positive affective climate in turn was related to organization-level aggregate (i.e., sum total of individual performance) task performance. The positive affective climate also predicted aggregate organizational citizenship behavior. The beneficial effects of positive affective climate were enhanced when the organization also had high levels of trust. In slightly simplified terms, their results indicate the following models:

Transformational Leadership Climate → Positive Affective Climate → Performance

Transformational Leadership Climate → Positive Affective Climate → Organizational Citizenship

These results suggest that one of the main ways transformational leadership influences organizational level productivity is by influencing the moods, emotions, and job satisfaction of their employees. As the next sections indicate, maintaining a positive climate isn't always easy, especially when undergoing change. Reorganizations and other change efforts have high failure rates, and one study found that only 25% of employees think their leaders always or usually implement change effectively (Gilley, McMillan, & Gilley, 2009).

PERSONAL REFLECTIONS: *CHANGE: GOOD, BAD, OR BOTH?*

Few things elicit such a bewildering mix of emotions, both positive and negative, as the thought of organizational change. Change brings uncertainty, and with uncertainty comes anxiety. But change can also bring hope and the promise of something better. Reorganization—merging or splitting departments, changing reporting relationships, reassigning work duties, and moving staff around—is one of the things that can create conflicting feelings of fear and hope. It is easy to see why people might fear reorganization: It could mean loss of status, loss of influence, loss of responsibility, loss of friends and social support, and even loss of one's job. It could also mean additional burdens: new chores, extra work for the same pay, doing two people's jobs instead of one, new and confusing work procedures, new and poorly tested or implemented technology, new people to train and help out, and a seemingly endless series of meetings to hash out the change. It is easy to understand why many people react to the thought of reorganization with an instinctive urge to reject and resist the change.

But change also brings hope. Hope that the inefficiencies, aggravations, and idiotic, outdated work procedures that you've endured for years can now be eliminated. Hope that confusing lines of communication can now be straightened out. Hope that new technologies and streamlined work processes can make your job easier and more efficient. Hope that you can escape the boredom or social isolation of your current position and find supportive, friendly, exciting coworkers. Hope that your organization can overcome declining market share, declining profits, layoffs, and stagnant wages. Hope that your organization can achieve growth and new opportunities. Hope for recognition, hope for advancement, hope for more meaningful work, hope for happiness.

Your Turn to Reflect: What does change mean to you? What emotions does the word "change" bring to mind? How about reorganization—does that arouse hope or anxiety? Not all reorganization efforts succeed. How often have reorganization attempts that you've experienced been successful? Have you ever initially opposed a change, only to find out that in the long run it was for the best? Have you supported a change, only to be disappointed? What can leaders do to make people more optimistic about change?

The following study shows that transformational leaders can help their followers feel more positive emotions about change. This is important because followers who feel more positive emotions are more likely to support change efforts.

Transformational Leadership, Affect, and Organizational Change

Seo and colleagues used a longitudinal (12 months) study to see how employees react to change (Seo et al., 2012). They surveyed employees in a governmental transportation-related agency that was undergoing reorganization. The reorganization involved merging multiple units into a single organization with a new identity. The goal was to increase cross-functional integration and make the organization run more like an innovative private sector business. The restructuring required reallocating resources, changing reporting relationships, and relocating personnel from low to high priority areas. At the beginning of the change effort (Time 1), the researchers surveyed 906 employees (these employees were under the supervision of 217 managers). Roughly 12 months later (Time 2), midway through the change effort, they resurveyed the employees; there were 430 employees who replied to both surveys. The surveys asked the employees to evaluate their emotional reactions to the change by rating themselves on seven positive emotions (happy, excited, active, energetic, interested, enthusiastic, and proud) and seven negative ones (afraid, scornful, resentful, nervous, threatened, irritable, and scared). The employees also rated their commitment to the change process, their behavioral support or resistance to the change, and their creative behavior in support of the change. Moreover, they rated their leaders on transformational leadership using items from the Transformational Leadership Inventory.

The results were as follows: At Time 1, employees with transformational leaders were more likely to experience positive emotions with regard to the change and less likely to experience negative emotions. The emotions that employees felt predicted to their level of support for the change: Employees with more positive emotions had higher levels of commitment to the change. Thus, transformational leaders influenced commitment to change by influencing their employees' moods and emotions. Transformational leadership also directly influenced the amount of commitment to change. The employees' emotions and level of commitment at Time 1 also predicted their commitment to change and their behaviors in support of the change at Time 2. As expected, commitment to change at Time 1 predicted commitment to change at Time 2. Moreover, positive affect at Time 1 predicted to behavioral support for the change and creative behavior in support of the change at Time 2. Thus, employees in positive moods were more likely to report being creative in coming up with ways to implement the change.

The positive effects of transformational leadership on follower moods is also supported by an experimental study; this study found that transformational leadership "was associated with enhanced task performance, higher social support perceptions, greater efficacy beliefs, lower negative affect, and lower threat appraisals compared to the transactional conditions" (Lyons & Schneider, 2009, p. 737). The Leader's Bookcase features an article with vivid quotes that show the importance of leaders' emotions to followers during organizational change.

> **The Leader's Bookcase:** Smollan, R., & Parry, K. (2011). Follower perceptions of the emotional intelligence of change leaders: A qualitative study. *Leadership*, *7*, 435–462.

As the preceding studies indicate, transformational leaders and change agents owe much of their success to their ability to influence followers. However, in order to be successful, these leaders also need to develop a vision that solves their organizations' problems. In order to develop their vision, they have to make sense of the environment they are in, something that is not always easy to do. The world is complex, and it's hard to predict the future. The following sections on sensemaking go over how leaders understand the complex world around them and develop their visions.

Sensemaking and Managing the Unexpected

Karl Weick demonstrated the importance of sensemaking in his classic study of the Mann Gulch disaster (1993). The forest firefighters who made sense of

This photo shows two elk in a stream in front of a wildfire in the Bitterroot National Forest in Montana, United States of America.

Source: U.S. Department of Agriculture/John McColgan.

the changing environmental conditions survived, whereas those who didn't perished. Firefighters are not the only ones who need to make sense of rapidly changing conditions. As the worldwide economic recession in 2008 demonstrated, businesses can go from making record profits to financial collapse in a matter of months, even weeks. There are also many organizations that need to function reliably day in and day out without exception. Air traffic controllers and nuclear power plant operators need to make sure their systems perform perfectly every time. One plane crash or one core reactor meltdown is one too many. Weick and his coauthor, Sutcliffe (2007), examined how these "high reliability organizations" handle crisis and environmental change in their book, *Managing the Unexpected*. Weick and Sutcliffe (2007) argued that high reliability organizations act **mindfully,** i.e., *"they organize themselves in such a way that they are better able to notice the unexpected in the making and halt its development"* (p. 18) [boldface and italics added]. The methods these organizations use to prevent catastrophes can also help other organizations notice early signs of customer dissatisfaction, employee problems, production problems, etc., that can grow into big problems. Two of the methods that Weick and Sutcliffe describe are as follows:

Preoccupation with failure: High reliability organizations treat even minor problems as signs that something could be seriously wrong. Many disasters occur when small problems are ignored. For example, the 1984 Union Carbide release of poisonous gas that killed 3,000 people in India was due to a collection of small problems:

> Small errors such as the failure to reinsert a water isolation plate, malfunctioning storage tanks, inoperative gauges and alarms, English-language manuals that could not be read by plant personnel, and high turnover with a consequent loss of experience all contributed to the disaster. (Weick & Sutcliffe, 2007, p. 9)

Reluctance to simplify: High reliability organizations are reluctant to accept oversimplified pictures of the environment. Reducing a problem to its simplest components helps people make sense of the world and helps people focus on key issues. But simplification can also cause decision makers to ignore problems and signs that something is wrong. High reliability organizations recognize "that the world they face is complex, unstable, unknowable, and unpredictable" and thus they "position themselves to see as much as possible" (Weick & Sutcliffe, 2007, p. 10). Weick and Sutcliffe (2007) state,

> There is no question that when you organize, you simplify. But you don't need to simplify casually or habitually or instantly. People can be more deliberate in their choices of what to simplify. To be more deliberate means to be more thorough in articulating mistakes you don't want to make. (p. 12)

Weick and Sutcliffe (2007) give as an example of a catastrophe due to oversimplification the Cerro Grande wildland fire in New Mexico (May, 2000), which caused a $1 billion loss. Firefighters had intentionally started a prescribed burn to burn off excess debris, but because they had underestimated the complexity of the situation, the fire escaped the planned burn area and threatened Los Alamos and the surrounding areas.

Like Weick and Sutcliffe, other researchers recognize that the world is complex and hard to understand. The next section on complexity theory further investigates how leaders make sense of the complex world around them.

Complexity Theory and Leadership

Osborn, Hunt, and Jauch (2002) argued that leaders need to consider the amount of change in the environment. They classified four types of environmental contexts: stability, crisis, dynamic equilibrium, and edge of chaos. There are still some organizations in stable environments that have no changes in their market conditions, their technology, or their organizational structure, but these organizations are growing increasingly rare. Many organizations find themselves in crisis situations every few years and have to make radical changes in their processes in a short period of time in order to survive—and some don't. Other organizations find themselves in a type of dynamic equilibrium, where they frequently make changes to take into account new technologies or market conditions. Finally, some organizations find themselves on the edge of chaos, balanced between order and chaos.

Changes in technology, market conditions, labor supplies, governmental regulations, etc., all require adaptive leadership. As Uhl-Bien and Marion (2009) state, "Adaptive leadership helps produce a rich flow of information (in the form of ideas, innovations, changes, technologies, etc.) to enhance dynamic complexity processes" (p. 638). Adaptive leaders have to support innovation at all levels of the organization and unleash the creative potential of all employees. Adaptive leaders also have to be good at reading the environment and making sense of complex interrelationships.

Once leaders make sense of the environment, they have to engage in *sense-giving* in order to help their followers understand the environment and the vision that will guide the organization through the change process (Akrivou & Bradbury-Huang, 2011). This is a dynamic, interactive process, and effective leaders have to enable all stakeholders to participate in the generation of the vision if they want to fully engage them in supporting the organizational change.

> **Applications:** How would you describe the environmental context for the organizations you belong to? Is their environment stable or undergoing considerable change? How hard is it to predict what the environment will be in a few months or years? Is it easy to understand what the organizational strategy should be? Are the leaders effective in helping organizational members understand the environmental pressures the organization faces?

The concluding case is about a transformational leader who understood that the environment was right for a new type of women's underwear. The leader is also high on many of the other leadership abilities that are featured in this book. As such, this case reviews many of the themes of this book.

Case: *Spanx's Sara Blakely*
Shapes Up Women (and an Industry)

Sara Blakely is the founder of Spanx, a company that sells women's undergarments in upscale stores. She also sells the Assets line of shapewear at Targets. *Forbes* has announced that she has joined the ranks of female billionaires, and at age 41, she's the youngest self-made woman to make the list. She's also a good example of a transformational leader.

Sara Blakely, founder of Spanx

Source: Wikipedia/David Shankbone (CC-BY)

Self-leadership and constructive thought patterns: During high school, it seemed like Sara had it made. She was a popular cheerleader and a champion debater. Then tragedies began falling on her like rain. First, she witnessed one of her best friends get run over and killed. To make matters even worse, her parents divorced. Then two of her prom dates were also killed. To cope with these tragedies, Sara began listening to audio tapes by Wayne Dyer. These tapes taught her to practice self-leadership and to replace negative, self-defeating thoughts with more constructive ones.

Intellectual stimulation, openness, and extraversion: Sara Blakely demonstrates what a woman with a vision can do. Like many inventors, she came up with her invention in order to solve a problem she had. She wanted to wear her new cream colored pants with sandals, but she discovered that embarrassing panty lines would show through the pants. If she wore pantyhose instead, the stocking feet would be visible with her open-toed sandals. Sara is most likely high on the Big Five personality trait of openness, so she tried something new: She cut off the feet of some control top pantyhose and wore them under her pants to a party (Sara does many extraverted activities). Unfortunately, the hose kept riding up her legs all night. That's when she decided to open her own business selling footless pantyhose that also have no visible waistlines. She knew there had to be some way to make footless pantyhose that would be comfortable and fashionable. Sara developed slimming, footless pantyhose that transformed the hosiery industry. When her business began to grow, Sara led her employees in designing over 200 products that revolutionized the shapewear industry.

Cognitive intelligence, emotional intelligence, and conscientiousness: Most people are afraid to tackle projects when they lack the education, training, and experience for the job. But Sara had the cognitive intelligence to learn what she needed to know to start Spanx and the emotional intelligence to overcome her fears and motivate herself. Sara was also very conscientious: For 2 years she worked during the day as a high performing full-time employee selling fax machines while working at night and on weekends developing Spanx. Sara had no experience in fashion design. Her degree was in communications. Her life savings only amounted to $5,000. But she didn't let her inexperience or lack of money stop her. She designed her footless pantyhose herself, and her mother (an artist) created the drawings of the hose. She read a book on patents and trademarks that she bought at the local bookstore. Sara also spent many evenings at the Georgia Tech library researching all of the patents she could find on hosiery. The first patent lawyers she talked to laughed at her idea—one thought it must be a Candid Camera prank—and wanted $3,000 to write the patent. She only had $5,000 to start the business, so she wrote most of the patent application herself, and she found a lawyer willing to write the rest for $700.

Individual consideration, empowerment, leader-member relationships, and task leadership: Sara's first employees worked with her while she was running her business out of her apartment. The informal atmosphere and Sara's friendly interpersonal style undoubtedly motivated her new employees and created warm leader-member relationships. She promoted many of them to important positions right from the start, and many are still working with her. When her business began to grow, she also hired a woman with industry experience to help her manage the business. She empowered these employees to run much of the daily production side of the business while she was out on the road promoting Spanx. Sara is high at task leadership as well. When starting the business she worked alongside her employees packing and shipping the product, and she continues to take a hands-on approach with regard to designing and marketing Spanx and Assets products. She still personally tries on prototype garments during staff meetings.

Idealized influence, inspirational motivation, charismatic emotional displays, persuasion, and identification: Sara inspires both her employees and her customers with her enthusiasm, optimism, and lively, emotionally expressive communication style. Sara's optimism and persuasive abilities helped her

(Continued)

(Continued)

overcome the frequent rejections she encountered while trying to sell fax machines and when trying to start Spanx. Sara had been so successful at selling fax machines that at the young age of 25 she had been promoted to be the national sales trainer for Danka (the fax company she worked for). She knew how to do cold calling and handle frequent rejection. Her determination and resilience helped her cope with the repeated rejections she had over the phone when she called up hosiery mills about developing her product. Finally, she drove to North Carolina to personally talk (unannounced) with mill owners. Her face-to-face personal charisma did the trick—2 weeks after a visit to a mill, the owner called her back offering to help make the prototypes of her footless pantyhose.

Blakely's charisma and persuasive flair helped her get her product in the stores. Sara put her prototype pantyhose in her lucky red backpack and flew to the Neiman Marcus headquarters to speak for 10 minutes with the head buyer. Sara invited the buyer into the ladies room and modeled wearing her cream pants with and without her Spanx pantyhose. Sara's charisma, along with the no visible waistline effect, won over the buyer. Blakely continued using her emotionally expressive interpersonal style to win customers. For 2 years she stood outside Neiman Marcus stores modeling her Spanx to potential customers. She would raise her pants leg to show off the hose and then demonstrate the no visible waistline effect while moving around. Many of her customers identify with the Spanx brand and with Sara personally. When Sara is traveling, many women approach her and show off their own Spanx undergarments!

Sara knew how to get free publicity back when she couldn't afford advertising. Her smiles and her friendly, emotionally expressive demeanor made her a wanted guest on TV shows. She appeared on Oprah after sending Oprah's stylist a gift basket full of Spanx. Sara had to get some friends to pretend to be employees and staff members when the Oprah crew showed up to interview her in her corporate headquarters (i.e., her kitchen). Sara also spent 3 months as a contestant on Richard Branson's show, *The Rebel Billionaire*. On the show, she had to overcome her fear of heights and regulate her emotions: One of her tasks was to climb a rope ladder (as long as a 17 story building) and scramble up the sides of a hot air balloon (the balloon was thousands of feet in the air at the time). She then had tea with Branson while sitting on top of the balloon. She also appeared as a judge on the American Inventor show and in numerous infomercials.

Authentic leadership, ethics, and empathy: In keeping with her core values, ethics, and empathic nature, Blakely has founded a charity, The Sara Blakely Foundation, which seeks to empower women and help them become entrepreneurs. Sara uses her life story to inspire others.

Applications: Which of Sara's skills do you think contributed most to her success? Do you think you would like to work for someone like Sara? Why or why not?

Sources: http://video.msnbc.msn.com/mitchell-reports/46761642/#46761642 (retrieved March 19, 2012).

http://www.forbes.com/sites/clareoconnor/2012/03/07/undercover-billionaire-sara-blakely-joins-the-rich-list-thanks-to-spanx/ (retrieved March 15, 2012).

http://www.marketwatch.com/story/worlds-first-self-made-female-billionaire-sara-blakely-credits-wayne-dyer-for-her-success-as-an-entrepreneur-2012-03-14 (retrieved March 14, 2012).

http://www.spanx.com/category/index.jsp?categoryId=4399478&clickId=topnav_aboutsara_text (retrieved March 15, 2012).

Put It in Practice

1. Use transformational and transactional leadership: Develop your vision by consulting others and learning all you can; then drive your vision home by setting goals, requiring people to work together, monitoring performance, and gaining trust.

2. Get everyone working together: Communicate your vision and build consensus to increase goal importance congruence and thus performance.

3. Use the four "I's": Become a transformational leader by using idealized influence, inspirational motivation, intellectual stimulation, and individualized consideration.

4. Don't be a monkey: Role model positive attitudes toward work, your customers, your company, and your fellow employees, and give employees a mission they can be proud of.

5. Articulate your vision to create a competitive performance-oriented culture and a climate for innovation.

6. Use contingent rewards backed up by transformational leadership to improve individual follower performance, and use transformational leadership backed up by contingent rewards to improve organizational citizenship behaviors, team performance, and follower satisfaction with the leader.

7. For a prosperous nation with high GDP, use transformational leadership and a low power distance culture.

8. Create a transformational leadership climate throughout your organization to form a positive affective climate which boosts performance and organizational citizenship behaviors.

9. Recognize that change brings conflicting feelings of fear and hope. Use transformational leadership to help followers feel positive emotions about the proposed change and to get them to commit to supporting the change.

10. Make sense of the unexpected: Act mindfully, watch out for even small failures, don't oversimplify, and be deliberate about mistakes you don't want to make.

11. The world is complex: Consider your organizational context and use adaptive leadership to handle environmental change. Engage in sense-giving to help your followers understand the environment and the need for change.

Exercises

1. **Leaders as Role Models**

   Think about all of the leaders that you have read about in this book. Which leaders would be good role models for you? What lessons have you learned from them? Make a list of your top five leaders from the book.

2. **Transformational Leadership and Change**

   Think about a change that you would like to see implemented in an organization that you are familiar with. How would you go about bringing about the change using the four "I's" of transformational leadership? For each "I" list a transformational behavior that could help bring about the change.

Visit the Student Study Site at **www.sagepub.com/humphreyel** for these additional tools:

- Learning Goals
- Leader's Book Case Articles
- Web Resources
- Student Self Assessments

References

Akrivou, K., & Bradbury-Huang, H. (2011). Executive catalysts: Predicting sustainable organizational performance amid complex demands. *The Leadership Quarterly, 22,* 995–1009.

Anonymous (2012). *Phone monkey: The secret diary of a frustrated call centre worker* [E-reader version]. Great Britain, UK: Underglow Books.

Avolio, B. J. (2011). *Full range leadership development* (2nd ed.). Thousand Oaks, CA: Sage.

Avolio, B. J., & Bass, B. M. (2004). *Multifactor Leadership Questionnaire: Manual and sampler set* (3rd ed.). Menlo Park, CA: Mind Garden.

Bass, B. M., & Riggio, R. E. (2006/2007). *Transformational leadership* (2nd ed.) [E-library edition]. Mahwah, NJ: Lawrence Erlbaum.

Colbert, A. E., Kristof-Brown, A. L., Bradley, B. H., & Barrick, M. R. (2008). CEO transformational leadership: The role of goal importance congruence in top management teams. *Academy of Management Journal, 51,* 81–96.

Epitropaki, O., & Martin, R. (2005). The moderating role of individual differences in the relation between transformational/transactional leadership perceptions and organizational identification. *The Leadership Quarterly, 16,* 569–589.

Gilley, A., McMillan, H. S., & Gilley, J. W. (2009). Organizational change and characteristics of leadership effectiveness. *Journal of Leadership & Organizational Studies, 16,* 38–47.

Hackman, J. R., & Oldham, G. R. (1976). Motivation through the design of work: Test of a theory. *Organizational Behavior and Human Performance, 16,* 250–279.

Hoffman, B. G. (2012). *American icon: Alan Mulally and the fight to save Ford Motor Company* [E-reader version]. New York, NY: Crown Business.

J.D. Power and Associates 2012 U.S. vehicle dependability study[SM] (VDS) (2011, December 30). Retrieved from http://autos.jdpower.com/content/study-auto/V8Ois5x/2012-vehicle-dependability-study-results.htm?page=2

Judge, T. A., & Piccolo, R. F. (2004). Transformational and transactional leadership: A meta-analytic test of their relative validity. *Journal of Applied Psychology, 89,* 755–768.

Leong, L. Y. C., & Fischer, R. (2011). Is transformational leadership universal? A meta-analytical investigation of multifactor leadership questionnaire means across cultures. *Journal of Leadership & Organizational Studies, 18*(2), 164–174.

Lyons, J. B., & Scheider, T. R. (2009). The effects of leadership style on stress outcomes. *The Leadership Quarterly, 20,* 737–748.

Matthew, C. T. (2009). Leader creativity as a predictor of leading change in organizations. *Journal of Applied Social Psychology, 39,* 1–41.

Menges, J. I., Walter, F., Vogel, B., & Bruch, H. (2011). Transformational leadership climate: Performance linkages, mechanisms, and boundary conditions at the organizational level. *The Leadership Quarterly, 22,* 893–909.

Moskowitz, M., & Levering, R. (2012, February). The 100 best companies to work for. *Fortune,* 117–127.

Osborn, R., Hunt, J. G., & Jauch, L. R. (2002). Toward a contextual theory of leadership. *The Leadership Quarterly, 13,* 797–837.

Piccolo, R. F., & Colquitt, J. A. (2006). Transformational leadership and job behaviors: The mediating role of core job characteristics. *Academy of Management Journal, 49,* 327–340.

Podsakoff, P. M., MacKenzie, S. B., Moorman, R. H., & Fetter, R. (1990). Transformational leader behaviors and their effects on followers' trust in leader, satisfaction, and organizational citizenship behaviors. *The Leadership Quarterly, 1,* 107–142.

Sarros, J. C., Cooper, B. K., & Santora, J. C. (2008). Building a climate for innovation through transformational leadership and organizational culture. *Journal of Leadership & Organizational Studies, 15,* 145–158.

Seo, M., Taylor, M. S., Hill, N. S., Zhang, X., Tesluk, P. E., & Lorinkova, N. M. (2012). The role of affect and leadership during organizational change. *Personnel Psychology, 65,* 121–165.

Smollan, R., & Parry, K. (2011). Follower perceptions of the emotional intelligence of change leaders: A qualitative study. *Leadership, 7,* 435–462.

Sosik, J. J., & Dinger, S. L. (2007). Relationships between leadership style and vision content: The moderating role of need for social approval, self-monitoring, and need for social power. *The Leadership Quarterly, 18,* 134–153.

Uhl-Bien, M., & Marion, R. (2009). Complexity leadership in bureaucratic forms of organizing: A meso model. *The Leadership Quarterly, 20,* 631–650.

USAA. Retrieved April 9, 2012 from https://www.usaa.com/inet/pages/why_choose_usaa_main?wa_ref=pub_global_usaaandu

Vlasic, B. (2011). *Once upon a car: The fall and resurrection of America's big three automakers—GM, Ford, and Chrysler.* New York, NY: HarperCollins.

Wang, G., Oh, I., Courtright, S. H., & Colbert, A. E. (2011). Transformational leadership and performance across criteria and levels: A meta-analytic review of 25 years of research. *Group & Organization Management, 36,* 223–270.

Weick, K. E. (1993). The collapse of sensemaking in organizations: The Mann Gulch disaster. *Administrative Science Quarterly, 38,* 628–652.

Weick, K. E., & Sutcliffe, K. M. (2007). *Managing the unexpected* (2nd ed.). San Francisco, CA: Wiley & Sons.

Concluding Thoughts:
Footprints on the Sands of Time

D ear Readers: I hope you have enjoyed the book as much as I have enjoyed writing it. And over the following years, I hope the book continues to be useful to you as you pursue your leadership careers. You are the future leaders of the world, and who knows, perhaps someday I'll be writing about you in future editions of this book. In the meantime, I hope you enjoy this concluding inspirational message from one of my favorite poets. I particularly like the stanza that begins "Lives of great men all remind us"—it is certainly appropriate for a leadership book like this one. Perhaps someday you'll be leaving your own footprints on the sands of time.

A PSALM OF LIFE
WHAT THE HEART OF THE YOUNG MAN
SAID TO THE PSALMIST

TELL me not, in mournful numbers,
Life is but an empty dream! —
For the soul is dead that slumbers,
And things are not what they seem.

Life is real! Life is earnest!
And the grave is not its goal;
Dust thou art, to dust returnest,
Was not spoken of the soul.

Not enjoyment, and not sorrow,
Is our destined end or way;
But to act, that each to-morrow
Find us farther than to-day.

Art is long, and Time is fleeting,
And our hearts, though stout and brave,
Still, like muffled drums, are beating
Funeral marches to the grave.

In the world's broad field of battle,
In the bivouac of Life,
Be not like dumb, driven cattle!
Be a hero in the strife!

Trust no Future, howe'er pleasant!
Let the dead Past bury its dead!
Act,— act in the living Present!
Heart within, and God o'erhead!

Lives of great men all remind us
We can make our lives sublime,
And, departing, leave behind us
Footprints on the sands of time;

Footprints, that perhaps another,
Sailing o'er life's solemn main,
A forlorn and shipwrecked brother,
Seeing, shall take heart again.

Let us, then, be up and doing,
With a heart for any fate;
Still achieving, still pursuing,
Learn to labor and to wait.

Henry Wadsworth Longfellow
(1807–1882)

Index

431

Environmental factors, in leadership, 12, 17, 123
  leader-member exchange, 149–150 (table)
  position power, 149–150 (table)
  situational factors in, 149–150 (table)
  task structure, 149–150 (table)
Epitropaki, O., 407
Erez, A., 44
Estefan, Emilio, 374–376
Ethics, 20, 181, 183, 262, 274, 396, 425
Euwema, M.C., 134–137
Evidence-based leadership, 21
Exemplification, 362
Expectancy theory of motivation, 154–155
Expert power, 321–322, 323, 324
External attributions, 186
External Locus of Control, 43
Extroversion, 39–40, 42 (table), 47, 48, 49 (table), 50, 382, 383

Facebook, 60–62
Face-to-face leadership, 10–11
Facilitation power, 324–325
Farmer, S. M., 182
Feelers, 48, 49 (table), 50
Feldman, D. C., 302–303
Fernandez, C.E., 153
Ferrin, D. L., 181
Ferris, G. R., 38, 330, 331
Fiedler, Fred, 149–152
Field, H. S., 38, 277
Fields, Mark, 403–404
Finkelstein, S., 75–77
Fischer, R., 413–414
Fischer, Scott, 249–251
Fishbein, M., 327
Fisher, C. D., 215
Five-Level Model of Emotion in Organizations, 206 (table)–208, 210–214
  between-persons, 206 (table), 210–212
  groups & teams, 206 (table), 213
  interpersonal, 206 (table), 212–213

  organization-wide, 206 (table), 214
  within-person, 206 (table), 207–208
Fleenor, J. W., 8–10
"Florence Nightingale: The Passionate Statistician" (Rehmeyer), 105–106
Follower level of leadership, 12
Follower readiness, 152, 153
Ford, Bill, 402
Ford, Henry, 68, 237
Ford Motor Company, 402–404
Forsyth, Donelson R., 249–251
Foti, R. J., 378
Fox, M. L., 130–131
Franklin, Benjamin, 72, 178
Freeman, D. M., 243
French, J. R. P., 321–322
French Revolution, 177, 178
Friedrich, T. L., 247–248
Fritz, C., 208
Fry, L. W., 159
Functional resistance, 244
Furlonger, B., 129

Galvin, Robert W., 73
Gardner, W. L., 48–50, 187, 268–269
Garin, K. A., 146
Gates, Bill, 64, 68, 73, 79, 307, 344
Gates Foundation, 79
Gatorade, 76
Gender differences
  in developmental opportunities, 137–138
  in initiating structure, 134–135, 136, 137
  in innovation and top management team, 138
General Electric, 163–165
Generalized Self-Efficacy, 43
Generating alternatives, 73, 75
Genuine emotional labor, 357, 358, 359
George, Bill, 261, 262
Gerstner, C. R., 174
Gladwell, Malcolm, 46
Global Leadership and Organizational Behavior Effectiveness (GLOBE) project, 8–9, 135, 306
Glynn, M. A., 305
Goal importance congruence, 405–406

Author Biography

Ronald H. Humphrey is a professor in the Department of Management at Virginia Commonwealth University. His research interests are on leadership, entrepreneurship, customer service, emotions in the workplace, empathy, emotional labor, emotional intelligence, person perception, identity theory, labeling theory, attribution theory, collective efficacy, careers, project management, assessment centers, job characteristics, and other topics. Ron is on the Editorial Board of *The Leadership Quarterly*, and he edited a special issue of *The Leadership Quarterly* on emotions and leadership. He was also one of the founding members of the Network of Leadership Scholars (also known as LDRNET) and was coprogram chair for the Professional Development Workshops organized by the Network at Academy of Management Conferences. In 2008, Ron also edited *Affect and Emotion: New Directions in Management Theory and Research*. Along with Neal Ashkanasy and Quy Huy, Ron will edit a forthcoming special issue of the *Academy of Management Review* on integrating affect and emotions in management theories. Ron has published in a wide range of journals including the *Academy of Management Review*, *Academy of Management Perspectives*, *American Sociological Review*, *Research in Organizational Behavior*, *Leadership Quarterly*, *Social Psychology Quarterly*, *Basic and Applied Social Psychology*, *Human Relations*, *Organization Science*, *Journal of Health and Social Behavior*, *Public Opinion Quarterly*, *Journal of Organizational Behavior*, and other journals.

Ron enjoys working with the business community doing corporate training and consulting, and his research and consulting activities have been with some of the largest corporations in America such as Chrysler, General Motors, and Northwest Airlines, as well as numerous small businesses and entrepreneurs.

Education: AB: University of Chicago; PhD: University of Michigan; Postdoctoral Fellow: Indiana University.

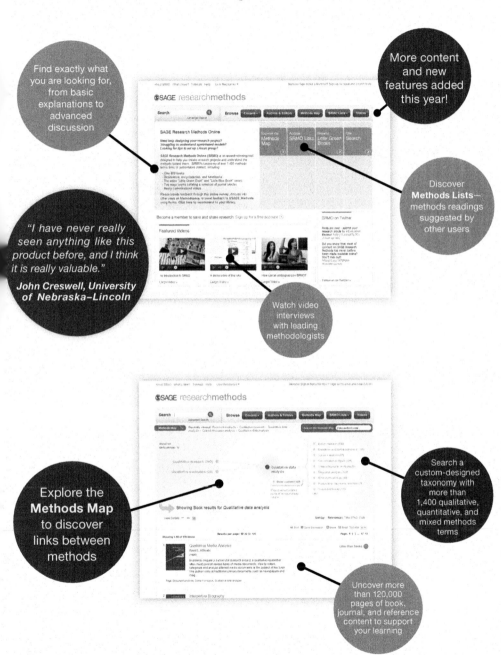